Python Essential Reference, Second Edition

Contents at a Glance

Python Essential Reference
Second Edition

David M. Beazley

www.newriders.com

201 West 103rd Street, Indianapolis, Indiana 46290
An Imprint of Pearson Education
Boston • Indianapolis • London • Munich • New York • San Francisco

Python Essential Reference

International Standard Book Number: 0-7357-1091-0

Library of Congress Catalog Card Number: 00-110880

05 04 03 02 01   7 6 5 4 3 2 1

Interpretation of the printing code: The rightmost double-digit number is the year of the book's printing; the rightmost single-digit number is the number of the book's printing. For example, the printing code 01-1 shows that the first printing of the book occurred in 2001.

Printed in the United States of America

Trademarks

Warning and Disclaimer

Publisher
David Dwyer

Associate Publisher
Al Valvano

Executive Editor
Stephanie Wall

Managing Editor
Gina Brown

Acquisitions Editor
Ann Quinn

Editor
Robin Drake

Product Marketing Manager
Stephanie Layton

Publicity Manager
Susan Petro

Manufacturing Coordinator
Jim Conway

Book Designer
Louisa Klucznik

Cover Designer
Brainstorm Design, Inc.

Cover Production
Aren Howell

Proofreaders
Debra Neel
Tim Bell

Composition
Ron Wise
Amy Parker

For my parents.

Table of Contents

About the Author

David M. Beazley is the developer of SWIG, a popular software package for integrating C programs with interpreted languages including Python, Perl, and Tcl. He has been actively involved with the Python community since 1996 and is currently working on projects related to mixed-mode debugging of scripting language extensions. Dave spent seven years working in the Theoretical Physics Division at Los Alamos National Laboratory, where he helped pioneer the use of Python with high-performance simulation software running on parallel computers. He is currently an assistant professor in the Department of Computer Science at the University of Chicago, where he enjoys tormenting students with insane programming projects in operating systems, networks, and compilers courses. He can be reached at `beazley@cs.uchicago.edu`.

About the Technical Reviewers

These reviewers contributed their considerable hands-on expertise to the entire development process for *Python Essential Reference, Second Edition*. As the book was being written, these dedicated professionals reviewed all the material for technical content, organization, and flow. Their feedback was critical to ensuring that *Python Essential Reference, Second Edition* fits our reader's need for the highest-quality technical information.

Paul F. Dubois graduated from the University of California at Berkeley with a degree in mathematics. He obtained a Ph.D. in mathematics from the University of California at Davis in 1970. After six years of teaching and research, in 1976 he joined Lawrence Livermore National Laboratory. He has held a variety of positions at LLNL as a technical leader in numerical mathematics and computer science. In 1999 he joined the Program for Climate Model Diagnosis and Intercomparison in the Atmospheric Sciences Division, where he is putting Python to work creating analysis tools for climate modelers.

Paul's work includes pioneering work on computational steering and the use of object technology for scientific programming. He is the Editor of the Scientific Programming Department for the journal *IEEE Computing in Science and Engineering*.

Mats Wichmann is a consultant and trainer. A 1980 computer science graduate of the University of California at Berkeley, he managed operating systems development for several UNIX companies in the 1980s before becoming a consultant. His search for a programming language that spans the range from scripting system administration tasks to developing serious applications has found a happy conclusion in Python. Mats is the author of a Python training course for a major training provider. Living in Questa, New Mexico, he can be reached at m.wichmann@ieee.org.

Acknowledgments

This book would not be possible without the input and support of many people. First, I would like to thank technical reviewers Mats Wichmann and Paul Dubois for their feedback. I would also like to thank the technical reviewers of the first edition, David Ascher and Paul Dubois, for their valuable comments and continued advice. Guido van Rossum, Jeremy Hylton, Fred Drake, Roger Masse, Barry Warsaw, and the rest of the Python developers also provided tremendous assistance with the first edition.

I'd also like to thank the folks at New Riders for their commitment to the project and assistance. A special thanks is in order for freelance editor Robin Drake for her amazing editing of both editions, and to compositors Ron Wise and Amy Parker (freelance and in-house, respectively), whose patience and stamina exceeded expectations and made it possible to finish this edition on time. I would also like to acknowledge the heroic efforts of Tim Bell, who not only provided a substantial number of suggestions for improving the first edition, but jumped in at the last moment to proofread this edition.

The following individuals also supplied feedback from the first edition: Jan Decaluwe, Mike Coleman, Andrew Kuchling, Greg Ward, Richard Wolff, Holger Dürer, Patrick Moran, Christian Norgaard Storm Pedersen, Dustin Mitchell, Benjamin Smith, Michael Drumheller, Brett Porter, Tim Bell, Michael Dyck, Ian Thomas Cohen, Steve Burns, David Morrill, Dennis McCoy, Paul DuBois, Peter Koren, Richard Gruet, Hamish Lawson, Michael Rodgers, Eric Rowe, Phil Austin, Aaron Digulla, Jack Gilbert, Joseph Sachs, Cecil Edwards, and Daniel Klein. I have done my best to incorporate your suggestions.

Tell Us What You Think

As the reader of this book, you are our most important critic and commentator. We value your opinion and want to know what we're doing right, what we could do better, what areas you'd like to see us publish in, and any other words of wisdom you're willing to pass our way.

As an Executive Editor for the Web Development team at New Riders Publishing, I welcome your comments. You can fax, email, or write me directly to let me know what you did or didn't like about this book—as well as what we can do to make our books stronger.

Please note that I cannot help you with technical problems related to the topic of this book, and that due to the high volume of mail I receive, I might not be able to reply to every message.

When you write, please be sure to include this book's title and author as well as your name and phone or fax number. I will carefully review your comments and share them with the author and editors who worked on the book.

Fax: 317-581-4663

Email: Stephanie.Wall@newriders.com

Mail: Stephanie Wall
          Executive Editor
          New Riders Publishing
          201 West 103rd Street
          Indianapolis, IN 46290 USA

Introduction

This book is intended to be a concise reference to the Python programming language. Although an experienced programmer will probably be able to learn Python from this book, it's not intended to be an extended tutorial or a treatise on how to program. Rather, the goal is to present the core Python language, the contents of the Python library, and the Python extension API in a manner that's accurate and succinct. This book assumes that the reader has prior programming experience with Python or other languages such as C or Java. In addition, a general familiarity with systems programming topics (for example, basic operating system concepts, process management, and network programming) may be useful in understanding certain parts of the library reference.

Python is freely available for download at `http://www.python.org`. Versions are available for UNIX, Windows, Macintosh, and Java. In addition, this site includes links to documentation, how-to guides, and a wide assortment of extension modules.

What's Inside?

The contents of this book are based on Python 2.1. However, readers should be aware that Python is a constantly evolving language. Most of the topics described herein are likely to be applicable to future versions of Python 2.x. In addition, most topics are applicable to earlier releases. To a lesser extent, the topics in this book also apply to JPython, an implementation of Python entirely in Java. However, that is not the primary focus of this book.

It should be noted that just as Python is an evolving language, the Second Edition of *Python Essential Reference* has evolved to make use of new language features and new library modules added in Python 2.1. Rather than merely describing new language features as an afterthought, recently added features have been freely used and incorporated throughout the text. Although no distinction is given to new additions, detailed descriptions of language changes can easily be found online.

Finally, note that Python is distributed with hundreds of pages of reference documentation. The contents of this book are largely based on that documentation, but with a number of enhancements, additions, and omissions. First, this reference presents most of the same material in a more compact form, with different examples and alternative descriptions of many topics. Second, a significant number of topics in the library reference have been expanded to include additional outside reference material. This is especially true for low-level system and networking modules in which effective use of a module normally relies on a myriad of options listed in UNIX manual pages and outside reference material. In addition, in order to produce a more concise reference, a number of deprecated and relatively obscure library modules have been omitted. Finally, this reference doesn't attempt to cover large frameworks such as Tkinter, XML, or the COM extensions, as these topics are beyond the scope of this book and are described in books of their own.

In writing this book, it has been my goal to produce a reference containing virtually everything I have needed to use Python and its large collection of modules. Although this is by no means a gentle introduction to the Python language, I hope that you find the contents of this book to be a useful addition to your programming reference library for many years to come. I welcome your comments.

—David Beazley
Chicago, IL
6/1/2001

Conventions Used in This Book

Convention	Usage
monospace text	Datatypes, classes, modules, constants, and so on—basically, anything that constitutes part of the Python language or any command you could present to the computer. The monospaced font is also used for Internet addresses such as www.python.org.
italic monospace	Variables such as x in abs(x).
[ ]	Brackets are used in syntax lines to indicate optional elements, such as object in dir([object]). In the syntax [arg = value], value indicates the default value of arg. Brackets are also used to denote Python lists; in all coding examples, this is the interpretation.
➡	Code-continuation characters are inserted into code when a line shouldn't be broken, but we simply ran out of room on the page.

Web Site

For downloadable source files from the code listings in this book, visit www.newriders.com.

1

A Tutorial Introduction

This chapter provides a quick introduction to Python. The goal is to illustrate Python's essential features without getting too bogged down in special rules or details. To do this, the chapter briefly covers basic concepts such as variables, expressions, control flow, functions, and input/output. This chapter is not intended to provide comprehensive coverage, nor does it cover many of Python's more advanced features. However, experienced programmers should be able to extrapolate from the material in this chapter to create more advanced programs. Beginners are encouraged to try a few examples to get a feel for the language.

Running Python

Python programs are executed by an interpreter. On UNIX machines, the interpreter is started by typing python. On Windows and the Macintosh, the interpreter is launched as an application (either from the Start menu or by double-clicking the interpreter's icon). When the interpreter starts, a prompt appears at which you can start typing programs into a simple read-evaluation loop. For example, in the following output, the interpreter displays its copyright message and presents the user with the >>> prompt, at which the user types the familiar "Hello World" command:

```
Python 2.1 (#1, Apr 20 2001, 14:34:45)
[GCC 2.95.2 19991024 (release)] on sunos5
Type "copyright", "credits" or "license" for more information.
>>> print "Hello World"
Hello World
>>>
```

Programs can also be placed in a file such as the following:

```
# helloworld.py
print "Hello World"
```

Python source files have a .py suffix. The # character denotes a comment that extends to the end of the line.

To execute the `helloworld.py` file, you provide the filename to the interpreter as follows:

```
% python helloworld.py
Hello World
%
```

On Windows, Python programs can be started by double-clicking a .py file. This launches the interpreter and runs the program in a console window. In this case, the console window disappears immediately after the program completes its execution (often before you can read its output). To prevent this problem, you should use an integrated development environment such as Idle or Pythonwin. An alternative approach is to launch the program using a `.bat` file containing a statement such as `python -i helloworld.py` that instructs the interpreter to enter interactive mode after program execution.

On the Macintosh, programs can be executed from the included integrated development environment. In addition, the `BuildApplet` utility (included in the distribution) turns a Python program into a document that automatically launches the interpreter when opened.

Within the interpreter, the `execfile()` function runs a program, as in the following example:

```
>>> execfile("helloworld.py")
Hello World
```

On UNIX, you can also invoke Python using `#!` in a shell script:

```
#!/usr/local/bin/python
print "Hello World"
```

The interpreter runs until it reaches the end of the input file. If running interactively, you can exit by typing the EOF (end of file) character or by selecting Exit from a pull-down menu. On UNIX, EOF is Ctrl+D; on Windows, Ctrl+Z. A program can also exit by calling the `sys.exit()` function or raising the `SystemExit` exception. For example:

```
>>> import sys
>>> sys.exit()
```

or

```
>>> raise SystemExit
```

Variables and Arithmetic Expressions

The program in Listing 1.1 shows the use of variables and expressions by performing a simple compound-interest calculation:

Listing 1.1   Simple Compound-Interest Calculation

```
principal = 1000        # Initial amount
rate = 0.05             # Interest rate
numyears = 5            # Number of years
year = 1
while year <= numyears:
        principal = principal*(1+rate)
        print year, principal
        year += 1
```

The output of this program is the following table:

```
1 1050.0
2 1102.5
3 1157.625
4 1215.50625
5 1276.2815625
```

Python is a dynamically typed language in which names can represent values of different types during the execution of the program. In fact, the names used in a program are really just labels for various quantities and objects. The assignment operator simply creates an association between that name and a value. This is different from C, for example, in which a name represents a fixed size and location in memory into which results are placed. The dynamic behavior of Python can be seen in Listing 1.1 with the `principal` variable. Initially, it's assigned to an integer value. However, later in the program it's reassigned as follows:

```
principal = principal*(1+rate)
```

This statement evaluates the expression and reassociates the name `principal` with the result. When this occurs, the original binding of `principal` to the integer `1000` is lost. Furthermore, the result of the assignment may change the *type* of a variable. In this case, the type of `principal` changes from an integer to a floating-point number because `rate` is a floating-point number.

A newline terminates each individual statement. You also can use a semicolon to separate statements, as shown here:

```
principal = 1000; rate = 0.05; numyears = 5;
```

The `while` statement tests the conditional expression that immediately follows. If the tested expression is true, the body of the `while` statement executes. The condition is then retested and the body executed again until the condition becomes false. Because the body of the loop is denoted by indentation, the three statements following the `while` in Listing 1.1 execute on each iteration. Python doesn't specify the amount of required indentation, as long as it's consistent within a block.

One problem with the program in Listing 1.1 is that the output isn't very pretty. To make it better, you could right-align the columns and limit the precision of `principal` to two digits by modifying the `print` to use a *format string*, like this:

```
print "%3d  %0.2f" % (year, principal)
```

Now the output of the program looks like this:

```
1   1050.00
2   1102.50
3   1157.63
4   1215.51
5   1276.28
```

Format strings contain ordinary text and special formatting-character sequences such as `"%d"`, `"%s"`, or `"%f"`. These sequences specify the formatting of a particular type of data such as an integer, string, or floating-point number, respectively. The special-character sequences can also contain modifiers that specify a width and precision. For example, `"%3d"` formats an integer right-aligned in a column of width 3, and `"%0.2f"` formats a floating-point number so that only two digits appear after the decimal point. The behavior of format strings is almost identical to the C `sprintf()` function and is described in detail in Chapter 4, "Operators and Expressions."

Conditionals

The `if` and `else` statements can perform simple tests. For example:

```
# Compute the maximum (z) of a and b
if a < b:
        z = b
else:
        z = a
```

The bodies of the `if` and `else` clauses are denoted by indentation. The `else` clause is optional.

To create an empty clause, use the `pass` statement as follows:

```
if a < b:
        pass        # Do nothing
else:
        z = a
```

You can form Boolean expressions by using the `or`, `and`, and `not` keywords:

```
if b >= a and b <= c:
        print "b is between a and c"
if not (b < a or b > c):
        print "b is still between a and c"
```

To handle multiple-test cases, use the `elif` statement, like this:

```
if a == '+':
        op = PLUS
elif a == '-':
        op = MINUS
elif a == '*':
        op = MULTIPLY
else:
        raise RuntimeError, "Unknown operator"
```

File Input and Output

The following program opens a file and reads its contents line by line:

```
f = open("foo.txt")         # Returns a file object
line = f.readline()         # Invokes readline() method on file
while line:
        print line,         # trailing ',' omits newline character
        line = f.readline()
f.close()
```

The `open()` function returns a new file object. By invoking methods on this object, you can perform various file operations. The `readline()` method reads a single line of input, including the terminating newline. The empty string is returned at the end of the file. To make the output of a program go to a file, you can give the file to the `print` statement using `>>` as shown in the following example:

```
f = open("out","w")         # Open file for writing
while year <= numyears:
        principal = principal*(1+rate)
        print >>f,"%3d    %0.2f" % (year,principal)
        year += 1
f.close()
```

In addition, files support a `write()` method that can be used to write raw data. For example, the `print` statement in the previous example could have been written this way:

```
f.write("%3d   %0.2f\n" % (year,principal))
```

Strings

To create *string literals*, enclose them in single, double, or triple quotes as follows:

```
a = 'Hello World'
b = "Python is groovy"
c = """What is footnote 5?"""
```

The same type of quote used to start a string must be used to terminate it. Triple-quoted strings capture all the text that appears prior to the terminating triple quote, as opposed to single- and double-quoted strings, which must be specified on one logical line. Triple quotes can be done with either single quotes (as in the following example) or double quotes (as in the above example). Triple-quoted strings are useful when the contents of a string literal span multiple lines of text such as the following:

```
print '''Content-type: text/html

<h1> Hello World </h1>
Click <a href="http://www.python.org">here</a>.
'''
```

Strings are sequences of characters indexed by integers starting at zero. To extract a single character, use the indexing operator `s[i]` like this:

```
a = "Hello World"
b = a[4]                # b = 'o'
```

To extract a *substring*, use the *slicing operator* `s[i:j]`. This extracts all elements from `s` whose index `k` is in the range $i <= k < j$. If either index is omitted, the beginning or end of the string is assumed, respectively:

```
c = a[0:5]              # c = "Hello"
d = a[6:]               # d = "World"
e = a[3:8]              # e = "lo Wo"
```

Strings are concatenated with the plus (+) operator:

```
g = a + " This is a test"
```

Other datatypes can be converted into a string by using either the `str()` or `repr()` function or backquotes (`` ` ``), which are a shortcut notation for `repr()`. For example:

```
s = "The value of x is " + str(x)
s = "The value of y is " + repr(y)
s = "The value of y is " + `y`
```

In many cases, `str()` and `repr()` return identical results. However, there are subtle differences in semantics that are described in later chapters.

Lists and Tuples

Just as strings are sequences of characters, lists and tuples are sequences of arbitrary objects. You create a list as follows:

```
names = [ "Dave", "Mark", "Ann", "Phil" ]
```

Lists are indexed by integers starting with zero. Use the indexing operator to access and modify individual items of the list:

```
a = names[2]           # Returns the third item of the list, "Ann"
names[0] = "Jeff"      # Changes the first item to "Jeff"
```

The length of a list can be obtained using the `len()` function:

```
print len(names)       # prints 4
```

To append new items to a list, use the `append()` method:

```
names.append("Kate")
```

To insert an item into the list, use the `insert()` method:

```
names.insert(2, "Sydney")
```

You can extract or reassign a portion of a list by using the slicing operator:

```
b = names[0:2]                          # Returns [ "Jeff", "Mark" ]
c = names[2:]                           # Returns [ "Sydney", "Ann", "Phil", "Kate" ]
names[1] = 'Jeff'                       # Replace the 2nd item in names with 'Jeff'
names[0:2] = ['Dave','Mark','Jeff']     # Replace the first two items of
                                        # the list with the list on the right.
```

Use the plus (+) operator to concatenate lists:

```
a = [1,2,3] + [4,5]      # Result is [1,2,3,4,5]
```

Lists can contain any kind of Python object, including other lists, as in the following example:

```
a = [1,"Dave",3.14, ["Mark", 7, 9, [100,101]], 10]
```

Nested lists are accessed as follows:

```
a[1]             # Returns "Dave"
a[3][2]          # Returns 9
a[3][3][1]       # Returns 101
```

The program in Listing 1.2 illustrates a few more advanced features of lists by reading a list of numbers from a file and outputting the minimum and maximum values.

Listing 1.2   Advanced List Features

```
import sys                     # Load the sys module
f = open(sys.argv[1])          # Filename on the command line
svalues = f.readlines()        # Read all lines into a list
f.close()

# Convert all of the input values from strings to floats
fvalues = [float(s) for s in svalues]

# Print min and max values
print "The minimum value is ", min(fvalues)
print "The maximum value is ", max(fvalues)
```

The first line of this program uses the `import` statement to load the `sys` module from the Python library.

The `open()` method uses a filename that has been supplied as a command-line option and stored in the list `sys.argv`. The `readlines()` method reads all the input lines into a list of strings.

The expression `[float(s) for s in svalues]` constructs a new list by looping over all the strings in the list `svalues` and applying the function `float()` to each element. This particularly powerful method of constructing a list is known as a *list comprehension*.

After the input lines have been converted into a list of floating-point numbers, the built-in `min()` and `max()` functions compute the minimum and maximum values.

Closely related to lists is the tuple datatype. You create tuples by enclosing a group of values in parentheses or with a comma-separated list, like this:

```
a = (1,4,5,-9,10)
b = (7,)                          # Singleton (note extra ,)
person = (first_name, last_name, phone)
```

Sometimes Python recognizes that a tuple is intended even if the parentheses are missing:

```
a = 1,4,5,-9,10
b = 7,
person = first_name, last_name, phone
```

Tuples support most of the same operations as lists, such as indexing, slicing, and concatenation. The only difference is that you cannot modify the contents of a tuple after creation—that is, you cannot modify individual elements, or append new elements to a tuple.

Loops

The simple loops shown earlier used the `while` statement. The other looping construct is the `for` statement, which iterates over the members of a sequence, such as a string, list, or tuple. Here's an example:

```
for i in range(1,10):
        print "2 to the %d power is %d" % (i, 2**i)
```

The `range(i,j)` function constructs a list of integers with values from `i` to `j-1`. If the starting value is omitted, it's taken to be zero. An optional stride can also be given as a third argument. For example:

```
a = range(5)        # a = [0,1,2,3,4]
b = range(1,8)      # b = [1,2,3,4,5,6,7]
c = range(0,14,3)   # c = [0,3,6,9,12]
d = range(8,1,-1)   # d = [8,7,6,5,4,3,2]
```

The `for` statement can iterate over any sequence type and isn't limited to sequences of integers:

```
a = "Hello World"
# Print out the characters in a
for c in a:
        print c

b = ["Dave","Mark","Ann","Phil"]
# Print out the members of a list
for name in b:
        print name
```

`range()` works by constructing a list and populating it with values according to the starting, ending, and stride values. For large ranges, this process is expensive in terms of both memory and runtime performance. To avoid this, you can use the `xrange()` function, as shown here:

```
for i in xrange(1,10):
        print "2 to the %d power is %d" % (i, 2**i)

a = xrange(100000000)       # a = [0,1,2, ..., 99999999]
b = xrange(0,100000000,5)   # b = [0,5,10, ...,99999995]
```

Rather than creating a sequence populated with values, the sequence returned by xrange() computes its values from the starting, ending, and stride values whenever it's accessed.

Dictionaries

A *dictionary* is an associative array or hash table that contains objects indexed by keys. Create a dictionary by enclosing the values in curly braces ({ }) like this:

```
a = {
        "username" : "beazley",
        "home" : "/home/beazley",
        "uid" : 500
    }
```

To access members of a dictionary, use the key-indexing operator as follows:

```
u = a["username"]
d = a["home"]
```

Inserting or modifying objects works like this:

```
a["username"] = "pxl"
a["home"] = "/home/pxl"
a["shell"] = "/usr/bin/tcsh"
```

Although strings are the most common type of key, you can use many other Python objects, including numbers and tuples. Some objects, including lists and dictionaries, cannot be used as keys, because their contents are allowed to change.

Dictionary membership is tested with the has_key() method, as in the following example:

```
if a.has_key("username"):
        username = a["username"]
else:
        username = "unknown user"
```

This particular sequence of steps can also be performed more compactly as follows:

```
username = a.get("username", "unknown user")
```

To obtain a list of dictionary keys, use the keys() method:

```
k = a.keys()          # k = ["username","home","uid","shell"]
```

Use the del statement to remove an element of a dictionary:

```
del a["username"]
```

Functions

You use the def statement to create a function, as shown in the following example:

```
def remainder(a,b):
        q = a/b
        r = a - q*b
        return r
```

To invoke a function, simply use the name of the function followed by its arguments enclosed in parentheses, such as result = remainder(37,15). You can use a tuple to return multiple values from a function, as in the following example:

```
def divide(a,b):
        q = a/b          # If a and b are integers, q is an integer
        r = a - q*b
        return (q,r)
```

When returning multiple values in a tuple, it's often useful to invoke the function as follows:

```
quotient, remainder = divide(1456,33)
```

To assign a default value to a parameter, use assignment:

```
def connect(hostname,port,timeout=300):
        # Function body
```

When default values are given in a function definition, they can be omitted from subsequent function calls. For example:

```
connect('www.python.org', 80)
```

You also can invoke functions by using keyword arguments and supplying the arguments in arbitrary order. For example:

```
connect(port=80,hostname="www.python.org")
```

When variables are created or assigned inside a function, their scope is local. To modify the value of a global variable from inside a function, use the `global` statement as follows:

```
a = 4.5
...
def foo():
        global a
        a - 8.0                  # Changes the global variable a
```

Classes

The `class` statement is used to define new types of objects and for object-oriented programming. For example, the following *class* defines a simple stack:

```
class Stack:
        def __init__(self):                 # Initialize the stack
                self.stack = [ ]
        def push(self,object):
                self.stack.append(object)
        def pop(self):
                return self.stack.pop()
        def length(self):
                return len(self.stack)
```

In the class definition, methods are defined using the `def` statement. The first argument in each method always refers to the object itself. By convention, `self` is the name used for this argument. All operations involving the attributes of an object must explicitly refer to the `self` variable. Methods with leading and trailing double underscores are special methods. For example, `__init__` is used to initialize an object after it's created.

To use a class, write code such as the following:

```
s = Stack()          # Create a stack
s.push("Dave")       # Push some things onto it
s.push(42)
s.push([3,4,5])
x = s.pop()          # x gets [3,4,5]
y - c.pop()          # y gets 42
del s                # Destroy s
```

Exceptions

If an error occurs in your program, an *exception* is raised and an error message such as the following appears:

```
Traceback (most recent call last):
  File "<interactive input>", line 42, in foo.py
NameError: a
```

The error message indicates the type of error that occurred, along with its location. Normally, errors cause a program to abort. However, you can catch and handle exceptions using the try and except statements, like this:

```
try:
    f = open("file.txt","r")
except IOError, e:
    print e
```

If an IOError occurs, details concerning the cause of the error are placed in e and control passes to the code in the except block. If some other kind of exception is raised, it's passed to the enclosing code block (if any). If no errors occur, the code in the except block is ignored.

The raise statement is used to signal an exception. When raising an exception, you can use one of the built-in exceptions, like this:

```
raise RuntimeError, "Unrecoverable error"
```

Or you can create your own exceptions, as described in the section "Defining New Exceptions" in Chapter 5, "Control Flow."

Modules

As your programs grow in size, you'll probably want to break them into multiple files for easier maintenance. To do this, Python allows you to put definitions in a file and use them as a *module* that can be imported into other programs and scripts. To create a module, put the relevant statements and definitions into a file that has the same name as the module. (*Note:* The file must have a .py suffix.) For example:

```
# file : div.py
def divide(a,b):
    q = a/b        # If a and b are integers, q is an integer
    r = a - q*b
    return (q,r)
```

To use your module in other programs, you can use the import statement:

```
import div
a, b = div.divide(2305, 29)
```

import creates a new namespace that contains all the objects defined in the module. To access this namespace, simply use the name of the module as a prefix, as in div.divide() in the preceding example.

If you want to import a module using a different name, supply the import statement with an optional as qualifier as follows:

```
import div as foo
a,b = foo.divide(2305,29)
```

To import specific definitions into the current namespace, use the `from` statement:

```
from div import divide
a,b = divide(2305,29)        # No longer need the div prefix
```

To load all of a module's contents into the current namespace, you can also use the following:

```
from div import *
```

Finally, the `dir()` function lists the contents of a module and is a useful tool for interactive experimentation, since it can be used to provide a list of available functions and variables:

```
>>> import string
>>> dir(string)
['__builtins__', '__doc__', '__file__', '__name__', '_idmap',
 '_idmapL', '_lower', '_swapcase', '_upper', 'atof', 'atof_error',
 'atoi', 'atoi_error', 'atol', 'atol_error', 'capitalize',
 'capwords', 'center', 'count', 'digits', 'expandtabs', 'find',
 ...
>>>
```

2

Lexical Conventions and Syntax

This chapter describes the syntactic and lexical conventions of a Python program. Topics include line structure, grouping of statements, reserved words, literals, operators, and tokens. In addition, the use of Unicode string literals is described in detail.

Line Structure and Indentation

Each statement in a program is terminated with a newline. Long statements can span multiple lines by using the line-continuation character (\), as shown in the following example:

```
a = math.cos(3*(x-n)) + \
    math.sin(3*(y-n))
```

You don't need the line-continuation character when the definition of a triple-quoted string, list, tuple, or dictionary spans multiple lines. More generally, any part of a program enclosed in parentheses (...), brackets [...], braces {...}, or triple quotes can span multiple lines without use of the line-continuation character.

Indentation is used to denote different blocks of code, such as the bodies of functions, conditionals, loops, and classes. The amount of indentation used for the first statement of a block is arbitrary, but the indentation of the entire block must be consistent. For example:

```
if a:
    statement1      # Consistent indentation
    statement2
else:
    statement3
      statement4    # Inconsistent indentation (error)
```

If the body of a function, conditional, loop, or class is short and contains only a few statements, they can be placed on the same line, like this:

```
if a:   statement1
else:   statement2
```

To denote an empty body or block, use the pass statement. For example:

```
if a:
    pass
else:
    statements
```

Although tabs can be used for indentation, this practice is discouraged. When tab characters are encountered, they're converted into the number of spaces required to move to the next column that's a multiple of 8. (For example, a tab appearing in column 11 inserts enough spaces to move to column 16.) Running Python with the -t option prints warning messages when tabs and spaces are mixed inconsistently within the same program block. The -tt option turns these warning messages into TabError exceptions.

To place more than one statement on a line, separate the statements with a semicolon (;). A line containing a single statement can also be terminated by a semicolon.

The # character denotes a comment that extends to the end of the line. A # appearing inside a quoted string doesn't start a comment, however.

Finally, the interpreter ignores all blank lines except when running in interactive mode.

Identifiers and Reserved Words

An *identifier* is a name used to identify variables, functions, classes, modules, and other objects. Identifiers can include letters, numbers, and the underscore character (_), but must always start with a non-numeric character. Letters are currently confined to the characters A–Z and a–z in the ISO-Latin character set. Because identifiers are case sensitive, FOO is different from foo. Special symbols such as $, %, and @ are not allowed in identifiers. In addition, words such as if, else, and for are reserved and cannot be used as identifier names. The following list shows all the reserved words:

and	elif	global	or
assert	else	if	pass
break	except	import	print
class	exec	in	raise
continue	finally	is	return
def	for	lambda	try
del	from	not	while

Identifiers starting or ending with underscores often have special meanings. For example, identifiers starting with a single underscore such as _foo are not imported by the from module import * statement. Identifiers with leading and trailing double underscores such as __init__ are reserved for special methods, and identifiers with leading double underscores such as __bar are used to implement private class members as described in Chapter 7, "Classes and Object-Oriented Programming." General-purpose use of similar identifiers should be avoided.

Literals

There are four built-in numeric types: integers, long integers, floating-point numbers, and complex numbers.

A number such as 1234 is interpreted as a decimal integer. To specify octal and hexadecimal integers, precede the value with 0 or 0x, respectively—0644 or 0x100fea8. Write a long integer using a trailing 1 (ell) or L character, as in 1234567890L. Unlike integers, which are limited by machine precision, long integers can be of any length (up to the maximum memory of the machine). Numbers such as 123.34 and 1.2334e+02 are interpreted as floating-point numbers. An integer or floating-point number with a trailing j or J, such as 12.34J, is an imaginary number. You can create complex numbers with real and imaginary parts by adding a real number and an imaginary number, as in 1.2 + 12.34J.

Python currently supports two types of string literals:

- 8-bit character data (ASCII)

- Unicode (16-bit wide character data)

The most commonly used string type is 8-bit character data, because of its use in representing characters from the ASCII or ISO-Latin character set as well as representing raw binary data as a sequence of bytes. By default, 8-bit string literals are defined by enclosing text in single ('), double ("), or triple (''' or """) quotes. You must use the same type of quote to start and terminate a string. The backslash (\) character is used to escape special characters such as newlines, the backslash itself, quotes, and nonprinting characters. Table 2.1 shows the accepted escape codes. Unrecognized escape sequences are left in the string unmodified and include the leading backslash. Furthermore, strings may contain embedded null bytes and binary data. Triple-quoted strings can span multiple lines and include unescaped newlines and quotes.

Table 2.1   Standard Character Escape Codes

Character	Description
\	Newline continuation
\\	Backslash
\'	Single quote
\"	Double quote
\a	Bell
\b	Backspace
\e	Escape
\0	Null
\n	Line feed
\v	Vertical tab
\t	Horizontal tab
\r	Carriage return
\f	Form feed
\000	Octal value (\000 to \377)
\xhh	Hexadecimal value (\x00 to \xff)
\uhhhh	Unicode character value (Unicode strings only)

Unicode strings are used to represent multibyte international character sets and allow for 65,536 unique characters. Unicode string literals are defined by preceding an ordinary string literal with a u or U, such as in u"hello". In Unicode, each character is internally represented by a 16-bit integer value. For the purposes of notation, this value is written as U+XXXX, where XXXX is a four-digit hexadecimal number. (*Note:* This notation is only a convention used to describe Unicode characters and is not Python syntax.) For example, u+0068 is the Unicode character for the letter h in the Latin-1 character set. When Unicode string literals are defined, ordinary characters and escape codes are directly mapped as Unicode ordinals in the range [U+0000, U+00FF]. For example, the string "hello\n" is mapped to the sequence of ASCII values 0x68, 0x65, 0x6c, 0x6c, 0x6f, 0x0a, whereas the Unicode string u"hello\n" is mapped to the sequence U+0068, U+0065, U+006C, U+006C, U+006F, U+000A. Arbitrary Unicode characters are defined using the \uxxxx escape sequence. This sequence can only appear inside a Unicode string literal and must always specify a four-digit hexadecimal value. For example:

```
s = u"\u0068\u0065\u006c\u006c\u006f\u000a"
```

In older versions of Python, the \xxxxx escape could be used to define Unicode characters. Although this is still allowed, the \uxxxx sequence should be used instead. In addition, the \000 octal escape sequence can be used to define Unicode characters in the range [U+0000, U+01FF].

Unicode string literals should not be defined using a sequence of raw bytes that correspond to a multibyte Unicode data encoding such as UTF-8 or UTF-16. For example, writing a raw UTF-8 encoded string such as u'M\303\274ller' produces the seven-character Unicode sequence U+004D, U+00C3, U+00BC, U+006C, U+006C, U+0065, U+0072, which is probably not what you wanted. This is because in UTF-8, the multibyte sequence \303\274 is supposed to represent U+00FC, not U+00C3, U+00BC. For more details about Unicode encodings, see Chapter 3, "Types and Objects," Chapter 4, "Operators and Expressions," and Chapter 9, "Input and Output."

Optionally, you can precede a string with an r or R, such as in r'\n\"'. These strings are known as *raw strings* because all their backslash characters are left intact—that is, the string literally contains the enclosed text, including the backslashes. Raw strings cannot end in a single backslash, such as r"\". When raw Unicode strings are defined by preceding the string with ur or UR, \uxxxx escape sequences are still interpreted as Unicode characters, provided that the number of preceding \ characters is odd. For instance, ur"\u1234" defines a raw Unicode string with the character U+1234, whereas ur"\\u1234" defines a seven-character Unicode string in which the first two characters are slashes and the remaining five characters are the literal "u1234". Also, when defining raw Unicode string literals the "r" must appear after the "u" as shown.

Adjacent strings (separated by white space or a newline continuation character) such as "hello" 'world' are concatenated to form a single string: "helloworld". String concatenation works with any mix of ordinary, raw, and Unicode strings. However, whenever one of the strings is Unicode, the final result is always coerced to Unicode. Therefore, "hello" u"world" is the same as u"hello" + u"world". In addition, due to subtle implementation aspects of Unicode, writing "s1" u"s2" may produce a result that's different from writing u"s1s2". The details of this coercion process are described further in Chapter 4 and Appendix A (the Python library).

If Python is run with the -u command-line option, all string literals are interpreted as Unicode.

Values enclosed in square brackets [...], parentheses (...), and braces {...} denote lists, tuples, and dictionaries, respectively, as in the following example:

```
a = [ 1, 3.4, 'hello' ]        # A list
b = ( 10, 20, 30 )             # A tuple
c = { 'a': 3, 'b':42 }         # A dictionary
```

Operators, Delimiters, and Special Symbols

The following operator tokens are recognized:

```
+       -       *       **      /       %       <<      >>      &       |       ^
+=      -=      *=      **=     /=      %=      <<=     >>=     &=      |=      ^=
~       <       >       <=      >=      ==      !=      <>
```

The following tokens serve as delimiters for expressions, lists, dictionaries, and various parts of a statement:

```
(       )       [       ]       {       }       ,       :       .       `       =       ;
```

For example, the equal (=) character serves as a delimiter between the name and value of an assignment, while the comma (,) character is used to delimit arguments to a function, elements in lists and tuples, and so on. The period (.) is also used in floating-point numbers and in the ellipsis (...) used in extended slicing operations.

Finally, the following special symbols are also used:

```
'       "       #       \
```

The characters @, $, and ? cannot appear in a program except inside a quoted string literal.

Documentation Strings

If the first statement of a module, class, or function definition is a string, that string becomes a *documentation string* for the associated object, as in the following example:

```
def fact(n):
    "This function computes a factorial"
    if (n <= 1): return 1
    else: return n*fact(n-1)
```

Code-browsing and documentation-generation tools sometimes use documentation strings. The strings are accessible in the _ _doc_ _ attribute of an object, as shown here:

```
>>> print fact._ _doc_ _
This function computes a factorial
>>>
```

The indentation of the documentation string must be consistent with all the other statements in a definition. Furthermore, adjacent strings appearing on different lines are not concatenated to form a single documentation string.

3

Types and Objects

All the data stored in a Python program is built around the concept of an *object*. Objects include fundamental datatypes such as numbers, strings, lists, and dictionaries. It's also possible to create user-defined objects in the form of classes or extension types. This chapter describes the Python object model and provides an overview of the built-in datatypes. Chapter 4, "Operators and Expressions," further describes operators and expressions.

Terminology

Every piece of data stored in a program is an object. Each object has an identity, a type, and a value.

For example, when you write a = 42, an integer object is created with the value of 42. You can view the *identity* of an object as a pointer to its location in memory. In this example, a is a name that refers to this specific location.

The *type* of an object (which is itself a special kind of object) describes the internal representation of the object as well as the methods and operations that it supports. When an object of a particular type is created, that object is sometimes called an *instance* of that type (although an instance of a type should not be confused with an instance of a user-defined class). After an object is created, its identity and type cannot be changed. If an object's value can be modified, the object is said to be *mutable*. If the value cannot be modified, the object is said to be *immutable*. An object that contains references to other objects is said to be a *container* or *collection*.

In addition to holding a value, many objects define a number of data attributes and methods. An *attribute* is a property or value associated with an object. A *method* is a function that performs some sort of operation on an object when the method is invoked. Attributes and methods are accessed using the dot (.) operator, as shown in the following example:

```
a = 3 + 4j        # Create a complex number
r = a.real        # Get the real part (an attribute)

b = [1, 2, 3]     # Create a list
b.append(7)       # Add a new element using the append method
```

Object Identity and Type

The built-in function id() returns the identity of an object as an integer. This integer usually corresponds to the object's location in memory, although this is specific to the implementation. The is operator compares the identity of two objects. The built-in function type() returns the type of an object. For example:

```
# Compare two objects
def compare(a,b):
    print 'The identity of a is ', id(a)
    print 'The identity of b is ', id(b)
    if a is b:
        print 'a and b are the same object'
    if a == b:
        print 'a and b have the same value'
    if type(a) is type(b):
        print 'a and b have the same type'
```

The type of an object is itself an object. This type object is uniquely defined and is always the same for all instances of a given type. Therefore, the type can be compared using the is operator. The standard module types contains the type objects for all the built-in types and can be used to perform type-checking. For example:

```
import types
if type(s) is types.ListType:
    print 'Is a list'
else:
    print 'Is not a list'
```

When comparing object types in which user-defined classes are involved, it may be better to use the isinstance() function as described in Chapter 7, "Classes and Object-Oriented Programming." The isinstance(s, c) function correctly detects instances s of classes descended from the class c, as well as instances of c itself.

Reference Counting and Garbage Collection

All objects are reference-counted. An object's reference count is increased whenever it's assigned to a new name or placed in a container such as a list, tuple, or dictionary, as shown here:

```
a = 3.4       # Creates an object '3.4'
b = a         # Increases reference count on '3.4'
c = []
c.append(b)   # Increases reference count on '3.4'
```

This example creates a single object containing the value 3.4. The variable a is merely a name that refers to the newly created object. When b is assigned a, b becomes a new name for the same object, and the object's reference count increases. Likewise, when you place b into a list, the object's reference count increases again. In the example, only one object contains 3.4. All other operations are simply creating new references to the object.

An object's reference count is decreased by the del statement or whenever a reference goes out of scope (or is reassigned). For example:

```
del a       # Decrease reference count of 3.4
b = 7.8     # Decrease reference count of 3.4
c[0]=2.0    # Decrease reference count of 3.4
```

When an object's reference count reaches zero, it is garbage collected. However, in some cases a circular dependency may exist among a collection of objects that are no longer in use. For example:

```
a = { }
b = { }
a['b'] = b      # a contains reference to b
b['a'] = a      # b contains reference to a
del a
del b
```

In this example, the del statements decrease the reference count of a and b and destroy the names used to refer to the underlying objects. However, because each object contains a reference to the other, the reference count doesn't drop to zero and the objects remain allocated. To address this problem, the interpreter periodically executes a cycle-detector that searches for cycles of inaccessible objects and deletes them. The cycle-detection algorithm can be fine-tuned and controlled using functions in the gc module described in Appendix A, "The Python Library."

References and Copies

When a program makes an assignment such as a = b, a new reference to b is created. For immutable objects such as numbers and strings, this assignment effectively creates a copy of b. However, the behavior is quite different for mutable objects such as lists and dictionaries. For example:

```
b = [1,2,3,4]
a = b          # a is a reference to b
a[2] = -100    # Change an element in 'a'
print b        # Produces '[1, 2, -100, 4]'
```

Because a and b refer to the same object in this example, a change made to one of the variables is reflected in the other. To avoid this, you have to create a copy of an object rather than a new reference.

Two types of copy operations are applied to container objects such as lists and dictionaries: a shallow copy and a deep copy. A *shallow copy* creates a new object, but populates it with references to the items contained in the original object. For example:

```
b = [ 1, 2, [3,4] ]
a = b[:]           # Create a shallow copy of b.
a.append(100)      # Append element to a.
print b            # Produces '[1,2, [3,4]]'. b unchanged.
a[2][0] = -100     # Modify an element of a.
print b            # Produces '[1,2, [-100,4]]'.
```

In this case, a and b are separate list objects, but the elements they contain are shared. Thus, a modification to one of the elements of a also modifies an element of b as shown.

A *deep copy* creates a new object and recursively copies all the objects it contains. There is no built-in function to create deep copies of objects. However, the copy.deepcopy() function in the standard library can be used, as shown in the following example:

```
import copy
b = [1, 2, [3, 4] ]
a = copy.deepcopy(b)
```

Built-in Types

Approximately two dozen types are built into the Python interpreter and grouped into a few major categories, as shown in Table 3.1. Some categories include familiar objects such as numbers and sequences. Others are used during program execution and are of little practical use to most programmers. The next few sections describe the most commonly used built-in types.

Table 3.1   Built-in Python Types

Type Category	Type Name	Description
None	NoneType	The null object
Numbers	IntType	Integer
	LongType	Arbitrary-precision integer
	FloatType	Floating-point number
	ComplexType	Complex number
Sequences	StringType	Character string
	UnicodeType	Unicode character string
	ListType	List
	TupleType	Tuple
	XRangeType	Returned by xrange()
	BufferType	Buffer; returned by buffer()
Mapping	DictType	Dictionary
Callable	BuiltinFunctionType	Built-in functions
	BuiltinMethodType	Built-in methods
	ClassType	Class object
	FunctionType	User-defined function
	InstanceType	Class object instance
	MethodType	Bound class method
	UnboundMethodType	Unbound class method
Modules	ModuleType	Module
Classes	ClassType	Class definition
Class Instance	InstanceType	Class instance
Files	FileType	File
Internal	CodeType	Byte-compiled code
	FrameType	Execution frame
	TracebackType	Stack traceback of an exception
	SliceType	Generated by extended slices
	EllipsisType	Used in extended slices

Note: ClassType and InstanceType appear twice in Table 3.1 because classes and instances are both callable under special circumstances.

The None Type

The None type denotes a null object. Python provides exactly one null object, which is written as None in a program. This object is returned by functions that don't explicitly return a value. None is frequently used as the default value of optional arguments, so that the function can detect whether the caller has actually passed a value for that argument. None has no attributes and evaluates to false in Boolean expressions.

Numeric Types

Python uses four numeric types: integers, long integers, floating-point numbers, and complex numbers. All numeric objects are signed and immutable.

Integers represent whole numbers in the range of −2147483648 to 2147483647 (the range may be larger on some machines). Internally, integers are stored as 2's complement binary values, in 32 or more bits. If the result of an operation exceeds the allowed range of values, an OverflowError exception is raised. Long integers represent whole numbers of unlimited range (limited only by available memory).

Floating-point numbers are represented using the native double-precision (64-bit) representation of floating-point numbers on the machine. Normally this is IEEE 754, which provides approximately 17 digits of precision and an exponent in the range of −308 to 308. This is the same as the double type in C. Python doesn't support 32-bit single-precision floating-point numbers. If space and precision are an issue in your program, consider using Numerical Python (http://numpy.sourceforge.net).

Complex numbers are represented as a pair of floating-point numbers. The real and imaginary parts of a complex number z are available in z.real and z.imag.

Sequence Types

Sequences represent ordered sets of objects indexed by non-negative integers and include strings, Unicode strings, lists, tuples, xrange objects, and buffer objects. Strings and buffers are sequences of characters, xrange objects are sequences of integers, and lists and tuples are sequences of arbitrary Python objects. Strings, Unicode strings, and tuples are immutable; lists allow insertion, deletion, and substitution of elements. Buffers are described later in this section.

Table 3.2 shows the operators and methods that you can apply to all sequence types. Element i of a sequence s is selected using the indexing operator s[i], and a subsequence is selected using the slicing operator s[i:j]. (These operations are described in Chapter 4.) The length of any sequence is returned using the built-in len(s) function. You can find the minimum and maximum values of a sequence by using the built-in min(s) and max(s) functions. However, these functions only work for sequences in which the elements can be ordered (typically numbers and strings).

Table 3.3 shows the additional operators that can be applied to mutable sequences such as lists.

Table 3.2   Operations and Methods Applicable to All Sequences

Item	Description
s[i]	Returns element i of a sequence
s[i:j]	Returns a slice
len(s)	Number of elements in s
min(s)	Minimum value in s
max(s)	Maximum value in s

Table 3.3   Operations Applicable to Mutable Sequences

Item	Description
s[i] = v	Item assignment
s[i:j] = t	Slice assignment
del s[i]	Item deletion
del s[i:j]	Slice deletion

Additionally, lists support the methods shown in Table 3.4. The built-in function list(s) converts any sequence type to a list. If s is already a list, this function constructs a new list that's a shallow copy of s. The s.append(x) method appends a new element x to the end of the list. The s.index(x) method searches the list for the first occurrence of x. If no such element is found, a ValueError exception is raised. Similarly, the s.remove(x) method removes the first occurrence of x from the list. The s.extend(t) method extends list s by appending the elements in sequence t. The s.sort() method sorts the elements of a list and optionally accepts a comparison function. This function should take two arguments and return negative, zero, or positive, depending on whether the first argument is smaller, equal to, or larger than the second argument, respectively. The s.reverse() method reverses the order of the items in the list. Both the sort() and reverse() methods operate on the list elements in place and return None.

Table 3.4   List Methods

Method	Description
list(s)	Converts sequence s to a list.
s.append(x)	Appends a new element x to the end of s.
s.extend(t)	Appends a new list t to the end of s.
s.count(x)	Counts occurrences of x in s.
s.index(x)	Returns the smallest i where s[i] == x.
s.insert(i,x)	Inserts x at index i.
s.pop([i])	Returns the element i and removes it from the list. If i is omitted, the last element is returned.
s.remove(x)	Searches for x and removes it from s.
s.reverse()	Reverses items of s in place.
s.sort([cmpfunc])	Sorts items of s in place. cmpfunc is a comparison function.

Python provides two string object types. Standard strings are sequences of bytes containing 8-bit data. They may contain binary data and embedded null bytes. Unicode strings are sequences of 16-bit characters encoded in a format known as *UCS-2*. This allows for 65,536 unique character values. Although the latest Unicode standard supports up to 1 million unique character values, these extra characters are not currently supported by Python. Instead, they must be encoded as a special two-character (4-byte) sequence known as a *surrogate pair*—the interpretation of which is up to the application. Python does not check data for Unicode compliance or the proper use of surrogates.

Both standard and Unicode strings support the methods shown in Table 3.5. Although these methods operate on string instances, none of these methods actually modifies the underlying string data. Thus, methods such as `s.capitalize()`, `s.center()`, and `s.expandtabs()` always return a new string as opposed to modifying the string `s`. Character tests such as `s.isalnum()` and `s.isupper()` return true or false if all the characters in the string `s` satisfy the test. Furthermore, these tests always return false if the length of the string is zero. The `s.find()`, `s.index()`, `s.rfind()`, and `s.rindex()` methods are used to search `s` for a substring. All these functions return an integer index to the substring in `s`. In addition, the `find()` method returns -1 if the substring isn't found, whereas the `index()` method raises a `ValueError` exception. Many of the string methods accept optional `start` and `end` parameters, which are integer values specifying the starting and ending indices in `s`. The `s.translate()` method is used to perform character substitutions, and is described in the `string` module in Appendix A. The `s.encode()` method is used to transform the string data into a specified character encoding. As input it accepts an encoding name such as `'ascii'`, `'utf-8'`, or `'utf-16'`. This method is most commonly used to convert Unicode strings into a data encoding suitable for I/O operations and is described further in Chapter 9, "Input and Output." More details about string methods can be found in the documentation for the `string` module (see Appendix A).

Table 3.5   String Methods

Method	Description
`s.capitalize()`	Capitalizes the first character of `s`.
`s.center(width)`	Centers the string in a field of length `width`.
`s.count(sub [,start [,end]])`	Counts occurrences of the specified substring `sub`.
`s.encode([encoding [,errors]])`	Returns an encoded version of the string.
`s.endswith(suffix [,start [,end]])`	Checks the end of the string for a suffix.
`s.expandtabs([tabsize])`	Expands tabs.
`s.find(sub [,start [,end]])`	Finds the first occurrence of the specified substring `sub`.
`s.index(sub [,start [,end]])`	Finds the first occurrence of `sub` or raises an exception.
`s.isalnum()`	Checks whether all characters are alphanumeric.

continues >>

Table 3.5   Continued

Method	Description
s.isalpha()	Checks whether all characters are alphabetic.
s.isdigit()	Checks whether all characters are digits.
s.islower()	Checks whether all characters are lowercase.
s.isspace()	Checks whether all characters are white-space.
s.istitle()	Checks whether the string is title-cased (first letter of each word capitalized).
s.isupper()	Checks whether all characters are uppercase.
s.join(t)	Joins the strings in list t using s as a delimiter.
s.ljust(width)	Left-aligns s in a string of size width.
s.lower()	Returns s converted to lowercase.
s.lstrip()	Removes leading whitespace.
s.replace(old, new [,maxreplace])	Replaces the substring old with new.
s.rfind(sub [,start [,end]])	Finds the last occurrence of a substring.
s.rindex(sub [,start [,end]])	Finds the last occurrence of sub or raises an exception.
s.rjust(width)	Right-aligns s in a string of length width.
s.rstrip()	Removes trailing whitespace.
s.split([sep [,maxsplit]])	Splits a string using sep as a delimiter. maxsplit is the maximum number of splits to perform.
s.splitlines([keepends])	Splits a string into a list of lines. If keepends is 1, trailing newlines are preserved.
s.startswith(prefix [,start [,end]])	Checks whether a string starts with prefix.
s.strip()	Removes leading and trailing whitespace.
s.swapcase()	Returns s with uppercase converted to lowercase and vice versa.
s.title()	Returns a title-cased version of the string.
s.translate(table [,deletechars])	Translates a string using a character translation table.
s.upper()	Returns s converted to uppercase.

The built-in function range([i,]j [,stride]) constructs a list and populates it with integers k such that $i <= k < j$. The first index i and the stride are optional and have default values of 0 and 1, respectively. The built-in function xrange([i,]j [,stride]) performs a similar operation, but returns an immutable sequence of type XRangeType. Rather than storing all the values in a list, this sequence calculates its values whenever it's accessed. Consequently, it's much more memory efficient when working with large sequences of integers. The XRangeType provides a single method, s.tolist(), that converts its values to a list.

Buffer objects are typically used to provide a sequence interface to a region of memory in which each byte is treated as an 8-bit character. Although there is no special syntax for creating a buffer object, they can be created using the built-in function buffer(*obj* [, *offset* [, *size*]]). Buffer objects usually share the same memory as that of the underlying object *obj*. Because of this, they can sometimes be used as a more memory-efficient mechanism for taking slices of strings and other byte-oriented data. In addition, buffers can sometimes be used to access the raw data used to store the contents of other Python types such as arrays in the array module and Unicode strings. Buffers may or may not be mutable, depending on the mutability of *obj*.

Mapping Types

A *mapping object* represents an arbitrary collection of objects that are indexed by another collection of nearly arbitrary key values. Unlike a sequence, a mapping object is unordered and can be indexed by numbers, strings, and other objects. Mappings are mutable.

Dictionaries are the only built-in mapping type and are Python's version of a hash table or associative array. You can use any immutable object as a dictionary key value (strings, numbers, tuples, and so on). Lists, dictionaries, or tuples containing mutable objects cannot be used as keys. (The dictionary type requires key values to remain constant.)

To select an item in a mapping object, use the key index operator *m*[*k*] where *k* is a key value. If the key is not found, a KeyError exception is raised. The len(*m*) function returns the number of items contained in a mapping object. Table 3.6 lists methods and operations.

Table 3.6 Methods and Operations for Mapping Types

Item	Description
len(*m*)	Returns the number of items in *m*.
m[*k*]	Returns the item of *m* with key *k*.
m[*k*] = *x*	Sets *m*[*k*] to *x*.
del *m*[*k*]	Removes *m*[*k*] from *m*.
m.clear()	Removes all items from *m*.
m.copy()	Returns a copy of *m*.
m.has_key(*k*)	Returns 1 if *m* has key *k*, 0 otherwise.
m.items()	Returns a list of (*key*,*value*) pairs.
m.keys()	Returns a list of key values.
m.update(*b*)	Adds all objects from dictionary *b* to *m*.
m.values()	Returns a list of all values in *m*.
m.get(*k* [,*v*])	Returns *m*[*k*] if found; otherwise, returns *v*.
m.setdefault(*k* [, *v*])	Returns *m*[*k*] if found; otherwise, returns *v* and sets *m*[*k*] = *v*.
m.popitem()	Removes a random (*key*,*value*) pair from *m* and returns it as a tuple.

The `m.clear()` method removes all items. The `m.copy()` method makes a shallow copy of the items contained in a mapping object and places them in a new mapping object. The `m.items()` method returns a list containing (*key,value*) pairs. The `m.keys()` method returns a list with all the key values and the `m.values()` method returns a list with all the objects. The `m.update(b)` method updates the current mapping object by inserting all the (*key,value*) pairs found in the mapping object *b*. The `m.get(k [,v])` method retrieves an object, but allows for an optional default value *v* that's returned if no such object exists. The `m.setdefault(k [,v])` method is similar to `m.get()` except that in addition to returning *v* if no object exists, it sets `m[k] = v`. If *v* is omitted, it defaults to `None`. The `m.popitem()` method is used to iteratively destroy the contents of a dictionary.

Callable Types

Callable types represent objects that support the function call operation. There are several flavors of objects with this property, including user-defined functions, built-in functions, and methods associated with classes.

User-defined functions are callable objects created at the module level by using the `def` statement or `lambda` operator. (Functions defined within class definitions are called *methods* and are described shortly.) Functions are first-class objects that behave just like any other Python object. As a result, you can assign them to variables or place them in lists, tuples, and dictionaries, as shown in the following example:

```
def foo(x,y):
    print '%s + %s is %s' % (str(x), str(y), str(x+y))

# Assign to a new variable
bar = foo
bar(3,4)             # Invokes 'foo' defined above

# Place in a container
d = { }
d['callback'] = foo
d['callback'](3,4)  # Invokes 'foo'
```

A user-defined function *f* has the following attributes:

Attribute(s)	Description
`f.__doc__` or `f.func_doc`	Documentation string
`f.__name__` or `f.func_name`	Function name
`f.__dict__` or `f.func_dict`	Dictionary containing function attributes
`f.func_code`	Byte-compiled code
`f.func_defaults`	Tuple containing the default arguments
`f.func_globals`	Dictionary defining the global namespace
`f.func_closure`	Tuple containing data related to nested scopes

Methods are functions that operate only on instances of an object. Typically, methods are defined inside a class definition, as shown in Listing 3.1.

Listing 3.1 *Defining a Method*

```
# A queue of objects ranked by priorities
class PriorityQueue:
    def __init__(self):
        self.items = [ ]                # List of (priority, item)
    def insert(self,priority,item):
        for i in range(len(self.items)):
            if self.items[i][0] > priority:
                self.items.insert(i,(priority,item))
                break
        else:
            self.items.append((priority,item))
    def remove(self):
        try:
            return self.items.pop(0)[1]
        except IndexError:
            raise RuntimeError, 'Queue is empty'
```

An *unbound method object* is a method that hasn't yet been associated with a specific instance of an object. The methods contained within a class definition are unbound until they're attached to a specific object. For example:

```
m = PriorityQueue.insert        # Unbound method
```

To invoke an unbound method, supply an instance of an object as the first argument:

```
pq = PriorityQueue()
m = PriorityQueue.insert
m(pq,5,"Python")                # Invokes pq.insert(5,"Python")
```

A *bound method object* is a function that has been bound to a specific object instance. For example:

```
pq = PriorityQueue()     # Create a PriorityQueue instance
n = pq.insert            # n is a method bound to pq
```

A bound method implicitly contains a reference to the associated instance, so it can be invoked as follows:

```
n(5,"Python")                   # Invokes pq.insert(5,"Python")
```

Bound and unbound methods are no more than a thin wrapper around an ordinary function object. The following attributes are defined for method objects:

Attribute	Description
m.__doc__	Documentation string
m.__name__	Method name
m.__dict__	Method attributes
m.im_class	Class in which this method was defined
m.im_func	Function object implementing the method
m.im_self	Instance associated with the method (None if unbound)

So far, this discussion has focused on functions and methods, but class objects (described shortly) are also callable. When a class is called, a new class instance is created. In addition, if the class defines an `__init__()` method, it's called to initialize the newly created instance. The creation of a `PriorityQueue` in the earlier example illustrates this behavior.

A class instance is also callable if its class defines a special method `__call__()`. If this method is defined for a class instance *x*, then *x(args)* invokes the method *x.__call__(args)*.

The final types of callable objects are *built-in functions* and *methods*. Built-in functions and methods correspond to code written in extension modules and are usually written in C or C++. The following attributes are available for built-in methods:

Attribute	Description
b.__doc__	Documentation string
b.__name__	Function/method name
b.__self__	Instance associated with the method
b.__members__	List of method attribute names

For built-in functions such as len(), the __self__ is set to None, indicating that the function isn't bound to any specific object. For built-in methods such as x.append() where x is a list object, __self__ is set to x.

Modules

The *module* type is a container that holds objects loaded with the import statement. When the statement import foo appears in a program, for example, the name foo is assigned to the corresponding module object. Modules define a namespace that's implemented using a dictionary accessible in the attribute __dict__. Whenever an attribute of a module is referenced (using the dot operator), it's translated into a dictionary lookup. For example, m.x is equivalent to m.__dict__["x"]. Likewise, assignment to an attribute such as m.x = y is equivalent to m.__dict__["x"] = y. The following attributes are available:

Attribute	Description
m.__dict__	Dictionary associated with the module
m.__doc__	Module documentation string
m.__name__	Name of the module
m.__file__	File from which the module was loaded
m.__path__	Fully qualified package name, defined when the module object refers to a package

Classes

Classes are created using the class statement, as described in Chapter 7. Like modules, classes are implemented using a dictionary that contains all the objects defined within the class, and defines a namespace. References to class attributes such as c.x are translated into a dictionary lookup c.__dict__["x"]. If an attribute isn't found in this dictionary, the search continues in the list of base classes. This search is depth first, left to right, in the order that base classes were specified in the class definition. Attribute assignment such as c.y = 5 always updates the __dict__ attribute of c, not the dictionaries of any base class.

The following attributes are defined by class objects:

Attribute	Description
c.__dict__	Dictionary associated with the class
c.__doc__	Class documentation string
c.__name__	Name of the class
c.__module__	Name of the module in which the class was defined
c.__bases__	Tuple containing base classes

Class Instances

A *class instance* is an object created by calling a class object. Each instance has its own local namespace that's implemented as a dictionary. This dictionary and the associated class object have the following attributes:

Attribute	Description
x.__dict__	Dictionary associated with an instance
x.__class__	Class to which an instance belongs

When the attribute of an object is referenced, such as in x.a, the interpreter first searches in the local dictionary for x.__dict__["a"]. If it doesn't find the name locally, the search continues by performing a lookup on the class defined in the __class__ attribute. If no match is found, the search continues with base classes as described earlier. If still no match is found and the object's class defines a __getattr__() method, it's used to perform the lookup. The assignment of attributes such as x.a = 4 always updates x.__dict__, not the dictionaries of classes or base classes.

Files

The file object represents an open file and is returned by the built-in open() function (as well as a number of functions in the standard library). For more details about this type, see Chapter 9.

Internal Types

A number of objects used by the interpreter are exposed to the user. These include traceback objects, code objects, frame objects, slice objects, and the Ellipsis object.

Code Objects

Code objects represent raw byte-compiled executable code or bytecode and are typically returned by the built-in compile() function. Code objects are similar to functions except that they don't contain any context related to the namespace in which the code was defined, nor do code objects store information about default argument values. A code object c has the read-only attributes described in the following table:

Attribute	Description
c.co_name	Function name.
c.co_argcount	Number of positional arguments (including default values).
c.co_nlocals	Number of local variables used by the function.
c.co_varnames	Tuple containing names of local variables.
c.co_code	String representing raw bytecode.
c.co_consts	Tuple containing the literals used by the bytecode.
c.co_names	Tuple containing names used by the bytecode.
c.co_filename	Filename of the file in which the code was compiled.
c.co_firstlineno	First line number of the function.
c.co_lnotab	String encoding bytecode offsets to line numbers.
c.co_stacksize	Required stack size (including local variables).
c.co_flags	Integer containing interpreter flags. Bit 2 is set if the function uses a variable number of positional arguments using "*args". Bit 3 is set if the function allows arbitrary keyword arguments using "**kwargs". All other bits are reserved.

Frame Objects

Frame objects are used to represent execution frames and most frequently occur in traceback objects (described next). A frame object f has the following read-only attributes:

Attribute	Description
f.f_back	Previous stack frame (toward the caller).
f.f_code	Code object being executed.
f.f_locals	Dictionary used for local variables.
f.f_globals	Dictionary used for global variables.
f.f_builtins	Dictionary used for built-in names.
f.f_restricted	Set to 1 if executing in restricted execution mode.
f.f_lineno	Line number.
f.f_lasti	Current instruction. This is an index into the bytecode string of f_code.

The following attributes can be modified (and are used by debuggers and other tools):

Attribute	Description
f.f_trace	Function called at the start of each source code line
f.f_exc_type	Most recent exception type
f.f_exc_value	Most recent exception value
f.f_exc_traceback	Most recent exception traceback

Traceback Objects

Traceback objects are created when an exception occurs and contains stack trace information. When an exception handler is entered, the stack trace can be retrieved using the `sys.exc_info()` function. The following read-only attributes are available in traceback objects:

Attribute	Description
t.tb_next	Next level in the stack trace (toward the execution frame where the exception occurred)
t.tb_frame	Execution frame object of the current level
t.tb_lineno	Line number where the exception occurred
t.tb_lasti	Instruction being executed in the current level

Slice Objects

Slice objects are used to represent slices given in extended slice syntax, such as `a[i:j:stride]`, `a[i:j, n:m]`, or `a[..., i:j]`. Slice objects are also created using the built-in `slice([i,] j [,stride])` function. The following read-only attributes are available:

Attribute	Description
s.start	Lower bound of the slice; none if omitted
s.stop	Upper bound of the slice; none if omitted
s.step	Stride of the slice; none if omitted

Ellipsis Object

The *Ellipsis object* is used to indicate the presence of an ellipsis (...) in a slice. There is a single object of this type, accessed through the built-in name `Ellipsis`. It has no attributes and evaluates as true.

Special Methods

All the built-in datatypes consist of some data and a collection of special object methods. The names of special methods are always preceded and followed by double underscores (_). These methods are automatically triggered by the interpreter as a program executes. For example, the operation `x + y` is mapped to an internal method `x.__add__(y)`, and an indexing operation `x[k]` is mapped to `x.__getitem__(k)`. The behavior of each datatype depends entirely on the set of special methods that it implements.

Although it's not possible to alter the behavior of built-in types (or even to invoke any of their special methods directly by name, as just suggested), it's possible to use class definitions to define new objects that behave like the built-in types. To do this, supply implementations of the special methods described in this section.

Object Creation, Destruction, and Representation

The methods in Table 3.7 initialize, destroy, and represent objects. The `__init__()` method initializes the attributes of an object and is called immediately after an object has been newly created. The `__del__()` method is invoked when an object is about to be destroyed. This method is invoked only when an object is no longer in use. It's important to note that the statement `del x` only decrements an object's reference count and doesn't necessarily result in a call to this function.

Table 3.7   Special Methods for Object Creation, Destruction, and Representation

Method	Description
`__init__(self [,args])`	Called to initialize a new instance
`__del__(self)`	Called to destroy an instance
`__repr__(self)`	Creates a full string representation of an object
`__str__(self)`	Creates an informal string representation
`__cmp__(self,other)`	Compares two objects and returns negative, zero, or positive
`__hash__(self)`	Computes a 32-bit hash index
`__nonzero__(self)`	Returns 0 or 1 for truth-value testing

The `__repr__()` and `__str__()` methods create string representations of an object. The `__repr__()` method normally returns an expression string that can be evaluated to re-create the object. This method is invoked by the built-in `repr()` function and by the backquotes operator (`` ` ``). For example:

```
a = [2,3,4,5]     # Create a list
s = repr(a)       # s = '[2, 3, 4, 5]'
                  # Note : could have also used s = `a`
b = eval(s)       # Turns s back into a list
```

If a string expression cannot be created, the convention is for `__repr__()` to return a string of the form <...*message*...>, as shown here:

```
f = open("foo")
a = repr(f)       # a = "<open file 'foo', mode 'r' at dc030>"
```

The `__str__()` method is called by the built-in `str()` function and by the `print` statement. It differs from `__repr__()` in that the string it returns can be more concise and informative to the user. If this method is undefined, the `__repr__()` method is invoked.

The `__cmp__(self,other)` method is used by the other comparison operators. It returns a negative number if *self* < *other*, zero if *self* == *other*, and positive if *self* > *other*. If this method is undefined for an object, the object will be compared by object identity. In addition, an object may define an alternative set of comparison functions for each of the relational operators. These are known as *rich comparisons*, and are described shortly. The `__nonzero__()` method is used for truth-value testing and should return 0 or 1. If undefined, the `__len__()` method is invoked to determine truth. Finally, the `__hash__()` method computes an integer hash key used in dictionary operations. (The hash value can also be returned using the built-in function `hash()`.) The value returned should be identical for two objects that compare as equal. Furthermore, mutable objects should not define this method; any changes to an object will alter the hash value and make it impossible to locate an object on subsequent dictionary lookups. An object should not define a `__hash__()` method without also defining `__cmp__()`.

Attribute Access

The methods in Table 3.8 read, write, and delete the attributes of an object using the dot (.) operator and the del operator, respectively.

Table 3.8   Special Methods for Attribute Access

Method	Description
__getattr__(self, name)	Returns the attribute self.name
__setattr__(self, name, value)	Sets the attribute self.name = value
__delattr__(self, name)	Deletes the attribute self.name

For example:

```
a = x.s      # Invokes __getattr__(x,"s")
x.s = b      # Invokes __setattr__(x,"s", b)
del x.s      # Invokes __delattr__(x,"s")
```

For class instances, the __getattr__() method is invoked only if the search for the attribute in the object's local dictionary or corresponding class definition fails. This method should return the attribute value or raise an AttributeError exception on failure.

Sequence and Mapping Methods

The methods in Table 3.9 are used by objects that want to emulate sequence and mapping objects.

Table 3.9   Methods for Sequences and Mappings

Method	Description
__len__(self)	Returns the length of self
__getitem__(self, key)	Returns self[key]
__setitem__(self, key, value)	Sets self[key] = value
__delitem__(self, key)	Deletes self[key]
__getslice__(self,i,j)	Returns self[i:j]
__setslice__(self,i,j,s)	Sets self[i:j] = s
__delslice__(self,i,j)	Deletes self[i:j]
__contains__(self,obj)	Returns obj in self

For example:

```
a = [1,2,3,4,5,6]
len(a)              # __len__(a)
x = a[2]            # __getitem__(a,2)
a[1] = 7            # __setitem__(a,1,7)
del a[2]            # __delitem__(a,2)
x = a[1:5]          # __getslice__(a,1,5)
a[1:3] = [10,11,12] # __setslice__(a,1,3,[10,11,12])
del a[1:4]          # __delslice__(a,1,4)
```

The __len__ method is called by the built-in len() function to return a non-negative length. This function also determines truth values unless the __nonzero__() method has also been defined.

For manipulating individual items, the __getitem__() method can return an item by key value. The key can be any Python object, but is typically an integer for sequences. The __setitem__() method assigns a value to an element. The __delitem__() method is invoked whenever the del operation is applied to a single element.

The slicing methods support the slicing operator s[i:j]. The __getslice__() method returns a slice, which is normally the same type of sequence as the original object. The indices i and j must be integers, but their interpretation is up to the method. Missing values for i and j are replaced with 0 and sys.maxint, respectively. The __setslice__() method assigns values to a slice. Similarly, __delslice__() deletes all the elements in a slice.

The __contains__() method is used to implement the in operator.

In addition to implementing the methods just described, sequences and mappings implement a number of mathematical methods, including __add__(), __radd__(), __mul__(), and __rmul__() to support concatenation and sequence replication. These methods are described shortly.

Finally, Python supports an extended slicing operation that's useful for working with multidimensional data structures such as matrices and arrays. Syntactically, you specify an extended slice as follows:

```
a = m[0:100:10]         # Strided slice (stride=10)
b = m[1:10, 3:20]       # Multidimensional slice
c = m[0:100:10, 50:75:5] # Multiple dimensions with strides
m[0:5, 5:10] = n        # extended slice assignment
del m[:10, 15:]         # extended slice deletion
```

The general format for each dimension of an extended slice is i:j[:stride], where stride is optional. As with ordinary slices, you can omit the starting or ending values for each part of a slice. In addition, a special object known as the Ellipsis and written as ... is available to denote any number of trailing or leading dimensions in an extended slice:

```
a = m[..., 10:20]    # extended slice access with Ellipsis
m[10:20, ...] = n
```

When using extended slices, the __getitem__(), __setitem__(), and __delitem__() methods implement access, modification, and deletion, respectively. However, instead of an integer, the value passed to these methods is a tuple containing one or more slice objects and at most one instance of the Ellipsis type. For example,

```
a = m[0:10, 0:100:5, ...]
```

invokes __getitem__() as follows:

```
a = __getitem__(m, (slice(0,10,None), slice(0,100,5), Ellipsis))
```

At this time, none of the built-in datatypes supports extended slices, so using them is likely to result in an error. However, special-purpose extensions, especially those with a scientific flavor, may provide new types and objects that support the extended slicing operation.

Mathematical Operations

Table 3.10 lists special methods that objects must implement to emulate numbers. Mathematical operations associate from left to right; when an expression such as *x* + *y* appears, the interpreter tries to invoke the method *x*.__add__(*y*). The special methods beginning with *r* support operations with reversed operands. These are invoked only if the left operand doesn't implement the specified operation. For example, if *x* in *x* + *y* doesn't support the __add__() method, the interpreter tries to invoke the method *y*.__radd__(*x*).

Table 3.10   Methods for Mathematical Operations

Method	Result
__add__(*self,other*)	*self + other*
__sub__(*self,other*)	*self - other*
__mul__(*self,other*)	*self * other*
__div__(*self,other*)	*self / other*
__mod__(*self,other*)	*self % other*
__divmod__(*self,other*)	divmod(*self,other*)
__pow__(*self,other* [*,modulo*])	*self ** other*, pow(*self, other, modulo*)
__lshift__(*self,other*)	*self << other*
__rshift__(*self,other*)	*self >> other*
__and__(*self,other*)	*self & other*
__or__(*self,other*)	*self ¦ other*
__xor__(*self,other*)	*self ^ other*
__radd__(*self,other*)	*other + self*
__rsub__(*self,other*)	*other - self*
__rmul__(*self,other*)	*other * self*
__rdiv__(*self,other*)	*other / self*
__rmod__(*self,other*)	*other % self*
__rdivmod__(*self,other*)	divmod(*other,self*)
__rpow__(*self,other*)	*other ** self*
__rlshift__(*self,other*)	*other << self*
__rrshift__(*self,other*)	*other >> self*
__rand__(*self,other*)	*other & self*
__ror__(*self,other*)	*other ¦ self*
__rxor__(*self,other*)	*other ^ self*
__iadd__(*self,other*)	*self += other*
__isub__(*self,other*)	*self -= other*
__imul__(*self,other*)	*self *= other*
__idiv__(*self,other*)	*self /= other*
__imod__(*self,other*)	*self %= other*
__ipow__(*self,other*)	*self **= other*
__iand__(*self,other*)	*self &= other*
__ior__(*self,other*)	*self ¦= other*
__ixor__(*self,other*)	*self ^= other*

continues>>

Table 3.10   Continued

Method	Result
`__ilshift__(self,other)`	`self <<= other`
`__irshift__(self,other)`	`self >>= other`
`__neg__(self)`	`-self`
`__pos__(self)`	`+self`
`__abs__(self)`	`abs(self)`
`__invert__(self)`	`~self`
`__int__(self)`	`int(self)`
`__long__(self)`	`long(self)`
`__float__(self)`	`float(self)`
`__complex__(self)`	`complex(self)`
`__oct__(self)`	`oct(self)`
`__hex__(self)`	`hex(self)`
`__coerce__(self,other)`	`Type coercion`

The methods `__iadd__()`, `__isub__()`, and so forth are used to support in-place arithmetic operators such as `a+=b` and `a-=b` (also known as *augmented assignment*). A distinction is made between these operators and the standard arithmetic methods because the implementation of the in-place operators might be able to provide certain customizations such as performance optimizations. For instance, if the `self` parameter is not shared, it might be possible to modify its value in place without having to allocate a newly created object for the result.

The conversion methods `__int__()`, `__long__()`, `__float__()`, and `__complex__()` convert an object into one of the four built-in numerical types. The `__oct__()` and `__hex__()` methods return strings representing the octal and hexadecimal values of an object, respectively.

The `__coerce__(x,y)` method is used in conjunction with mixed-mode numerical arithmetic. This method returns either a 2-tuple containing the values of x and y converted to a common numerical type, or `None` if no such conversion is possible. To evaluate an operation x `op` y where `op` is an operation such as +, the following rules are applied, in order:

1. If x has a `__coerce__()` method, replace x and y with the values returned by `x.__coerce__(y)`. If `None` is returned, skip to step 3.

2. If x has a method `__op__()`, return `x.__op__(y)`. Otherwise, restore x and y to their original values and continue.

3. If y has a `__coerce__()` method, replace x and y with the values returned by `y.__coerce__(x)`. If `None` is returned, raise an exception.

4. If y has a method `__rop__()`, return `y.__rop__(x)`. Otherwise, raise an exception.

Although strings define a few arithmetic operations, the `__coerce__()` method is not used in operations involving standard and Unicode strings.

The interpreter supports only a limited number of mixed-type operations involving the built-in types, in particular the following:

- If *x* is a string, *x* % *y* invokes the string-formatting operation, regardless of the type of *y*.

- If *x* is a sequence, *x* + *y* invokes sequence concatenation.

- If either *x* or *y* is a sequence and the other operand is an integer, *x* * *y* invokes sequence repetition.

Comparison Operations

Table 3.11 lists special methods that objects can implement to provide individualized versions of the relational operators (<, >, <=, >=, ==, !=). These are known as *rich comparisons* and were first introduced in Python 2.1. Each of these functions takes two arguments and can return any kind of object, including a Boolean value, a list, or any other Python type. For instance, a numerical package might use this to perform an element-wise comparison of two matrices, returning a matrix with the results. If a comparison cannot be made, these functions may also raise an exception.

Table 3.11   Methods for Comparisons

Method	Result
__lt__(*self,other*)	*self < other*
__le__(*self,other*)	*self <= other*
__gt__(*self,other*)	*self > other*
__ge__(*self,other*)	*self >= other*
__eq__(*self,other*)	*self == other*
__ne__(*self,other*)	*self != other*

Callable Objects

Finally, an object can emulate a function by providing the __call__(*self* [,*args*]) method. If an object *x* provides this method, it can be invoked like a function. That is, *x(arg1, arg2, ...)* invokes *x.*__call__(*self, arg1, arg2, ...*).

Performance and Memory Considerations

All Python objects minimally include an integer reference count, a descriptor defining the type, and the representation of the actual data. Table 3.12 shows the approximate memory requirements of various built-in objects based on the C implementation of Python 2.0 running on a 32-bit machine. The precise values may vary slightly according to the implementation of the interpreter and machine architecture. (For instance, the memory requirements may double on a 64-bit machine.) Although you may never need to think about memory utilization, Python is used in a variety of high-performance and memory-critical applications ranging from supercomputing to mobile computing. The memory footprint of the built-in types is presented here to help programmers make informed design decisions in memory-critical settings.

Table 3.12   Memory Size of Built-in Datatypes

Type	Size
Integer	12 bytes
Long integer	12 bytes + ($n$bits/16 + 1)*2 bytes
Floats	16 bytes
Complex	24 bytes
List	16 bytes + 4 bytes for each item
Tuple	16 bytes + 4 bytes for each item
String	20 bytes + 1 byte per character
Unicode string	24 bytes + 2 bytes per character
Dictionary	24 bytes + $12*2^n$ bytes, $n = \log_2(n\text{items})+1$
Class instance	16 bytes plus a dictionary object
Xrange object	24 bytes

Because strings are used so frequently, the interpreter uses a number of optimizations. First, a string s can be *interned* using the built-in function intern(s). This function looks in an internal hash table to see whether the string value already exists. If so, a reference to that string—instead of a copy of the string data—is stored in the string object. If not, the data in s is added to the hash table. Interned strings live until the interpreter exits; if you're concerned about memory, you shouldn't intern infrequently used strings. Also, to increase the performance of dictionary lookups, strings cache their last computed hash-table value.

Dictionaries are implemented using a hash table with open indexing. The number of entries allocated to a dictionary is equal to twice the smallest power of 2 that's greater than the number of objects stored in the dictionary. When a dictionary expands, its size doubles. On average, about half of the entries allocated to a dictionary are unused.

The execution of a Python program is primarily a sequence of function calls involving the special methods described in the earlier section "Special Methods." Next to choosing the most efficient algorithm, performance improvements can be made by understanding Python's object model and trying to minimize the number of special method calls that occur during execution. This is especially true for name lookups on modules and classes. For example, consider the following code:

```
import math
d = 0.0
for i in xrange(1000000):
    d = d + math.sqrt(i)
```

In this case, each iteration of the loop involves two name lookups. First, the math module is located in the global namespace; then it's searched for a function object named sqrt. Now consider the following modification:

```
from math import sqrt
d = 0.0
for i in xrange(1000000):
    d = d + sqrt(i)
```

In this case, one name lookup is eliminated from the inner loop. In fact, when running on the author's speedy 200 MHz PC, this simple change makes the code run more than twice as fast as before.

Unnecessary method calls can also be eliminated by making careful use of temporary values and avoiding unnecessary lookups in sequences and dictionaries. For example, consider the two classes shown in Listing 3.2:

Listing 3.2   Unnecessary Method Calls

```
class Point:
    def __init__(self,x,y,z):
        self.x = x
        self.y = y
        self.z = z

class Poly:
    def __init__(self):
        self.pts = [ ]
    def addpoint(self,pt):
        self.pts.append(pt)
    def perimeter(self):
        d = 0.0
        self.pts.append(self.pts[0])       # Temporarily close the polygon
        for i in xrange(len(self.pts)-1):
            d2 = (self.pts[i+1].x - self.pts[i].x)**2 + \
                 (self.pts[i+1].y - self.pts[i].y)**2 + \
                 (self.pts[i+1].z - self.pts[i].z)**2
            d = d + math.sqrt(d2)
        self.pts.pop()                      # Restore original list of points
        return d
```

In the `perimeter()` method, each occurrence of `self.pts[i]` involves two special-method lookups—one involving a dictionary and another involving a sequence. You can reduce the number of lookups by rewriting the method as shown in Listing 3.3:

Listing 3.3   Improved Version of Listing 3.2

```
class Poly:
    ...
    def perimeter(self):
        d = 0.0
        pts = self.pts
        pts.append(pts[0])
        for i in xrange(len(pts)-1):
            p1 = pts[i+1]
            p2 = pts[i]
            d2 = (p1.x - p2.x)**2 + \
                 (p1.y - p2.y)**2 + \
                 (p1.z - p2.z)**2
            d = d + math.sqrt(d2)
        pts.pop()
        return d
```

Although the performance gains made by such modifications are often modest (15–20%), an understanding of the underlying object model and the manner in which special methods are invoked can result in faster programs. Of course, if performance is extremely critical, you often can export functionality to a Python extension module written in C.

4

Operators and Expressions

This chapter describes Python's built-in operators as well as precedence rules used in the evaluation of expressions.

Operations on Numbers

The following operations can be applied to all numeric types:

Operation	Description
x + y	Addition
x - y	Subtraction
x * y	Multiplication
x / y	Division
x ** y	Power (x^y)
x % y	Modulo (x mod y)
-x	Unary minus
+x	Unary plus

For integers, division truncates the result to an integer. Thus, 7/4 is 1, not 1.75. The modulo operator returns the remainder of the division x / y. For example, 7 % 4 is 3. For floating-point numbers, the modulo operator returns the floating-point remainder of x / y, which is x - int(x / y) * y. For complex numbers, the modulo operator returns x - int((x / y).real) * y.

The following shifting and bitwise logical operators can only be applied to integers and long integers:

Operation	Description
x << y	Left shift
x >> y	Right shift
x & y	Bitwise and
x ¦ y	Bitwise or
x ^ y	Bitwise xor (exclusive or)
~x	Bitwise negation

The bitwise operators assume that integers are represented in a 2's complement binary representation. For long integers, the bitwise operators operate as if the sign bit is infinitely extended to the left.

In addition, you can apply the following built-in functions to all the numerical types:

Function	Description
abs(x)	Absolute value
divmod(x,y)	Returns (int(x / y), x % y)
pow(x,y [,modulo])	Returns (x ** y) % modulo
round(x,[n])	Rounds to the nearest multiple of 10^{-n} (floating-point numbers only)

The abs() function returns the absolute value of a number. The divmod() function returns the quotient and remainder of a division operation. The pow() function can be used in place of the ** operator, but also supports the ternary power-modulo function (often used in cryptographic algorithms). The round() function rounds a floating-point number x to the nearest multiple of 10 to the power of -n. If n is omitted, it's set to 0. If x is equally close to two multiples, rounding is performed away from zero (for example, 0.5 is rounded to 1 and -0.5 is rounded to -1).

The following comparison operators have the standard mathematical interpretation and return an integer value of 1 for true, 0 for false:

Operation	Description
x < y	Less than
x > y	Greater than
x == y	Equal to
x != y	Not equal to (same as <>)
x >= y	Greater than or equal to
x <= y	Less than or equal to

Comparisons can be chained together, such as in w < x < y < z. Such expressions are evaluated as w < x and x < y and y < z. Expressions such as x < y > z are legal, but are likely to confuse anyone else reading the code (it's important to note that no comparison is made between x and z in such an expression).

Comparisons involving complex numbers are only valid for equality (==) and inequality (!=). Attempts to compare complex numbers with <, <=, >, and >= are mathematically meaningless and will raise a TypeError exception.

Operations involving numbers are valid only if the operands are of the same type. If the types differ, a coercion operation is performed to convert one of the types to the other:

1. If either operand is a complex number, the other operand is converted to a complex number.
2. If either operand is a floating-point number, the other is converted to a float.
3. If either operand is a long integer, the other is converted to a long integer.
4. Otherwise, both numbers must be integers and no conversion is performed.

Operations on Sequences

The following operators can be applied to sequence types, including strings, lists, and tuples:

Operation	Description
s + r	Concatenation
s * n, n * s	Makes *n* copies of *s*, where *n* is an integer
s % d	String formatting (strings only)
s[i]	Indexing
o[i:j]	Slicing
x in s, x not in s	Membership
for x in s:	Iteration
len(s)	Length
min(s)	Minimum item
max(s)	Maximum item

The + operator concatenates two sequences of the same type. The s * n operator makes *n* copies of a sequence. However, these are shallow copies that replicate elements by reference only. For example, consider the following code:

```
a = [3,4,5]        # A list
b = [a]            # A list containing a
c = 4*b            # Make four copies of b

# Now modify a
a[0] = -7

# Look at c
print c
```

The output of this program is the following:

```
[[-7, 4, 5], [-7, 4, 5], [-7, 4, 5], [-7, 4, 5]]
```

In this case, a reference to the list a was placed in the list b. When b was replicated, four additional references to a were created. Finally, when a was modified, this change was propagated to all of the other "copies" of a. This behavior of sequence multiplication is often unexpected and not the intent of the programmer. One way to work around the problem is to manually construct the replicated sequence by duplicating the contents of a. For example:

```
a = [ 3, 4, 5 ]
c = [a[:] for j in range(4)]   # [:] makes a copy of a list
```

The copy module in the standard library can also be used to make copies of objects.

The indexing operator s[n] returns the *n*th object from a sequence in which s[0] is the first object. Negative indices can be used to fetch items from the end of a sequence. For example, s[-1] returns the last item. Otherwise, attempts to access elements that are out of range result in an IndexError exception.

The slicing operator s[i:j] extracts a subsequence from s consisting of the elements with index *k* where *i* <= *k* < *j*. Both *i* and *j* must be integers or long integers. If the starting or ending index is omitted, the beginning or end of the sequence is assumed, respectively. Negative indices are allowed and assumed to be relative to the end of the sequence. If *i* or *j* is out of range, they're assumed to refer to the beginning or end of a sequence, depending on whether their value refers to an element before the first item or after the last item, respectively.

The *x* in *s* operator tests to see whether the object *x* is in the sequence *s* and returns 1 if true, 0 if false. Similarly, the *x* not in *s* operator tests whether *x* is not in the sequence *s*. The for *x* in *s* operator iterates over all the elements of a sequence and is described further in Chapter 5, "Control Flow." len(s) returns the number of elements in a sequence. min(s) and max(s) return the minimum and maximum values of a sequence, although the result may only make sense if the elements can be ordered with respect to the < operator. (For example, it would make little sense to find the maximum value of a list of file objects.)

Strings and tuples are immutable and cannot be modified after creation. Lists can be modified with the following operators:

Operation	Description
s[i] = x	Index assignment
s[i:j] = r	Slice assignment
del s[i]	Deletes an element
del s[i:j]	Deletes a slice

The s[i] = x operator changes element *i* of a list to refer to object *x*, increasing the reference count of *x*. Negative indices are relative to the end of the list and attempts to assign a value to an out-of-range index result in an IndexError exception. The slicing assignment operator s[i:j] = r replaces elements *k* where *i* <= *k* < *j* with elements from sequence *r*. Indices may have the same values as for slicing and are adjusted to the beginning or end of the list if they're out of range. If necessary, the sequence *s* is expanded or reduced to accommodate all the elements in *r*. For example:

```
a = [1,2,3,4,5]
a[1] = 6          # a = [1,6,3,4,5]
a[2:4] = [10,11]  # a = [1,6,10,11,5]
a[3:4] = [-1,-2,-3] # a = [1,6,10,-1,-2,-3,5]
a[2:] = [0]       # a = [1,6,0]
```

The del s[i] operator removes element *i* from a list and decrements its reference count. del s[i:j] removes all the elements in a slice.

Sequences are compared using the operators <, >, <=, >=, ==, and !=. When comparing two sequences, the first elements of each sequence are compared. If they differ, this determines the result. If they're the same, the comparison moves to the second element of each sequence. This process continues until two different elements are found or no more elements exist in either of the sequences. If *a* is an initial subsequence of *b*, then *a* < *b*. Strings are compared using lexicographical ordering. Each character is assigned a unique index determined by the machine's character set (such as ASCII or Unicode). A character is less than another character if its index is less.

The modulo operator *s* % *d* produces a formatted string, given a format string *s* and a collection of objects in a tuple or mapping object (dictionary). The string *s* may be a standard or a Unicode string. The behavior of this operator is similar to the C `sprintf()` function. The format string contains two types of objects: ordinary characters (which are left unmodified) and conversion specifiers—each of which is replaced with a formatted string representing an element of the associated tuple or mapping. If d is a tuple, the number of conversion specifiers must exactly match the number of objects in d. If d is a mapping, each conversion specifier must be associated with a valid key name in the mapping (using parentheses, as described shortly). Each conversion specifier starts with the % character and ends with one of the conversion characters shown in Table 4.1.

Table 4.1   String Formatting Conversions

Character	Output Format
d,i	Decimal integer or long integer.
u	Unsigned integer or long integer.
o	Octal integer or long integer.
x	Hexadecimal integer or long integer.
X	Hexadecimal integer (uppercase letters).
f	Floating point as [-]m.dddddd.
e	Floating point as [-]m.dddddde±xx.
E	Floating point as [-]m.ddddddE±xx.
g,G	Use %e or %E for exponents less than -4 or greater than the precision; otherwise, use %f.
s	String or any object. The formatting code uses str() to generate strings.
r	Produces the same string as produced by repr().
c	Single character.
%	Literal %.

Between the % and the conversion character, the following modifiers may appear, in this order:

1. A key name in parentheses, which selects a specific item out of the mapping object. If no such element exists, a KeyError exception is raised.

2. One or more of the following:

   - - sign, indicating left alignment.

   - + sign, indicating that the numeric sign should be included (even if positive).

   - 0, indicating a zero fill.

3. A number specifying the minimum field width. The converted value will be printed in a field at least this wide and padded on the left (or right if the - flag is given) to make up the field width.

4. A period separating the field width from a precision.

5. A number specifying the maximum number of characters to be printed from a string, the number of digits following the decimal point in a floating-point number, or the minimum number of digits for an integer.

In addition, the asterisk (*) character may be used in place of a number in any width field. If present, the width will be read from the next item in the tuple.

The following code illustrates a few examples:

```
a = 42
b = 13.142783
c = "hello"
d = {'x':13, 'y':1.54321, 'z':'world'}
e = 5628398123741234L

print 'a is %d' % a              #  "a is 42"
print '%10d %f' % (a,b)          #  "        42 13.142783"
print '%+010d %E' % (a,b)        #  "+000000042 1.314278E+01"
print '%(x)-10d %(y)0.3g' % d    #  "13         1.54"
print '%0.4s %s' % (c, d['z'])   #  "hell world"
print '%*.*f' % (5,3,b)          #  "13.143"
print 'e = %d' % e               #  "e = 5628398123741234"
```

Operations on Dictionaries

Dictionaries provide a mapping between names and objects. You can apply the following operations to dictionaries:

Operation	Description
x = d[k]	Indexing by key
d[k] = x	Key assignment
del d[k]	Deletes an item by key
len(d)	Number of items in the dictionary

Key values can be any immutable object, such as strings, numbers, and tuples. In addition, dictionary keys can be specified as a comma-separated list of values like this:

```
d = { }
d[1,2,3] = "foo"
d[1,0,3] = "bar"
```

In this case, the key values represent a tuple, making the above assignments identical to the following:

```
d[(1,2,3)] = "foo"
d[(1,0,3)] = "bar"
```

Augmented Assignment

Python provides the following set of augmented assignment operators:

Operation	Description
x += y	x = x + y
x -= y	x = x - y
x *= y	x = x * y
x /= y	x = x / y
x **= y	x = x ** y
x %= y	x = x % y

Operation	Description
x &= y	x = x & y
x |= y	x = x | y
x ^= y	x = x ^ y
x >>= y	x = x >> y
x <<= y	x = x << y

These operators can be used anywhere that ordinary assignment is used. For example:

```
a = 3
b = [1,2]
c = "%s %s"
a += 1                      # a = 4
b[1] += 10                  # b = [1, 12]
c %= ("Douglas", "Adams")   # c = "Douglas Adams"
```

Augmented assignment doesn't violate mutability or perform in-place modification of objects. Therefore, writing *x += y* creates an entirely new object *x* with the value *x + y*. User-defined classes can redefine the augmented assignment operators using the special methods described in Chapter 3, "Types and Objects."

The Attribute (.) Operator

The dot (.) operator is used to access the attributes of an object. For example:

```
foo.x = 3
print foo.y
a = foo.bar(3,4,5)
del foo.x
```

More than one dot operator can appear in a single expression, such as in foo.y.a.b. The dot operator can also be applied to the intermediate results of functions, as in a = foo.bar(3,4,5).spam. An attribute can be deleted using the del statement as in del foo.x.

Type Conversion

Sometimes it's necessary to perform conversions between the built-in types. The following built-in functions perform explicit type conversions:

Function	Description
int(x [,*base*])	Converts x to an integer
long(x [,*base*])	Converts x to a long integer
float(x)	Converts x to a floating-point number
complex(*real* [,*imag*])	Creates a complex number
str(x)	Converts object x to a string representation
repr(x)	Converts object x to an expression string
eval(*str*)	Evaluates a string and returns an object
tuple(s)	Converts sequence s to a tuple
list(s)	Converts sequence s to a list

continues >>

>> *continued*

Function	Description
chr(x)	Converts an integer to a character
unichr(x)	Convert an integer to a Unicode character
ord(x)	Converts a single character to its integer value
hex(x)	Converts an integer to a hexadecimal string
oct(x)	Converts an integer to an octal string

You also can write the repr(x) function using backquotes as `x`. Note that the str() and repr() functions may return different results. repr() typically creates an expression string that can be evaluated with eval() to re-create the object. On the other hand, str() produces a concise or nicely formatted representation of the object (and is used by the print statement). The ord() function returns the integer ordinal value for a standard or Unicode character. The chr() and unichr() functions convert integers back into standard or Unicode characters, respectively.

To convert strings back into numbers and other objects, use the int(), long(), and float() functions. The eval() function can also convert a string containing a valid expression to an object. For example:

```
a = int("34")            # a = 34
b = long("0xfe76214", 16) # b = 266822164L (0xfe76214L)
b = float("3.1415926")   # b = 3.1415926
c = eval("3, 5, 6")      # c = (3,5,6)
```

Unicode Strings

The use of standard strings and Unicode strings in the same program presents a number of subtle complications. This is because such strings may be used in a variety of operations, including string concatenation, comparisons, dictionary key lookups, and as arguments to built-in functions.

To convert a standard string *s* to a Unicode string, the built-in function unicode(s [, *encoding* [,*errors*]]) is used. To convert a Unicode string *u* to a standard string, the string method *u*.encode([*encoding* [, *errors*]]) is used. Both of these conversion operators require the use of a special encoding rule that specifies how 16-bit Unicode character values are mapped to a sequence of 8-bit characters in standard strings and vice versa. The encoding parameter is specified as a string and consists of one of the following values:

Value	Description
'ascii'	7-bit ASCII
'latin-1' or 'iso-8859-1'	ISO 8859-1 Latin-1
'utf-8'	8-bit variable-length encoding
'utf-16'	16-bit variable-length encoding (may be little or big endian)
'utf-16-le'	UTF-16, little-endian encoding
'utf-16-be'	UTF-16, big-endian encoding
'unicode-escape'	Same format as Unicode literals u"string"
'raw-unicode-escape'	Same format as raw Unicode literals ur"string"

The default encoding is set in the site module and can be queried using
sys.getdefaultencoding(). In most cases, the default encoding is 'ascii', which
means that ASCII characters with values in the range [0x00,0x7f] are directly
mapped to Unicode characters in the range [U+0000, U+007F]. Details about
the other encodings can be found in Chapter 9, "Input and Output."

When converting string values, a UnicodeError exception may be raised if a character that can't be converted is encountered. For instance, if the encoding rule is
'ascii', a Unicode character such as U+1F28 can't be converted because its value
is too large. Similarly, the string "\xfc" can't be converted to Unicode because it
contains a character outside the range of valid ASCII character values. The errors
parameter determines how encoding errors are handled. It's a string with one of
the following values:

Value	Description
'strict'	Raises a UnicodeError exception for decoding errors
'ignore'	Ignores invalid characters
'replace'	Replaces invalid characters with a replacement character (U+FFFD in Unicode, '?' in standard strings)

The default error handling is 'strict'.

When standard strings and Unicode strings are mixed in an expression, standard
strings are automatically coerced to Unicode using the built-in unicode() function.
For example:

```
s = "hello"
t = u"world"
w = s + t          # w = unicode(s) + t
```

When Unicode strings are used in string methods that return new strings (as
described in Chapter 3), the result is always coerced to Unicode. For example:

```
a = "Hello World"
b = a.replace("World", u"Bob")  # Produces u"Hello Bob"
```

Furthermore, even if zero replacements are made and the result is identical to the
original string, the final result is still a Unicode string.

If a Unicode string is used as the format string with the % operator, all the arguments are first coerced to Unicode and then put together according to the given
format rules. If a Unicode object is passed as one of the arguments to the % operator, the entire result is coerced to Unicode at the point at which the Unicode
object is expanded. For example:

```
c = "%s %s" % ("Hello", u"World") # c = "Hello " + u"World"
d = u"%s %s" % ("Hello", "World") # d = u"Hello " + u"World"
```

When applied to Unicode strings, the str() and repr() functions automatically
coerce the value back to a standard string. For Unicode string u, str(u) produces
the value u.encode() and repr(u) produces u"%s" % repr(u.encode('unicode-escape')).

In addition, most library and built-in functions that only operate with standard
strings will automatically coerce Unicode strings to a standard string using the
default encoding. If such a coercion is not possible, a UnicodeError exception is raised.

Standard and Unicode strings can be compared. In this case, standard strings are coerced to Unicode using the default encoding before any comparison is made. This coercion also occurs whenever comparisons are made during list and dictionary operations. For example, 'x' in [u'x', u'y', u'z'] coerces 'x' to Unicode and returns true. For character containment tests such as 'W' in u'Hello World' the character 'W' is coerced to Unicode before the test.

When computing hash values with the hash() function, standard strings and Unicode strings produce identical values, provided that the Unicode string only contains characters in the range [U+0000, U+007F]. This allows standard strings and Unicode strings to be used interchangeably as dictionary keys, provided that the Unicode strings are confined to ASCII characters. For example:

```
a = { }
a[u"foo"] = 1234
print a["foo"]         # Prints 1234
```

However, it should be noted that this dictionary key behavior may not hold if the default encoding is ever changed to something other than 'ascii' or if Unicode strings contain non–ASCII characters. For example, if 'utf-8' is used as a default character encoding, it's possible to produce pathological examples in which strings compare as equal, but have different hash values. For example:

```
a = u"M\u00fcller"        # Unicode string
b = "M\303\274ller"       # utf-8 encoded version of a
print a == b              # Prints '1', true
print hash(a)==hash(b)    # Prints '0', false
```

Boolean Expressions and Truth Values

The and, or, and not keywords can form Boolean expressions. The behavior of these operators is as follows:

Operator	Description
x or y	If x is false, return y; otherwise, return x.
x and y	If x is false, return x; otherwise, return y.
not x	If x is false, return 1; otherwise, return 0.

When you use an expression to determine a true or false value, any nonzero number or nonempty string, list, tuple, or dictionary is taken to be true. Zero, None, and empty lists, tuples, and dictionaries evaluate as false. Boolean expressions are evaluated from left to right and consume the right operand only if it's needed to determine the final value. For example, a and b evaluates b only if a is true.

Object Equality and Identity

The equality operator x == y tests the values of x and y for equality. In the case of lists and tuples, all the elements are compared and evaluated as true if they're of equal value. For dictionaries, a true value is returned only if x and y have the same set of keys and all the objects with the same key have equal values.

The identity operators x is y and x is not y test two objects to see whether they refer to the same object in memory. In general, it may be the case that x == y, but x is not y.

Comparison between objects of non-compatible types such as a file and a floating-point number may be allowed, but the outcome is arbitrary and may not make any sense. In addition, comparison between incompatible types may result in an exception.

Order of Evaluation

Table 4.2 lists the order of operation (precedence rules) for Python operators. All operators except the power (**) operator are evaluated from left to right and are listed in the table from highest to lowest precedence. That is, operators listed first in the table are evaluated before operators listed later. (*Note:* Operators included together within subsections—such as x * y, x / y, and x % y, have equal precedence.)

Table 4.2   Order of Evaluation (Highest to Lowest)

Operator	Name
(...), [...], {...}	Tuple, list, and dictionary creation
`...`	String conversion
s[i], s[i:j], s.attr	Indexing and slicing attributes
f(...)	Function calls
+x, -x, ~x	Unary operators
x ** y	Power (right associative)
x * y, x / y, x % y	Multiplication, division, modulo
x + y, x - y	Addition, subtraction
x << y, x >> y	Bit shifting
x & y	Bitwise and
x ^ y	Bitwise exclusive or
x ¦ y	Bitwise or
x < y, x <= y,	Comparison, identity, and sequence membership tests
x > y, x >= y,	
x == y, x != y	
x <> y	
x is y, x is not y	
x in s, x not in s	
not x	Logical negation
x and y	Logical and
x or y	Logical or
lambda args: expr	Anonymous function

5

Control Flow

This chapter describes statements related to the control flow of a program. Topics include conditionals, loops, and exceptions.

Conditionals

The if, else, and elif statements control conditional code execution. The general format of a conditional statement is as follows:

```
if expression:
    statements
elif expression:
    statements
elif expression:
    statements
...
else:
    statements
```

If no action is to be taken, you can omit both the else and elif clauses of a conditional. Use the pass statement if no statements exist for a particular clause:

```
if expression:
    pass            # Do nothing
else:
    statements
```

Loops

You implement loops using the for and while statements. For example:

```
while expression:
    statements

for i in s:
    statements
```

The while statement executes statements until the associated expression evaluates to false. The for statement iterates over all the elements in a sequence until no more elements are available. If the elements of the sequence are tuples of identical size, you can use the following variation of the for statement:

```
for x,y,z in s:
    statements
```

In this case, s must be a sequence of tuples, each with three elements. On each iteration, the contents of the variables x, y, and z are assigned the contents of the corresponding tuple.

To break out of a loop, use the break statement. For example, the following function reads lines of text from the user until an empty line of text is entered:

```
while 1:
    cmd = raw_input('Enter command > ')
    if not cmd:
        break               # No input, stop loop
    # process the command
    ...
```

To jump to the next iteration of a loop (skipping the remainder of the loop body), use the continue statement. This statement tends to be used less often, but is sometimes useful when the process of reversing a test and indenting another level would make the program too deeply nested or unnecessarily complicated. As an example, the following loop prints only the non-negative elements of a list:

```
for a in s:
    if a < 0:
        continue       # Skip negative elements
    print a
```

The break and continue statements apply only to the innermost loop being executed. If it's necessary to break out of a deeply nested loop structure, you can use an exception. Python doesn't provide a goto statement.

You can also attach the else statement to loop constructs, as in the following example:

```
# while-else
while i < 10:
    do something
    i = i + 1
else:
    print 'Done'

# for-else
for a in s:
    if a == 'Foo':
        break
else:
    print 'Not found!'
```

The else clause of a loop executes only if the loop runs to completion. This either occurs immediately (if the loop wouldn't execute at all) or after the last iteration. On the other hand, if the loop is terminated early using the break statement, the else clause is skipped.

Exceptions

Exceptions indicate errors and break out of the normal control flow of a program. An exception is raised using the raise statement. The general format of the raise statement is raise *exception* [, *value*] where *exception* is the exception type and *value* is an optional value giving specific details about the exception. For example:

```
raise RuntimeError, 'Unrecoverable Error'
```

If the raise statement is used without any arguments, the last exception generated is raised again (although this works only while handling a previously raised exception).

To catch an exception, use the try and except statements, as shown here:

```
try:
    f = open('foo')
except IOError, e:
    print "Unable to open 'foo': ", e
```

When an exception occurs, the interpreter stops executing statements in the try block and looks for an except clause that matches the exception that has occurred. If found, control is passed to the first statement in the except clause. Otherwise, the exception is propagated up to the block of code in which the try statement appeared. This code may itself be enclosed in a try-except that can handle the exception. If an exception works its way up to the top level of a program without being caught, the interpreter aborts with an error message. If desired, uncaught exceptions can also be passed to a user–defined function sys.excepthook() as described in Appendix A, "The Python Library," sys module.

The optional second argument to the except statement is the name of a variable in which the argument supplied to the raise statement is placed if an exception occurs. Exception handlers can examine this value to find out more about the cause of the exception.

Multiple exception-handling blocks are specified using multiple except clauses, such as in the following example:

```
try:
    do something
except IOError, e:
    # Handle I/O error
    ...
except TypeError, e:
    # Handle Type error
    ...
except NameError, e:
    # Handle Name error
    ...
```

A single handler can catch multiple exception types like this:

```
try:
    do something
except (IOError, TypeError, NameError), e:
    # Handle I/O, Type, or Name errors
    ...
```

To ignore an exception, use the pass statement as follows:

```
try:
    do something
except IOError:
    pass                # Do nothing (oh well).
```

To catch all exceptions, omit the exception name and value:

```
try:
    do something
except:
    print 'An error occurred'
```

Table 5.1   Built-in Exceptions

Exception	Description
Exception	The root of all exceptions
SystemExit	Generated by sys.exit()
StandardError	Base for all built-in exceptions
ArithmeticError	Base for arithmetic exceptions
FloatingPointError	Failure of a floating-point operation
OverflowError	Arithmetic overflow
ZeroDivisionError	Division or modulus operation with 0
AssertionError	Raised by the assert statement
AttributeError	Raised when an attribute name is invalid
EnvironmentError	Errors that occur externally to Python
IOError	I/O or file-related error
OSError	Operating system error
WindowsError	Error in Windows
EOFError	Raised when the end of the file is reached
ImportError	Failure of the import statement
KeyboardInterrupt	Generated by the interrupt key (usually Ctrl+C)
LookupError	Indexing and key errors
IndexError	Out-of-range sequence offset
KeyError	Nonexistent dictionary key
MemoryError	Out of memory
NameError	Failure to find a local or global name
UnboundLocalError	Unbound local variable
RuntimeError	A generic catch-all error
NotImplementedError	Unimplemented feature
SyntaxError	Parsing error
TabError	Inconsistent tab usage (generated with -tt option)
IndentationError	Indentation error
SystemError	Nonfatal system error in the interpreter
TypeError	Passing an inappropriate type to an operation
ValueError	Inappropriate or missing value
UnicodeError	Unicode encoding error

The try statement also supports an else clause, which must follow the last except clause. This code is executed if the code in the try block doesn't raise an exception. Here's an example:

```
try:
    f = open('foo', 'r')
except IOError:
    print 'Unable to open foo'
else:
    data = f.read()
    f.close()
```

The `finally` statement defines a cleanup action for code contained in a `try` block. For example:

```
f = open('foo','r')
try:
    # Do some stuff
    ...
finally:
    f.close()
    print "File closed regardless of what happened."
```

The `finally` clause isn't used to catch errors. Rather, it's used to provide code that must always be executed, regardless of whether an error occurs. If no exception is raised, the code in the `finally` clause is executed immediately after the code in the `try` block. If an exception occurs, control is first passed to the first statement of the `finally` clause. After this code has executed, the exception is re-raised to be caught by another exception handler. The `finally` and `except` statements cannot appear together within a single `try` statement.

Python defines the built-in exceptions listed in Table 5.1. (For specific details about these exceptions, see Appendix A.)

All the exceptions in a particular group can be caught by specifying the group name in an `except` clause. For example,

```
try:
    statements
except LookupError:      # Catch IndexError or KeyError
    statements
```

or

```
try:
    statements
except StandardError:    # Catch any built-in exception
    statements
```

Defining New Exceptions

All the built-in exceptions are defined in terms of classes. To create a new exception, create a new class definition that inherits from `exceptions.Exception` such as the following:

```
import exceptions
# Exception class
class NetworkError(exceptions.Exception):
    def __init__(self,args=None):
        self.args = args
```

The name `args` should be used as shown. This allows the value used in the `raise` statement to be properly printed in tracebacks and other diagnostics. In other words,

```
raise NetworkError, "Cannot find host."
```

creates an instance of `NetworkError` using the call

```
NetworkError("Cannot find host.")
```

The object that is created will print itself as `NetworkError: Cannot find host.`. If you use a name other than `self.args` or you don't store the argument, this feature won't work correctly.

When an exception is raised, the optional value supplied in the raise statement is used as the argument to the exception's class constructor. If the constructor for an exception requires more than one argument, it can be raised in two ways:

```
import exceptions
# Exception class
class NetworkError(exceptions.Exception):
        def __init__(self,errno,msg):
            self.args = (errno, msg)
            self.errno = errno
            self.errmsg = msg

# Raises an exception (multiple arguments)
def error2():
    raise NetworkError(1, 'Host not found')

# Raises an exception (multiple arguments)
def error3():
    raise NetworkError, (1, 'Host not found')
```

Class-based exceptions enable you to create hierarchies of exceptions. For instance, the NetworkError exception defined earlier could serve as a base class for a variety of more specific errors. For example:

```
class HostnameError(NetworkError):
    pass

class TimeoutError(NetworkError):
    pass

def error3():
    raise HostnameError

def error4():
    raise TimeoutError

try:
    error3()
except NetworkError:
    import sys
    print sys.exc_type    # Prints exception type
```

In this case, the except NetworkError statement catches any exception derived from NetworkError. To find the specific type of error that was raised, examine the variable sys.exc_type. Similarly, the sys.exc_value variable contains the value of the last exception. Alternatively, the sys.exc_info() function can be used to retrieve exception information in a manner that doesn't rely on global variables and is thread-safe.

Assertions and __debug__

The assert statement is used to add debugging code into a program. The general form of assert is

```
assert test [, data]
```

where test is an expression that should evaluate to true or false. If test evaluates to false, assert raises an AssertionError exception with the optional data supplied to the assert statement. For example:

```
def write_data(file,data):
    assert file, "write_data: file is None!"
    ...
```

Internally, the `assert` statement is translated into the following code:

```
if __debug__:
   if not (test):
       raise AssertionError, data
```

_ _debug_ _ is a built-in read-only value that's set to 1 unless the interpreter is running in optimized mode (specified with the -o option). Although _ _debug_ _ is used by assertions, you also can use it to include any sort of debugging code.

The `assert` statement should not be used for code that must be executed to make the program correct, since it won't be executed if Python is run in optimized mode. In particular, it's an error to use `assert` to check user input. Instead, `assert` statements are used to check things that should always be true; if one is violated, it represents a bug in the program, not an error by the user.

For example, if the function `write_data()` shown here were intended for use by an end user, the `assert` statement should be replaced by a conventional `if` statement and the desired error handling.

6

Functions and Functional Programming

Most substantial programs are broken up into functions for better modularity and ease of maintenance. Python makes it easy to define functions, but borrows a number of ideas from functional programming languages that simplify certain tasks. This chapter describes functions, anonymous functions, and functional programming features, as well as the eval() and execfile() functions and the exec statement. It also describes list comprehensions, a powerful list-construction technique.

Functions

Functions are defined with the def statement:

```
def add(x,y):
    return x+y
```

Invoke the function by writing the function name followed by a tuple of function arguments, such as a = add(3,4). The order and number of arguments must match those given in the function definition. If a mismatch exists, a TypeError exception is raised.

By assigning values, you can attach default arguments to function parameters:

```
def foo(x,y,z = 42):
```

When a function defines a parameter with a default value, that parameter and all the parameters that follow are optional. If values are not assigned to all the optional parameters in the function definition, a SyntaxError exception is raised.

Default parameter values are always set to the objects that were supplied as values when the function was defined. For example:

```
a = 10
def foo(x = a):
    print x

a = 5              # Reassign 'a'.
foo()              # Prints '10' (default value not changed)
```

However, the use of mutable objects as default values can lead to unintended behavior:

```
a = [10]
def foo(x = a):
    print x
a.append(20)
foo()              # Prints '[10, 20]'
```

A function can accept a variable number of parameters if an asterisk (*) is added to the last parameter name:

```
def fprintf(file, fmt, *args):
    file.write(fmt % args)

# Use fprintf. args gets (42, "hello world", 3.45)
fprintf(out,"%d %s %f", 42, "hello world", 3.45)
```

In this case, all the remaining arguments are placed into the args variable as a tuple. To pass a tuple args to another function as if they were parameters, the *args syntax can be used as follows:

```
def printf(fmt, *args):
        # Call another function and pass along args
        fprintf(sys.stdout, fmt, *args)
```

You can also pass function arguments by explicitly naming each parameter and specifying a value:

```
def foo(w,x,y,z):
    print w,x,y,z

# Keyword invocation
foo(x=3, y=22, w='hello', z=[1,2])
```

With keyword arguments, the order of the parameters doesn't matter. However, unless you're using default values, you must explicitly name all the function parameters. If you omit any of the required parameters or if the name of a keyword doesn't match any of the parameter names in the function definition, a TypeError exception is raised.

Positional arguments and keyword arguments can appear in the same function call, provided that all the positional arguments appear first. For example:

```
foo('hello', 3, z=[1,2], y=22)
```

If the last argument of a function definition begins with **, all the additional keyword arguments (those that don't match any of the parameter names) are placed in a dictionary and passed to the function. For example:

```
def spam(**parms):
    print "You supplied the following args:"
    for k in parms.keys():
        print "%s = %s" % (k, parms[k])

spam(x=3, a="hello", foobar=(2, 3))
```

You can combine extra keyword arguments with variable-length argument lists, as long as the ** parameter appears last:

```
# Accept variable number of positional or keyword arguments
def spam(x, *args, **keywords):
    print x, args, keywords
```

Keyword arguments can also be passed to another function using the **keywords syntax:

```
def callfunc(func, *args, **kwargs):
    print args
    print kwargs
    func(*args, **kwargs)
```

Finally, starting in Python 2.1, functions and methods can have arbitrary attributes attached to them. For example:

```
def foo():
    print "Hello world"

foo.secure = 1
foo.private = 1
```

Function attributes are stored in a dictionary that's available as the `__dict__` attribute of a function or method.

The primary use of function attributes is in specialized applications such as parser generators or network applications that would like to attach additional information to a function. Previously, the docstring was the only place to store such information.

Parameter Passing and Return Values

When a function is invoked, its parameters are passed by reference. If a mutable object (such as a list or dictionary) is passed to a function where it's then modified, those changes will be reflected in the caller. For example:

```
a = [1,2,3,4,5]
def foo(x):
    x[3] = -55     # Modify an element of x

foo(a)             # Pass a
print a            # Produces [1,2,3,-55,5]
```

The `return` statement returns a value from a function. If no value is specified or you omit the `return` statement, the `None` object is returned. To return multiple values, place them in a tuple:

```
def factor(a):
    d = 2
    while (d <= (a/2)):
        if ((a/d)*d == a):
            return ((a/d),d)
        d = d + 1
    return (a,1)
```

Multiple return values returned in a tuple can be assigned to individual variables:

```
x,y = factor(1243)     # Return values placed in x and y.
(x,y) = factor(1243)   # Alternate version. Same behavior.
```

Scoping Rules

Each time a function executes, a new local namespace is created. This namespace contains the names of the function parameters, as well as the names of variables that are assigned inside the function body. When resolving names, the interpreter first searches the local namespace. (See the comments on the next page regarding nested scopes.) If no match exists, it searches the global namespace. The global namespace for a function is always the module in which the function was defined. If the interpreter finds no match in the global namespace, it makes a final check in the built-in namespace. If this fails, a `NameError` exception is raised.

One peculiarity of namespaces is the manipulation of global variables from within a function. For example, consider the following code:

```
a = 42
def foo():
    a = 13
foo()
print a
```

When executed, the value 42 prints, despite the appearance that we might be modifying the variable a inside the function foo. When variables are assigned in a function, they're always bound to the function's local namespace; as a result, the variable a in the function body refers to an entirely new object containing the value 13. To alter this behavior, use the global statement. global simply marks a list of names as belonging to the global namespace, and is necessary only when global variables will be modified. It can be placed anywhere in a function body and used repeatedly. For example:

```
a = 42
def foo():
    global a        # 'a' is in global namespace
    a = 13
foo()
print a
```

All versions of Python allow nested function definitions. However, prior to Python 2.1, nested functions didn't provide nested scopes. As a result, a program using a nested function might not work as you expect. For example in Python 2.0, the following program is legal, but doesn't execute properly:

```
def bar():
    x = 10
    def spam():              # Nested function definition
        print 'x is ', x    # Looks for x in global scope of bar()
    while x > 0:
        spam()              # Fails with a NameError on 'x'
        x -= 1
```

In this case, when the nested function spam() executes, its global namespace is the same as the global namespace for bar(), the module in which the function is defined. As a result, spam() is unable to resolve any symbols in the namespace of bar() and fails with a NameError.

Starting with Python 2.1, support for nested scopes is provided (so the above example will work). With nested scopes, names are resolved by first checking the local scope and then all enclosing scopes. If no match is found, the global and built-in namespaces are checked as before. Note that in Python 2.1 nested scopes are an optional feature that must be enabled by including from __future__ import nested_scopes in your program (see Chapter 10, "Execution Environment"). In addition, if you care about compatibility with older versions of Python, avoid using nested functions.

If a local variable is used before it's assigned a value, an UnboundLocalError exception is raised. For example:

```
def foo():
    print i         # Results in UnboundLocalError exception
    i = 0
```

Recursion

Python places a limit on the depth of recursive function calls. The function `sys.getrecursionlimit()` returns the current maximum recursion depth and the function `sys.setrecursionlimit()` can be used to change the value. The default value is 1000. When the recursion depth is exceeded, a `RuntimeError` exception is raised.

The `apply()` Function

The `apply(func [, args [, kwargs]])` function is used to invoke a function indirectly where the arguments have been constructed in the form of a tuple or dictionary. `args` is a tuple containing the positional argument to be supplied to the function. If omitted, no arguments are passed. `kwargs` is a dictionary containing keyword arguments. The following statements produce identical results:

```
foo(3,"x", name='Dave', id=12345)
apply(foo, (3,"x"), { 'name': 'Dave', 'id': 12345 })
```

In older versions of Python, `apply()` was the only mechanism for calling a function in which the arguments were contained in a tuple or dictionary. This capability is now handled by the following syntax:

```
a = (3,"x")
b = { 'name' : 'Dave', 'id': 12345 }
foo(*a,**b)      # Same as code above
```

The `lambda` Operator

To create an anonymous function in the form of an expression, use the `lambda` statement:

```
lambda args : expression
```

`args` is a comma-separated list of arguments and `expression` is an expression involving those arguments. For example:

```
a = lambda x,y : x+y
print a(2,3)              # produces 5
```

The code defined with `lambda` must be a valid expression. Multiple statements and other nonexpression statements such as `print`, `for`, and `while` cannot appear in a `lambda` statement. `lambda` expressions follow the same scoping rules as functions.

`map(), zip(), reduce(),` and `filter()`

The `t = map(func, s)` function applies the function `func` to each of the elements in `s` and returns a new list `t`. Each element of `t` is `t[i] = func(s[i])`. The function given to `map()` should require only one argument. For example:

```
a = [1, 2, 3, 4, 5, 6]
def foo(x):
    return 3*x

b = map(foo,a)    # b = [3, 6, 9, 12, 15, 18]
```

Alternatively, this could be calculated using an anonymous function as follows:

```
b = map(lambda x: 3*x, a)    # b = [3, 6, 9, 12, 15, 18]
```

The map() function can also be applied to multiple lists such as t = map(func, s1, s2, ..., sn). In this case, each element of t is t[i] = func(s1[i], s2[i], ..., sn[i]), and the function given to map() must accept the same number of arguments as the number of lists given. The result has the same number of elements as the longest list in s1, s2, ... sn. During the calculation, short lists are extended with values of None to match the length of the longest list, if necessary.

If the function is set to None, the identity function is assumed. If multiple lists are passed to map(None, s1, s2, ... sn), the function returns a list of tuples in which each tuple contains an element from each list. For example:

```
a = [1,2,3,4]
b = [100,101,102,103]
c = map(None, a, b)   # c = [(1,100), (2,101), (3,102), (4,103)]
```

As an alternative to map(), a list of tuples can also be created using the zip(s1, s2, ..., sn) function. zip() takes a collection of sequences and returns a new list t in which each element of t is t[i] = (s1[i], s2[i], ..., sn[i]). Unlike map(), zip() truncates the length of t to the shortest sequence in s1, s2, ... sn. For example:

```
d = [1,2,3,4,5,6,7]
e = [10,11,12]
f = zip(d,e)   # f = [(1,10), (2,11), (3,12)]
```

The reduce(func, s) function collects information from a sequence and returns a single value (for example, a sum, maximum value, and so on). reduce() works by applying the function func to the first two elements of s. This value is then combined with the third element to yield a new value. This result is then combined with the fourth element, and so forth until the end of the sequence. The function func must accept two arguments and return a single value. For example:

```
def sum(x,y):
    return x+y

b = reduce(sum, a)   # b = (((1+2)+3)+4) = 10
```

The filter(func,s) function filters the elements of s using a filter function func() that returns true or false. A new sequence is returned consisting of all elements x of s for which func(x) is true. For example:

```
c = filter(lambda x: x < 4, a)   # c = [1, 2, 3]
```

If func is set to None, the identity function is assumed and filter() returns all elements of s that evaluate to true.

List Comprehensions

Many operations involving map() and filter() can be replaced with a list construction operator known as a *list comprehension*. The syntax for a list comprehension is as follows:

```
[expression for item1 in sequence1
            for item2 in sequence2
            ...
            for itemN in sequenceN
            if condition]
```

This syntax is roughly equivalent to the following code:

```
s = []
for item1 in sequence1:
    for item2 in sequence2:
        ...
            for itemN in sequenceN:
                if condition: s.append(expression)
```

To illustrate, consider the example in Listing 6.1:

Listing 6.1   List Comprehensions

```
a = [-3,5,2,-10,7,8]
b = 'abc'

c = [2*s for s in a]        # c = [-6,10,4,-20,14,16]
d = [s for s in a if s >= 0] # d = [5,2,7,8]
e = [(x,y) for x in a       # e = [(5,'a'),(5,'b'),(5,'c'),
         for y in b         #      (2,'a'),(2,'b'),(2,'c'),
         if x > 0]          #      (7,'a'),(7,'b'),(7,'c'),
                            #      (8,'a'),(8,'b'),(8,'c')]

f = [(1,2), (3,4), (5,6)]
g = [math.sqrt(x*x+y*y)     # f = [2.23606, 5.0, 7.81024]
         for x,y in f]

h = reduce(lambda x,y: x+y,  # Sum of squares
           [math.sqrt(x*x+y*y)
            for x,y in f])
```

The sequences supplied to a list comprehension don't have to be the same length because they're iterated over their contents using a nested set of for loops, as previously shown. The resulting list contains successive values of expressions. The if clause is optional; however, if it's used, *expression* is evaluated and appended to the result only if *condition* is true.

If a list comprehension is used to construct a list of tuples, the tuple values must be enclosed in parentheses. For example, [(x,y) for x in a for y in b] is legal syntax, whereas [x,y for x in a for y in b] is not.

Finally, it is important to note that the variables defined within a list comprehension are evaluated within the current scope and remain defined after the list comprehension has executed. For example, in [x for x in a], the iteration variable x overwrites any previously defined value of x and is set to the value of the last item in a after the list is created.

eval(), exec, execfile(), and compile()

The eval(str [,*globals* [,*locals*]]) function executes an expression string and returns the result. For example:

```
a = eval('3*math.sin(3.5+x) + 7.2')
```

Similarly, the exec statement executes a string containing arbitrary Python code. The code supplied to exec is executed within the namespace of the caller as if the code actually appeared in place of the exec statement. For example:

```
a = [3, 5, 10, 13]
exec "for i in a: print i"
```

Finally, the execfile(*filename* [,*globals* [,*locals*]]) function executes the contents of a file. For example:

```
execfile("foo.py")
```

All these functions execute within the namespace of the caller (which is used to resolve any symbols that appear within a string or file). Optionally, eval(), exec, and execfile() can accept one or two dictionaries that serve as the global and local namespaces for the code to be executed, respectively. For example:

```
globals = {'x': 7,
           'y': 10,
           'birds': ['Parrot', 'Swallow', 'Albatross']
          }

locals = { }

# Execute using the above dictionaries as the global and local namespace
a = eval("3*x + 4*y", globals, locals)
exec "for b in birds: print b" in globals, locals    # Note unusual syntax
execfile("foo.py", globals, locals)
```

If you omit one or both namespaces, the current values of the global and local namespaces are used. Also, due to issues related to nested scopes, the use of exec or execfile() inside a function body may result in a SyntaxError exception if that function also contains nested function definitions or uses the lambda operator.

Note that the syntax of the exec statement in the example is different from that of eval() and execfile(). exec is a statement (much like print or while), whereas eval() and execfile() are built-in functions.

When a string is passed to exec, eval(), or execfile(), the parser first compiles it into bytecode. Because this process is expensive, it may be better to precompile the code and reuse the bytecode on subsequent calls if the code will be executed multiple times.

The compile(*str*,*filename*,*kind*) function compiles a string into bytecode in which *str* is a string containing the code to be compiled and *filename* is the file in which the string is defined (for use in traceback generation). The *kind* argument specifies the type of code being compiled—'single' for a single statement, 'exec' for a set of statements, or 'eval' for an expression. The code object returned by the compile() function can also be passed to the eval() function and exec statement. For example:

```
str = "for i in range(0,10): print i"
c = compile(str,'','exec')      # Compile into a code object
exec c                          # Execute it

str2 = "3*x + 4*y"
c2 = compile(str2, '', 'eval')  # Compile into an expression
result = eval(c2)               # Execute it
```

7

Classes and Object-Oriented Programming

Classes are the primary mechanism used to create data structures and new kinds of objects. This chapter covers the details of classes, but is not intended to be an introduction to object-oriented programming and design. It's assumed that the reader has prior experience with data structures and object-oriented programming in other languages such as C or Java. (Chapter 3, "Types and Objects," contains additional information about the terminology and internal implementation of objects.)

The class statement

A *class* defines a set of attributes that are associated with a collection of objects known as *instances*. These attributes typically include variables that are known as *class variables* and functions that are known as *methods*.

Classes are defined using the class statement. The body of a class contains a series of statements that are executed when the class is first defined (see Listing 7.1).

Listing 7.1   Classes

```
class Account:
    "A simple class"
    account_type = "Basic"
    def _ _init_ _(self,name,balance):
        "Initialize a new Account instance"
        self.name = name
        self.balance = balance
    def deposit(self,amt):
        "Add to the balance"
        self.balance = self.balance + amt
    def withdraw(self,amt):
        "Subtract from the balance"
        self.balance = self.balance - amt
    def inquiry(self):
        "Return the current balance"
        return self.balance
```

The objects created during the execution of the class body are placed into a class object that serves as a namespace. For example, the members of the Account class are accessible as follows:

```
Account.account_type
Account._ _init_ _
Account.deposit
Account.withdraw
Account.inquiry
```

It's important to note that a class statement doesn't create any instances of a class (for example, no accounts are actually created in the preceding example). Rather, a class only defines the set of attributes that are shared by all of the instances that will be created.

The functions defined within a class (methods) always operate on a class instance that's passed as the first argument. By convention, this argument is called self, although any legal identifier name can be used. Class variables such as account_type are shared among all instances of a class (that is, they're not individually assigned to each instance). Although a class defines a namespace, this namespace is not a scope for code appearing inside the class body. Thus, references to other attributes of a class must use a fully qualified name, as shown in the following example:

```
class Foo:
    def bar(self):
        print "bar!"
    def spam(self):
        bar(self)      # Incorrect! 'bar' generates a NameError
        Foo.bar(self) # This works
```

Finally, you cannot define class methods that don't operate on instances:

```
class Foo:
    def add(x,y):
        return x+y

a = Foo.add(3,4)      # TypeError.  Need class instance as first argument
```

Class Instances

Instances of a class are created by calling a class object as a function. This creates a new instance and calls the __init__() method of the class (if defined). For example:

```
# Create a few accounts
a = Account("Guido", 1000.00)      # Invokes Account.__init__(a,"Guido",1000.00)
b = Account("Bill", 100000000000L)
```

Once created, the attributes and methods of the newly created instances are accessible using the dot (.) operator as follows:

```
a.deposit(100.00)        # Call Account.deposit(a,100.00)
b.withdraw(sys.maxint)   # Call Account.withdraw(b,sys.maxint)
name = a.name            # Get account name
print a.account_type     # Print account type
```

Internally, each instance is implemented using a dictionary that's accessible as the instance's __dict__ attribute (described in detail in Chapter 3). This dictionary contains the information that's unique to each instance. For example:

```
>>> print a.__dict__
{'balance': 1100.0, 'name': 'Guido'}
>>> print b.__dict__
{'balance': 97852516353L, 'name': 'Bill'}
```

Whenever the attributes of an instance are modified, these changes are made to the instance's local dictionary. Within methods defined in the class, attributes are changed through assignment to the self variable as shown in the __init__(), deposit(), and withdraw() methods of Account. However, new attributes can be added to an instance at any time, like this:

```
a.number = 123456    # Add attribute 'number' to a.__dict__
```

Although the assignment of attributes is always performed on the local dictionary of an instance, attribute access is somewhat more complicated. Whenever an attribute is accessed, the interpreter first searches the dictionary of the instance. If no match is found, the interpreter searches the dictionary of the class object used to create the instance. If this fails, a search of base classes is performed. (See the later section "Inheritance" for details on base classes.) If this fails, a final attempt to find the attribute is made by attempting to invoke the __getattr__() method of the class (if defined). If this fails, an AttributeError exception is raised.

Reference Counting and Instance Destruction

All instances have a reference count. If the reference count reaches zero, the instance is destroyed. When the instance is about to be destroyed, the interpreter looks for a __del__() method associated with the object and calls it. In practice, it's rarely necessary for a class to define a __del__() method. The only exception is when the destruction of an object requires a cleanup action such as closing a file, shutting down a network connection, or releasing other system resources. Even in these cases, it's dangerous to rely on __del__() for a clean shutdown, as there's no guarantee that this method will be called when the interpreter exits. A better approach may be to define a method such as close() that a program can use to explicitly perform a shutdown. Finally, note that instances for which __del__() is defined cannot be collected by Python's cyclic garbage collector (which is a strong reason not to define __del__ unless you need it). See Appendix A, "The Python Library," gc module for details.

Occasionally, a program will use the del statement to delete a reference to an object. If this causes the reference count of the object to reach zero, the __del__() method is called. However, in general, the del statement doesn't directly call __del__().

Inheritance

Inheritance is a mechanism for creating a new class that specializes or modifies the behavior of an existing class. The original class is called a *base class* or a *superclass*. The new class is called a *derived class* or a *subclass*. When a class is created via inheritance, it "inherits" the attributes defined by its base classes. However, a derived class may redefine any of these attributes and add new attributes of its own.

Inheritance is specified with a comma-separated list of base-class names in the class statement. For example:

```
class A:
    varA = 42
    def method1(self):
        print "Class A : method1"

class B:
    varB = 37
    def method1(self):
        print "Class B : method1"
    def method2(self):
        print "Class B : method2"
```

continues >>

>> *continued*

```
class C(A,B):      # Inherits from A and B
    varC = 3.3
    def method3(self):
        print "Class C : method3"

class D: pass
class E(C,D): pass
```

When searching for an attribute defined in a base class, the base classes are searched using a depth-first search algorithm in the same order as specified in the class definition. For example, in class E in the preceding example, base classes are searched in the order C, A, B, D. In the event that multiple base classes define the same symbol, the first symbol encountered in the search process is used. For example:

```
c = C()              # Create a 'C'
c.method3()          # Invoke C.method3(c)
c.method1()          # Invoke A.method1(c)
c.varB               # Access B.varB
```

If a derived class defines an attribute with the same name as an attribute in a base class, instances of the derived class use the attributes in the derived class. If it's ever necessary to access the original attribute, a fully qualified name can be used as follows:

```
class D(A):
    def method1(self):
        print "Class D : method1"
        A.method1(self)              # Invoke base class method
```

One notable use of this is in the initialization of class instances. When an instance is created, the __init__() methods of base classes are not invoked. Thus, it's up to a derived class to perform the proper initialization of its base classes, if necessary. For example:

```
class D(A):
    def __init__(self, args1):
        # Initialize the base class
        A.__init__(self)
        # Initialize myself
        ...
```

Similar steps may also be necessary when defining cleanup actions in the __del__() method.

Polymorphism

Polymorphism, or *dynamic binding*, is handled entirely through the attribute lookup process described for inheritance in the preceding section. Whenever a method is accessed as *obj.method()*, *method* is located by searching the __dict__ attribute of the instance, the instance's class definition, and base classes, in that order. The first match found is used as the method.

Information Hiding

By default, all attributes are "public." This means that all attributes of a class instance are accessible without any restrictions. It also implies that everything defined in a base class is inherited and accessible within a derived class. This behavior is often undesirable in object-oriented applications because it exposes the internal implementation of an object and it can lead to namespace conflicts between objects defined in a derived class and those defined in a base class.

To fix this problem, all names in a class that start with a double underscore, such as _ _Foo, are mangled to form a new name of the form _*Classname*_ _Foo. This effectively provides a way for a class to have private attributes, since private names used in a derived class won't collide with the same private names used in a base class. For example:

```
class A:
    def _ _init_ _(self):
        self._ _X = 3          # Mangled to self._A_ _X

class B(A):
    def _ _init_ _(self):
        A._ _init_ _(self)
        self._ _X = 37         # Mangled to self._B_ _X
```

Although this scheme provides the illusion of data hiding, there's no strict mechanism in place to prevent access to the "private" attributes of a class. In particular, if the name of the class and corresponding private attribute are known, they can be accessed using the mangled name.

Operator Overloading

User-defined objects can be made to work with all of Python's built-in operators by adding implementations of the special methods described in Chapter 3 to a class. For example, the class in Listing 7.2 implements the complex numbers with some of the standard mathematical operators and type coercion to allow complex numbers to be mixed with integers and floats.

Listing 7.2   Mathematical Operators and Type Coercion

```
class Complex:
    def _ _init_ _(self,real,imag=0):
        self.real = float(real)
        self.imag = float(imag)
    def _ _repr_ _(self):
        return "Complex(%s,%s)" % (self.real, self.imag)
    def _ _str_ _(self):
        return "(%g+%gj)" % (self.real, self.imag)
    # self + other
    def _ _add_ _(self,other):
        return Complex(self.real + other.real, self.imag + other.imag)
    # self - other
    def _ _sub_ _(self,other):
        return Complex(self.real - other.real, self.imag - other.imag)
    # -self
    def _ _neg_ _(self):
        return Complex(-self.real, -self.imag)
    # other + self
    def _ _radd_ _(self,other):
        return Complex._ _add_ _(other,self)
    # other - self
    def _ _rsub_ _(self,other):
        return Complex._ _sub_ _(other,self)
    # Coerce other numerical types to complex
    def _ _coerce_ _(self,other):
        if isinstance(other,Complex):
            return self,other
        try:    # See if it can be converted to float
            return self, Complex(float(other))
        except ValueError:
```

```
                   pass
```

In this example, there are a few items of interest:

- First, the normal behavior of `__repr__()` is to create a string that can be evaluated to re-create the object. In this case, a string of the form `"Complex(r,i)"` is created. On the other hand, the `__str__()` method creates a string that's intended for nice output formatting (this is the string that would be produced by the `print` statement).

- Second, to handle operators in which complex numbers appear on both the left and right side of operators, both the `__op__()` and `__rop__()` methods for each operation must be provided.

- Finally, the `__coerce__` method is used to handle operations involving mixed types. In this case, other numeric types are converted to complex numbers so that they can be used in the complex arithmetic methods.

Classes, Types, and Membership Tests

Currently, there's a separation between types and classes. In particular, built-in types such as lists and dictionaries cannot be specialized via inheritance, nor does a class define a new type. In fact, all class definitions have a type of `ClassType`, while all class instances have a type of `InstanceType`. Thus, the following expression is true for any two objects that are instances of a class (even if they were created by different classes):

```
type(a) == type(b)
```

To test for membership in a class, use the built-in function `isinstance(obj,cname)`. This function returns true if an object `obj` belongs to the class `cname` or any class derived from `cname`. For example:

```
class A: pass
class B(A): pass
class C: pass

a = A()          # Instance of 'A'
b = B()          # Instance of 'B'
c = C()          # Instance of 'C'

isinstance(a,A)  # Returns 1
isinstance(b,A)  # Returns 1, B derives from A
isinstance(b,C)  # Returns 0, C not derived from A
```

Similarly, the built-in function `issubclass(A,B)` returns true if the class `A` is a subclass of class `B`. For example:

```
issubclass(B,A)   # Returns 1
issubclass(C,A)   # Returns 0
```

The `isinstance()` function can be used to perform type-checking against any of the built-in types:

```
import types
isinstance(3, types.IntType)     # Returns 1
isinstance(3, types.FloatType)   # Returns 0
```

This is the recommended way to perform type-checking with the built-in types, as the distinction between types and classes may disappear in a future release.

8

Modules and Packages

Large Python programs are often organized as a package of modules. In addition, a large number of modules are included in the Python library. This chapter describes the module and package system in more detail.

Modules

You can turn any valid source file into a module by loading it with the `import` statement. For example, consider the following code:

```
# file : spam.py
a = 37                  # A variable
def foo:                # A function
    print "I'm foo"
class bar:              # A class
    def grok(self):
        print "I'm bar.grok"
b = bar()               # Create an instance
```

To load this code as a module, you use the statement `import spam`. The first time `import` is used to load a module, it does three things:

1. It creates a new namespace that serves as a namespace to all the objects defined in the corresponding source file. This is the namespace accessed when functions and methods defined within the module use the `global` statement.

2. It executes the code contained in the module within the newly created namespace.

3. It creates a name within the caller that refers to the module namespace. This name matches the name of the module and is used as follows:

```
import spam            # Loads and executes the module 'spam'
print spam.a           # Accesses a member of module 'spam'
spam.foo()
c = spam.bar()
...
```

To import multiple modules, supply `import` with a comma-separated list of module names, like this:

```
import socket, os, regex
```

Modules can be imported using alternative names by using the as qualifier. For example:

```
import os as system
import socket as net, thread as threads
system.chdir("..")
net.gethostname()
```

Use the from statement to load specific definitions within a module into the current namespace. The from statement is identical to import except that instead of creating a name referring to the newly created module namespace, references to one or more of the objects defined in the module are placed into the current namespace:

```
from socket import gethostname
                                # Put gethostname in current namespace

print gethostname()             # Use without module name
socket.gethostname()            # NameError: socket
```

The from statement also accepts a comma-separated list of object names. The asterisk (*) wildcard character can also be used to load all the definitions in a module except those that start with an underscore. For example:

```
from socket import gethostname, socket
from socket import *   # Load all definitions into current namespace
```

Modules can more precisely control the set of names that are imported by from *module* import * by defining a list __all__. For example:

```
# module: foo.py
__all__ = [ 'bar', 'spam' ]    # Names to be imported by *
```

In addition, the as qualifier can be used to rename specific objects imported with from. For example:

```
from socket import gethostname as hostname
h = hostname()
```

The import statement can appear at any point in a program. However, the code in each module is loaded and executed only once, regardless of how often you use the import statement. Subsequent import statements simply create a reference to the module namespace created on a previous import. You can find a dictionary containing all currently loaded modules in the variable sys.modules, which is a dictionary that maps module names to module objects. The contents of this dictionary are used to determine whether import loads a fresh copy of a module.

The from *module* import * statement can only be used at the top level of a module. In particular, it's illegal to use this form of import inside function bodies, due to the way in which it interacts with function scoping rules.

Each module defines a variable __name__ that contains the module name. Programs can examine this variable to determine the module in which they're executing. The top-level module of the interpreter is named __main__. Programs specified on the command line or entered interactively run inside the __main__ module. Sometimes, a program may alter its behavior, depending on whether it has been imported as a module or is running in __main__. This can be done as follows:

```
# Check if running as a program
if __name__ == '__main__':
    # Yes
    statements
else:
    # No, I must have been imported as a module
    statements
```

The Module Search Path

When loading modules, the interpreter searches the list of directories in `sys.path`.
The following is a typical value of `sys.path`:

```
['', '/usr/local/lib/python2.0',
    '/usr/local/lib/python2.0/plat-sunos5',
    '/usr/local/lib/python2.0/lib-tk',
    '/usr/local/lib/python2.0/lib-dynload',
    '/usr/local/lib/python2.0/site-packages']
```

The empty string `''` refers to the current directory.

To add new directories to the search path, simply append them to this list.

Module Loading and Compilation

So far, this chapter has presented modules as files containing Python code.
However, modules loaded with `import` really fall into four general categories:

- Programs written in Python (`.py` files)

- C or C++ extensions that have been compiled into shared libraries or DLLs

- Packages containing a collection of modules

- Built-in modules written in C and linked into the Python interpreter

When looking for a module `foo`, the interpreter searches each of the directories in
`sys.path` for the following files (listed in search order):

1. A directory `foo` defining a package
2. `foo.so`, `foomodule.so`, `foomodule.sl`, or `foomodule.dll` (compiled extensions)
3. `foo.pyo` (only if the `-O` or `-OO` option has been used)
4. `foo.pyc`
5. `foo.py`

Packages are described shortly; compiled extensions are described in Appendix B,
"Extending and Embedding Python." For `.py` files, when a module is first imported,
it's compiled into bytecode and written back to disk as a `.pyc` file. On subsequent
imports, the interpreter loads this precompiled bytecode unless the modification
date of the `.py` file is more recent (in which case, the `.pyc` file is regenerated). Files
ending in `.pyo` are used in conjunction with the interpreter's `-O` option. These files
contain bytecode stripped of line numbers, assertions, and other debugging information. As a result, they're somewhat smaller and allow the interpreter to run
slightly faster. If the `-OO` option is specified instead of `-O`, documentation strings are
also stripped from the file. This removal of documentation strings occurs only
when `.pyo` files are created—not when they're loaded. If none of these files exists
in any of the directories in `sys.path`, the interpreter checks whether the name corresponds to a built-in module name. If no match exists, an `ImportError` exception
is raised.

The compilation of files into `.pyc` and `.pyo` files occurs only in conjunction with
the `import` statement. Programs specified on the command line or standard input
don't produce such files.

When import searches for files, it matches filenames in a case-sensitive manner—even on machines where the underlying filesystem is not case-sensitive, such as Windows. (Such systems are case-preserving, however.) Thus, import foo will only import a file foo.py and not a file FOO.PY. However, note that versions of Python prior to 2.1 didn't handle this case correctly on all platforms. If you're concerned about backward compatibility, avoid the use of module names that differ in case only.

Module Reloading

The built-in function reload() can be used to reload and execute the code contained within a module previously loaded with import. It accepts a module object as a single argument. For example:

```
import foo
... some code ...
reload(foo)            # Reloads foo
```

All operations involving the module after the execution of reload() will utilize the newly loaded code. However, reload() doesn't retroactively update objects created using the old module. Thus, it's possible for references to coexist for objects in both the old and new versions of a module. Furthermore, compiled extensions written in C or C++ cannot be reloaded using reload().

As a general rule, avoid module reloading except during debugging and development.

Packages

Packages allow a collection of modules to be grouped under a common package name. This technique helps resolve namespace conflicts between module names used in different applications. A package is defined by creating a directory with the same name as the package and creating a file _ _init_ _.py in that directory. You can then place additional source files, compiled extensions, and subpackages in this directory as needed. For example, a package might be organized as follows:

```
Graphics/
       _ _init_ _.py
       Primitive/
           _ _init_ _.py
           lines.py
           fill.py
           text.py
           ...
       Graph2d/
           _ _init_ _.py
           plot2d.py
           ...
       Graph3d/
           _ _init_ _.py
           plot3d.py
           ...
       Formats/
           _ _init_ _.py
           gif.py
           png.py
           tiff.py
           jpeg.py
```

The `import` statement is used to load modules from a package in a number of ways:

- `import Graphics.Primitive.fill`

  This loads the submodule `Graphics.Primitive.fill`. The contents of this module have to be explicitly named, such as

  `Graphics.Primitive.fill.floodfill(img,x,y,color)`.

- `from Graphics.Primitive import fill`

  This loads the submodule `fill` but makes it available without the package prefix; for example, `fill.floodfill(img,x,y,color)`.

- `from Graphics.Primitive.fill import floodfill`

  This loads the submodule `fill` but makes the `floodfill` function directly accessible; for example, `floodfill(img,x,y,color)`.

Whenever any part of a package is imported, the code in the file `__init__.py` is executed. Minimally, this file may be empty, but it can also contain code to perform package-specific initializations. All the `__init__.py` files encountered during an import are executed. Thus, the statement `import Graphics.Primitive.fill` shown earlier would execute the `__init__.py` files in both the `Graphics` directory and the `Primitive` directory.

One peculiar problem with packages is the handling of this statement:

```
from Graphics.Primitive import *
```

The intended outcome of this statement is to import all the modules associated with a package into the current namespace. However, because filename conventions vary from system to system (especially with regard to case sensitivity), Python cannot accurately determine what modules those might be. As a result, this statement just imports all the references defined in the `__init__.py` file in the `Primitive` directory. This behavior can be modified by defining a list `__all__` that contains all the module names associated with the package. This list should be defined in the package `__init__.py` file, like this:

```
# Graphics/Primitive/__init__.py
__all__ = ["lines","text","fill",...]
```

Now when the user issues a `from Graphics.Primitive import *` statement, all the listed submodules are loaded as expected.

Importing a package name alone doesn't import all the submodules contained in the package. For example, the following code doesn't work:

```
import Graphics
Graphics.Primitive.fill.floodfill(img,x,y,color)  # Fails!
```

However, because the `import Graphics` statement executes the `__init__.py` file in the `Graphics` directory, it could be modified to import all the submodules automatically as follows:

```
# Graphics/__init__.py
import Primitive, Graph2d, Graph3d

# Graphics/Primitive/__init__.py
import lines, fill, text, ...
```

Now the `import Graphics` statement imports all the submodules and makes them available using their fully qualified names.

The modules contained within the same directory of a package can refer to each other without supplying a full package name. For example, the Graphics.Primitive.fill module could import the Graphics.Primitive.lines module simply by using import lines. However, if a module is located in a different subdirectory, its full package name must be used. For example, if the plot2d module of Graphics.Graph2d needs to use the lines module of Graphics.Primitive, it must use a statement such as from Graphics.Primitive import lines. If necessary, a module can examine its __name__ variable to find its fully qualified module name. For example, the following code imports a module from a sibling subpackage knowing only the name of the sibling (and not that of its top-level package):

```
# Graphics/Graph2d/plot2d.py

# Determine the name of the package where my package is located
import string
base_package = string.join(string.split(__name__,'.')[:-2],'.')

# Import the ../Primitive/fill.py module
exec "from %s.Primitive import fill" % (base_package,)
```

Finally, when Python imports a package, it defines a special variable __path__ that contains a list of directories that are searched when looking for package submodules. (The variable __path__ is a package-specific version of the sys.path variable.) __path__ is accessible to the code contained in __init__.py files and initially contains a single item with the directory name of the package. If necessary, a package can add additional directories to the __path__ list to alter the search path used for finding submodules.

9

Input and Output

This chapter describes the details of Python input/output, including command-line options, environment variables, file I/O, Unicode, and object persistence.

Reading Options and Environment Variables

When the interpreter starts, command-line options are placed in the list sys.argv. The first element is the name of the program. Subsequent elements are the options presented on the command line *after* the program name. The following program shows how to access command-line options:

```
# printopt.py
# Print all of the command-line options
import sys
for i in range(len(sys.argv)):
    print "sys.argv[%d] = %s" % (i, sys.argv[i])
```

Running the program produces the following:

```
% python printopt.py foo bar -p
sys.argv[0] = printopt.py
sys.argv[1] = foo
sys.argv[2] = bar
sys.argv[3] = -p
%
```

Environment variables are accessed in the dictionary os.environ. For example:

```
import os
path = os.environ["PATH"]
user = os.environ["USER"]
editor = os.environ["EDITOR"]
... etc ...
```

To modify the environment variables, set the os.environ variable. Alternatively, you can use the os.putenv() function. For example:

```
os.environ["FOO"] = "BAR"
os.putenv("FOO","BAR")
```

Files

The built-in function open(*name* [,*mode*]) opens and creates files, as shown here:

```
f = open('foo')        # Opens 'foo' for reading
f = open('foo','w')    # Open for writing
```

The file mode is 'r' for read, 'w' for write, or 'a' for append. The mode character can be followed by 'b' for binary data, such as 'rb' or 'wb'. This is optional on UNIX, but required on Windows, and should be included if you're concerned about portability. In addition, a file can be opened for updates by supplying a plus (+) character, such as 'r+' or 'w+'. When a file is opened for update, you can perform both input and output, as long as all output operations flush their data before any subsequent input operations. If a file is opened using 'w+' mode, its length is first truncated to zero.

open() returns a file object that supports the methods shown in Table 9.1.

Table 9.1   File Methods

Method	Description
f.read([*n*])	Reads at most *n* bytes.
f.readline([*n*])	Reads a single line of input up to *n* characters. If *n* is omitted, reads the entire line.
f.readlines()	Reads all the lines and returns a list.
f.xreadlines()	Returns an opaque sequence object where each iteration reads a new line from the file.
f.write(*s*)	Writes string *s*.
f.writelines(*l*)	Writes all strings in list *l*.
f.close()	Closes the file.
f.tell()	Returns the current file pointer.
f.seek(*offset* [, *where*])	Seeks to a new file position.
f.isatty()	Returns 1 if *f* is an interactive terminal.
f.flush()	Flushes the output buffers.
f.truncate([*size*])	Truncates the file to at most *size* bytes.
f.fileno()	Returns an integer file descriptor.
f.readinto(*buffer*,*nbytes*)	Read *nbytes* of data into a writable buffer object.

The read() method returns the entire file as a string unless an optional *length* parameter is given specifying the maximum number of bytes. The readline() method returns the next line of input, including the terminating newline; the readlines() method returns all the input lines as a list of strings. The readline() method optionally accepts a maximum line length *n*. If a line longer than *n* bytes is read, the first *n* bytes are returned. The remaining line data is not discarded and will be returned on subsequent read operations. Both the readline() and readlines() methods are platform-aware and handle different representations of newlines properly (for example, '\n' versus '\r\n'). The xreadlines() method returns a special opaque sequence object that allows the lines of a file to be read using iteration instead of first being read entirely into memory, as with the readlines() method. For example:

```
for line in f.xreadlines():
    # Do something with line
    ...
```

The `write()` method writes a string to the file, and the `writelines()` method writes a list of strings to the file. In all these cases, the string can contain binary data, including embedded null characters.

The `seek()` method is used to randomly access parts of a file given an *offset* and a placement rule in *where*. If *where* is 0 (the default), `seek()` assumes that *offset* is relative to the start of the file; if *where* is 1, the position is moved relative to the current position; and if *where* is 2, the offset is taken from the end of the file. The `fileno()` method returns the integer file-descriptor for a file and is sometimes used in low-level I/O operations in certain library modules. On machines that support large files (greater than 2GB), the `seek()` and `tell()` methods use long integers. However, enabling such support may require a reconfiguration and recompilation of the Python interpreter.

File objects also have the data attributes shown in the following table.

Attribute	Description
f.closed	Boolean value indicates the file state: 0 if the file is open, 1 if closed.
f.mode	The I/O mode for the file.
f.name	Name of the file if created using open(). Otherwise, it will be a string indicating the source of the file.
f.softspace	Boolean value indicating whether a space character needs to be printed before another value when using the print statement. Classes that emulate files must provide a writable attribute of this name that's initially initialized to zero.

Standard Input, Output, and Error

The interpreter provides three standard file objects, known as *standard input*, *standard output*, and *standard error*, which are available in the sys module as `sys.stdin`, `sys.stdout`, and `sys.stderr`, respectively. `stdin` is a file object corresponding to the stream of input characters supplied to the interpreter. `stdout` is the file object that receives output produced by print. `stderr` is a file that receives error messages. More often than not, `stdin` is mapped to the user's keyboard, while `stdout` and `stderr` produce text onscreen.

The methods described in the preceding section can be used to perform raw I/O with the user. For example, the following function reads a line of input from standard input:

```
def gets():
    text = ""
    while 1:
        c = sys.stdin.read(1)
        text = text + c
        if c == '\n': break
    return text
```

Alternatively, the built-in function `raw_input(prompt)` can read a line of text from `stdin`:

```
s = raw_input("type something : ")
print "You typed '%s'" % (s,)
```

Finally, keyboard interrupts (often generated by Ctrl+C) result in a `KeyboardInterrupt` exception that can be caught using an exception handler.

If necessary, the values of `sys.stdout`, `sys.stdin`, and `sys.stderr` can be replaced with other file objects, in which case the `print` statement and raw input functions use the new values. The original values of `sys.stdout`, `sys.stdin`, and `sys.stderr` at interpreter startup are also available in `sys.__stdout__`, `sys.__stdin__`, and `sys.__stderr__`, respectively.

Note that in some cases `sys.stdin`, `sys.stdout`, and `sys.stderr` may be altered by the use of an integrated development environment (IDE). For example, when running Python under Idle, `sys.stdin` is replaced with an object that behaves like a file, but is really an object in the development environment. In this case, certain low-level methods such as `read()` and `seek()` may be unavailable.

The print Statement

The `print` statement produces output on the file contained in `sys.stdout`. `print` accepts a comma-separated list of objects such as the following:

```
print "The values are", x, y, z
```

For each object, the `str()` function is invoked to produce an output string. These output strings are then joined and separated by a single space to produce the final output string. The output is terminated by a newline unless a trailing comma is supplied to the `print` statement. In this case, only a trailing space is printed. For example:

```
print "The values are ", x, y, z, w
# Print the same text, using two print statements
print "The values are ", x, y,    # Omits trailing newline
print z, w
```

To produce formatted output, use the string-formatting operator (`%`) as described in Chapter 4, "Operators and Expressions." For example:

```
print "The values are %d %7.5f %s" % (x,y,z) # Formatted I/O
```

You can change the destination of the `print` statement by adding the special `>>file` modifier, where `file` is a file object that allows writes. Here's an example:

```
f = open("output","w")
print >>f, "hello world"
...
f.close()
```

Combining formatted I/O using dictionaries with triple-quoted strings is a powerful way to write computer-generated text. For example, you might want to write a short form letter, filling in a `name`, an `item` name, and an `amount`, like this:

```
Dear Mr. Bush,
Please send back my blender or pay me $50.00.

                        Sincerely yours,


                        Joe Python User
```

To do this, you can form a triple-quoted string containing text and dictionary-based format specifiers such as this:

```
form = """\
Dear  %(name)s,

Please send back my %(item)s or pay me $%(amount)0.2f.


                        Sincerely yours,


                        Joe Python User
"""
print form % { 'name': 'Mr. Bush',
               'item': 'blender',
               'amount': 50.00,
               }
```

For forms involving many lines and many items to be substituted, this is much clearer than using one `print` statement per line or a large tuple of items to format.

Persistence

It's often necessary to save and restore the contents of an object to a file. One approach to this problem is to write a pair of functions that read and write data from a file in a special format. An alternative approach is to use the `pickle` and `shelve` modules.

The `pickle` module serializes an object into a stream of bytes that can be written to a file. For example, the following code writes an object to a file:

```
import pickle
object = someObject()
f = open(filename,'w')
pickle.dump(object, f)        # Save object
```

To restore the object, you can use the following code:

```
import pickle
f = open(filename,'r')
object = pickle.load(f)   # Restore the object
```

The `shelve` module is similar, but saves objects in a dictionary-like database:

```
import shelve
object = someObject()
dbase = shelve.open(filename)     # Open a database
dbase['key'] = object             # Save object in database
...
object = dbase['key']             # Retrieve it
dbase.close()                     # Close the database
```

In both cases, only serializable objects can be saved to a file. Most Python objects can be serialized, but special-purpose objects such as files maintain an internal state that cannot be saved and restored in this manner. For more details about the pickle and shelve modules, see Appendix A, "The Python Library."

Unicode I/O

Internally, Unicode strings are represented as sequences of 16-bit integer character values. As in 8-bit strings, all characters are the same size, and most common string operations are simply extended to handle strings with a larger range of character values. However, whenever Unicode strings are converted to a stream of bytes, a number of issues arise. First, to preserve compatibility with existing software, it may be desirable to convert Unicode to an 8-bit representation compatible with software that expects to receive ASCII or other 8-bit data. Second, the use of 16-bit characters introduces problems related to byte ordering. For a Unicode character U+HHLL, little endian encoding places the low-order byte first, as in LL HH. Big endian encoding places the high-order byte first, as in HH LL. Because of this difference, it's generally not possible to simply write raw Unicode data to a file without also specifying the encoding used.

To address these problems, external representation of Unicode strings is always done according to a specific encoding rule. This rule precisely defines how Unicode characters are to be represented as a byte sequence. In Chapter 4, encoding rules were first described for the unicode() function and the s.encode() string method. For example:

```
a = u"M\u00fcller"
b = "Hello World"
c = a.encode('utf-8')    # Convert a to a UTF-8 string
d = unicode(b)           # Convert b to a Unicode string
```

For Unicode I/O, a similar technique is implemented through the use of the built-in codecs module. The codecs module contains a collection of functions for converting byte-oriented data to and from Unicode strings under a variety of different data-encoding schemes. A specific codec is selected by calling the codecs.lookup(encoding) function. This function returns a four-element tuple (enc_func, decode_func, stream_reader, stream_writer). For example:

```
import codecs
(utf8_encode, utf8_decode, utf8_reader, utf8_writer) = \
        codecs.lookup('utf-8')
```

The enc_func(u [,errors]) function takes a Unicode string u and returns a tuple (s, len) in which s is an 8-bit string containing a portion or all of the Unicode string u, converted into the desired encoding, and len contains the number of Unicode characters converted. The decode_func(s [,errors]) function takes an 8-bit string s and returns a tuple (u, len) containing a Unicode string u and the number of characters in s that were converted. The errors parameter determines how errors are handled and is one of 'strict', 'ignore', or 'replace'. In 'strict' mode, encoding errors raise a UnicodeError exception. In 'ignore' mode, encoding errors are ignored. In 'replace' mode, characters that can't be converted are replaced by a replacement character. The replacement character is U+FFFD in Unicode and '?' in 8-bit strings.

stream_reader is a class that implements a wrapper for reading Unicode data from a file object. Calling *stream_reader(file)* returns an object in which the read(), readline(), and readlines() methods read Unicode string data. *stream_writer* is a class that provides a wrapper for writing Unicode to a file object. Calling *stream_writer(file)* returns a file object in which the write() and writelines() methods translate Unicode strings to the given encoding on the output stream.

The following example illustrates how to read and write UTF-8 encoded Unicode data using these functions:

```
# Output Unicode data to a file
ustr = u'M\u00fcller'          # A Unicode string

outf = utf8_writer(open('foo','w'))    # Create UTF-8 output stream
outf.write(ustr)
outf.close()

# Read Unicode data from a file
infile = utf8_reader(open('bar'))
ustr = infile.read()
infile.close()
```

When working with Unicode files, the data encoding is usually embedded in the file itself. For example, XML parsers may look at the first few bytes of the string '<?xml ...>' to determine the document encoding. If the first four values are 3C 3F 78 6D ('<?xm'), the encoding is assumed to be UTF-8. If the first four values are 00 3C 00 3F or 3C 00 3F 00, the encoding is assumed to be UTF-16 big endian or UTF-16 little endian, respectively. Alternatively, a document encoding may appear in MIME headers or as an attribute of other document elements. For example:

```
<?xml ... encoding="ISO 8859-1" ... ?>
```

When the encoding is read from a document, code similar to the following might be used:

```
f = open("somefile")
# Determine encoding
...
(encoder,decoder,reader,writer) = codecs.lookup(encoding)
f = reader(f)    # Wrap file with Unicode reader
data = f.read()  # Read Unicode data
f.close()
```

Unicode Data Encoding

Table 9.2 lists all of the currently available encoders in the codecs module.

Table 9.2   Encoders in the codecs Module

Encoder	Description
'ascii'	ASCII encoding
'latin-1', 'iso-8859-1'	Latin-1 or ISO-8859-1 encoding
'utf-8'	8-bit variable length encoding
'utf-16'	16-bit variable length encoding

continues >>

Table 9.2   Continued

Encoder	Description
'utf-16-le'	UTF-16, but with explicit little endian encoding
'utf-16-be'	UTF-16, but with explicit big endian encoding
'unicode-escape'	Same format as u"*string*"
'raw-unicode-escape'	Same format as ur"*string*"

The following paragraphs describe each of the encoders in more detail.

'ascii' encoding:

In 'ascii' encoding, character values are confined to the ranges [0,0x7f] and [U+0000, U+007F]. Any character outside this range is invalid.

'iso-8859-1' or 'latin-1' encoding:

Characters can be any 8-bit value in the ranges [0,0xff] and [U+0000, U+00FF]. Values in the range [0,0x7f] correspond to characters from the ASCII character set. Values in the range [0x80,0xff] correspond to characters from the ISO-8859-1 or extended ASCII character set. Any characters with values outside the range [0,0xff] result in an error.

'utf-8' encoding:

UTF-8 is a variable-length encoding that allows all Unicode characters to be represented. A single byte is used to represent ASCII characters in the range 0–127. All other characters are represented by multibyte sequences of two or three bytes. The encoding of these bytes is shown in the following table.

Unicode Characters	Byte 0	Byte 1	Byte 2
U+0000 - U+007F	0*nnnnnnn*		
U+007F - U+07FF	110*nnnnn*	10*nnnnnn*	
U+0800 - U+FFFF	1110*nnnn*	10*nnnnnn*	10*nnnnnn*

For two-byte sequences, the first byte always starts with the bit sequence 110. For three-byte sequences, the first byte starts with the bit sequence 1110. All subsequent data bytes in multibyte sequences start with the bit sequence 10.

In full generality, the UTF-8 format allows for multibyte sequences of up to six bytes. In Python, four-byte UTF-8 sequences are used to encode a pair of Unicode characters known as a *surrogate pair*. Both characters have values in the range [U+D800, U+DFFF] and are combined to encode a 20-bit character value. The surrogate encoding is as follows: The four-byte sequence 111100*nn* 10*nnnnnn* 10*nnmmmm* 10*mmmmmm* is encoded as the pair U+D800 + *N*, U+DC00 + *M*, where *N* is the upper 10 bits and *M* is the lower 10 bits of the 20-bit character encoded in the four-byte UTF-8 sequence. Five- and six-byte UTF-8 sequences (denoted by starting bit sequences of 111110 and 1111110, respectively) are used to encode character values up to 32 bits in length. These values are not supported by Python and currently result in a UnicodeError exception if they appear in an encoded data stream.

UTF–8 encoding has a number of useful properties that allow it to be used by older software. First, the standard ASCII characters are represented in their standard encoding. This means that a UTF–8 encoded ASCII string is indistinguishable from a traditional ASCII string. Second, UTF–8 doesn't introduce embedded null bytes for multibyte character sequences. Thus, existing software based on the C library and programs that expect null-terminated 8-bit strings will work with UTF–8 strings. Finally, UTF–8 encoding preserves the lexicographic ordering of strings. That is, if a and b are Unicode strings and a < b, then a < b also holds when a and b are converted to UTF–8. Therefore, sorting algorithms and other ordering algorithms written for 8-bit strings will also work for UTF–8.

`'utf-16'`, `'utf-16-be'`, and `'utf-16-le'` **encoding:**

UTF–16 is a variable-length 16-bit encoding in which Unicode characters are written as 16-bit values. Unless a byte ordering is specified, big endian encoding is assumed. In addition, a byte-order marker of U+FEFF can be used to explicitly specify the byte ordering in a UTF–16 data stream. In big endian encoding, U+FEFF is the Unicode character for a zero-width nonbreaking space, whereas the reversed value U+FFFE is an illegal Unicode character. Thus, the encoder can use the byte sequence FE FF or FF FE to determine the byte ordering of a data stream. When reading Unicode data, Python removes the byte-order markers from the final Unicode string.

`'utf-16-be'` encoding explicitly selects UTF–16 big endian encoding. `'utf-16-le'` encoding explicitly selects UTF–16 little ending encoding.

Although there are extensions to UTF–16 to support character values greater than 16 bits, none of these extensions are currently supported.

`'unicode-escape'` and `'raw-unicode-escape'` **encoding:**

These encoding methods are used to convert Unicode strings to the same format as used in Python Unicode string literals and Unicode raw string literals. For example:

```
s = u'u\14a8\u0345\u2a34'
t = s.encode('unicode-escape')    #t = '\u14a8\u0345\u2a34'
```

Unicode Character Properties

In addition to performing I/O, programs that use Unicode may need to test Unicode characters for various properties such as capitalization, numbers, and whitespace. The `unicodedata` module provides access to a database of character properties. General character properties can be obtained with the `unicodedata.category(c)` function. For example, `unicodedata.category(u"A")` returns `'Lu'`, signifying that the character is an uppercase letter. Further details about the Unicode character database and the `unicodedata` module can be found in Appendix A.

10

Execution Environment

This chapter describes the environment in which Python programs are executed. The goal is to describe the runtime behavior of the interpreter, including program startup, site configuration, and program termination.

Interpreter Options and Environment

The interpreter has a number of options that control its runtime behavior and environment. On UNIX and Windows, options are given to the interpreter in the form of command-line options such as the following:

```
python [options] [-c cmd ¦ filename ¦ - ] [args]
```

On the Macintosh, options to the Python interpreter are set using a separate program, EditPythonPrefs.

The following command-line options are available:

Option	Description
-d	Generates parser debugging information.
-h	Prints a list of all available command-line options.
-i	Enters interactive mode after program execution.
-O	Optimized mode.
-OO	Optimized mode plus removal of documentation strings.
-S	Prevents inclusion of the site initialization module.
-t	Reports warnings about inconsistent tab usage.
-tt	Inconsistent tab usage results in a TabError exception.
-u	Unbuffered binary stdout and stdin.
-U	Unicode literals. All string literals are handled as Unicode.
-v	Verbose mode.
-V	Prints the version number and exits.
-x	Skips the first line of the source program.
-c cmd	Executes cmd as a string.
-Wfilter	Adds a warning filter.

The -d option debugs the interpreter and is of limited use to most programmers. The -i option starts an interactive session immediately after a program has finished execution, and is useful for debugging. The -0 and -00 options apply some optimization to byte-compiled files, and are described in Chapter 8, "Modules and Packages." The -s option omits the site initialization module described in the later section "Site Configuration Files." The -t, -tt, and -v options report additional warnings and debugging information. The -x optionP 94 ignores the first line of a program in the event that it's not a valid Python statement (for example, when the first line starts the Python interpreter in a script). The -U option forces the interpreter to treat all string literals as Unicode. The -W option is used to specify a warning filter and is described further in the warnings module in Appendix A, "The Python Library."

The program name appears after all the interpreter options. If no name is given, or the hyphen (-) character is used as a filename, the interpreter reads the program from standard input. If standard input is an interactive terminal, a banner and prompt are presented. Otherwise, the interpreter opens the specified file and executes its statements until an end-of-file marker is reached. The -c cmd option can be used to execute short programs in the form of a command-line option.

Command-line options appearing after the program name or hyphen (-) are passed to the program in sys.argv, as described in the section "Reading Options and Environment Variables" in Chapter 9, "Input and Output."

Additionally, the interpreter reads the following environment variables:

Variable	Description
PYTHONPATH	Colon-separated module search path
PYTHONSTARTUP	File executed on interactive startup
PYTHONHOME	Location of the Python installation
PYTHONINSPECT	Implies the -i option
PYTHONUNBUFFERED	Implies the -u option
PYTHONCASEOK	Use non–case-sensitive matching for module names used by import (Python 2.1)

PYTHONPATH specifies a module search path that is inserted into the beginning of sys.path, which is described in Chapter 8. PYTHONSTARTUP specifies a file to execute when the interpreter runs in interactive mode. The PYTHONHOME variable is used to set the location of the Python installation but is rarely needed, since Python knows how to find its own libraries and the site-packages directory where extensions are normally installed. If a single directory such as /usr/local is given, the interpreter expects to find all files in that location. If two directories are given, such as /usr/local:/usr/local/sparc-solaris-2.6, the interpreter searches for platform-independent files in the first directory and platform-dependent files in the second. PYTHONHOME has no effect if no valid Python installation exists at the specified location.

On Windows, some of the environment variables such as PYTHONPATH are read from Registry entries found in HKEY_LOCAL_MACHINE/Software/Python. On the Macintosh, the environment variables can be adjusted using the EditPythonPrefs program.

Interactive Sessions

If no program name is given and the standard input to the interpreter is an interactive terminal, Python starts in interactive mode. In this mode, a banner message
is printed and the user is presented with a prompt. In addition, the interpreter
evaluates the script contained in the PYTHONSTARTUP environment variable (if set).
This script is evaluated as if part of the input program (that is, it isn't loaded using
an import statement). One application of this script might be to read a user configuration file such as .pythonrc.

When accepting interactive input, two user prompts appear. The >>> prompt
appears at the beginning of a new statement; the ... prompt indicates a statement
continuation. For example:

```
Python 2.0 (#1, Oct 27 2000, 14:34:45)
[GCC 2.95.2 19991024 (release)] on sunos5
Type "copyright", "credits" or "license" for more information.
>>> for i in range(0,4):
...     print i
...
0
1
2
3
>>>
```

In customized applications, you can change the prompts by modifying the values
of sys.ps1 and sys.ps2.

On some systems, Python may be compiled to use the GNU readline library. If
enabled, this library provides command histories, completion, and other additions
to Python's interactive mode. The special key bindings provided by the readline
library are described in the readline module in Appendix A.

By default, the output of commands issued in interactive mode is generated
by printing the output of the built-in repr() function on the result. Starting
with Python 2.1, this can be changed by setting the variable sys.displayhook. For
example:

```
>>> def my_display(x):
...     print "result = %s" % repr(x)
...
>>> sys.displayhook = my_display
>>> 3+4
result = 7
>>>
```

Launching Python Applications

In most cases, you'll want programs to start the interpreter automatically, rather
than first having to start the interpreter manually. On UNIX, this is done using
shell scripts by setting the first line of a program to something like this:

```
#!/usr/local/bin/python
# Python code from this point on...
import string
print "Hello world"
...
```

On Windows, double-clicking a .py, .pyw, .wpy, .pyc, or .pyo file automatically launches the interpreter. Normally, programs run in a console window unless they're renamed with a .pyw suffix (in which case the program runs silently). If it's necessary to supply options to the interpreter, Python can also be started from a .bat file.

On the Macintosh, clicking a .py file normally launches the editor that was used to create the file. However, two special programs in the Macintosh distribution can be used to build applications. Dropping a .py file on the BuildApplet program converts the program into a file that automatically launches the Python interpreter when opened. The BuildApplication program converts a Python program into a standalone application that can be distributed and executed on machines that don't have a Python installation.

Site Configuration Files

A typical Python installation may include a number of third-party modules and packages. To configure these packages, the interpreter first imports the module site. The role of site is to search for package files and to add additional directories to the module search path sys.path. In addition, the site module sets the default encoding for Unicode string conversions. For details on the site module, see Appendix A.

Enabling Future Features

Starting in Python 2.1, new language features that affect compatibility with older versions of Python may be disabled when they first appear in a release. To enable these features, the statement from __future__ import *feature* can be used. For example:

```
# Enable nested scopes in Python 2.1
from __future__ import nested_scopes
```

When used, this statement should appear as the first statement of a module or program. Furthermore, the intent of the __future__ module is to introduce features that will eventually be a standard part of the Python language (in which case, the use of __future__ will not be required).

Program Termination

A program terminates when no more statements exist to execute in the input program, when an uncaught SystemExit exception is raised (as generated by sys.exit()), or when the interpreter receives a SIGTERM or SIGHUP signal (on UNIX). On exit, the interpreter decrements the reference count of all objects in all the currently known namespaces (and destroys each namespace as well). If the reference count of an object reaches zero, the object is destroyed and its __del__() method is invoked. It's important to note that in some cases the __del__()

method might not be invoked at program termination. This can occur if circular references exist between objects (in which case objects may be allocated, but accessible from no known namespace). Although Python's garbage collector can reclaim unused circular references during execution, it isn't normally invoked on program termination.

Because there's no guarantee that _ _del_ _() will be invoked at termination, it may be a good idea to explicitly clean up certain objects, such as open files and network connections. To accomplish this, add specialized cleanup methods (for example, close()) to user-defined objects. Another possibility is to write a termination function and register it with the atexit module, as follows:

```
import atexit
connection = open_connection("deaddot.com")

def cleanup():
    print "Going away..."
    close_connection(connection)

atexit.register(cleanup)
```

The garbage collector can also be invoked in this manner:

```
import atexit, gc
atexit.register(gc.collect)
```

One final peculiarity about program termination is that the _ _del_ _ method for some objects may try to access global data or methods defined in other modules. Since these objects may already have been destroyed, a NameError exception occurs in _ _del_ _, and you may get an error such as the following:

```
Exception exceptions.NameError: 'c' in <method Bar._ _ del_ _
of Bar instance at c0310> ignored
```

If this occurs, it means that _ _del_ _ has aborted prematurely. It also implies that it may have failed in an attempt to perform an important operation (such as cleanly shutting down a server connection). If this is a concern, it's probably a good idea to perform an explicit shutdown step in your code, rather than relying on the interpreter to destroy objects cleanly at program termination. The peculiar NameError exception can also be eliminated by declaring default arguments in the declaration of the _ _del_ _() method:

```
import foo
class Bar:
    def _ _ del_ _ (self, foo=foo):
        foo.bar()          # Use something in module foo
```

In some cases, it may be useful to terminate program execution without performing any cleanup actions. This can be accomplished by calling os._exit(status). This function provides an interface to the low-level exit() system call responsible for killing the Python interpreter process. When invoked, the program immediately terminates.

A

The Python Library

Python is bundled with a large collection of modules that provide a wide range of services ranging from interacting with the operating system to multimedia support. These modules are collectively known as the *Python library*. Currently, the library consists of approximately 200 modules that have been contributed by dozens of users.

This appendix describes most of the more frequently used modules in the Python library, with a focus on built-in functions, Python services, string processing, operating system interfaces, threads, and network programming. A brief overview of background material is introduced as necessary, but the reader is assumed to be reasonably familiar with basic operating system and programming concepts. Furthermore, because much of the library is based on C programming APIs, a good C programming book may help with some of the finer points of some modules. Extensive online documentation for the library is also available at http://www.python.org/doc/lib.

This appendix is largely based on the contents of the online library documentation as of Python version 2.1. However, a number of substantial modifications have been made:

- The library reference has been abridged to fit into a more compact format.

- Additional reference material has been added to better describe certain modules—especially with respect to operating system interfaces and network programming.

- Several modules require significant understanding of outside topics such as low-level network protocols and data formats. In these cases, only a brief description is given, along with references to related information.

- Special-purpose modules applicable to a single platform are omitted (for instance, SGI multimedia extensions).

- Large frameworks such as Tkinter, XML processing, and the Win32 extensions are omitted because they're beyond the scope of this book (and they're covered in books of their own).

- Obsolete modules are omitted, even though these modules are still included in the standard distribution.

It's also important to note that the Python library is always being improved and extended with new functionality. Although the modules covered here are the most stable, their contents are still likely to change slightly over time. When in doubt, consult the online documentation.

Finally, a few words on compatibility and availability. Unless otherwise indicated, each module is available on all platforms. When platform-specific issues are discussed, they're clearly marked.

Built-in Functions and Exceptions

This section describes Python's built-in functions and exceptions. Much of this material is covered less formally in the chapters of this book. Additional details and some of the more subtle aspects of many built-in functions can be found here.

Built-in Functions

The functions in this section are always available to the interpreter and are contained within the `__builtin__` module. In addition, the `__builtins__` attribute of each module usually refers to this module (except when running in a restricted execution environment as described in the "Restricted Execution" section).

_ (Underscore)

By default, the _ variable is set to the result of the last expression evaluated when the interpreter is running in interactive mode.

▶ **See Also** `sys.displayhook` (118).

`__import__(name [, globals [, locals [, fromlist]]])`

This function is invoked by the `import` statement to load a module. *name* is a string containing the module name, *globals* is an optional dictionary defining the global namespace, *locals* is a dictionary defining the local namespace, and *fromlist* is a list of targets given to the `from` statement. For example, the statement `import spam` results in a call to `__import__('spam', globals(), locals(), [])`, while the statement `from spam import foo` results in a call `__import__ ('spam', globals(), locals(), ['foo'])`. If the module name is prefixed by a package name such as `foo.bar` and *fromlist* is empty, the corresponding module object is returned. If *fromlist* is not empty, only the top-level package is returned.

This function is intended to be a low-level interface to the module loader. It doesn't perform all the steps performed by an `import` statement (in particular, the local namespace is not updated with names referring to objects contained within the module). This function can be redefined by the user to implement new behaviors for `import`. The default implementation doesn't even look at the `locals` parameter, while `globals` is only used to determine package context (these parameters are supplied so that alternative implementations of `__import__()` have full access to the global and local namespace information where `import` statements appear).

`abs(x)`

Returns the absolute value of *x*.

`apply(func [, args [, keywords]])`

Performs a function call operation on a callable object `func`. `args` is a tuple containing positional arguments and `keywords` is a dictionary containing keyword arguments. The `apply()` function can also be written as `func(*args,**keywords)`.

`buffer(sequence [, offset [, size]])`

Creates a new buffer object. A buffer is typically a byte-oriented subsequence of another sequence such as a string. For the most part, buffers appear like strings except that they don't support string methods and can't be used with the functions in the `string` module.

`callable(object)`

Returns 1 if `object` is a callable object, 0 otherwise.

`chr(i)`

Converts an integer or long integer value i, $0 <= i <= 255$, into a one-character string.

`cmp(x, y)`

Compares x and y and returns a negative number if $x < y$, 0 if $x == y$, and a positive number if $x > y$. Any two objects can be compared, although the result may be meaningless if the two objects have no meaningful comparison method defined (for example, comparing a number with a file object). In certain circumstances, such comparisons may also raise an exception.

`coerce(x, y)`

Returns a tuple containing the values of x and y converted to a common numerical type. See the section "Mathematical Operations" in Chapter 3, "Types and Objects."

`compile(string, filename, kind)`

Compiles `string` into a code object for use with `exec` or `eval()`. `filename` is a string containing the name of the file in which the string was defined. `kind` is `'exec'` for a sequence of statements, `'eval'` for a single expression, or `'single'` for a single executable statement.

`complex(real [, imag])`

Creates a complex number.

`delattr(object, attr)`

Deletes an attribute of an object. `attr` is a string. Same as `del object.attr`.

`dir([object])`

Returns a sorted list of attribute names. These are taken from the object's `__dict__`, `__methods__`, and `__members__` attributes. If no argument is given, the names in the current local symbol table are returned.

`divmod(a, b)`

Returns the quotient and remainder of long division as a tuple. For integers, the value `(a / b, a % b)` is returned. For floats, `(math.floor(a / b), a % b)` is returned.

`eval(expr [, globals [, locals]])`

Evaluates an expression. `expr` is a string or a code object created by `compile()`. `globals` and `locals` define the global and local namespaces for the operation. If omitted, the expression is evaluated in the namespace of the caller.

Appendix A   The Python Library

execfile(*filename* [, *globals* [, *locals*]])

Executes the statements in the file *filename*. *globals* and *locals* define the global and local namespaces in which the file is executed. If omitted, the file's contents are executed in the namespace of the caller. This function should not be used inside a function body because it is incompatible with nested scopes.

filter(*function*, *list*)

Creates a new list consisting of the objects from *list* for which *function* evaluates to true. If *function* is None, the identity function is used and all the elements of *list* that are false are removed.

float(*x*)

Converts *x* to a floating-point number.

getattr(*object*, *name* [, *default*])

Returns an attribute of an object. *name* is a string. *default* is an optional value to return if no such attribute exists. Same as *object.name*.

globals()

Returns a dictionary corresponding to the global namespace of the caller.

hasattr(*object*, *name*)

Returns 1 if *name* is the name of an attribute of *object*, 0 otherwise. *name* is a string.

hash(*object*)

Returns an integer hash value for an object (if possible). The hash value is the same for any two objects that compare as equals. Mutable objects don't define a hash value.

hex(*x*)

Converts an integer or long integer *x* to a hexadecimal string.

id(*object*)

Returns the unique integer identity of *object*.

input([*prompt*])

Same as eval(raw_input(*prompt*)).

int(*x* [, *base*])

Converts a number or string *x* to an integer. *base* optionally specifies a base when converting from a string.

intern(*string*)

Checks to see whether *string* is contained in an internal table of strings. If found, a copy of the internal string is returned. If not, *string* is added to the internal table and returned. This function is primarily used to get better performance in operations involving dictionary lookups. Interned strings are never garbage-collected. Not applicable to Unicode strings.

isinstance(*object*, *classobj*)

Returns true if *object* is an instance of *classobj* or a subclass of *classobj*. Can also be used for type checking if *classobj* is a type object.

issubclass(*class1*, *class2*)

Returns true if *class1* is a subclass of (derived from) *class2*.
Note: issubclass(A, A) is true.

len(*s*)

Returns the number of items contained in the sequence *s*.

`list(s)`

Returns a new list consisting of the items in the sequence s.

`locals()`

Returns a dictionary corresponding to the local namespace of the caller.

`long(x [, base])`

Converts a number or string x to a long integer. base optionally specifies the base of the conversion when converting from a string.

`map(function, list, ...)`

Applies function to every item of list and returns a list of results. If multiple lists are supplied, function is assumed to take that many arguments, with each argument taken from a different list. If function is None, the identity function is assumed. If None is mapped to multiple lists, a list of tuples is returned, wherein each tuple contains an element from each list. Short lists are extended with values of None to match the length of the longest list, if necessary. Consider using list comprehensions instead of map. For example, map(function, alist) can be replaced by [function(x) for x in alist].

▶ **See Also** zip (105).

`max(s [, args, ...])`

For a single argument s, returns the maximum value of the sequence s. For multiple arguments, returns the largest of the arguments.

`min(s [, args, ...])`

For a single argument s, returns the minimum value of the sequence s. For multiple arguments, returns the smallest of the arguments.

`oct(x)`

Converts an integer or long integer x to an octal string.

`open(filename [, mode [, bufsize]])`

Opens the file filename and returns a new file object (see Chapter 10, "Execution Environment"). mode indicates how the file should be opened: 'r' for reading, 'w' for writing, and 'a' for appending. An optional '+' can be added to the mode to open the file for updating (which allows both reading and writing). A mode of 'w+' truncates the file to zero length if it already exists. A mode of 'r+' or 'a+' opens the file for both reading and writing, but leaves the original contents intact when the file is opened. Append 'b' to the mode to indicate binary mode on platforms such as Windows, where a distinction is made between text and binary files. If the mode is omitted, a mode of 'r' is assumed. The bufsize argument specifies the buffering behavior, where 0 is unbuffered, 1 is line buffered, and any other positive number indicates an approximate buffer size in bytes. A negative number indicates that the system default buffering should be used (this is the default behavior).

`ord(c)`

Returns the integer ordinal value of a single character c. For ordinary characters, a value in the range [0,255] is returned. For Unicode characters, a value in the range [0,65535] is returned.

`pow(x, y [, z])`

Returns x ** y. If z is supplied, returns (x ** y) % z.

range([*start*,] *stop* [, *step*])

Creates a list of integers from *start* to *stop*. *step* indicates a stride and is set to 1 if omitted. If *start* is omitted (when range() is called with one argument), it defaults to 0. A negative *step* creates a list of numbers in descending order.

▶ **See Also** xrange (105).

raw_input([*prompt*])

Reads a line of input from standard input (sys.stdin) and returns it as a string. If *prompt* is supplied, it's first printed to standard output (sys.stdout). Trailing newlines are stripped and an EOFError exception is raised if an EOF is read. If the readline module is loaded, this function will use it to provide advanced line-editing and command-completion features.

reduce(*func*, *seq* [, *initializer*])

Applies a function *func* cumulatively to the items in the sequence *seq* and returns a single value. *func* is expected to take two arguments and is first applied to the first two items of *seq*. This result and subsequent elements of *seq* are then combined one at a time in a similar manner, until all elements of *seq* have been consumed. *initializer* is an optional starting value used in the first computation and when *seq* is empty.

reload(*module*)

Reloads an already imported module. *module* must refer to an existing module object. The use of this function is discouraged except for debugging. Keep the following issues in mind:

- When a module is reloaded, the dictionary defining its global namespace is retained. Thus, definitions in the old module that aren't part of the newly reloaded module are retained. Modules can exploit this to see if they have been previously loaded.

- It's usually illegal to reload dynamically loaded modules written in C.

- If any other modules have imported this module by using the from statement, they'll continue to use the definitions in the previously imported module. This problem can be avoided by either reissuing the from statement after a module has been reloaded or using fully qualified names such as *module.name*.

- If there are any object instances created by classes in the old module, they'll continue to use methods defined in the old module.

repr(*object*)

Returns a string representation of *object*. This is the same string generated by backquotes (`` `object` ``). In most cases, the returned string is an expression that can be passed to eval() to re-create the object.

round(*x* [, *n*])

Returns the result of rounding the floating-point number *x* to the closest multiple of 10 to the power minus *n*. If *n* is omitted, it defaults to 0. If two multiples are equally close, rounding is done away from 0 (for example, 0.5 is rounded to 1.0 and -0.5 is rounded to -1.0).

setattr(*object*, *name*, *value*)

Sets an attribute of an object. *name* is a string. Same as *object.name* = *value*.

slice([*start*,] *stop* [, *step*])

Returns a slice object representing integers in the specified range. Slice objects are also generated by extended slice syntax. See the section "Sequence and Mapping Methods" in Chapter 3 for details.

str(*object*)

Returns a string representing the printable form of an object. This is the same string as would be produced by the print statement.

tuple(*s*)

Creates a tuple whose items are taken from the sequence *s*. If *s* is already a tuple, it's returned unmodified.

type(*object*)

Returns the type of object. The type is returned as a type object as defined in the types module.

▶ **See Also** isinstance (102).

unichr(*i*)

Converts the integer or long integer *i*, 0 <= *i* <= 65535, to a single Unicode character.

unicode(*string* [,*encoding* [,*errors*]])

Converts *string* to a Unicode string. *encoding* specifies the data encoding of *string*. If omitted, the default encoding as returned by sys.getdefaultencoding() is used. *errors* specifies how encoding errors are handled and is one of 'strict', 'ignore', or 'replace'. See Chapter 9 ("Input and Output") and Chapter 3 ("Types and Objects") for details.

vars([*object*])

Returns the symbol table of *object* (usually found in its __dict__ attribute). If no argument is given, a dictionary corresponding to the local namespace is returned.

xrange([*start*,] *stop* [, *step*])

Works like range() except that an XRangeType object is returned. This object produces the same values as stored in the list created by range(), but without actually storing them. This is useful when working with very large ranges of integers that would consume a large amount of memory.

zip(*s1* [, *s2* [,..]])

Returns a list of tuples where the *n*th tuple is (*s1*[*n*], *s2*[*n*], ...). The resulting list is truncated to the length of the shortest argument sequence.

Built-in Exceptions

Built-in exceptions are contained in the exceptions module, which is always loaded prior to the execution of any program. Exceptions are defined as classes. The following exceptions serve as base classes for all the other exceptions:

Exception

The root class for all exceptions. All built-in exceptions are derived from this class. User-defined exceptions are encouraged to use this as a base class.

StandardError

The base class for all built-in exceptions except for SystemExit.

ArithmeticError

Base class for arithmetic exceptions, including OverflowError, ZeroDivisionError, and FloatingPointError.

LookupError

Base class for indexing and key errors, including IndexError and KeyError.

EnvironmentError

Base class for errors that occur outside Python, including IOError and OSError.

The preceding exceptions are never raised explicitly. However, they can be used to catch certain classes of errors. For instance, the following code would catch any sort of numerical error:

```
try:
    # Some operation
    ...
except ArithmeticError, e:
    # Math error
```

When an exception is raised, an instance of an exception class is created. This instance is placed in the optional variable supplied to the except statement. For example:

```
except IOError, e:
    # Handle error
    # 'e' has an instance of IOError
```

Most exceptions have an associated value that can be found in the args attribute of the exception instance ('e.args' in the preceding example). In most cases, this is a string describing the error. For EnvironmentError exceptions, the value is a 2-tuple or 3-tuple containing an integer error number, string error message, and an optional filename (these values are also available as exception attributes as described below).

The following exceptions are raised by programs:

AssertionError

Failed assert statement.

AttributeError

Failed attribute reference or assignment.

EOFError

End of file. Generated by the built-in functions input() and raw_input(). *Note:* A number of I/O methods such as read() and readlines() return an empty string for EOF.

FloatingPointError

Failed floating-point operation. A subclass of ArithmeticError.

IOError

Failed I/O operation. The value is an IOError instance with attributes errno, strerror, and filename. errno is an integer error number, strerror is a string error message, and filename is an optional filename. A subclass of EnvironmentError.

ImportError

Raised when an import statement can't find a module or when from can't find a name in a module.

`IndentationError`

Indentation error. A subclass of `SyntaxError`.

`IndexError`

Sequence subscript out of range. A subclass of `LookupError`.

`KeyError`

Key not found in a dictionary. A subclass of `LookupError`.

`KeyboardInterrupt`

Raised when the user hits the interrupt key (usually Ctrl+C).

`MemoryError`

Recoverable out-of-memory error.

`NameError`

Name not found in local or global namespaces.

`NotImplementedError`

Unimplemented feature. Can be raised by base classes that require derived classes to implement certain methods. A subclass of `RuntimeError`.

`OSError`

Operating system error. Primarily raised by functions in the `os` module. The value is the same as for `IOError`. A subclass of `EnvironmentError`.

`OverflowError`

Result of arithmetic operation is too large to be represented. A subclass of `ArithmeticError`.

`RuntimeError`

A generic error not covered by any of the other categories.

`SyntaxError`

Parser syntax error. Instances have the attributes `filename`, `lineno`, `offset`, and `text` that can be used to gather more information.

`SystemError`

Internal error in the interpreter. The value is a string indicating the problem.

`SystemExit`

Raised by the `sys.exit()` function. The value is an integer indicating the return code. If it's necessary to exit immediately, `os._exit()` can be used.

`TabError`

Inconsistent tab usage. Generated when Python is run with the `-tt` option. A subclass of `SyntaxError`.

`TypeError`

Operation or function applied to an object of inappropriate type.

`UnboundLocalError`

Unbound local variable referenced. This error occurs if a variable is referenced before it's defined in a function. A subclass of `NameError`.

`UnicodeError`

Unicode encoding or decoding error. A subclass of `ValueError`.

Appendix A   The Python Library

`ValueError`

Generated when the argument to a function or operation is the right type, but of inappropriate value.

`WindowsError`

Generated by failed system calls on Windows. A subclass of `OSError`.

`ZeroDivisionError`

Dividing by zero. A subclass of `ArithmeticError`.

The `exceptions` module also defines the exception objects `Warning`, `UserWarning`, `DeprecationWarning`, `RuntimeWarning`, and `SyntaxWarning`. These exceptions are used as part of the Python warning framework and are described further in the `warnings` module.

▶ **See Also** warnings (121).

Python Services

The modules in this section are primarily used to interact with the Python interpreter and its environment.

atexit

The `atexit` module is used to register functions to execute when the Python interpreter exits. A single function is provided:

`register(func [,args [,kwargs]])`

Adds function `func` to a list of functions that will execute when the interpreter exits. `args` is a tuple of arguments to pass to the function. `kwargs` is a dictionary of keyword arguments. The function is invoked as `func(*args,**kwargs)`.

Note

■ The `atexit` module should be used instead of setting the `sys.exitfunc` variable.

▶ **See Also** sys (116).

copy

The `copy` module provides functions for making shallow and deep copies of compound objects, including lists, tuples, dictionaries, and class instances.

`copy(x)`

Makes a shallow copy of *x* by creating a new compound object and duplicating the members of *x* by reference.

`deepcopy(x [, visit])`

Makes a deep copy of *x* by creating a new compound object and recursively duplicating all the members of *x*. *visit* is an optional dictionary that's used internally to detect and avoid cycles in recursively defined data structures.

A class can implement its own copy methods by implementing the methods `__copy__(self)` and `__deepcopy__(self, visit)`. Both methods should return a copy of the object. In addition, the `__deepcopy__()` method must accept a dictionary *visit* as described for the `deepcopy()` function. When writing `__deepcopy__()`, it's not necessary to modify *visit*. However, *visit* should be passed to subsequent calls to deepcopy() (if any) performed inside the __deepcopy__() method.

Notes

- This module can be used with simple types such as integers and strings, but there's little need to do so.

- The copy functions don't work with modules, class objects, functions, methods, tracebacks, stack frames, files, sockets, or other similar types. When an object can't be copied, the copy.error exception is raised.

- The copy_reg module is not used by this module.

▶ **See Also** pickle (113).

copy_reg

The copy_reg module extends the capabilities of the pickle and cPickle modules to handle the serialization of objects described by extension types (as defined in C extension modules). To do this, extension writers use this module to register reduction and construction functions that are used to serialize and unserialize an object, respectively.

constructor(*cfunc*)

Declares *cfunc* to be a valid constructor function. *cfunc* must be a callable object that accepts the tuple of values returned by the reduction function given to the pickle() function.

pickle(*type, rfunc* [, *cfunc*])

Registers *rfunc* as a reduction function for objects of type *type*. *rfunc* is a function that takes an object of the specified type and returns a tuple containing the constructor function and a tuple of arguments to pass to that function in order to reassemble the object. If supplied, *cfunc* is the constructor function that's registered using the constructor() function.

Example

The following example shows how this module would be used to pickle complex numbers. (*Note:* Because complex numbers are already pickleable, this example is only intended to illustrate the use of this module.)

```
# Register a method for pickling complex numbers
import copy_reg

# Create a complex number from two reals
def construct_complex(real,imag):
    return complex(real,imag)        # Built-in function

# Take a complex number 'c' and turn it into a tuple of floats
def reduce_complex(c):
    return construct_complex, (c.real, c.imag)

# Register our handler
copy_reg.pickle(type(1j),reduce_complex, construct_complex)
```

When complex numbers are pickled, the reduce_complex() function is called. When the object is later unpickled, the function construct_complex() is called, using the tuple of values originally returned by reduce_complex().

Notes

- copy_reg is a misnomer—this module isn't used by the copy module.
- It's not necessary to use this module when pickling instances of user-defined classes.

▶ **See Also** pickle (113).

gc

The gc module provides an interface for controlling the garbage collector used to collect cycles in objects such as lists, tuples, dictionaries, and instances. As various types of container objects are created, they're placed on a list that's internal to the interpreter. Whenever container objects are deallocated, they're removed from this list. If the number of allocations exceeds the number of deallocations by a user-definable threshold value, the garbage collector is invoked. The garbage collector works by scanning this list and identifying collections of objects that are no longer being used, but that haven't been deallocated due to circular dependencies. In addition, the garbage collector uses a three-level generational scheme in which objects that survive the initial garbage-collection step are placed onto lists of objects that are checked less frequently. This provides better performance for programs that have a large number of long-lived objects.

collect()

Runs a full garbage collection. This function checks all generations and returns the number of unreachable objects found.

disable()

Disables garbage collection.

enable()

Enables garbage collection.

garbage

A variable containing a read-only list of the uncollectable objects that the garbage collector could not release for some reason. See notes.

isenabled()

Returns true if garbage collection is enabled.

set_debug(*flags***)**

Set the garbage-collection debugging flags, which can be used to debug the behavior of the garbage collector. *flags* is the bitwise-or of the constants DEBUG_STATS, DEBUG_COLLECTABLE, DEBUG_UNCOLLECTABLE, DEBUG_INSTANCES, DEBUG_OBJECTS, DEBUG_SAVEALL, and DEBUG_LEAK.

get_debug()

Returns the debugging flags currently set.

get_threshold()

Returns the current collection threshold as a tuple.

```
set_threshold(threshold0 [, threshold1[, threshold2]])
```

Sets the collection frequency of garbage collection. Objects are classified into three generations, where generation 0 contains the youngest objects and generation 2 contains the oldest objects. Objects that survive a garbage-collection step are moved to the next-oldest generation. Once an object reaches generation 2, it stays in that generation. *threshold0* is the difference between the number of allocations and deallocations that must be reached before garbage collection occurs in generation 0. *threshold1* is the number of collections of generation 0 that must occur before generation 1 is scanned. *threshold2* is the number of collections that must occur in generation 1 before generation 2 is collected. The default threshold is currently set to (700,10,10). Setting *threshold0* to zero disables garbage collection.

Notes

- Circular references involving objects with a __del__() method are not garbage-collected and are placed on the list gc.garbage (uncollectable objects). These objects are not collected due to difficulties related to object finalization and the order in which __del__() methods should be invoked.

- To debug a leaky program, use gc.set_debug(gc.DEBUG_LEAK).

- The gc module first appeared in Python 2.0.

marshal

The marshal module is used to serialize Python objects. marshal is similar to the pickle and shelve modules, but is less powerful and intended for use only with simple objects. It shouldn't be used to implement persistent objects in general (use pickle instead).

```
dump(value, file)
```

Writes the object *value* to the open file object *file*. If *value* is an unsupported type, a ValueError exception is raised.

```
dumps(value)
```

Returns the string written by the dump() function. If *value* is an unsupported type, a ValueError exception is raised.

```
load(file)
```

Reads and returns the next value from the open file object *file*. If no valid value is read, an EOFError, ValueError, or TypeError exception will be raised.

```
loads(string)
```

Reads and returns the next value from the string *string*.

Notes

- Data is stored in a binary architecture-independent format.

- Only None, integers, long integers, floats, complex numbers, strings, Unicode strings, tuples, lists, dictionaries, and code objects are supported. Lists, tuples, and dictionaries can only contain supported objects. Class instances and recursive references in lists, tuples, and dictionaries are not supported.

- marshal is significantly faster than pickle, but isn't as flexible.

▶ **See Also** pickle (113), shelve (153).

new

The new module is used to create various types of objects used by the interpreter. The primary use of this module is by applications that need to create objects in a nonstandard manner (such as when unmarshalling data).

instance(*class*, *dict*)

Creates a class instance of *class* with dictionary *dict* without calling the __init__() method.

instancemethod(*function*, *instance*, *class*)

Creates a method object, bound to *instance*. *function* must be a callable object. If *instance* is None, an unbound instance method is created.

function(*code*, *globals* [, *name* [, *argdefs*]])

Creates a function object with the given *code* object and global namespace. *name* is the name of the function or None (in which case the function name is taken from *code*.co_name). *argdefs* is a tuple containing default parameter values.

code(*argcount*, *nlocals*, *stacksize*, *flags*, *codestring*, *constants*, *names*, *varnames*, *filename*, *name*, *firstlineno*, *lnotab*)

Creates a new code object. See the section "Code Objects" in Chapter 3 for a description of the arguments.

module(*name*)

Creates a new module object. *name* is the module name.

classobj(*name*, *baseclasses*, *dict*)

Creates a new class object. *name* is the class name, *baseclasses* is a tuple of base classes, and *dict* is a dictionary defining the class namespace.

▶ **See Also** Chapter 3.

operator

The operator module provides functions that access the built-in operators and special methods of the interpreter described in Chapter 3. For example, add(3, 4) is the same as 3 + 4. When the name of a function matches the name of a special method, it can also be invoked using its name with double underscores—for example, __add__(3, 4).

Function	Description
add(*a*, *b*)	Returns $a + b$ for numbers
sub(*a*, *b*)	Returns $a - b$
mul(*a*, *b*)	Returns $a * b$ for numbers
div(*a*, *b*)	Returns a / b
mod(*a*, *b*)	Returns $a \% b$
neg(*a*)	Returns $-a$
pos(*a*)	Returns $+a$
abs(*a*)	Returns the absolute value of a
inv(*a*)	Returns the inverse of a
lshift(*a*, *b*)	Returns $a \ll b$

Function	Description
rshift(a, b)	Returns a >> b
and_(a, b)	Returns a & b (bitwise and)
or_(a, b)	Returns a ¦ b (bitwise or)
xor(a, b)	Returns a ^ b (bitwise xor)
not_(a)	Returns not a
truth(a)	Returns 1 if a is true, 0 otherwise
concat(a, b)	Returns a + b for sequences
repeat(a, b)	Returns a * b for a sequence a and integer b
contains(a, b)	Returns the result of b in a
sequenceIncludes(a, b)	Returns the result of b in a (deprecated)
countOf(a, b)	Returns the number of occurrences of b in a
indexOf(a, b)	Returns the index of the first occurrence of b in a
getitem(a, b)	Returns a[b]
setitem(a, b, c)	a[b] = c
delitem(a, b)	del a[b]
getslice(a, b, c)	Returns a[b:c]
setslice(a, b, c, v)	Sets a[b:c] = v
delslice(a, b, c)	del a[b:c]

In addition, the `operator` module defines the following functions for testing object properties. *Note:* These functions are not entirely reliable for user-defined instances, since they don't perform an exhaustive test of the interface to see whether all functions are implemented.

Function	Description
isMappingType(o)	Tests whether o supports the mapping interface
isNumberType(o)	Tests whether o supports the number interface
isSequenceType(o)	Tests whether o supports the sequence interface

▶ **See Also** "Special Methods" in Chapter 3.

pickle and cPickle

The `pickle` and `cPickle` modules are used to serialize Python objects into a stream of bytes suitable for storing in a file, transferring across a network, or placing in a database. This process is variously called *pickling, serializing, marshalling,* or *flattening*. The resulting byte stream can also be converted back into a series of Python objects using an unpickling process.

The pickling and unpickling process is controlled by using `Pickler` and `Unpickler` objects as created by the following two functions:

```
Pickler(file [, bin])
```

Creates a pickling object that writes data to the file object *file*. *bin* specifies that data should be written in binary format. By default, a less efficient—but readable—text format is used.

Unpickler(*file*)

Creates an unpickling object that reads data from the file object *file*. The unpickler automatically detects whether the incoming data is in binary or text format.

To serialize an object *x* onto a file *f*, the dump() method of the pickler object is used. For example:

```
f = open('myfile', 'w')
p = pickle.Pickler(f)      # Send pickled data to file f
p.dump(x)                  # Dump x
```

To later unpickle the object from the file, do the following:

```
f = open('myfile')
u = pickle.Unpickler(f)
x = u.load()                # Restore x from file f
```

Multiple calls to the dump() and load() methods are allowed, provided that the sequence of load() calls used to restore a collection of previously stored objects matches the sequence of dump() calls used during the pickling process.

The following functions are available as shortcuts to common pickling operations:

dump(*object, file* [, *bin*])

Dumps a pickled representation of *object* to the file object *file*. Same as Pickler(*file, bin*).dump(*object*).

dumps(*object* [, *bin*])

Same as dump(), but returns a string containing the pickled data.

load(*file*)

Loads a pickled representation of an object from the file object *file*. Same as Unpickler(*file*).load().

loads(*string*)

Same as load(), but reads the pickled representation of an object from a string.

The following objects can be pickled:

- None
- Integers, long integers, floating-point numbers, and complex numbers
- Tuples, lists, and dictionaries containing only pickleable objects
- Normal and Unicode strings
- Classes defined at the top level of a module
- Instances of classes defined at the top level of a module

When class instances are pickled, their corresponding class definition must appear at the top level of a module (that is, no nested classes). When instances are unpickled, the module in which their class definition appeared is automatically imported. In addition, when instances are re-created, their __init__() method is not invoked. If it's necessary to call __init__() when unpickling, the class must define a special method __getinitargs__() that returns a tuple of arguments to be supplied to __init__(). If present, pickle will call this function and encode the constructor arguments in the byte stream for use when unpickling.

It's also worth noting that when pickling class instances in which the corresponding class definition appears in __main__, that class definition must be manually reloaded prior to unpickling a saved object (because there's no way for the interpreter to know how to automatically load the necessary class definitions back into __main__ when unpickling).

A class can define customized methods for saving and restoring its state by implementing the special methods __getstate__() and __setstate__(). The __getstate__() method must return a pickleable object (such as a string) representing the state of the object. The __setstate__() method accepts the pickled object and restores its state. If no __getstate__() method is found, pickle simply pickles an object's __dict__ attribute.

When an attempt is made to pickle an unsupported object type, the pickle.PicklingError exception is raised. If an error occurs while unpickling, the pickle.UnpicklingError exception is raised.

Notes

- Recursive objects (objects containing references to themselves) and object sharing are handled correctly. However, if the same object is dumped to a Pickler object more than once, only the first instance is saved (even if the object has changed between dumps).

- When class instances are pickled, their class definitions and associated code for methods are not saved. This allows classes to be modified or upgraded while still being able to read data saved from older versions.

- pickle defines Pickler and Unpickler as classes that can be subclassed if necessary.

- The cPickle module is significantly faster than pickle, but doesn't allow subclassing of the Pickler and Unpickler objects.

- The data format used by pickle is Python-specific and shouldn't be assumed to be compatible with any external standards such as XDR.

- Any object that provides write(), read(), and readline() methods can be used in place of a file.

- The copy_reg module is used to register new types with the pickle module.

▶ **See Also** shelve (153), marshal (111), copy_reg (109).

site

The site module is automatically imported when the interpreter starts and is used to perform site-wide initialization of packages and to set the default Unicode encoding. The module works by first creating a list of up to four directory names created from the values of sys.prefix and sys.exec_prefix. On Windows or Macintosh platforms, the list of directories is as follows:

```
[ sys.prefix,
    sys.exec_prefix ]
```

On UNIX, the directories are as follows:

```
[ sys.prefix + '/lib/pythonvers/site-packages',
  sys.prefix + '/lib/site-python',
  sys.exec_prefix + '/lib/pythonvers/site-packages',
  sys.exec_prefix + '/lib/site-python' ]
```

For each directory in the list, a check is made to see whether the directory exists. If so, it's added to the sys.path variable. Next, a check is made to see whether it contains any path configuration files (files with a .pth suffix). A path configuration file contains a list of directories relative to the location of the path file that should be added to sys.path. For example:

```
# foo package configuration file 'foo.pth'
foo
bar
```

Each directory in the path configuration file must be listed on a separate line. Comments and blank lines are ignored. When the site module loads the file, it checks to see whether each directory exists. If so, the directory is added to sys.path. Duplicated items are added to the path only once.

After all paths have been added to sys.path, an attempt is made to import a module named sitecustomize. The purpose of this module is to perform any additional (and arbitrary) site customization. If the import of sitecustomize fails with an ImportError, the error is silently ignored.

The site module is also responsible for setting the default Unicode encoding. By default, the encoding is set to 'ascii'. However, the encoding can be changed by placing code in sitecustomize.py that calls sys.setdefaultencoding() with a new encoding such as 'utf-8'. If you're willing to experiment, the source code of site can also be modified to automatically set the encoding based on the machine's locale settings.

▶ **See Also** sys (116), Chapter 8, Chapter 10.

sys

The sys module contains variables and functions that pertain to the operation of the interpreter and its environment. The following variables are defined:

argv

List of command-line options passed to a program. argv[0] is the name of the program.

builtin_module_names

Tuple containing names of modules built into the Python executable.

byteorder

Native byte-ordering of the machine—'little' for little-endian or 'big' for big-endian.

copyright

String containing copyright message.

__displayhook__

Original value of the displayhook() function.

__excepthook__

Original value of the excepthook() function.

dllhandle

Integer handle for the Python DLL (Windows).

exec_prefix

Directory where platform-dependent Python files are installed.

executable

String containing the name of the interpreter executable.

exitfunc

Function object that's called when the interpreter exits. It can be set to a function taking no parameters. By default, exitfunc is not defined. Direct use of this variable is discouraged—use the atexit module instead.

▶ **See Also** atexit (108).

hexversion

Integer whose hexadecimal representation encodes the version information contained in sys.version_info. The value of this integer is always guaranteed to increase with newer versions of the interpreter.

last_type, last_value, last_traceback

These variables are set when an unhandled exception is encountered and the interpreter prints an error message. last_type is the last exception type, last_value is the last exception value, and last_traceback is a stack trace. *Note:* The use of these variables is not thread-safe. sys.exc_info() should be used instead.

maxint

Largest integer supported by the integer type.

modules

Dictionary mapping module names to module objects.

path

List of strings specifying the search path for modules. See Chapter 8, "Modules and Packages."

platform

Platform identifier string, such as 'linux-i386'.

prefix

Directory where platform-independent Python files are installed.

ps1, ps2

Strings containing the text for the primary and secondary prompts of the interpreter. Initially, ps1 is set to '>>> ' and ps2 is set to '... '. The str() method of whatever object is assigned to these values is evaluated to generate the prompt text.

stdin, stdout, stderr

File objects corresponding to standard input, standard output, and standard error. stdin is used for the raw_input() and input() functions. stdout is used for print and the prompts of raw_input() and input(). stderr is used for the interpreter's prompts and error messages. These variables can be assigned to any object that supports a write() method operating on a single string argument.

__stdin__, __stdout__, __stderr__

File objects containing the values of stdin, stdout, and stderr at the start of the interpreter.

tracebacklimit

Maximum number of levels of traceback information printed when an unhandled exception occurs. The default value is 1000. A value of 0 suppresses all traceback information and causes only the exception type and value to be printed.

version

Version string.

version_info

Version information represented as a tuple (major, minor, micro, releaselevel, serial). All values are integers except releaselevel, which is a string 'alpha', 'beta', 'candidate', or 'final'.

warnoptions

List of warning options supplied to the interpreter with the -W command-line option.

winver

The version number used to form registry keys on Windows.

The following functions are available:

displayhook([value])

This function is called to print the result of an expression when the interpreter is running in interactive mode. By default, the value of repr(value) is printed to standard output and value is saved in the variable __builtin__._. displayhook can be redefined to provide different behavior if desired.

excepthook(type,value,traceback)

This function is called when an uncaught exception occurs. type is the exception class, value is the value supplied by the raise statement, and traceback is a traceback object. The default behavior is to print the exception and traceback to standard error. However, this function can be redefined to provide alternative handling of uncaught exceptions (which may be useful in specialized applications such as debuggers or CGI scripts).

exc_info()

Returns a tuple (type, value, traceback) containing information about the exception that's currently being handled. type is the exception type, value is the exception parameter passed to raise, and traceback is a traceback object containing the call stack at the point where the exception occurred. Returns None if no exception is currently being handled.

exit([n])

Exits from Python by raising the SystemExit exception. n is an integer exit code indicating a status code. A value of 0 is considered normal (the default); nonzero values are considered abnormal. If a noninteger value is given to n, it's printed to sys.stderr and an exit code of 1 is used.

getdefaultencoding()

Gets the default string encoding in Unicode conversions. Returns a value such as 'ascii' or 'utf-8'. The default encoding is set by the site module.

_getframe([depth])

Returns a frame object from the call stack. If depth is omitted or is zero, the topmost frame is returned. Otherwise, the frame for that many calls below the current frame is returned. For example, _getframe(1) returns the caller's frame. Raises ValueError if depth is invalid.

getrecursionlimit()

Returns the recursion limit for functions.

getrefcount(object)

Returns the reference count of object.

setcheckinterval(n)

Sets the number of Python virtual machine instructions that must be executed by the interpreter before it checks for periodic events such as signals and thread context switches. The default value is 10.

setdefaultencoding(enc)

Sets the default encoding. enc is a string such as 'ascii' or 'utf-8'. This function is only defined inside the site module. It can be called from user-definable sitecustomize modules.

▶ **See Also** site (115).

setprofile(pfunc)

Sets the system profile function that can be used to implement a source code profiler. See the later section "The Python Profiler" for information about the Python profiler.

setrecursionlimit(n)

Changes the recursion limit for functions. The default value is 1000.

settrace(tfunc)

Sets the system trace function, which can be used to implement a debugger. See the later section "The Python Debugger" for information about the Python debugger.

traceback

The traceback module is used to gather and print stack traces of a program after an exception has occurred. The functions in this module operate on traceback objects such as the third item returned by the sys.exc_info() function.

print_tb(traceback [, limit [, file]])

Prints up to limit stack trace entries from traceback to the file file. If limit is omitted, all the entries are printed. If file is omitted, the output is sent to sys.stderr.

print_exception(type, value, traceback [, limit [, file]])

Prints exception information and a stack trace to file. type is the exception type and *value* is the exception value. *limit* and *file* are the same as in print_tb().

print_exc([*limit* [, *file*]])

Same as print_exception() applied to the information returned by the sys.exc_info() function.

print_last([*limit* [, *file*]])

Same as print_exception(sys.last_type, sys.last_value, sys.last_traceback, *limit*, *file*).

print_stack([*frame* [, *limit* [, *file*]]])

Prints a stack trace from the point at which it's invoked. *frame* specifies an optional stack frame from which to start. *limit* and *file* have the same meaning as for print_tb().

extract_tb(*traceback* [, *limit*])

Extracts the stack trace information used by print_tb().

extract_stack([*frame* [, *limit*]])

Extracts the stack trace information used by print_stack().

format_list(*list*)

Formats stack trace information for printing.

format_exception_only(*type*, *value*)

Formats exception information for printing.

format_exception(*type*, *value*, *traceback* [, *limit*])

Formats an exception and stack trace for printing.

format_tb(*traceback* [, *limit*])

Same as format_list(extract_tb(*traceback*, *limit*)).

format_stack([*frame* [, *limit*]])

Same as format_list(extract_stack(*frame*, *limit*)).

tb_lineno(*traceback*)

Returns the line number set in a traceback object.

Additional details are available in the online documentation.

▶ **See Also** sys (116), "The Python Debugger" (289), Chapter 3, and
http://www.python.org/doc/lib/module-traceback.html.

types

The types module defines names for all the built-in object types. The contents of this module are often used in conjunction with the built-in isinstance() function and other type-related operations. The module defines the following variables:

Variable	Description
BufferType	Buffer object.
BuiltinFunctionType	Built-in functions.
CodeType	Code object.
Variable	**Description**

ComplexType	Complex numbers.
ClassType	User-defined class.
DictType	Dictionaries.
DictionaryType	Alternative name for dictionaries.
EllipsisType	Type of Ellipsis.
FileType	File object.
FloatType	Floating-point numbers.
FrameType	Execution frame object.
FunctionType	User-defined functions and lambdas.
InstanceType	Instance of a user-defined class.
IntType	Integers.
LambdaType	Alternative name for FunctionType.
ListType	Lists.
LongType	Long integers.
MethodType	User-defined class method.
ModuleType	Modules.
NoneType	Type of None.
SliceType	Extended slice object. Returned by slice().
StringType	Strings.
TracebackType	Traceback objects.
TupleType	Tuples.
TypeType	Type of type objects.
UnboundMethodType	Alternative name for MethodType.
UnicodeType	Unicode string.
XRangeType	Object created by using xrange().

Example

```
import types
if isinstance(s, types.ListType):
    print 'Is a list'
else:
    print 'Is not a list'
```

▶ **See Also** Chapter 3.

warnings

The warnings module provides functions to issue and filter warning messages. Unlike exceptions, warnings are intended to alert the user to potential problems, but without generating an exception or causing execution to stop. One of the primary uses of the warnings module is to inform users about deprecated language features that may not be supported in future versions of Python. For example:

```
>>> import regex
__main__:1: DeprecationWarning: the regex module is
➥deprecated; please use the re module
>>>
```

Like exceptions, warnings are organized into a class hierarchy that describe general categories of warnings. The following table lists the currently supported categories:

Category	Description
Warning	Base class of all warning types
UserWarning	User-defined warning
DeprecationWarning	Deprecated feature
SyntaxWarning	Potential syntax problem
RuntimeWarning	Potential runtime problem

Each of these classes is available in the __builtin__ module as well as the exceptions module. In addition, they're instances of Exception. This makes it possible to easily convert warnings into errors.

Warnings are issued using the warn() function. For example:

```
warnings.warn("feature X is deprecated.")
warnings.warn("feature Y might be broken.", RuntimeWarning)
```

If desired, warnings can be filtered. The filtering process can be used to alter the output behavior of warning messages, ignore warnings, or turn warnings into exceptions. The filterwarnings() function is used to add a filter for a specific type of warning. For example:

```
warnings.filterwarnings(action="ignore",
                        message=".*regex.*",
                        category=DeprecationWarning)
import regex        # Warning message disappears
```

Limited forms of filtering can also be specified using the -W option to the interpreter. For example:

```
% python -Wignore:the\ regex:DeprecationWarning
```

The following functions are defined in the warnings module:

warn(message[, category[, stacklevel]])

Issues a warning. message is a string containing the warning message. category is the warning class, such as DeprecationWarning. stacklevel is an integer that specifies the stack frame from which the warning message should originate. By default, category is UserWarning and stacklevel is 1.

warn_explicit(message, category, filename, lineno[, module[, registry]])

This is a low-level version of the warn() function. message and category have the same meaning as for warn(). filename, lineno, and module explicitly specify the location of the warning. registry is an object representing all the currently active filters. If registry is omitted, the warning message is not suppressed.

showwarning(message, category, filename, lineno[, file])

Writes a warning to a file. If *file* is omitted, the warning is printed to
sys.stderr.

   formatwarning(*message*, *category*, *filename*, *lineno*)

Creates the formatted string that's printed when a warning is issued.

   filterwarnings(*action*[, *message*[, *category*[, *module*[, *lineno*[, *append*]]]]])

Adds an entry to the list of warning filters. *action* is one of 'error', 'ignore',
'always', 'default', 'once', or 'module', as described in the following table. *message* is
a regular expression string used to match against the warning message. *category* is a
warning class such as DeprecationError. *module* is a regular expression string that's
matched against the module name. *lineno* is a specific line number or 0 to match
against all lines. *append* specifies that the filter should be appended to the list of all
filters (checked last). By default, new filters are added to the beginning of the filter
list. If any argument is omitted, it defaults to a value that matches all warnings.

Action	Description
'error'	Convert the warning into an exception.
'ignore'	Ignore the warning.
'always'	Always print a warning message.
'default'	Print the warning once for each location where the warning occurs.
'module'	Print the warning once for each module in which the warning occurs.
'once'	Print the warning once regardless of where it occurs.

   resetwarnings()

Resets all the warning filters. This discards all previous calls to filterwarnings()
as well as options specified with -w.

Notes

- The list of currently active filters is found in the warnings.filters variable.

- The warnings module was first added to Python 2.1.

- When warnings are converted to exceptions, the warning category becomes
  the exception type. For instance, an error on DeprecationWarning raises a
  DeprecationWarning exception.

- The -W option can be used to specify a warning filter on the command line.
  The general format of this option is as follows:

  -Waction:message:category:module:lineno

  Each part has the same meaning as in the filterwarning() function. However,
  in this case the *message* and *module* fields specify substrings (instead of regular
  expressions) for the first part of the warning message and module name to
  be filtered.

weakref

The weakref module provides support for weak references. Normally, a reference to an object causes its reference count to increase—effectively keeping the object alive until the reference goes away. A *weak reference*, on the other hand, provides a way of referring to an object without increasing its reference count. A weak reference is created using the weakref.ref() function as follows:

```
>>> class A: pass
>>> a = A()
>>> ar = weakref.ref(a)        # Create a weak reference to a
>>> print ar
<weakref at 0x135a24; to 'instance' at 0x12ce0c>
```

Once created, the original object can be obtained from a weak reference by simply calling it as a function with no arguments. If the underlying object still exists, it will be returned. Otherwise, None is returned to indicate that the original object no longer exists. For example:

```
>>> print ar()                 # Print original object
<__main__.A instance at 12ce0c>
>>> del a                      # Delete the original object
>>> print ar()                 # a is gone, so this now returns None
None
>>>
```

The following functions are defined by the weakref module:

ref(*object*[, *callback*])

Creates a weak reference to *object*. *callback* is an optional function that will be called when *object* is about to be destroyed. If supplied, this function should accept a single argument that's the corresponding weak reference object. More than one weak reference may refer to the same object. In this case, the *callback* functions will be called in order from the most recently applied reference to the oldest reference. *object* can be obtained from a weak reference by calling the returned weak reference object as a function with no arguments. If the original object no longer exists, None will be returned.

proxy(*object*[, *callback*])

Creates a proxy using a weak reference to *object*. The returned proxy object is really a wrapper around the original object that provides access to its attributes and methods. As long as the original object exists, manipulation of the proxy object will transparently mimic the behavior of the underlying object. On the other hand, if the original object has been destroyed, operations on the proxy will raise a weakref.ReferenceError to indicate that the object no longer exists. *callback* is a callback function with the same meaning as for the ref() function. The type of a proxy object is either ProxyType or CallableProxyType, depending on whether the original object is callable.

getweakrefcount(*object*)

Returns the number of weak references and proxies that refer to *object*.

getweakrefs(*object*)

Returns a list of all weak reference and proxy objects that refer to *object*.

WeakKeyDictionary([*dict*])

Creates a dictionary in which the keys are referenced weakly. When there are no more strong references to a key, the corresponding entry in the dictionary is automatically removed. If supplied, the items in *dict* are initially added to the returned WeakKeyDictionary object. Because only certain types of objects can be weakly referenced, there are many restrictions on acceptable key values. In particular, built-in strings cannot be used as weak keys. However, instances of user-defined classes that define a __hash__() method can be used as keys.

WeakValueDictionary([*dict*])

Creates a dictionary in which the values are referenced weakly. When there are no more strong references to a value, corresponding entries in the dictionary will be discarded. If supplied, the entries in *dict* are added to the returned WeakValueDictionary.

Example

One application of weak references is to create caches of recently computed results. For instance, if a function takes a long time to compute a result, it might make sense to cache these results and reuse them as long as they're still in use someplace in the application. For example:

```
_resultcache = { }
def fooaache(x):
    if _resultcache.has_key(x):
        r = _resultcache[x]()         # Get weak ref and dereference it
        if r is not None: return r
    r = foo(x)
    _resultcache[x] = weakref.ref(r)
    return r
```

Notes

- Only class instances, functions, and methods currently support weak references. Built-in functions and most built-in types such as lists, dictionaries, strings, and numbers cannot be used.

- The dictionaries returned by WeakKeyDictionary and WeakValueDictionary are subclasses of UserDict in the UserDict module. WeakKeyDictionary and WeakValueDictionary can also be subclassed.

- If an exception occurs during the execution of a callback registered with ref() or proxy(), the exception is printed to standard error and ignored.

- Weak references are hashable as long as the original object is hashable. Moreover, the weak reference will maintain its hash value after the original object has been deleted, provided that the original hash value is computed while the object still exists.

- Weak references can be tested for equality, but not for ordering. If the objects are still alive, references are equal if the underlying objects have the same value. Otherwise, references are equal if they are the same reference.

- Weak references were first added to Python 2.1.

UserDict, UserList, and UserString

The UserDict, UserList, and UserString modules provide class wrappers around the built-in dictionary, list, and string types. These wrappers can be used as a base class for classes that want to override or add new methods to these types. Each module defines a single class UserDict, UserList, and UserString, respectively:

UserDict([*initialdata*])

Returns a class instance that simulates a dictionary.

UserList([*list*])

Returns a class instance that simulates a list. *list* is an optional list that will be used to set the initial value. If omitted, the list will be set to [ ].

UserString([*sequence*])

Returns a class instance that simulates a string. The initial value of the string is set to the value of str(*sequence*).

In all cases, the real dictionary, list, or string object can be accessed in the data attribute of the instance.

Example

```
# A dictionary with case-insensitive keys
from UserDict import UserDict
import string


class MyDict(UserDict):

    # Perform a case-insensitive lookup
    def __getitem__(self,key):
        return self.data[key.lower()]
    def __setitem__(self,key,value):
        self.data[key.lower()] = value
    def __delitem__(self,key):
        del self.data[key.lower()]
    def has_key(self,key):
        return self.data.has_key(key.lower())


# Use new dictionary-like class
d = MyDict()
d['Content-Type'] = 'text/html'
print d['content-type']         # Returns 'text/html'
```

The UserString module also defines a class MutableString that provides an implementation of mutable strings. For example:

```
a = UserString.MutableString("Hello World!")

a[1] = 'a'        # a = "Hallo World!"
a[6:] = 'Welt!'   # a = "Hallo Welt!"
```

Although mutable strings are a frequently requested Python feature, the implementation provided by MutableString has a number of drawbacks. First, the standard string methods such as s.replace() and s.upper() return new strings as opposed to modifying the string in place. Second, mutable strings cannot be used as dictionary keys. Finally, the mutable string implementation doesn't provide extra memory efficiency or runtime performance, as you might expect. For instance, all changes to a MutableString object involve a full memory copy of the underlying string, as opposed to simply modifying the contents in place.

Notes

- Use of the MutableString class should generally be discouraged, since it provides no significant benefit over the use of standard strings. In fact, it will probably make your application run more slowly.

- Subclasses of UserList should provide a constructor that takes one or no arguments.

Mathematics

The modules in this section provide a variety of mathematical functions.

array

The array module defines a new object type ArrayType that works almost exactly like other sequence types except that its contents are constrained to a single type. The type of an array is determined at the time of creation, using one of the following typecodes:

Type Code	Description	C Type	Minimum Size (in bytes)
'c'	8-bit character	char	1
'b'	8-bit integer	signed char	1
'B'	8-bit unsigned integer	unsigned char	1
'h'	16-bit integer	short	2
'H'	16-bit unsigned integer	unsigned short	2
'i'	integer	int	4 or 8
'I'	unsigned integer	unsigned int	4 or 8
'l'	long integer	long	4 or 8
'L'	unsigned long integer	unsigned long	4 or 8
'f'	single-precision float	float	4
'd'	double-precision float	double	8

The representation of integers and long integers is determined by the machine architecture (they may be 32 or 64 bits). When values stored as 'L' or 'I' are returned, they're returned as Python long integers.

The module defines the following function:

```
array(typecode [, initializer])
```

Creates an array of type *typecode*. *initializer* is a string or list of values used to initialize values in the array. The following attributes and methods apply to an array object `a`:

Item	Description
`a.typecode`	Typecode character used to create the array.
`a.itemsize`	Size of items stored in the array (in bytes).
`a.append(x)`	Appends `x` to the end of the array.
`a.buffer_info()`	Returns (*address*, *length*), giving the memory location and length of the buffer used to store the array.
`a.byteswap()`	Swaps the byte ordering of all items in the array from big-endian to little-endian or vice versa. This is only supported for integer values.
`a.count(x)`	Returns the number of occurrences of `x` in `a`.
`a.extend(b)`	Appends array `b` to the end of array `a`.
`a.fromfile(f, n)`	Reads `n` items (in binary format) from the file object `f` and appends to the end of the array. `f` must be a file object. Raises `EOFError` if fewer than `n` items can be read.
`a.fromlist(list)`	Appends items from `list` to the end of the array.
`a.fromstring(s)`	Appends items from string `s` where `s` is interpreted as a string of binary values—same as would have been read using `fromfile()`.
`a.index(x)`	Returns the index of the first occurrence of `x` in `a`. Raises `ValueError` if not found.
`a.insert(i, x)`	Inserts `x` before position `i`.
`a.pop([i])`	Removes item `i` from the array and returns it. If `i` is omitted, the last element is removed.
`a.remove(x)`	Remove the first occurrence of `x` from the array. Raises `ValueError` if not found.
`a.reverse()`	Reverses the order of the array.
`a.tofile(f)`	Writes all items to file `f`. Data is saved in native binary format.
`a.tolist()`	Converts the array to an ordinary list of values.
`a.tostring()`	Converts to a string of binary data—the same data as would be written using `tofile()`.

When items are inserted into an array, a `TypeError` exception is generated if the type of the item doesn't match the type used to create the array.

Notes

- This module is used to create large lists in a storage-efficient manner. The resulting arrays are not suitable for numeric work. For example, the addition operator doesn't add the corresponding elements of the arrays; it appends one array to the other. To create storage- and calculation-efficient arrays, use the `Numeric` extension available at `http://numpy.sourceforge.net/`. Note that the `Numeric` API is completely different.

- The type of an array object is `array.ArrayType`.

▶ **See Also** `struct` (144), `xdrlib` (277).

cmath

The cmath module provides mathematical functions for complex numbers. All functions accept and return complex numbers.

Function	Description
acos(x)	Returns the arccosine of x
acosh(x)	Returns the arc hyperbolic cosine of x
asin(x)	Returns the arcsine of x
asinh(x)	Returns the arc hyperbolic sine of x
atan(x)	Returns the arctangent of x
atanh(x)	Returns the arc hyperbolic tangent of x
cos(x)	Returns the cosine of x
cosh(x)	Returns the hyperbolic cosine of x
exp(x)	Returns e ** x
log(x)	Returns the natural logarithm of x
log10(x)	Returns the base 10 logarithm of x
sin(x)	Returns the sine of x
sinh(x)	Returns the hyperbolic sine of x
sqrt(x)	Returns the square root of x
tan(x)	Returns the tangent of x
tanh(x)	Returns the hyperbolic tangent of x

The following constants are defined:

Constant	Description
pi	Mathematical constant pi, as a real
e	Mathematical constant e, as a real

▶ **See Also** math (129).

math

The math module defines standard mathematical functions. These functions operate on integers and floats, but don't work with complex numbers.

Function	Description
acos(x)	Returns the arccosine of x
asin(x)	Returns the arcsine of x
atan(x)	Returns the arctangent of x
atan2(y, x)	Returns atan(y / x)
ceil(x)	Returns the ceiling of x
cos(x)	Returns the cosine of x

continues >>

>> *continued*

Function	Description
cosh(x)	Returns the hyperbolic cosine of x
exp(x)	Returns e ** x
fabs(x)	Returns the absolute value of x
floor(x)	Returns the floor of x
fmod(x, y)	Returns x % y
frexp(x)	Returns the positive mantissa and exponent of x
hypot(x, y)	Returns the Euclidean distance, sqrt(x * x + y * y)
ldexp(x, i)	Returns x * (2 ** i)
log(x)	Returns the natural logarithm of x
log10(x)	Returns the base 10 logarithm of x
modf(x)	Returns the fractional and integer parts of x (both have the same sign as x)
pow(x, y)	Returns x ** y
sin(x)	Returns the sine of x
sinh(x)	Returns the hyperbolic sine of x
sqrt(x)	Returns the square root of x
tan(x)	Returns the tangent of x
tanh(x)	Returns the hyperbolic tangent of x

The following constants are defined:

Constant	Description
pi	Mathematical constant pi
e	Mathematical constant e

▶ **See Also** cmath (129).

random

The random module provides a variety of functions for generating pseudo-random numbers as well as functions for randomly generating values according to various distributions on the real numbers. Most of the functions in this module depend on the function random(), which generates uniformly distributed numbers in the range (0.0, 1.0) using the standard Wichmann-Hill generator.

The following functions are used to control the state of the underlying random-number generator:

seed([x])

Initializes the random-number generator. If x is omitted or is None, the system time is used to seed the generator. Otherwise, if x is an integer or long integer, its value is used. If x is not an integer, it must be a hashable object and the value of hash(x) is used as a seed.

`getstate()`

Returns an object representing the current state of the generator. This object can later be passed to `setstate()` to restore the state.

`setstate(state)`

Restores the state of the random-number generator from an object returned by `getstate()`.

`jumpahead(n)`

Quickly changes the state of the generator to what it would be if `random()` were called *n* times in a row. *n* must be a non-negative integer.

The following function can be used to generate random integers:

`randrange(start,stop [,step])`

Returns a random integer in `range(start,stop,step)`. Doesn't include the endpoint.

The following functions can be used to randomly manipulate sequences:

`choice(seq)`

Returns a random element from the nonempty sequence *seq*.

`shuffle(x [,random])`

Randomly shuffles the items in the list *x* in place. *random* is an optional argument that specifies a random-generation function. If supplied, it must be a function that takes no arguments and that returns a floating-point number in the range (0.0, 1.0).

The following functions generate random numbers on real numbers. Parameter names correspond to the names in the distribution's standard mathematical equation.

`betavariate(alpha, beta)`

Returns a value between 0 and 1 from the Beta distribution. *alpha* > -1 and *beta* > -1.

`cunifvariate(mean, arc)`

Circular uniform distribution. *mean* is the mean angle and *arc* is the range of the distribution, centered around the mean angle. Both of these values must be specified in radians in the range between 0 and *pi*. Returned values are in the range (*mean* - *arc*/2, *mean* + *arc*/2).

`expovariate(lambd)`

Exponential distribution. *lambd* is 1.0 divided by the desired mean. Returns values in the range (0, +∞).

`gamma(alpha, beta)`

Gamma distribution. *alpha* > -1, *beta* > 0.

`gauss(mu, sigma)`

Gaussian distribution with mean *mu* and standard deviation *sigma*. Slightly faster than `normalvariate()`.

`lognormvariate(mu, sigma)`

Log normal distribution. Taking the natural logarithm of this distribution results in a normal distribution with mean *mu*, standard deviation *sigma*.

`normalvariate(mu, sigma)`

Normal distribution with mean *mu* and standard deviation *sigma*.

Appendix A   The Python Library

paretovariate(*alpha*)

Pareto distribution with shape parameter *alpha*.

vonmisesvariate(*mu*, *kappa*)

von Mises distribution where *mu* is the mean angle in radians between 0 and
2 * pi, and *kappa* is a non-negative concentration factor. If *kappa* is zero, the
distribution reduces to a uniform random angle over the range 0 to 2 * pi.

weibullvariate(*alpha*, *beta*)

Weibull distribution with scale parameter *alpha* and shape parameter *beta*.

Notes

- The Numeric extension also provides a number of efficient generators for large
  samples and creating independent random-number streams.

- The functions in this module are not thread-safe. If you're generating random
  numbers in different threads, you should use locking to prevent concurrent
  access.

- The period of the random-number generator (before numbers start repeat-
  ing) is 6,953,607,871,644. Although this is better than that found in many
  programming libraries, it's not suitable for all applications—especially those
  related to cryptography.

- New types of random-number generators can be created by subclassing
  random.Random and implementing the random(), seed(), getstate(), getstate(),
  and jumpahead() methods. All the other functions in this module are actually
  internally implemented as methods of Random. Thus, they could be accessed
  as methods on an instance of the new random-number generator.

- Significant modifications were made to this module in Python 2.1.
  Furthermore, some of its functionality was previously found in the deprecated whrandom module. Please refer to the online documentation for details of
  these changes.

String Handling

The modules in this section are used for string processing.

codecs

The codecs module provides an interface for accessing different string encoding
and decoding functions (*codecs*) as well as a collection of base classes that can be
used to define new codecs. The following functions are available:

register(*search_function*)

Registers a new codec search function. This function should take a single argument in the form of an encoding string (for example, 'utf-8') and return a tuple
of functions (*encoder*, *decoder*, *streamreader*, *streamwriter*).

lookup(*encoding***)**

Looks up a codec in the codec registry. *encoding* is a string such as 'utf-8'.
Returns a tuple of functions (*encoder, decoder, streamreader, streamwriter*).
Internally, this function keeps a cache of previously used encodings. If a match is
not found in the cache, all the registered search functions are invoked until a
match is found. If no match is found, LookupError is raised.

open(*filename, mode***[,** *encoding***[,** *errors***[,** *buffering***]]])**

Opens *filename* in the given *mode* and provides transparent data encoding/
decoding according to the encoding specified in *encoding*. *errors* is one of 'strict',
'ignore', or 'replace'. The default is 'strict'. *buffering* has the same meaning as for
the built-in open() function.

EncodedFile(*file, inputenc***[,** *outputenc* **[,** *errors***]])**

A class that provides an encoding wrapper around a file object *file*. Data written to the file is first interpreted according to the input encoding *inputenc* and
then written to the file using the output encoding *outputenc*. Data read from the
file is decoded according to *inputenc*. If *outputenc* is omitted, it defaults to *inputenc*.
errors has the same meaning as for open() and defaults to 'strict'.

To define new codecs, the codecs module defines a base class Codec that is subclassed when defining encoders and decoders. The interface to a Codec object *c* is
as follows:

c.encode(*self, input* **[,** *errors***])**

Encodes input and returns a tuple (*output, length*) where *length* is the length of
the data in *input* that was consumed in the encoding. *errors* is one of 'strict',
'ignore', or 'replace' and defaults to 'strict'.

c.decode(*self, input* **[,** *errors***])**

Decodes input and returns a tuple (*output, length*) where *length* is the length of
the data that was consumed in the decoding. *errors* defaults to 'strict'.

Neither the encode() nor decode() method should maintain internal state. In addition, both methods must be able to operate with zero-length input, producing a
zero-length output object of the proper type.

In addition, the codecs module provides base classes for four different types of I/O
interfaces. All of these classes are subclasses of Codec.

StreamWriter(*stream* **[,** *errors***])**

Provides a wrapper around *stream* for producing an encoded output stream. An
instance *w* of StreamWriter provides the same methods as *stream*. In addition, the following methods are defined:

w.write(*object***)**

Writes an encoded version of *object* to *w*.

w.writelines(*list***)**

Writes a concatenated list of strings to *w*.

`w.reset()`

Flushes the output buffers and resets the internal encoding state.

`StreamReader(stream [, errors])`

Provides a wrapper around `stream` for reading an encoded input stream. An instance `r` of `StreamReader` provides the same methods as `stream` in addition to the following methods:

`r.read([size])`

Reads decoded data from `r`. `size` is the approximate number of bytes to read. The decoder may adjust this value slightly to accommodate the underlying encoding. If `size` is omitted, all data is read and decoded.

`r.readline([size])`

Reads a single line of input using the underlying stream's `readline()` method and returns as decoded data. `size` is simply passed to the underlying `readline()` method.

`r.readlines([size])`

Reads all lines and returns as a list of decoded lines.

`r.reset()`

Resets the codec buffers. This is usually used to recover from decoding errors.

`StreamReaderWriter(stream, reader, writer [, errors])`

Provides a wrapper around a stream that provides both encoding and decoding. `stream` is any file object. `reader` must be a factory function or class implementing the `StreamReader` interface. `writer` must be a factory function or class implementing the `StreamWriter` interface. A `StreamWriter` instance provides the combined interface of `StreamReader` and `StreamWriter`.

`StreamRecoder(stream, encode, decode, reader, writer [,errors])`

Provides a wrapper around `stream` that allows for conversion between two different encodings (for example, UTF-8 to and from UTF-16). `stream` may be any file-like object. The `encode` and `decode` arguments define the encoding and decoding functions that are returned or accepted by the `read()` and `write()` methods, respectively; that is, data returned by `read()` is encoded according to `encode` and data given to `write()` is decoded according to `decode`. `reader` and `writer` are the `StreamReader` and `StreamWriter` classes used to read and write the actual contents of the data stream. A `StreamRecoder` object provides the combined interface of `StreamReader` and `StreamWriter`.

codecs also defines the following byte-order marker constants that can be used to help interpret platform-specific files:

Constant	Description
BOM	Native byte-order marker for the machine
BOM_BE	Big-endian byte-order marker
BOM_LE	Little-endian byte-order marker
BOM32_BE	32-bit big-endian marker

Constant	Description
BOM32_LE	32-bit little-endian marker
BOM64_BE	64-bit big-endian marker
BOM64_LE	64-bit little-endian marker

Example

The following example illustrates the implementation of a new encoding using simple exclusive-or (XOR) based encryption. This only works for 8-bit strings, but it could be extended to support Unicode:

```
# xor.py: Simple encryption using XOR
import codecs

# Encoding/decoding function (works both ways)
def xor_encode(input, errors = 'strict', key=0xff):
    output = "".join([chr(ord(c) ^ key) for c in input])
    return (output,len(input))

# XOR Codec class
class Codec(codecs.Codec):
    key = 0xff
    def encode(self,input, errors='strict'):
        return xor_encode(input,errors,self.key)
    def decode(self,input, errors='strict'):
        return xor_encode(input,errors,self.key)

# StreamWriter and StreamReader classes
class StreamWriter(Codec,codecs.StreamWriter):
    pass

class StreamReader(Codec,codecs.StreamReader):
    pass

# Factory functions for creating StreamWriter and
# StreamReader objects with a given key value.

def xor_writer_factory(stream,errors,key=0xff):
    s = StreamWriter(stream,errors)
    s.key = key
    return s;

def xor_reader_factory(stream,errors,key=0xff):
    r = StreamReader(stream,errors)
    r.key = key
    return r

# Function registered with the codecs module.  Recognizes any
# encoding of the form 'xor-hh' where hh is a hexadecimal number.

def lookup(s):
    if (s[:4] == 'xor-'):
        key = int(s[4:],16)
    # Create some functions with key set to desired value
    e = lambda x,err='strict',key=key:xor_encode(x,err,key)
    r = lambda x,err='strict',key=key:xor_reader_factory(x,err,key)
    w = lambda x,err='strict',key=key:xor_writer_factory(x,err,key)
    return (e,e,r,w)

# Register with the codec module
codecs.register(lookup)
```

Appendix A   The Python Library

Now, here's a short program that uses the encoding:

```
import xor, codecs
f = codecs.open("foo","w","xor-37")
f.write("Hello World\n")          # Writes an "encrypted" version
f.close()

(enc,dec,r,w) = codecs.lookup("xor-ae")
a = enc("Hello World")
# a = ('\346\313\302\302\301\216\371\301\334\302\312', 11)
```

Notes

- Further use of the codecs module is described in Chapter 9.

- Most of the built-in encodings are provided to support Unicode string encoding. In this case, the encoding functions produce 8-bit strings and the decoding functions produce Unicode strings.

▶ **See Also** Chapter 9.

re

The re module is used to perform regular-expression pattern matching and replacement in strings. Both ordinary and Unicode strings are supported. Regular-expression patterns are specified as strings containing a mix of text and special-character sequences. Since patterns often make extensive use of special characters and the backslash, they're usually written as "raw" strings such as r'(?P<*int*>\d+)\.(\d*)'. For the remainder of this section, all regular-expression patterns are denoted using the raw string syntax.

The following special-character sequences are recognized in regular expression patterns:

Character(s)	Description
text	Matches the literal string *text*.
.	Matches any character except newline.
^	Matches the start of a string.
$	Matches the end of the string.
*	Matches zero or more repetitions of the preceding expression, matching as many repetitions as possible.
+	Matches one or more repetitions of the preceding expression, matching as many repetitions as possible.
?	Matches zero repetitions or one repetition of the preceding expression.
*?	Matches zero or more repetitions of the preceding expression, matching as few repetitions as possible.

Character(s)	Description
+?	Matches one or more repetitions of the preceding expression, matching as few repetitions as possible.
??	Matches zero or one repetitions of the preceding expression, matching as few repetitions as possible.
{m, n}	Matches from *m* to *n* repetitions of the preceding expression, matching as many repetitions as possible.
{m, n}?	Matches from *m* to *n* repetitions of the preceding expression, matching as few repetitions as possible.
[...]	Matches a set of characters such as r'[abcdef]' or r'[a-zA-z]'. Special characters such as * are not active inside a set.
[^...]	Matches the characters not in the set, such as r'[^0-9]'.
A¦B	Matches either *A* or *B* where *A* and *B* are both regular expressions.
(...)	Matches the regular expression inside the parentheses as a group and saves the matched substring.
(?iLmsux)	Interprets the letters "i", "L", "m", "s", "u", and "x" as flag settings corresponding to the re.I, re.L, re.M, re.S, re.U, re.X flag settings given to re.compile().
(?:...)	Matches the regular expression inside the parentheses, but discards the matched substring.
(?P<name>...)	Matches the regular expression in the parentheses and creates a named group. The group name must be a valid Python identifier.
(?P=name)	Matches the same text that was matched by an earlier named group.
(?#...)	A comment. The contents of the parentheses are ignored.
(?=...)	Matches the preceding expression only if followed by the pattern in the parentheses. For example, r'Hello (?=World)' matches 'Hello ' only if followed by 'World'.
(?!...)	Matches the preceding expression only if it's *not* followed by the pattern in parentheses. For example, r'Hello (?!World)' matches 'Hello ' only if it's not followed by 'World'.
(?<=...)	Matches the following expression if it's preceded by a match of the pattern in parentheses. For example, r'(?<=abc)def' matches 'def' only if it's preceded by 'abc'.
(?<!...)	Matches the following expression only if it's *not* preceded by a match of the pattern in parentheses. For example, r'(?<!abc)def' matches 'def' only if it's not preceded by 'abc'.

Standard character escape sequences such as '\n' or '\t' are recognized as standard characters in a regular expression; for example, r'\n+' would match one or more newline characters. In addition, literal symbols that normally have special meaning in a regular expression can be specified by preceding them with a backslash. For example, r'*' matches the character *. In addition, a number of backslash sequences correspond to special sets of characters:

Appendix A   The Python Library

Character(s)	Description
\number	Matches the text that was matched by a previous group number. Groups are numbered from 1 to 99, starting from the left.
\A	Matches only at the start of the string.
\b	Matches the empty string at the beginning or end of a word. A *word* is a sequence of alphanumeric characters terminated by whitespace or any other non-alphanumeric character.
\B	Matches the empty string not at the beginning or end of a word.
\d	Matches any decimal digit. Same as r'[0-9]'.
\D	Matches any non-digit character. Same as r'[^0-9]'.
\s	Matches any whitespace character. Same as r'[\t\n\r\f\v]'.
\S	Matches any non-whitespace character. Same as r'[^ \t\n\r\f\v]'.
\w	Matches any alphanumeric character.
\W	Matches any character not contained in the set defined by \w.
\Z	Matches only at the end of the string.
\\	Matches a literal backslash.

The following functions are used to perform pattern matching and replacement.

compile(str [, flags])

Compiles a regular-expression pattern string into a regular-expression object. This object can be passed as the pattern argument to all the functions that follow. flags is the bitwise-or of the following:

Flag	Description
I or IGNORECASE	Performs non–case-sensitive matching.
L or LOCALE	Uses locale settings for \w, \W, \b, and \B.
M or MULTILINE	Makes ^ and $ apply to each line in addition to the beginning and end of the entire string. (Normally ^ and $ apply only to the beginning and end of an entire string.)
S or DOTALL	Makes the dot (.) character match all characters, including the newline.
U or UNICODE	Uses information from the Unicode character properties database for \w, \W, \b, and \B.
X or VERBOSE	Ignores unescaped whitespace and comments.

search(pattern, string [, flags])

Searches string for the first match of pattern. flags has the same meaning as for compile(). Returns a MatchObject on success, None if no match was found.

match(pattern, string [, flags])

Checks whether zero or more characters at the beginning of string match pattern. Returns a MatchObject on success, or None.

`split(pattern, string [, maxsplit = 0])`

Splits *string* by the occurrences of *pattern*. Returns a list of strings including the text matched by any groups in the pattern. *maxsplit* is the maximum number of splits to perform. By default, all possible splits are performed.

`findall(pattern, string)`

Returns a list of all non-overlapping matches of *pattern* in *string*, including empty matches. If the pattern has groups, a list of the text matched by the groups is returned. If more than one group is used, each item in the list is a tuple containing the text for each group.

`sub(pattern, repl, string [, count = 0])`

Replaces the leftmost non-overlapping occurrences of *pattern* in *string* by the replacement *repl*. *repl* can be a string or a function. If it's a function, it's called with a `MatchObject` and should return the replacement string. If *repl* is a string, back references such as `'\6'` are used to refer to groups in the pattern. The sequence `'\g<name>'` is used to refer to a named group. *count* is the maximum number of substitutions to perform. By default, all occurrences are replaced. Although these functions don't accept a *flags* parameter like `compile()`, the same effect can be achieved by using the `(?iLmsux)` notation described earlier in this section.

`subn(pattern, repl, string [, count = 0])`

Same as `sub()`, but returns a tuple containing the new string and the number of substitutions.

`escape(string)`

Returns a string with all non-alphanumerics backslashed.

A compiled regular-expression object *r* created by the `compile()` function has the following methods and attributes:

`r.search(string [, pos [, endpos]])`

Searches *string* for a match. *pos* and *endpos* specify the starting and ending positions for the search. Returns a `MatchObject` for a match, `None` otherwise.

`r.match(string [, pos [, endpos]])`

Checks whether zero or more characters at the beginning of *string* match. *pos* and *endpos* specify the range of *string* to be searched. Returns a `MatchObject` for a match, `None` otherwise.

`r.split(string [, maxsplit = 0])`

Identical to the `split()` function.

`r.findall(string)`

Identical to the `findall()` function.

`r.sub(repl, string [, count = 0])`

Identical to the `sub()` function.

`r.subn(repl, string [, count = 0])`

Identical to the `subn()` function.

`r.flags`

The *flags* argument used when the regular expression object was compiled, or `0`.

r.groupindex

A dictionary mapping symbolic group names defined by r'(?P<*id*>)' to group numbers.

r.pattern

The pattern string from which the regular expression object was compiled.

The MatchObject instances returned by search() and match() contain information about the contents of groups as well as positional data about where matches occurred. A MatchObject instance *m* has the following methods and attributes:

m.expand(*template*)

Returns a string that would be obtained by doing regular-expression backslash substitution on the string *template*. Numeric back-references such as "\1" and "\2" and named references such as "\g<*n*>" and "\g<*name*>" are replaced by the contents of the corresponding group. *Note:* These sequences should be specified using raw strings or with a literal backslash character such as r'\1' or '\\1'.

m.group([*group1*, *group2*, ...])

Returns one or more subgroups of the match. The arguments specify group numbers or group names. If no group name is given, the entire match is returned. If only one group is given, a string containing the text matched by the group is returned. Otherwise, a tuple containing the text matched by each of the requested groups is returned. An IndexError is raised if an invalid group number or name is given.

m.groups([*default*])

Returns a tuple containing the text matched by all groups in a pattern. *default* is the value returned for groups that didn't participate in the match (the default is None).

m.groupdict([*default*])

Returns a dictionary containing all the named subgroups of the match. *default* is the value returned for groups that didn't participate in the match (the default is None).

m.start([*group*])

m.end([*group*])

Returns the indices of the start and end of the substring matched by a group. If *group* is omitted, the entire matched substring is used. Returns None if the group exists but didn't participate in the match.

m.span([*group*])

Returns a 2-tuple (*m*.start(*group*), *m*.end(*group*)). If *group* didn't contribute to the match, this returns (None, None). If *group* is omitted, the entire matched substring is used.

m.pos

The value of *pos* passed to the search() or match() function.

m.endpos

The value of *endpos* passed to the search() or match() function.

m.re

The regular-expression object whose match() or search() method produced this MatchObject instance.

m.string

The string passed to match() or search().

When pattern strings don't specify a valid regular expression, the re.error exception is raised.

m.lastindex

The integer index of the last matched capturing group. None if no group was matched.

m.lastgroup

The name of the last matched capturing group. None if the group didn't have a name or no group was matched.

Examples

```
import re
s = open('foo').read()              # Read some text

# Replace all occurrences of 'foo' with 'bar'
t = re.sub('foo','bar',s)

# Get the title of an HTML document
tmatch = re.search(r'<title>(.*?)</title>',s, re.IGNORECASE)
if tmatch: title = tmatch.group(1)

# Extract a list of possible e-mail addresses from s
pat = re.compile(r'([a-zA-Z][\w-]*@[\w-]+(?:\.[\w-]+)*)')
addrs = re.findall(pat,s)

# Replace strings that look like URLs such as 'http://www.python.org'
# with an HTML anchor tag of the form
# <a href='http://www.python.org'>http://www.python.org</a>

pat = re.compile(r'((ftp|http)://[\w-]+(?:\.[\w-]+)*(?:/[\w-]*)*)')
t = pat.sub('<a href="\\1">\\1</a>', s)
```

Notes

- The implementation of the re module is actually found in the module sre, which provides support for standard and Unicode strings. An older implementation of re that supports only standard strings is available in the pre module.

- Detailed information about the theory and implementation of regular expressions can be found in textbooks on compiler construction. The book *Mastering Regular Expressions* by Jeffrey Friedl (O'Reilly & Associates, 1997) may also be useful.

- The re module is 8-bit clean and can process strings that contain null bytes and characters whose high bit is set. Regular expression patterns cannot contain null bytes, but can match against the null byte by writing the escape sequence '\000'.

▶ **See Also** string (142).

string

The string module contains a number of useful constants and functions for manipulating strings. Most of the functionality of this module is also available in the form of string methods. The following constants are defined:

Constant	Description
digits	The string '0123456789'.
hexdigits	The string '0123456789abcdefABCDEF'.
letters	Concatenation of lowercase and uppercase.
lowercase	String containing all lowercase letters.
octdigits	The string '01234567'.
punctuation	String of ASCII punctuation characters.
printable	String of ASCII characters considered to be printable.
uppercase	String containing all uppercase letters.
whitespace	String containing all whitespace characters. This usually includes space, tab, linefeed, return, formfeed, and vertical tab.

The following functions are available:

atof(s)

Converts string s to a floating-point number. See the built-in float() function.

atoi(s [, base])

Converts string s to an integer. base is an optional base. See the built-in int() function.

atol(s [, base])

Converts string s to a long integer. base is an optional base. See the built-in long() function.

capitalize(s)

Capitalizes the first character of s. Same as s.capitalize().

capwords(s)

Capitalizes the first letter of each word in s, replaces repeated whitespace characters with a single space, and removes leading and trailing whitespace.

count(s, sub [, start [, end]])

Counts the number of non-overlapping occurrences of sub in s[start:end]. Same as s.count(sub, start, end).

expandtabs(s [, tabsize=8])

Expands tabs in string s with whitespace. tabsize specifies the number of characters between tab stops. Same as s.expandtab(tabsize).

find(s, sub [, start [, end]])
index(s, sub [, start [, end]])

Returns the first index in s[start:end] where the substring sub is found. If start and end are omitted, the entire string is searched. find() returns -1 if not found, while index() raises a ValueError exception. Same as s.find(sub,start,end) and s.index(sub,start,end).

```
rfind(s, sub [, start [, end]])
rindex(s, sub [, start [, end]])
```

Like find() and index(), but finds the highest index. Same as
s.rfind(*sub,start,end*) and s.rindex(*sub,start,end*).

```
lower(s)
```

Converts all uppercase characters in s to lowercase. Same as s.lower().

```
maketrans(from, to)
```

Creates a translation table that maps each character in *from* to the character in
the same position in *to*. *from* and *to* must be the same length.

```
split(s [, sep [, maxsplit]])
splitfields(s [, sep [, maxsplit]])
```

Returns a list of words in s. If *sep* is omitted or None, the words are separated by
whitespace. Otherwise, the string in *sep* is used as a delimiter. *maxsplit* specifies the
maximum number of splits that can occur. The remainder of the string will be
returned as the last element. split() is the same as s.split(*sep,maxsplit*).

```
join(words [, sep])
joinfields(words [, sep])
```

Concatenates a sequence of words into a string, with words separated by the
string in *sep*. If omitted, the words are separated by whitespace. Same as
sep.join(*words*).

```
lstrip(s)
rstrip(s)
strip(s)
```

Strips leading and/or trailing whitespace from s. Same as s.lstrip(), s.rstrip(),
and s.strip().

```
swapcase(s)
```

Changes uppercase to lowercase and lowercase to uppercase in s. Same as
s.swapcase().

```
translate(s, table [, delchars])
```

Deletes all characters from s that are in *delchars* and translates the remaining
characters using *table*. *table* must be a 256-character string mapping characters to
characters as created by maketrans(). Same as s.translate(*table,delchars*).

```
upper(s)
```

Converts all lowercase characters in s to uppercase. Same as s.upper().

```
ljust(s, width)
rjust(s, width)
center(s, width)
```

Left-aligns, right-aligns, or centers s in a field of width *width*. Same as
s.ljust(*width*), s.rjust(*width*), and s.center(*width*).

```
zfill(s, width)
```

Pads a numeric string on the left with 0 digits up to the given width.

```
replace(str, old, new [, max])
```

Replaces *max* occurrences of *old* with *new* in *str*. If *max* is omitted, all occurrences
are replaced. Same as s.replace(*old,new,max*).

Appendix A   The Python Library

Notes

- This module is officially considered to be deprecated due to the addition of string methods in Python 2.0, but is still widely used in existing Python programs.
- Unicode and standard strings are supported by the module, but standard strings are coerced to Unicode when necessary.

▶ **See Also** re (136), Chapter 3.

StringIO and cStringIO

The `StringIO` and `cStringIO` modules define an object that behaves like a file but reads and writes data from a string buffer.

StringIO([*buffer*])

Creates a new `StringIO` object. *buffer* is an initial value (by default, the empty string).

A `StringIO` object supports all the standard file operations—read(), write(), and so on—and the following methods:

s.getvalue()

Returns the contents of the string buffer before close() is called.

s.close()

Releases the memory buffer.

Note

- The `StringIO` module defines `StringIO` as a class. `cStringIO` defines it as an extension type and provides significantly faster performance.

▶ **See Also** Chapter 9, the section "Files" (for file methods).

struct

The `struct` module is used to convert data between Python and binary data structures (represented as Python strings). These data structures are often used when interacting with functions written in C or with binary network protocols.

pack(*fmt*, *v1*, *v2*, ...)

Packs the values *v1*, *v2*, and so on into a string according to the format string in *fmt*.

unpack(*fmt*, *string*)

Unpacks the contents of *string* according to the format string in *fmt*. Returns a tuple of the unpacked values.

calcsize(*fmt*)

Calculates the size in bytes of the structure corresponding to a format string *fmt*.

The format string is a sequence of characters with the following interpretations:

Format	C Type	Python Type
'x'	pad byte	No value
'c'	char	String of length 1
'b'	signed char	Integer
'B'	unsigned char	Integer
'h'	short	Integer
'H'	unsigned short	Integer
'i'	int	Integer
'I'	unsigned int	Integer
'l'	long	Integer
'L'	unsigned long	Integer
'f'	float	Float
'd'	double	Float
's'	char[]	String
'p'	char[]	String with length encoded in the first byte
'P'	void *	Integer

Each format character can be preceded by an integer to indicate a repeat count (for example, '4i' is the same as 'iiii'). For the 's' format, the count represents the maximum length of the string, so '10s' represents a 10-byte string. A format of '0s' indicates a string of zero length. The 'p' format is used to encode a string in which the length appears in the first byte, followed by the string data. This is useful when dealing with Pascal code, as is sometimes necessary on the Macintosh. *Note:* The length of the string in this case is limited to 255 characters.

When the 'I' and 'L' formats are used to unpack a value, the return value is a Python long integer. In addition, the 'P' format may return an integer or long integer, depending on the word size of the machine.

The first character of each format string can also specify a byte ordering and alignment of the packed data, as shown in the following table.

Format	Byte Order	Size and Alignment
'@'	Native	Native
'='	Native	Standard
'<'	Little-endian	Standard
'>'	Big-endian	Standard
'!'	Network (big-endian)	Standard

Native byte ordering may be little-endian or big-endian, depending on the machine architecture. The native sizes and alignment correspond to the values used by the C compiler and are implementation-specific. The standard alignment assumes that no alignment is needed for any type. The standard size assumes that short is 2 bytes, int is 4 bytes, long is 4 bytes, float is 32 bits, and double is 64 bits. The 'P' format can only use native byte ordering.

Sometimes it's necessary to align the end of a structure to the alignment requirements of a particular type. To do this, end the structure-format string with the code
for that type with a repeat count of zero. For example, the format 'llh0l' specifies
a structure that ends on a four-byte boundary (assuming that longs are aligned on
four-byte boundaries). In this case, two pad bytes would be inserted after the short
value specified by the 'h' code. This only works when native size and alignment
are being used—standard size and alignment don't enforce alignment rules.

▶ **See Also** array (127), xdrlib (277).

unicodedata

The unicodedata modules provide access to the Unicode character database, which
contains character properties for all Unicode characters.

decimal(unichr[, default]**)**

Returns the decimal integer value assigned to the character unichr. If unichr is
not a decimal digit, default is returned or ValueError is raised.

digit(unichr[, default]**)**

Returns the integer digit value assigned to the character unichr. If unichr is not a
digit, default is returned or ValueError is raised. This function differs from decimal() in
that it works with characters that may represent digits, but that are not decimal digits.

numeric(unichr[, default]**)**

Returns the value assigned to the Unicode character unichr as a floating-point
number. If no numeric value is defined, default is returned or ValueError is raised.
For example, the numeric value of U+2155 (the character for the fraction "1/5")
is 0.2.

category(unichr**)**

Returns a string describing the general category of unichr. The returned string
is one of the following values:

Value	Description
Lu	Letter, Uppercase
Ll	Letter, Lowercase
Lt	Letter, Titlecase
Mn	Mark, Non-Spacing
Mc	Mark, Spacing Combining
Me	Mark, Enclosing
Nd	Number, Decimal Digit
Nl	Number, Letter
No	Number, Other
Zs	Separator, Space
Zl	Separator, Line
Zp	Separator, Paragraph
Cc	Other, Control
Cf	Other, Format

Value	Description
Cs	Other, Surrogate
Co	Other, Private Use
Cn	Other, Not Assigned
Lm	Letter, Modifier
Lo	Letter, Other
Pc	Punctuation, Connector
Pd	Punctuation, Dash
Ps	Punctuation, Open
Pe	Punctuation, Close
Pi	Punctuation, Initial quote
Pf	Punctuation, Final quote
Po	Punctuation, Other
Sm	Symbol, Math
Sc	Symbol, Currency
Sk	Symbol, Modifier
So	Symbol, Other

bidirectional(*unichr*)

Returns the bi-directional category assigned to *unichr* as a string, or an empty string if no such value is defined. Returns one of the following:

Value	Description
L	Left-to-Right
LRE	Left-to-Right Embedding
LRO	Left-to-Right Override
R	Right-to-Left
AL	Right-to-Left Arabic
RLE	Right-to-Left Embedding
RLO	Right-to-Left Override
PDF	Pop Directional Format
EN	European Number
ES	European Number Separator
ET	European Number Terminator
AN	Arabic Number
CS	Common Number Separator
NSM	Non-Spacing Mark
BN	Boundary Neutral
B	Paragraph Separator
S	Segment Separator
WS	Whitespace
ON	Other Neutrals

Appendix A   The Python Library

`combining(`*`unichr`*`)`

Returns an integer describing the combining class for *unichr*, or 0 if no combining class is defined. One of the following values is returned:

Value	Description
0	Spacing, split, enclosing, reordrant, and Tibetan subjoined
1	Overlays and interior
7	Nuktas
8	Hiragana/Katakana voicing marks
9	Viramas
10-199	Fixed position classes
200	Below left attached
202	Below attached
204	Below right attached
208	Left attached
210	Right attached
212	Above left attached
214	Above attached
216	Above right attached
218	Below left
220	Below
222	Below right
224	Left
226	Right
228	Above left
230	Above
232	Above right
233	Double below
234	Double above
240	Below (iota subscript)

`mirrored(`*`unichr`*`)`

Returns 1 if *unichr* is a "mirrored" character in bi-directional text, 0 otherwise.

`decomposition(`*`unichr`*`)`

Returns a string containing the decomposition mapping of *unichr*, or the empty string if no such mapping is defined. Typically, characters containing accent marks can be decomposed into multicharacter sequences. For example, `decomposition(u"\u00fc")` ("ü") returns the string `"0075 0308"` corresponding to the letter *u* and the umlaut (¨) accent mark. The string returned by this function may also include the following strings:

Value	Description
<font>	A font variant (for example, a blackletter form)
<noBreak>	A nonbreaking version of a space or hyphen
<initial>	An initial presentation form (Arabic)
<medial>	A medial presentation form (Arabic)
<final>	A final presentation form (Arabic)
<isolated>	An isolated presentation form (Arabic)
<circle>	An encircled form
<super>	A superscript form
<sub>	A subscript form
<vertical>	A vertical layout presentation form
<wide>	A wide (or zenkaku) compatibility character
<narrow>	A narrow (or hankaku) compatibility character
<small>	A small variant form (CNS compatibility)
<square>	A CJK squared-font variant
<fraction>	A vulgar fraction form
<compat>	Otherwise unspecified compatibility character

Note

- For further details about the Unicode character database, see
  http://www.unicode.org.

Data Management and Object Persistence

The modules in this section are used to store data in a variety of DBM-style database formats. These databases operate like a large disk-based hash table in which objects are stored and retrieved using unique keys represented by standard strings. Most of these modules are optional Python extensions that require third-party libraries and that must be enabled when Python is built. See Appendix B, "Extending and Embedding Python," for details on enabling optional modules.

All the databases are opened using a variation of the open() function (defined in each database module):

```
open(filename [, flag [, mode]])
```

Opens the database file *filename* and returns a database object. *flag* is 'r' for read-only access, 'w' for read-write access, 'c' to create the database if it doesn't exist, or 'n' to force the creation of a new database. *mode* is the file-access mode (the default is 0666 on UNIX).

The object returned by the open() function supports the following dictionary-like operations:

Operation	Description
d[key] = value	Inserts value into the database
value = d[key]	Gets data from the database
del d[key]	Removes a database entry
d.close()	Closes the database
d.has_key(key)	Tests for a key
d.keys()	Returns a list of keys

In all cases, key must be a standard string. In addition, value must be a standard string for all the database modules except the shelve module. Unicode strings cannot be used for keys in any of the modules and cannot be used for values in any module except shelve.

Note

- Most of the database packages described rely on third-party libraries that must be installed in addition to Python.

anydbm

The anydbm module provides a generic interface that's used to open a database without knowing which of the lower-level database packages are actually installed and available. When imported, it looks for one of the bsddb, gdbm, or dbm modules. If none are installed, the dumbdbm module is loaded.

A database object is created using the open() function:

    open(filename [, flag='r' [, mode]])

Opens the database file *filename* and returns a database object. If the database already exists, the whichdb module is used to determine its type and the corresponding database module to use. If the database doesn't exist, an attempt is made to create it using the first installed module in the above list of database modules. *flags* and *mode* are as described in the introduction to this section, "Data Management and Object Persistence" (p. 149).

    error

A tuple containing the exceptions that can be raised by each of the supported database modules.

Programs wanting to catch errors should use this tuple as an argument to except. For example:

```
try:
    d = anydbm.open('foo','r')
except anydbm.error:
    # Handle error
```

Note

- If the dumbdbm module is the only installed database module, attempts to reopen a previously created database with anydbm might fail in certain older versions of Python. Use dumbdbm.open() instead.

▶ **See Also** dumbdbm (152), whichdb (154).

bsddb

The bsddb module provides an interface to the Berkeley DB library. Hash, btree, or record-based files can be created using the appropriate open() call:

hashopen(*filename* [, *flag*='r' [, *mode*]])

Opens the hash format file named *filename*.

btopen(*filename* [, *flag*='r' [, *mode*]])

Opens the btree format file named *filename*.

rnopen(*filename* [, *flag*='r' [, *mode*]])

Opens a DB record format file named *filename*.

Databases created by this module behave like dictionaries, as described in the introduction to this section ("Data Management and Object Persistence," p. 149), and additionally provide methods for moving a "cursor" through records:

Method	Description
d.set_location(*key*)	Sets the cursor to the item indicated by the key and returns it.
d.first()	Sets the cursor to the first item in the database and returns it.
d.next()	Sets the cursor to the next item in the database and returns it.
d.previous()	Sets the cursor to the previous item in the DB file and returns it. Not supported on hash table databases.
d.last()	Sets the cursor to the last item in the DB file and returns it. Not supported on hash table databases.
d.sync()	Synchronizes the database on disk.

Exception

error

Exception raised on non–key-related database errors.

Notes

- This module uses the version 1.85 API of the Berkeley DB package available at http://www.sleepycat.com.
- All the open() functions accept additional optional arguments that are rarely used. Consult the online documentation for details.
- Consult New Riders' *Berkeley DB* (2001, ISBN 0-7357-1064-3).

   ▶ **See Also** dbhash (151), http://www.python.org/doc/lib/module-bsddb.html.

dbhash

The dbhash module is used to open databases using the bsddb module, but with an interface that closely matches the interface of the other database modules.

open(*filename* [, *flag*='r' [, *mode*])

Opens a DB database and returns the database object.

A database object *d* returned by open() behaves like a dictionary and also provides the following methods:

Method	Description
d.first()	Returns the first key in the database
d.last()	Returns the last key in a database traversal
d.next(*key*)	Returns the next key following *key* in the database
d.previous(*key*)	Returns the item that comes before *key* in a forward traversal of the database
d.sync()	Writes unsaved data to the disk

Exception

error

Exception raised on database errors other than KeyError. Same as bsddb.error.

Note

■ The bsddb module must be installed.

▶ **See Also** bsddb (151).

dbm

The dbm module provides an interface to the UNIX dbm library.

open(*filename* [, *flag*='r' [, *mode*]])

Opens a dbm database and returns a dbm object. *filename* is the name of the database file (without the .dir or .pag extension). The returned object behaves like a dictionary, as described in the section introduction ("Data Management and Object Persistence," p. 149).

Exception

error

Exception raised for dbm-specific errors other than KeyError.

▶ **See Also** anydbm (150), gdbm (153).

dumbdbm

The dumbdbm module is a simple DBM-style database implemented in Python. It should only be used when no other DBM database modules are available.

open(*filename* [, *flag* [, *mode*]])

Opens the database file *filename*. *filename* should not include any suffixes such as .dat or .dir. The returned database object behaves like a dictionary, as described in the section introduction ("Data Management and Object Persistence," p. 149).

Exception

error

Exception raised for database-related errors other than KeyError.

▶ **See Also** anydbm (150), whichdb (154).

gdbm

The gdbm module provides an interface to the GNU DBM library.

open(*filename* [, *flag*='r' [, *mode*]])

Opens a gdbm database with filename *filename*. Appending 'f' to the flag opens the database in fast mode. In this mode, altered data is not automatically written to disk after every change, resulting in better performance. If used, the sync() method should be used to force unwritten data to be written to disk on program termination.

A gdbm object *d* behaves like a dictionary as described in the section introduction ("Data Management and Object Persistence," p. 149), but also supports the following methods:

Method	Description
d.firstkey()	Returns the starting key in the database.
d.nextkey(*key*)	Returns the key that follows *key* in a traversal of the database.
d.reorganize()	Reorganizes the database and reclaims unused space. This can be used to shrink the size of the gdbm file after a lot of deletions have occurred.
d.sync()	Forces unwritten data to be written to disk.

Exception

error

Exception raised for gdbm-specific errors.

Note

■ The GNU DBM library is available at www.gnu.org/software/gdbm/gdbm.html.

▶ **See Also** anydbm (150), whichdb (154).

shelve

The shelve module provides support for persistent objects using a special "shelf" object. This object behaves like a dictionary except that all the objects it contains are stored on disk using a database such as dbm or gdbm. A shelf is created using the shelve.open() function.

open(*filename* [,*flag*='c'])

Opens a shelf file. If the file doesn't exist, it's created. *filename* should be the database filename and should not include a suffix. *flag* has the same meaning as in the open() function and is one of 'r', 'w', 'c', or 'n'. If the database file doesn't exist, it is created. Returns a shelf object.

Once opened, the following dictionary operations can be performed on a shelf:

Operation	Description
d[*key*] = *data*	Stores data at *key*. Overwrites existing data.
data = *d*[*key*]	Retrieves data at *key*.

continues >>

Appendix A   The Python Library

>> *continued*

Operation	Description
del *d*[*key*]	Deletes data at *key*.
d.has_key(*key*)	Tests for the existence of *key*.
d.keys()	Returns all keys.
d.close()	Closes the shelf.
d.sync()	Write unsaved data to disk.

The key values for a shelf must be strings. The objects stored in a shelf must be serializable using the pickle module.

▶ **See Also** open (103).

Shelf(*dict*)

A class that implements the functionality of a shelf. *dict* is an existing dictionary object. This function can be used to create a shelf object that utilizes a preferred database engine. For example, s = Shelf(dbm.open("foo","c")).

Note

■ The shelve module differs from other database modules in that it allows almost any Python object to be stored.

▶ **See Also** pickle (113), Chapter 9.

whichdb

The whichdb module provides a function that attempts to guess which of the several simple database modules (dbm, gdbm, or dbhash) should be used to open a database file.

whichdb(*filename*)

filename is a filename without any suffixes. Returns None if the file cannot be opened because it's unreadable or doesn't exist. Returns the empty string if the file format cannot be guessed. Otherwise, a string containing the required module name is returned, such as 'dbm' or 'gdbm'.

▶ **See Also** anydbm (150).

Operating System Services

The modules in this section provide access to a wide variety of operating system services with an emphasis on file, process, and terminal management.

Note: A general familiarity with basic operating system concepts is assumed in this section. Furthermore, a number of modules provide advanced functionality which is beyond the scope of this book to introduce, but which is presented for readers who know what they're doing.

Most of Python's operating system modules are based on POSIX interfaces. POSIX is a standard that defines a core set of operating system interfaces. Most UNIX systems support POSIX, and other platforms such as Windows and Macintosh support large portions of the interface.

Readers may want to supplement the material presented here with additional references. *The C Programming Language, Second Edition* by Brian W. Kernighan and Dennis M. Ritchie (Prentice Hall, 1989, ISBN 0-13-110362-8) provides a good overview of files, file descriptors, and the low-level interfaces on which many of the modules in this section are based. More advanced readers may want to consult a book such as W. Richard Stevens' *Advanced Programming in the UNIX Environment* (Addison-Wesley, 1992, ISBN 0-201-56317-7). Background material regarding operating system concepts can be found in a text such as *Operating Systems Concepts, 5th Edition* by Abraham Silberschatz and Peter Baer Galvin (John Wiley & Sons, 1998). Threads and network programming are presented in separate sections of this appendix.

commands

The commands module is used to execute system commands as a string and return their output as a string.

getoutput(*cmd***)**

Executes *cmd* in a shell and returns a string containing both the standard output and standard error streams of the command.

getstatus(*filename***)**

Returns the output of 'ls -ld *filename*' as a string. UNIX.

getstatusoutput(*cmd***)**

Like getoutput() except that a 2-tuple (*status*, *output*) is returned, where *status* is the exit code as returned by the os.wait() function and *output* is the string returned by getoutput().

mkarg(*str***)**

Turns *str* into an argument that can be safely used within a command string (using quoting rules of the shell).

Notes

- The os.popen2() call is used to execute commands. This module is available on most UNIX systems, but is not supported on all versions of Windows.

- The returned output strings don't include a trailing newline.

▶ **See Also** os (180), popen2 (195).

crypt

The crypt module provides an interface to the UNIX crypt() routine that's used to encrypt passwords on many UNIX systems.

crypt(*word***,** *salt***)**

Encrypts *word* using a modified DES algorithm. *salt* is a two-character seed used to initialize the algorithm. Returns the encrypted word as a string. Only the first eight characters of *word* are significant.

Example

The following code reads a password from the user and compares it against the value in the system password database:

```
import getpass
import pwd
import crypt
uname = getpass.getuser()          # Get username from environment
pw    = getpass.getpass()          # Get entered password
realpw = pwd.getpwnam(uname)[1]    # Get real password
entrpw = crypt.crypt(pw,realpw[:2])# Encrypt
if realpw == entrpw:               # Compare
     print 'Password Accepted'
else:
     print 'Get lost.'
```

Note

- Many modern UNIX systems use MD5 or other crytographic hashing algorithms to store passwords.

▶ **See Also** pwd (196), getpass (167).

errno

The errno module defines symbolic names for the integer error codes returned by various operating system calls. These codes are typically found in the errno attribute of an OSError or IOError exception. The os.strerror() function can be used to translate an error code into a string error message. The following dictionary can also be used to translate an integer error code into its symbolic name:

errorcode

Dictionary mapping errno integers to symbolic names (such as 'EPERM').

The following list shows the POSIX symbolic names for many system error codes. Not all names are available on all machines. Some platforms may define additional codes. The codes U, W, M, and A are used to indicate availability of the following codes for UNIX, Windows, Macintosh, and all platforms, respectively.

Error Code	Platform	Description
E2BIG	A	Arg list too long.
EACCES	A	Permission denied.
EADDRINUSE	A	Address already in use.
EADDRNOTAVAIL	A	Cannot assign requested address.
EADV	U	Advertise error.
EAFNOSUPPORT	A	Address family not supported by protocol.
EAGAIN	A	Try again.
EALREADY	A	Operation already in progress.
EBADE	U	Invalid exchange.
EBADF	A	Bad file number.
EBADFD	U	File descriptor in bad state.
EBADMSG	U	Not a data message.
EBADR	U	Invalid request descriptor.

Error Code	Platform	Description
EBADRQC	U	Invalid request code.
EBADSLT	U	Invalid slot.
EBFONT	U	Bad font file format.
EBUSY	A	Device or resource busy.
ECHILD	A	No child processes.
ECHRNG	U	Channel number out of range.
ECOMM	U	Communication error on send.
ECONNABORTED	A	Software caused connection abort.
ECONNREFUSED	A	Connection refused.
ECONNRESET	A	Connection reset by peer.
EDEADLK	A	Resource deadlock would occur.
EDEADLOCK	U, W	File-locking deadlock error.
EDESTADDRREQ	A	Destination address required.
EDOM	A	Math argument out of domain of func.
EDOTDOT	U	RFS-specific error.
EDQUOT	A	Quota exceeded.
EEXIST	A	File exists.
EFAULT	A	Bad address.
EFBIG	A	File too large.
EHOSTDOWN	A	Host is down.
EHOSTUNREACH	A	No route to host.
EIDRM	U	Identifier removed.
EILSEQ	U, W	Illegal byte sequence.
EINPROGRESS	U, W	Operation now in progress.
EINTR	A	Interrupted system call.
EINVAL	A	Invalid argument.
EIO	A	I/O error.
EISCONN	A	Transport endpoint is already connected.
EISDIR	A	Is a directory.
EISNAM	U	Is a named type file.
EL2HLT	U	Level 2 halted.
EL2NSYNC	U	Level 2 not synchronized.
EL3HLT	U	Level 3 halted.
EL3RST	U	Level 3 reset.
ELIBACC	U	Cannot access a needed shared library.
ELIBBAD	U	Accessing a corrupted shared library.
ELIBEXEC	U	Cannot exec a shared library directly.
ELIBMAX	U	Attempting to link in too many shared libraries.
ELIBSCN	U	.lib section in a.out corrupted.

continues >>

Appendix A   The Python Library

>> continued

Error Code	Platform	Description
ELNRNG	U	Link number out of range.
ELOOP	A	Too many symbolic links encountered.
EMFILE	A	Too many open files.
EMLINK	U, W	Too many links.
EMSGSIZE	U, W	Message too long.
EMULTIHOP	U	Multihop attempted.
ENAMETOOLONG	U	Filename too long.
ENAVAIL	U	No XENIX semaphores available.
ENETDOWN	U, W	Network is down.
ENETRESET	U, W	Network dropped connection because of reset.
ENETUNREACH	U, W	Network is unreachable.
ENFILE	U, W	File table overflow.
ENOANO	U	No anode.
ENOBUFS	A	No buffer space available.
ENOCSI	U	No CSI structure available.
ENODATA	U	No data available.
ENODEV	A	No such device.
ENOENT	A	No such file or directory.
ENOEXEC	A	exec format error.
ENOLCK	A	No record locks available.
ENOLINK	U	Link has been severed.
ENOMEM	A	Out of memory.
ENOMSG	U	No message of desired type.
ENONET	U	Machine is not on the network.
ENOPKG	U	Package not installed.
ENOPROTOOPT	A	Protocol not available.
ENOSPC	A	No space left on device.
ENOSR	U	Out of streams resources.
ENOSTR	U	Device not a stream.
ENOSYS	A	Function not implemented.
ENOTBLK	U, M	Block device required.
ENOTCONN	A	Transport endpoint is not connected.
ENOTDIR	A	Not a directory.
ENOTEMPTY	A	Directory not empty.
ENOTNAM	U	Not a XENIX named type file.
ENOTSOCK	A	Socket operation on non-socket.
ENOTTY	A	Not a terminal.
ENOTUNIQ	U	Name not unique on network.
ENXIO	A	No such device or address.
EOPNOTSUPP	A	Operation not supported on transport endpoint.

Error Code	Platform	Description
EOVERFLOW	U	Value too large for defined data type.
EPERM	A	Operation not permitted.
EPFNOSUPPORT	A	Protocol family not supported.
EPIPE	A	Broken pipe.
EPROTO	U	Protocol error.
EPROTONOSUPPORT	A	Protocol not supported.
EPROTOTYPE	A	Protocol wrong type for socket.
ERANGE	A	Math result not representable.
EREMCHG	U	Remote address changed.
EREMOTE	A	Object is remote.
EREMOTEIO	U	Remote I/O error.
ERESTART	U	Interrupted system call should be restarted.
EROFS	A	Read-only filesystem.
ESHUTDOWN	A	Cannot send after transport endpoint shutdown.
ESOCKTNOSUPPORT	A	Socket type not supported.
ESPIPE	A	Illegal seek.
ESRCH	A	No such process.
ESRMNT	U	srmount error.
ESTALE	A	Stale NFS file handle.
ESTRPIPE	U	Streams pipe error.
ETIME	U	Timer expired.
ETIMEDOUT	A	Connection timed out.
ETOOMANYREFS	A	Too many references: Cannot splice.
ETXTBSY	U, M	Text file busy.
EUCLEAN	U	Structure needs cleaning.
EUNATCH	U	Protocol driver not attached.
EUSERS	A	Too many users.
EWOULDBLOCK	A	Operation would block.
EXDEV	A	Cross-device link.
EXFULL	U	Exchange full.
WSAEACCES	W	Permission denied.
WSAEADDRINUSE	W	Address already in use.
WSAEADDRNOTAVAIL	W	Cannot assign requested address.
WSAEAFNOSUPPORT	W	Address family not supported by protocol family.
WSAEALREADY	W	Operation already in progress.
WSAEBADF	W	Invalid file handle.
WSAECONNABORTED	W	Software caused connection abort.
WSAECONNREFUSED	W	Connection refused.

continues >>

Appendix A   The Python Library

>> *continued*

Error Code	Platform	Description
WSAECONNRESET	W	Connection reset by peer.
WSAEDESTADDRREQ	W	Destination address required.
WSAEDISCON	W	Remote shutdown.
WSAEDQUOT	W	Disk quota exceeded.
WSAEFAULT	W	Bad address.
WSAEHOSTDOWN	W	Host is down.
WSAEHOSTUNREACH	W	No route to host.
WSAEINPROGRESS	W	Operation now in progress.
WSAEINTR	W	Interrupted system call.
WSAEINVAL	W	Invalid argument.
WSAEISCONN	W	Socket already connected.
WSAELOOP	W	Cannot translate name.
WSAEMFILE	W	Too many open files.
WSAEMSGSIZE	W	Message too long.
WSAENAMETOOLONG	W	Name too long.
WSAENETDOWN	W	Network is down.
WSAENETRESET	W	Network dropped connection on reset.
WSAENETUNREACH	W	Network is unreachable.
WSAENOBUFS	W	No buffer space is available.
WSAENOPROTOOPT	W	Bad protocol option.
WSAENOTCONN	W	Socket is not connected.
WSAENOTEMPTY	W	Cannot remove non-empty directory.
WSAENOTSOCK	W	Socket operation on non-socket.
WSAEOPNOTSUPP	W	Operation not supported.
WSAEPFNOSUPPORT	W	Protocol family not supported.
WSAEPROCLIM	W	Too many processes.
WSAEPROTONOSUPPORT	W	Protocol not supported.
WSAEPROTOTYPE	W	Protocol wrong type for socket.
WSAEREMOTE	W	Item not available locally.
WSAESHUTDOWN	W	Cannot send after socket shutdown.
WSAESOCKTNOSUPPORT	W	Socket type not supported.
WSAESTALE	W	File handle no longer available.
WSAETIMEDOUT	W	Connection timed out.
WSAETOOMANYREFS	W	Too many references to a kernel object.
WSAEUSERS	W	Quota exceeded.
WSAEWOULDBLOCK	W	Resource temporaily unavailable.
WSANOTINITIALISED	W	Successful WSA Startup not performed.
WSASYSNOTREADY	W	Network subsystem not available.
WSAVERNOTSUPPORTED	W	Winsock.dll version out of range.

▶ **See Also** os (180).

fcntl

The fcntl module performs file and I/O control on UNIX file descriptors. File descriptors can be obtained using the fileno() method of a file or socket object. This module relies on a large number of constants defined in the FCNTL module (that should also be imported).

fcntl(fd, cmd [, arg])

Performs command cmd on an open file descriptor fd. cmd is an integer command code. arg is an optional argument that's either an integer or a string. If arg is passed as an integer, the return value of this function is an integer. If arg is a string, it's interpreted as a binary data structure, and the return value of the call is the contents of the buffer converted back into a string object. The following commands are available (these constants are defined in the FCNTL module):

Command	Description
F_DUPFD	Duplicates a file descriptor. arg is the lowest number that the new file descriptor can assume. Similar to the os.dup() system call.
F_SETFD	Sets the close-on-exec flag to arg (0 or 1). If set, the file is closed on an exec() system call.
F_GETFD	Returns the close-on-exec flag.
F_SETFL	Sets status flags to arg, which is the bitwise-or of the following:
	O_NDELAY—Nonblocking I/O (System V).
	O_APPEND—Append mode (System V).
	O_SYNC—Synchronous write (System V).
	FNDELAY—Nonblocking I/O (BSD).
	FAPPEND—Append mode (BSD).
	FASYNC—Sends SIGIO signal to process group when I/O is possible (BSD).
F_GETFL	Gets status flags as set by F_SETFL.
F_GETOWN	Gets process ID or process group ID set to receive SIGIO and SIGURG signals (BSD).
F_SETOWN	Sets process ID or process group ID to receive SIGIO and SIGURG signals (BSD).
F_GETLK	Returns flock structure used in file locking operations.
F_SETLK	Locks a file, returning -1 if the file is already locked.
F_SETLKW	Locks a file, but waits if the lock cannot be acquired.

An IOError exception is raised if the fcntl() function fails. The F_GETLK and F_SETLK commands are supported through the lockf() function.

ioctl(fd, op, arg)

This function is like the fcntl() function, except that the operations are defined in the library module IOCTL. The IOCTL module may be unavailable on some platforms.

flock(fd, op)

Performs a lock operation op on file descriptor fd. op is the bitwise-or of the following constants found in fcntl:

Item	Description
LOCK_EX	Exclusive lock.
LOCK_NB	Don't lock when locking.
LOCK_SH	Shared lock.
LOCK_UN	Unlock.

In nonblocking mode, an IOError exception is raised if the lock cannot be acquired.

lockf(_fd_, _op_ [, _len_ [, _start_ [, _whence_]]])

Performs record or range locking on part of a file. _op_ is the same as for the flock() function. _len_ is the number of bytes to lock. _start_ is the starting position of the lock relative to the value of _whence_. _whence_ is 0 for the beginning of the file, 1 for the current position, and 2 for the end of the file.

Examples

```
import fcntl, FCNTL

# Set the close-on-exec bit for a file object f
fcntl.fcntl(f.fileno(), FCNTL.F_SETFD, 1)

# Lock a file (blocking)
fcntl.flock(f.fileno(), fcntl.LOCK_EX)

# Lock the first 8192 bytes of a file (nonblocking)
try:
    fcntl.lockf(f.fileno(), fcntl.LOCK_EX | fcntl.LOCK_NB, 8192, 0, 0)
except IOError,e:
    print "Unable to acquire lock", e
```

Notes

- The set of available fcntl() commands and options is system-dependent. The FCNTL module may contain well over 100 constants on some platforms.

- Many of the functions in this module can also be applied to the file descriptors of sockets.

▶ **See Also** os (180), socket (252).

filecmp

The filecmp module provides functions that can be used to compare files and directories.

cmp(_file1_, _file2_[, _shallow_[, _use_statcache_]]])

Compares the files _file1_ and _file2_ and returns 1 if they're equal, 0 if not. By default, files that have identical attributes as returned by os.stat() are considered to be equal. If the _shallow_ parameter is specified and is false, the contents of the two files are compared to determine equality. In this case, subsequent comparisons between the same two files will return a cached result unless the os.stat() data for one of the files changes. If _use_statcache_ is given, values of os.stat() are cached and used in subsequent comparisons. This latter option improves performance, but prevents the module from detecting changes to previously compared files.

> `cmpfiles(dir1, dir2, common[, shallow[, use_statcache]])`

Compares the contents of the files contained in the list `common` in the two directories `dir1` and `dir2`. Returns a tuple containing three lists of filenames (`match`, `mismatch`, `errors`). `match` lists the files that are the same in both directories, `mismatch` lists the files that don't match, and `errors` lists the files that could not be compared for some reason. The `shallow` and `use_statcache` parameters have the same meaning as for `cmp()`.

> `dircmp(dir1, dir2 [, ignore[, hide]])`

Creates a directory comparison object that can be used to perform various comparison operations on the directories `dir1` and `dir2`. `ignore` is a list of filenames to ignore and has a default value of `['RCS','CVS','tags']`. `hide` is a list of filenames to find and defaults to the list `[os.curdir, os.pardir]` (`['.', '..']` on UNIX).

A directory object `d` returned by `dircmp()` has the following methods and attributes:

> `d.report()`

Compares directories `dir1` and `dir2` and prints a report to `sys.stdout`.

> `d.report_partial_closure()`

Compares `dir1` and `dir2` and common immediate subdirectories.

> `d.report_full_closure()`

Compares `dir1` and `dir2` and all subdirectories recursively.

> `d.left_list`

Lists the files and subdirectories in `dir1`. The contents are filtered by `hide` and `ignore`.

> `d.right_list`

Lists the files and subdirectories in `dir2`. The contents are filtered by `hide` and `ignore`.

> `d.common`

Lists the files and subdirectories found in both `dir1` and `dir2`.

> `d.left_only`

Lists the files and subdirectories found only in `dir1`.

> `d.right_only`

Lists the files and subdirectories found only in `dir2`.

> `d.common_dirs`

Lists the subdirectories that are common to `dir1` and `dir2`.

> `d.common_files`

Lists the files that are common to `dir1` and `dir2`.

> `d.common_funny`

Lists the files in `dir1` and `dir2` with different types or for which no information can be obtained from `os.stat()`.

> `d.same_files`

Lists the files with identical contents in `dir1` and `dir2`.

d.diff_files

Lists the files with different contents in *dir1* and *dir2*.

d.funny_files

Lists the files that are in both *dir1* and *dir2*, but that could not be compared.

d.subdirs

A dictionary that maps names in *d*.common_dirs to additional dircmp objects.

Note

- The attributes of a dircmp object are evaluated lazily and not determined at the time the dircmp object is first created.

fileinput

The fileinput module iterates over a list of input files and reads their contents line by line. The main interface to the module is the following function:

input([*files* [, *inplace* [, *backup*]]])

Creates an instance of the FileInput class. *files* is an optional list of filenames to be read (a single filename is also permitted). If omitted, the filenames are read from the command line in sys.argv[1:]. An empty list implies input from stdin, as does a filename of '-'. If *inplace* is set to 1, each input file is moved to a backup file and sys.stdout is redirected to overwrite the original input file. The backup file is then removed when the output is closed. The *backup* option specifies a filename extension such as .bak that is appended to each filename in order to create the names of backup files. When given, the backup files are not deleted. By default, *backup* is the empty string and no backup files are created.

All FileInput instances have the following methods. These methods are also available as functions that apply to the last instance created by the input() function.

Method	Description
filename()	Returns the name of the file currently being read
lineno()	Returns the cumulative line number just read
filelineno()	Returns the line number in the current file
isfirstline()	Returns true if the line just read was the first line of a file
isstdin()	Returns true if the input is stdin
nextfile()	Closes the current file and skips to the next file
close()	Closes the file sequence

In addition, the FileInput instance returned by input() can be used as an iterator for reading all input lines.

Example

The following code reads and prints all the input lines from a list of files supplied on the command line:

```
import fileinput
for line in fileinput.input():
    print '%5d %s' % (fileinput.lineno(), line),
```

Notes

- All files opened by this module are opened in text mode.
- An IOError is raised if a file cannot be opened.
- Empty files are opened and closed immediately.
- All lines returned include trailing newlines unless the last line of an input file doesn't include a newline.
- MS-DOS/Windows short filenames (eight characters plus a three-letter suffix) are not supported.

▶ **See Also** glob (170), fnmatch (165).

findertools

The findertools module is used to access some of the functionality in the Macintosh Finder. All file and folder parameters can be specified either as full pathname strings or as FSSpec objects as created using the macfs module.

launch(*file*)

Launches a file either by launching an application or by opening a document in the correct application.

Print(*file*)

Prints a file.

copy(*file*, *destdir*)

Copies *file* to the folder *destdir*.

move(*file*, *destdir*)

Moves *file* to the folder *destdir*.

sleep()

Puts the Macintosh to sleep (if supported).

restart()

Restarts the machine.

shutdown()

Shuts down the machine.

▶ **See Also** macfs (173), macostools (176).

fnmatch

The fnmatch module provides support for matching filenames using UNIX shell-style wildcard characters:

Character(s)	Description
*	Matches everything
?	Matches any single character
[*seq*]	Matches any character in *seq*
[!*seq*]	Matches any character not in *seq*

The following functions can be used to test for a wildcard match:

fnmatch(`filename, pattern`)

Returns true or false depending on whether `filename` matches `pattern`. Case sensitivity depends on the operating system (certain platforms, such as Windows, are not case sensitive).

fnmatchcase(`filename, pattern`)

Performs a case-sensitive comparison of `filename` against `pattern`.

Examples

```
fnmatch('foo.gif', '*.gif')               # Returns true
fnmatch('part37.html', 'part3[0-5].html') # Returns false
```

▶ **See Also** glob (170).

getopt

The getopt module is used to parse command-line options (typically passed in sys.argv).

getopt(`args, options [, long_options]`)

Parses the command-line options supplied in the list `args`. `options` is a string of letters corresponding to the single-letter options that a program wants to recognize (for example, '`-x`'). If an option requires an argument, the option letter must be followed by a colon. If supplied, `long_options` is a list of strings corresponding to long option names. When supplied in `args`, these options are always preceded by a double hyphen (--) such as in '`--exclude`' (the leading -- is not supplied in `long_options`). Long option names requiring an argument should be followed by an equal sign (=). The function returns a list of (`option, value`) pairs matched and a list of program arguments supplied after all of the options. The options are placed in the list in the same order in which they were found. Long and short options can be mixed. Option names are returned with the leading hyphen (-) or double hyphen (--).

Exception

error

Exception raised when an unrecognized option is found or when an option requiring an argument is given none. The exception argument is a string indicating the cause of the error.

Example

```
>>> import getopt
>>> args = ['-a', '-b', 'foo', '-cd', 'blah', '--exclude','bar', 'x1', 'x2']
>>> opts, pargs = getopt.getopt(args, 'ab:cd:', ['exclude='])
>>> opts
[('-a', ''), ('-b', 'foo'), ('-c',''), ('-d','blah'),('--exclude', 'bar')]
>>> pargs
['x1', 'x2']
>>>
```

Notes

- Only single-letter command-line options can be recognized with a single hyphen (-). For example, '-n 3' is legal, but '-name 3' isn't.
- More than one single-letter option can be combined, provided that all but the last option take no arguments. The '-cd blah' option in the example illustrates this behavior.

▶ **See Also** sys (116).

getpass

The getpass module provides support for reading passwords and usernames.

getpass([prompt])

Prompts the user for a password without echoing. The default prompt is 'Password: '. Returns the entered password as a string.

getuser()

Returns the login name of the user by first checking the environment variables $LOGNAME, $USER, $LNAME, and $USERNAME and then checking the system password database. Raises a KeyError exception if no name can be found. UNIX and Windows.

Notes

- An example of getpass is shown in the documentation for the crypt module.
- On UNIX, the getpass module depends on the termios module, which is disabled by default on some systems.

▶ **See Also** pwd (196), crypt (155).

gettext

The gettext module provides an interface to the GNU gettext library, which is used to provide support for internationalization (i18n). The primary use of gettext is to provide translation of selected program text in a way that's easy to extend and that's mostly transparent to the programmer. For example, if you're writing a program that prompts a user for a password, you might want it to print password in English, passwort in German, contraseña in Spanish, and so forth.

gettext works by making simple string substitutions of selected program text. To do this, it consults a specially constructed locale database that contains mappings of the original program text to translated versions in various languages. This database is application-specific and must be constructed with special tools (described shortly).

The standard interface to gettext relies on the following functions, which are used to both locate the translation database and produce translated strings.

bindtextdomain(domain [, localedir])

Sets the location of the locale directory for a given domain. *domain* is typically the name of the application and *localedir* is a path such as /usr/local/share/locale.

When searching for translation text, gettext looks for a file in the directory *localedir*/*language*/LC_MESSAGES/domain.mo where *language* is a language name such as en, de, fr, etc. Normally, the value of *language* is determined according to one of the following environment variables: $LANGUAGE, $LANG, $LC_MESSAGES, $LC_ALL. The *language* parameter and environment variables can also be a colon-separated list of acceptable languages. If *localedir* is omitted, the current binding for *domain* is returned.

textdomain([*domain*])

Sets the domain that will be used for subsequent text translations. If *domain* is omitted, the name of the current domain is returned.

gettext(*message*)

Returns the translated version of *message* according to the values of the current domain, locale database location, and language. If no suitable translation can be found, *message* is returned unmodified. This function is usually aliased to _() as described below.

dgettext(*domain*, *message*)

Like gettext(), but *message* is looked up in the specified *domain*.

Example

The following example shows how the gettext module is used in an application and how a programmer can construct the translation database.

```
# myapp.py
import getpass
import gettext

gettext.bindtextdomain("myapp","./locale")    # Set locale directory
gettext.textdomain("myapp")                    # Enabled 'myapp'
_ = gettext.gettext                            # Alias _() to gettext()

pw = getpass.getpass(_("password:"))
if pw != "spam":
    print _("Authorization failed.\n");
    raise SystemExit
```

The use of the _() alias is a critical feature of the application. For one thing, this shortens the amount of code that needs to be typed. More importantly, in order to construct the translation database, automatic tools are used to extract translation text from program source by looking for special sequences such as _("..."). For Python, the program pygettext.py (found in the Tools/i18n directory of the Python distribution) is used to do this. For example:

```
% pygettext.py -o myapp.po myapp.py
```

The output of pygettext.py is a human-readable .po file that contains information about the translation strings marked by _("...") in the original source. To support a new language, the entries of this file are edited by supplying a foreign language translation. For example, an edited version of myapp.po might look like this:

```
#: myapp.py:8
msgid "Password:"
msgstr "Passwort:"
```

```
#: myapp.py:10
msgid  "Authorization failed.\n"
msgstr "Authorisierung fehlgeschlagen.\n"
```

Once the translations for a specific language are entered, the myapp.po file is converted to a binary form using the special msgfmt.py program (found in the same directory as pygettext.py). For example:

```
% msgfmt.py myapp
```

This produces a file myapp.mo that can be copied to an appropriate subdirectory with the locale directory; for example, locale/de/LC_MESSAGES/myapp.mo. At this point, you can test the translation by setting the $LANGUAGE environment variable to the string "de" and running the application. You should now see translated text being printed instead of the original program text.

Class-Based Interface

In addition to the standard gettext interface, Python provides a class-based interface that provides better support for Unicode and is more flexible. The following functions are used for this interface:

find(*domain***[,** *localedir***[,** *languages***]])**

Locates the appropriate translation file (.mo file) based on the given domain, locale directory, and languages setting. *domain* and *localedir* are the same strings as used with the bindtextdomain() function. *languages* is a list of language strings to be searched. If *localedir* and *languages* are omitted, they default to the same values as for bindtextdomain(). Returns the filename of the translation file on success or None if no match is found.

install(*domain***[,** *localedir***[,** *unicode***]])**

Installs the _() function in the built-in namespace using the settings of *domain* and *localedir*. The *unicode* flag makes translation strings return as Unicode strings.

translation(*domain***[,** *localedir***[,** *languages***[,** *class_***]]])**

Returns an instance of a translation object for the given *domain*, *localedir*, and *languages* parameters. *domain* and *localedir* are strings and *languages* is a list of language names. The *class_* parameter specifies alternative translation implementations and is primarily reserved for future expansion. The default value is GNUTranslations.

The translation object *t* returned by translation() supports the following methods and attributes:

t.gettext(*message***)**

Returns the translated version of *message* as a standard string.

t.ugettext(*message***)**

Returns the translated version of *message* as a Unicode string.

t.info()

Returns a dictionary containing meta-data about the translation, including the character set, author, creation date, and so forth.

`t.charset()`

Returns the character set encoding for the translation, such as 'ISO-8859-1'.

Example

The following example illustrates the use of the class-based interface:

```
# myapp.py
import getpass
import gettext

gettext.install("myapp","./locale")
pw = getpass.getpass(_("password:"))
if pw != "spam":
    print _("Authorization failed.\n");
    raise SystemExit
```

Alternatively, you can directly control a translation instance as follows:

```
import gettext
t = gettext.translation("myapp","./locale", ["de"])
a = t.gettext("password:")
```

Notes

- Currently, only the GNU `gettext` format is supported by this module. However, the module may be modified to support alternative translation encoding at a later date.

- When Python is run interactively, the _ variable is used to hold the result of the last evaluated expression. This has the potential to clash with the _() function installed by the `gettext` module. However, such clashes are probably unlikely in practice.

glob

The `glob` module returns all filenames in a directory that match a pattern specified using the rules of the UNIX shell (as described in the `fnmatch` module).

glob(*pattern*)

Returns a list of pathnames that match *pattern*.

Examples

```
glob('*.html')
glob('image[0-5]*.gif')
```

Note

- Tilde (~) and shell variable expansion are not performed. Use `os.path.expanduser()` and `os.path.expandvars()`, respectively, to perform these expansions prior to calling `glob()`.

▶ **See Also** `fnmatch` (165), `os.path` (193).

grp

The grp module provides access to the UNIX group database.

getgrgid(*gid*)

Returns the group database entry for a group ID as a 4-tuple (*gr_name*, *gr_passwd*, *gr_gid*, *gr_mem*):

- *gr_name* is the group name.
- *gr_passwd* is the group password (if any).
- *gr_gid* is the integer group ID.
- *gr_mem* is a list of usernames in the group.

Raises KeyError if the group doesn't exist.

getgrnam(*name*)

Same as getgrgid(), but looks up a group by name.

getgrall()

Returns all available group entries as a list of tuples as returned by getgrgid().

▶ **See Also** pwd (196).

gzip

The gzip module provides a class GzipFile that can be used to read and write files compatible with the GNU gzip program. GzipFile objects work like ordinary files except that data is automatically compressed or decompressed.

GzipFile([*filename* [, *mode* [, *compresslevel* [, *fileobj*]]]])

Opens a GzipFile. *filename* is the name of a file and *mode* is one of 'r', 'rb', 'a', 'ab', 'w', or 'wb'. The default is 'rb'. *compresslevel* is an integer from 1 to 9 that controls the level of compression. 1 is the fastest and produces the least compression. 9 is the slowest and produces the most compression (the default). *fileobj* is an existing file object that should be used. If supplied, it's used instead of the file named by *filename*.

open(*filename* [, *mode* [, *compresslevel*]])

Same as GzipFile(*filename*, *mode*, *compresslevel*). The default mode is 'rb'. The default *compresslevel* is 9.

Notes

- Calling the close() method of a GzipFile object doesn't close files passed in *fileobj*. This allows additional information to be written to a file after the compressed data.
- Files produced by the UNIX compress program are not supported.
- This module requires the zlib module.

▶ **See Also** zlib (217), zipfile (214).

Appendix A   The Python Library

locale

The `locale` module provides access to the POSIX locale database, which allows programmers to handle certain cultural issues in an application without knowing all the specifics of each country where the software is executed. A "locale" defines a set of parameters that describe the representation of strings, time, numbers, and currency. These parameters are grouped into the following category codes:

Category	Description
LC_CTYPE	Character conversion and comparison.
LC_COLLATE	String sorting. Affects `strcoll()` and `strxfrm()`.
LC_TIME	Time formatting. Affects `time.strftime()`.
LC_MONETARY	Formatting of monetary values.
LC_MESSAGES	Message display. This may affect error messages returned by functions such as `os.strerror()`.
LC_NUMERIC	Number formatting. Affects `format()`, `atoi()`, `atof()`, and `str()`.
LC_ALL	A combination of all locale settings.

The following functions are available:

setlocale(*category* [, *locale*])

If *locale* is specified, this function changes the locale setting for a particular category. *locale* is a string that specifies the locale name. If set to `'C'`, the portable locale is selected (the default). If the empty string, the default locale from the user's environment is selected. If *locale* is omitted, a string representing the setting for the given category is returned. Raises the exception `locale.Error` on failure.

localeconv()

Returns the database of local conventions as a dictionary.

strcoll(*string1*, *string2*)

Compares two strings according to the current LC_COLLATE setting. Returns a negative, positive, or zero value depending on whether *string1* collates before or after *string2* or is equal to it.

strxfrm(*string*)

Transforms a string to one that can be used for the built-in function `cmp()` and still return locale-aware results.

format(*format*, *val* [, *grouping* = 0])

Formats a number *val* according to the current LC_NUMERIC setting. The *format* follows the conventions of the % operator. For floating-point values, the decimal point is modified, if appropriate. If *grouping* is true, the locale grouping is taken into account.

str(*float*)

Formats a floating-point number using the same format as the built-in function `str(float)`, but takes the decimal point into account.

atof(*string*)

Converts a string to a floating-point number according to the LC_NUMERIC settings.

atoi(*string*)

Converts a string to an integer according to the LC_NUMERIC conventions.

Exception

Error

Raised on failure of the `setlocale()` function.

Note

- Additional information about this module is available in the online library reference.

  ▶ **See Also** `http://www.python.org/doc/lib/module-locale.html`.

macfs

The `macfs` module is used to manipulate files and aliases on the Macintosh. For any function or method that expects a file argument, the argument may be a full or partial Macintosh pathname string, an `FSSpec` object, or a 3-tuple (*wdRefNum, parID, name*).

FSSpec(*file*)

Creates an `FSSpec` object for the specified file.

RawFSSpec(*data*)

Creates an `FSSpec` object, given the raw data for the underlying `FSSpec` C data structure as a string.

RawAlias(*data*)

Creates an `Alias` object, given the raw data for the underlying `alias` C data structure as a string.

FInfo()

Creates a zero-filled `FInfo` object.

ResolveAliasFile(*file*)

Resolves an alias file. Returns a 3-tuple (*fsspec, isfolder, aliased*) in which *fsspec* is the resulting `FSSpec` object, *isfolder* is true if *fsspec* points to a folder, and *aliased* is true if the file was an alias.

StandardGetFile([*type1* [, *type2* [, ...]]])

Presents an "open input file" dialog and requests the user to select a file. Up to four four-character file types can be passed to limit the types of files from which the user can choose. Returns a tuple containing an `FSSpec` object and a flag indicating whether the user completed the dialog without canceling.

PromptGetFile(*prompt type1* [, *type2*, [, ...]])

Similar to `StandardGetFile()`, but allows a prompt to be specified.

StandardPutFile(*prompt* [, *default*])

Presents an "open output file" dialog and requests the user to select a filename. *prompt* is a prompt string and *default* is the default filename. Returns a tuple containing an `FSSpec` object and a flag indicating whether the user completed the dialog without canceling.

GetDirectory([*prompt*])

Presents a "select a directory" dialog. *prompt* is a prompt string. Returns a tuple containing an `FSSpec` object and a success indicator.

SetFolder([fsspec])

Sets the folder that's initially presented to the user when one of the file selection dialogs is presented. fsspec should point to a file in the folder, not the folder itself (the file need not exist, though). If no argument is passed, the folder will be set to the current directory.

FindFolder(where, which, create)

Locates a special Macintosh folder such as the Trash or Preferences folder. where is the disk to search and is typically set to MACFS.kOnSystemDisk. which is a four character string specifying the folder to locate. (These strings are often specified using one of the symbols in the following table.) create, if set to 1, causes the folder to be created if it doesn't exist. Returns a tuple (vrefnum, dirid). The contents of this tuple can be used as the first two elements of the 3-tuple (vrefnum, dirid, name) suitable for use as a filename.

The following list shows the symbolic names in the MACFS module used for the which parameter of FindFolder():

kALMLocationsFolderType	kModemScriptsFolderType
kALMModulesFolderType	kOpenDocEditorsFolderType
kALMPreferencesFolderType	kOpenDocFolderType
kAppleExtrasFolderType	kOpenDocLibrariesFolderType
kAppleMenuFolderType	kOpenDocShellPlugInsFolderType
kApplicationAliasType	kPreferencesFolderType
kApplicationSupportFolderType	kPrintMonitorDocsFolderType
kApplicationsFolderType	kPrinterDescriptionFolderType
kAssistantsFolderType	kPrinterDriverFolderType
kChewableItemsFolderType	kScriptingAdditionsFolderType
kColorSyncProfilesFolderType	kSharedLibrariesFolderType
kContextualMenuItemsFolderType	kShutdownItemsDisabledFolderType
kControlPanelDisabledFolderType	kStartupFolderType
kControlPanelFolderType	kStartupItemsDisabledFolderType
kControlStripModulesFolderType	kStationeryFolderType
kDesktopFolderType	kSystemExtensionDisabledFolderType
kDocumentsFolderType	kSystemFolderType
kEditorsFolderType	kTemporaryFolderType
kExtensionDisabledFolderType	kTextEncodingsFolderType
kExtensionFolderType	kThemesFolderType
kFavoritesFolderType	kTrashFolderType
kFontsFolderType	kUtilitiesFolderType
kGenEditorsFolderType	kVoicesFolderType
kHelpFolderType	kVolumeRootFolderType
kInternetPlugInFolderType	kWhereToEmptyTrashFolderType
kMacOSReadMesFolderType	

NewAliasMinimalFromFullPath(pathname)

Returns a minimal alias object that points to the given file, which must be specified as a full pathname. This is the only way to create an alias pointing to a nonexistent file.

`FindApplication(creator)`

Locates the application with the four-character creator code `creator`. The function returns an FSSpec object pointing to the application.

An instance `f` of an FSSpec object has the following attributes and methods:

`f.data`

The raw data from the underlying FSSpec object.

`f.as_pathname()`

Returns the full pathname.

`f.as_tuple()`

Returns the (*wdRefNum*, *parID*, *name*) tuple of the file.

`f.NewAlias([file])`

Creates an Alias object pointing to the file described by `f`. If the optional `file` parameter is given, the alias is created relative to that file; otherwise, it's absolute.

`f.NewAliasMinimal()`

Creates a minimal alias pointing to this file.

`f.GetCreatorType()`

Returns the four-character creator code and file type.

`f.SetCreatorType(creator, type)`

Sets the four-character `creator` and `type` of the file.

`f.GetFInfo()`

Returns the FInfo object describing the finder information for the file.

`f.SetFInfo(finfo)`

Sets the finder info for the file to the values in the FInifo object `finfo`.

`f.GetDates()`

Returns a tuple with three floating-point values representing the creation date, modification date, and backup date of the file.

`f.SetDates(crdate, moddate, backupdate)`

Sets the creation, modification, and backup dates of the file.

An Alias object `a` has the following attributes and methods:

`a.data`

The raw data for the Alias record as a binary string.

`a.Resolve([file])`

Resolves the alias and returns a tuple containing the FSSpec for the file pointed to and a flag indicating whether the Alias object was modified during the search process. If the file doesn't exist but the path leading up to it does, a valid FSSpec is returned. `file` is an optional file that must be supplied if the alias was originally created as a relative alias.

`a.GetInfo(index)`

Retrieves alias information. `index` is an integer code that specifies the information to retrieve, and is one of the following values:

Value	Description
-3	Zone name
-2	Server name
-1	Volume name
0	Target name
1	Parent directory name

a.Update(*file* [, *file2*])

Updates the alias to point to *file*. If *file2* is present, a relative alias will be created.

An FInfo object *finfo* has the following attributes:

finfo.Creator

The four-character creator code of the file.

finfo.Type

The four-character type code of the file.

finfo.Flags

The finder flags for the file, as 16-bit integers. The bit values in Flags are defined by the following constants defined in the module MACFS: kHasBeenInited, kHasBundle, kHasCustomIcon, kIsAlias, kIsInvisible, kIsOnDesk, kIsShared, kIsStationary, kNameLocked.

finfo.Location

A pointer giving the position of the file's icon in its folder.

finfo.Fldr

The folder the file is in (as an integer).

▶ **See Also** macostools (176), findertools (165),
http://www.python.org/doc/mac (Macintosh Library Reference).

macostools

The macostools module contains functions for file manipulation on the Macintosh.

copy(*src*, *dst* [, *createpath* [, *copytimes*]])

Copies file *src* to *dst*. If *createpath* is nonzero, *dst* must be a pathname, and the folders leading to the destination are created if necessary. By default, the data and resource forks are copied in addition to some Finder information. If *copytimes* is nonzero, the creation, modification, and backup times are copied as well. Custom icons, comments, and icon positions are not copied. If *src* is an alias, the original to which the alias points is copied, not the alias file.

copytree(*src*, *dst*)

Recursively copies a file tree from *src* to *dst*, creating folders as needed. *src* and *dst* must be pathname strings.

mkalias(*src*, *dst*)

Creates a Finder alias *dst* pointing to *src*.

touched(*dst*)

Tells the finder that the Finder information of *dst* has changed and that the Finder should update the file's icon and other currently viewable information.

BUFSIZ

The buffer size used for copying (in bytes). The default is 1 megabyte.

Note

- Except for copytree(), filenames can be specified as strings or as FSSpec objects created by the macfs module.

▶ **See Also** macfs (173).

mmap

The mmap module provides support for a memory-mapped file object. This object behaves both like a file and a string and can be used in most places where an ordinary file or string is expected. Furthermore, the contents of a memory-mapped file are mutable. This means that modifications can be made using index-assignment and slice-assignment operators. Unless a private mapping of the file has been made, such changes directly alter the contents of the underlying file.

A memory-mapping file is created by the mmap() function, which is slightly different on UNIX and Windows.

mmap(fileno, length [, flags, prot])

(UNIX) Returns an mmap object that maps length bytes from the file with integer file descriptor fileno. flags specifies the nature of the mapping and is the bitwise-or of the following:

Flag	Meaning
MAP_PRIVATE	Create a private copy-on-write mapping. Changes to the object will be private to this process.
MAP_SHARED	Share the mapping with all other processes mapping the same areas of the file. Changes to the object will affect all mappings.
MAP_ANON	Used when creating an anonymous shared-memory region on BSD.
MAP_DENYWRITE	Disallow writes (not available on all platforms).
MAP_EXECUTABLE	Map memory as executable (not available on all platforms).

The default flags setting is MAP_SHARED. prot specifies the memory protections of the object and is the bitwise-or of the following:

Setting	Meaning
PROT_READ	Data can be read from the object.
PROT_WRITE	Modifications can be made to the object.
PROT_EXEC	The object can contain executable instructions.

The default value of prot is PROT_READ ¦ PROT_WRITE. The modes specified in prot must match the access permissions used to open the underlying file descriptor fileno. In most cases, this means that the file should be opened in read/write mode (for example, os.open(name, os.O_RDWR)).

`mmap(fileno, length[, tagname])`

(Windows) Returns an mmap object that maps *length* bytes from the file specified by the integer file descriptor *fileno*. This file should be open for both reading and writing or an error will be generated. *tagname* is an optional string that can be used to name the mapping. If the *tagname* refers to an existing mapping, that mapping is opened. Otherwise, a new mapping is created. If *tagname* is None, an unnamed mapping is created.

A memory-mapped file object *m* supports the following methods.

`m.close()`

Closes the file. Subsequent operations will result in an exception.

`m.find(string[, start])`

Returns the index of the first occurrence of *string*. *start* specifies an optional starting position. Returns -1 if no match is found.

`m.flush([offset, size])`

Flushes modifications of the in-memory copy back to the filesystem. *offset* and *size* specify an optional range of bytes to flush. Otherwise, the entire mapping is flushed.

`m.move(dst,src,count)`

Copies *count* bytes starting at index *src* to the destination index *dst*. This copy is performed using the C memmove() function, which is guaranteed to work correctly when the source and destination regions happen to overlap.

`m.read(n)`

Reads up to *n* bytes from the current file position and returns the data as a string.

`m.read_byte()`

Reads a single byte from the current file position and returns it as a string of length 1.

`m.readline()`

Returns a line of input starting at the current file position.

`m.resize(newsize)`

Resizes the memory-mapped object to contain *newsize* bytes.

`m.seek(pos[, whence])`

Sets the file position to a new value. *pos* and *whence* have the same meaning as for the seek() method on file objects.

`m.size()`

Returns the length of the file. This value may be larger than the size of the memory-mapped region.

`m.tell()`

Returns the value of the file pointer.

`m.write(string)`

Writes a string of bytes to the file at the current file pointer.

`m.write_byte(byte)`

Writes a single byte into memory at the current file pointer.

Notes

- Certain memory mappings may only work with a length that's a multiple of the system pagesize, which is contained in the constant mmap.PAGESIZE.

- On UNIX SVR4 systems, anonymous mapped memory can be obtained by calling mmap() on the file /dev/zero, opened with appropriate permissions.

- On UNIX BSD systems, anonymous mapped memory can be obtained by calling mmap() with a negative file descriptor and the flag mmap.MAP_ANON.

msvcrt

The msvcrt module provides access to a number of useful functions in the Microsoft Visual C runtime library. This module is available only on Windows.

getch()

Reads a keypress and returns the resulting character. This call blocks if a keypress is not available. If the pressed key was a special function key, the call returns '\000' or '\xe0' and the next call returns the keycode. This function doesn't echo characters to the console, nor can the function be used to read Ctrl+C.

getche()

Like getch() except that characters are echoed (if printable).

get_osfhandle(*fd*)

Returns the file handle for file descriptor *fd*. Raises IOError if *fd* is not recognized.

heapmin()

Forces the internal Python memory manager to return unused blocks to the operating system. This works only on Windows NT and raises IOError on failure.

kbhit()

Returns true if a keypress is waiting to be read.

locking(*fd*, *mode*, *nbytes*)

Locks part of a file, given a file descriptor from the C runtime. *nbytes* is the number of bytes to lock relative to the current file pointer. *mode* is one of the following integers:

Setting	Description
0	Unlocks the file region (LK_UNLCK)
1	Locks the file region (LK_LOCK)
2	Locks the file region; nonblocking (LK_NBLCK)
3	Locks for writing (LK_RLCK)
4	Locks for writing; nonblocking (LK_NBRLCK)

Attempts to acquire a lock that take more than approximately 10 seconds result in an error.

open_osfhandle(*handle*, *flags*)

Creates a C runtime file descriptor from the file handle *handle*. *flags* is the bitwise-or of os.O_APPEND, os.O_RDONLY, and os.O_TEXT. Returns an integer file descriptor that can be used as a parameter to os.fdopen() to create a file object.

putch(*char*)

Prints the character *char* to the console without buffering.

setmode(*fd, flags*)

Sets the line-end translation mode for file descriptor *fd*. *flags* is os.O_TEXT for text mode and os.O_BINARY for binary mode.

ungetch(*char*)

Causes the character *char* to be "pushed back" into the console buffer. It will be the next character read by getch() or getche().

Note

- A wide variety of Win32 extensions are available that provide access to the Microsoft Foundation Classes, COM components, graphical user interfaces, and so forth. These topics are far beyond the scope of this book, but detailed information about many of these topics is available in *Python Programming on Win32* by Mark Hammond and Andy Robinson (O'Reilly & Associates, 1999). http://www.python.org also maintains an extensive list of contributed modules for use under Windows.

▶ **See Also** _winreg (211).

os

The os module provides a portable interface to common operating-system services. It does this by searching for an OS-dependent built-in module such as mac or posix and exporting the functions and data as found there. Unless otherwise noted, functions are available on Windows, Macintosh, and UNIX.

The following general-purpose variables are defined:

environ

A mapping object representing the current environment variables. Changes to the mapping are reflected in the current environment.

linesep

The string used to separate lines on the current platform. May be a single character such as '\n' for POSIX or '\r' for MacOS, or multiple characters such as '\r\n' for Windows.

name

The name of the OS-dependent module imported: 'posix', 'nt', 'dos', 'mac', or 'os2'.

path

The OS-dependent standard module for pathname operations. This module can also be loaded using import os.path.

Process Environment

The following functions are used to access and modify various parameters related to the environment in which a process runs. Process, group, process group, and session IDs are integers unless otherwise noted.

`chdir(path)`

Changes the current working directory to `path`.

`ctermid()`

Returns a string with the filename of the control terminal for the process. UNIX.

`getcwd()`

Returns a string with the current working directory.

`getegid()`

Returns the effective group ID. UNIX.

`geteuid()`

Returns the effective user ID. UNIX.

`getgid()`

Returns the real group ID of the process. UNIX.

`getgroups()`

Return a list of integer group IDs to which the process owner belongs. UNIX.

`getpgrp()`

Returns the ID of the current process group. Process groups are typically used in conjunction with job control. The process group is not necessarily the same as the group ID of the process. UNIX.

`getpid()`

Returns the real process ID of the current process. UNIX and Windows.

`getppid()`

Returns the process ID of the parent process. UNIX.

`getuid()`

Returns the real user ID of the current process. UNIX.

`putenv(varname, value)`

Sets environment variable `varname` to `value`. Changes affect subprocesses started with `os.system()`, `popen()`, `fork()`, and `execv()`. Assignments to items in `os.environ` automatically call `putenv()`. However, calls to `putenv()` don't update `os.environ`. UNIX and Windows.

`setgid(gid)`

Sets the group ID of the current process. UNIX.

`setpgrp()`

Creates a new process group by calling the system call `setpgrp()` or `setpgrp(0, 0)`, depending on which version is implemented (if any). Returns the ID of the new process group. UNIX.

`setpgid(pid, pgrp)`

Assigns process `pid` to process group `pgrp`. If `pid` is equal to `pgrp`, the process becomes a new process group leader. If `pid` is not equal to `pgrp`, the process joins an existing group. If `pid` is `0`, the process ID of the calling process is used. If `pgrp` is `0`, the process specified by `pid` becomes a process group leader. UNIX.

`setreuid(ruid,euid)`

Set the real and effective user ID of the calling process. UNIX.

setregid(*rgid*,*egid*)

Set the real and effective group ID of the calling process. UNIX.

setsid()

Creates a new session and returns the newly created session ID. Sessions are typically associated with terminal devices and the job control of processes that are started within them. UNIX.

setuid(*uid*)

Sets the real user ID of the current process. This function is privileged and often can be performed only by processes running as root. UNIX.

strerror(*code*)

Returns the error message corresponding to the integer error *code*. UNIX and Windows.

▶ **See Also** errno (156).

umask(*mask*)

Sets the current numeric umask and returns the previous umask. The umask is used to clear permissions bits on files created by the process. UNIX and Windows.

▶ **See Also** os.open (184).

uname()

Returns a tuple of strings (*sysname*, *nodename*, *release*, *version*, *machine*) identifying the system type. UNIX.

File Creation and File Descriptors

The following functions provide a low-level interface for manipulating files and pipes. In these functions, files are manipulated in terms of an integer file descriptor *fd*. The file descriptor can be extracted from a file object by invoking its fileno() method.

close(*fd*)

Closes the file descriptor *fd* previously returned by open() or pipe().

dup(*fd*)

Duplicates file descriptor *fd*. Returns a new file descriptor that's the lowest-numbered unused file descriptor for the process. The new and old file descriptors can be used interchangeably. Furthermore, they share state such as the current file pointer and locks. UNIX and Windows.

dup2(*oldfd*, *newfd*)

Duplicates file descriptor *oldfd* to *newfd*. If *newfd* already corresponds to a valid file descriptor, it's closed first. UNIX and Windows.

fdopen(*fd* [, *mode* [, *bufsize*]])

Returns an open file object connected to file descriptor *fd*. The *mode* and *bufsize* arguments have the same meaning as in the built-in open() function.

fpathconf(*fd*, *name*)

Returns configurable pathname variables associated with the open file with descriptor *fd*. *name* is a string that specifies the name of the value to retrieve. The values are usually taken from parameters contained in system header files such as <limits.h> and <unistd.h>. POSIX defines the following constants for *name*:

Constant	Description
`"PC_ASYNC_IO"`	Indicates whether asynchronous I/O can be performed on *fd*.
`"PC_CHOWN_RESTRICTED"`	Indicates whether the `chown()` function can be used. If *fd* refers to a directory, this applies to all files in the directory.
`"PC_FILESIZEBITS"`	Maximum size of a file.
`"PC_LINK_MAX"`	Maximum value of the file's link count.
`"PC_MAX_CANON"`	Maximum length of a formatted input line. *fd* refers to a terminal.
`"PC_MAX_INPUT"`	Maximum length of an input line. *fd* refers to a terminal.
`"PC_NAME_MAX"`	Maximum length of a filename in a directory.
`"PC_NO_TRUNC"`	Indicates whether an attempt to create a file with a name longer than `PC_NAME_MAX` for a directory will fail with an `ENAMETOOLONG` error.
`"PC_PATH_MAX"`	Maximum length of a relative pathname when the directory *fd* is the current working directory.
`"PC_PIPE_BUF"`	Size of the pipe buffer when *fd* refers to a pipe or FIFO.
`"PC_PRIO_IO"`	Indicates whether priority I/O can be performed on *fd*.
`"PC_SYNC_IO"`	Indicates whether synchronous I/O can be performed on *fd*.
`"PC_VDISABLE"`	Indicates whether *fd* allows special-character processing to be disabled. *fd* must refer to a terminal.

Not all names are available on all platforms, and some systems may define additional configuration parameters. However, a list of the names known to the operating system can be found in the directory os.pathconf_names. If a known configuration name is not included in os.pathconf_names, its integer value can also be passed as *name*. Even if a name is recognized by Python, this function may still raise an OSError if the host operating system doesn't recognize the parameter or associate it with the file *fd*. This function is available only on some versions of UNIX.

fstat(*fd*)

Returns the status for file descriptor *fd*. Returns the same values as the os.stat() function. UNIX and Windows.

fstatvfs(*fd*)

Returns information about the filesystem containing the file associated with file descriptor *fd*. Returns the same values as the os.statvfs() function. UNIX.

ftruncate(*fd*, *length*)

Truncates the file corresponding to file descriptor *fd*, so that it's at most *length* bytes in size. UNIX.

lseek(*fd*, *pos*, *how*)

Sets the current position of file descriptor *fd* to position *pos*. Values of *how* are as follows: 0 sets the position relative to the beginning of the file, 1 sets it relative to the current position, and 2 sets it relative to the end of the file.

Appendix A   The Python Library

open(*file* [, *flags* [, *mode*]])

Opens the file *file*. *flags* is the bitwise-or of the following constant values:

Value	Description
O_RDONLY	Open the file for reading.
O_WRONLY	Open the file for writing.
O_RDWR	Open for reading and writing (updates).
O_APPEND	Append bytes to the end of the file.
O_CREAT	Create the file if it doesn't exist.
O_NONBLOCK	Don't block on open, read,or write (UNIX).
O_NDELAY	Same as O_NONBLOCK (UNIX).
O_DSYNC	Synchronous writes (UNIX).
O_NOCTTY	When opening a device, don't set controlling terminal (UNIX).
O_TRUNC	If the file exists, truncates to zero length.
O_RSYNC	Synchronous reads (UNIX).
O_SYNC	Synchronous writes (UNIX).
O_EXCL	Error if O_CREAT and the file already exists.
O_TEXT	Text mode (Windows).
O_BINARY	Binary mode (Windows).

Synchronous I/O modes (O_SYNC, O_DSYNC, O_RSYNC) force I/O operations to block until they've been completed at the hardware level (for example, a write will block until the bytes have been physically written to disk). The *mode* parameter contains the file permissions represented as the bitwise-or of the following octal values:

Mode	Meaning
0100	User has execute permission.
0200	User has write permission.
0400	User has read permission.
0010	Group has execute permission.
0020	Group has write permission.
0040	Group has read permission.
0001	Others have execute permission.
0002	Others have write permission.
0004	Others have read permission.

The default mode of a file is (0777 & ~umask) where the umask setting is used to remove selected permissions. For example, a umask of 0022 removes write permission for groups and others. The umask can be changed using the os.umask() function. The umask setting has no effect on Windows and Macintosh.

openpty()

Opens a pseudo-terminal and returns a pair of file descriptors (*master*,*slave*) for the PTY and TTY. Available on some versions of UNIX.

pipe()

Creates a pipe that can be used to establish unidirectional communication with another process. Returns a pair of file descriptors (*r*, *w*) usable for reading and writing, respectively. This function is usually called prior to executing a fork() function. After the fork(), the sending process closes the read end of the pipe and the receiving process closes the write end of the pipe. At this point, the pipe is activated and data can be sent from one process to another using read() and write() functions. UNIX.

popen(*command* [, *mode* [, *bufsize*]])

Opens a pipe to or from a command. The return value is an open file object connected to the pipe, which can be read or written depending on whether *mode* is 'r' (the default) or 'w'. *bufsize* has the same meaning as in the built-in open() function. The exit status of the command is returned by the close() method of the returned file object, except that when the exit status is zero, None is returned.

popen2(*cmd*[, *bufsize*[, *mode*]])

Executes *cmd* as a subprocess and returns the file objects (*child_stdin*, *child_stdout*). *bufsize* is the buffer size. *mode* is 't' or 'b' to indicate text or binary mode, which is needed on Windows.

popen3(*cmd*[, *bufsize*[, *mode*]])

Executes *cmd* as a subprocess and returns three file objects (*child_stdin*, *child_stdout*, *child_stderr*).

popen4(*cmd*[, *bufsize*[, *mode*]])

Executes *cmd* as a subprocess and returns two file objects (*child_stdin*, *child_stdout_stderr*), in which the standard output and standard error of the child are combined.

read(*fd*, *n*)

Reads at most *n* bytes from file descriptor *fd*. Returns a string containing the bytes read.

tcgetpgrp(*fd*)

Returns the process group associated with the control terminal given by *fd*. UNIX.

tcsetpgrp(*fd*, *pg*)

Sets the process group associated with the control terminal given by *fd*. UNIX.

ttyname(*fd*)

Returns a string that specifies the terminal device associated with file descriptor *fd*. If *fd* is not associated with a terminal device, an exception is raised. UNIX.

write(*fd*, *str*)

Writes the string *str* to file descriptor *fd*. Returns the number of bytes actually written.

Files and Directories

The following functions and variables are used to manipulate files and directories on the filesystem. To handle variances in file-naming schemes, the following variables contain information about the construction of pathnames:

Variable	Description
altsep	An alternative character used by the OS to separate pathname components, or None if only one separator character exists. This is set to '/' on DOS and Windows systems, where sep is a backslash.
curdir	The string used to refer to the current working directory: '.' for UNIX and Windows and ':' for Macintosh.
pardir	The string used to refer to the parent directory: '..' for UNIX and Windows and '::' for Macintosh.
pathsep	The character used to separate search path components (as contained in the $PATH environment variable): ':' for UNIX and ';' for DOS and Windows.
sep	The character used to separate pathname components: '/' for UNIX and Windows and ':' for Macintosh.

The following functions are used to manipulate files:

access(path, accessmode)

Checks read/write/execute permissions for this process or file path. accessmode is R_OK, W_OK, X_OK, or F_OK for read, write, execute, or existence, respectively. Returns 1 if access is granted, 0 if not. UNIX.

chmod(path, mode)

Changes the mode of path. mode has the same values as described for the open() function. UNIX and Windows.

chown(path, uid, gid)

Changes the owner and group ID of path to the numeric uid and gid. UNIX.

getbootvol()

Returns the name of the boot disk. Macintosh.

link(src, dst)

Creates a hard link named dst that points to src. UNIX.

listdir(path)

Returns a list containing the names of the entries in the directory path. The list is returned in arbitrary order and doesn't include the special entries of '.' and '..'.

lstat(path)

Like stat(), but doesn't follow symbolic links. UNIX.

mkfifo(path [, mode])

Creates a FIFO (a named pipe) named path with numeric mode mode. The default mode is 0666. UNIX.

mkdir(path [, mode])

Creates a directory named path with numeric mode mode. The default mode is 0777. On non–UNIX systems, the mode setting may have no effect or be ignored.

makedirs(path [, mode])

Recursive directory-creation function. Like mkdir(), but makes all the intermediate-level directories needed to contain the leaf directory. Raises an OSError exception if the leaf directory already exists or cannot be created.

`pathconf(path, name)`

Returns configurable system parameters related to the pathname `path`. `name` is a string that specifies the name of the parameter and is the same as described for the `fpathconf()` function. UNIX.

▶ **See Also** `fpathconf` (182).

`readlink(path)`

Returns a string representing the path to which a symbolic link `path` points. UNIX.

`remove(path)`

Removes the file `path`. This is identical to the `unlink()` function.

`removedirs(path)`

Recursive directory-removal function. Works like `rmdir()` except that, if the leaf directory is successfully removed, directories corresponding to the rightmost path segments will be pruned away until either the whole path is consumed or an error is raised (which is ignored, because it generally means that a parent directory isn't empty). Raises an `OSError` exception if the leaf directory could not be removed successfully.

`rename(src, dst)`

Renames the file or directory `src` to `dst`.

`renames(old, new)`

Recursive directory-renaming or file-renaming function. Works like `rename()` except first attempting to create any intermediate directories needed to make the new pathname. After the rename, directories corresponding to the rightmost path segments of the old name will be pruned away using `removedirs()`.

`rmdir(path)`

Removes the directory `path`.

`stat(path)`

Performs a `stat()` system call on the given `path` to extract information about a file. The return value is a tuple of at least 10 integers in the order `st_mode`, `st_ino`, `st_dev`, `st_nlink`, `st_uid`, `st_gid`, `st_size`, `st_atime`, `st_mtime`, `st_ctime`. More items may be added at the end by some implementations, and on non–UNIX platforms some items are filled with dummy values. The standard module `stat` defines functions and constants that are useful for extracting information from a stat tuple.

`statvfs(path)`

Performs a `statvfs()` system call on the given `path` to get information about the filesystem. The return value is a tuple of 10 integers in the order `f_bsize`, `f_frsize`, `f_blocks`, `f_bfree`, `f_bavail`, `f_files`, `f_ffree`, `f_favail`, `f_flag`, `f_namemax`. The standard module `statvfs` defines constants that can be used to extract information from the returned `statvfs` data. UNIX.

`symlink(src, dst)`

Creates a symbolic link named `dst` that points to `src`.

`sync()`

Syncs the filesystem. Macintosh.

`unlink(path)`

Removes the file `path`. Same as `remove()`.

`utime(path, (atime, mtime))`

Sets the access and modified time of the file to the given values. (The second argument is a tuple of two items.) The time arguments are specified in terms of the numbers returned by the `time.time()` function.

`xstat(path)`

Like `stat()`, but the returned tuple includes three additional fields containing the size of the resource fork and the four-character creator and type codes. Macintosh.

Process Management

The following functions and variables are used to create, destroy, and manage processes.

`abort()`

Generates a SIGABRT signal that's sent to the calling process. Unless the signal is caught with a signal handler, the default is for the process to terminate with an error.

`defpath`

This variable contains the default search path used by the `exec*p*()` functions if the environment doesn't have a `'PATH'` variable.

`execl(path, arg0, arg1, ...)`

Equivalent to `execv(path, (arg0, arg1, ...))`. UNIX and Windows.

`execle(path, arg0, arg1, ..., env)`

Equivalent to `execve(path, (arg0, arg1, ...), env)`. UNIX and Windows.

`execlp(path, arg0, arg1, ...)`

Equivalent to `execvp(path, (arg0, arg1, ...))`. UNIX and Windows.

`execv(path, args)`

Executes the executable program `path` with argument list `args`, replacing the current process (that is, the Python interpreter). The argument list may be a tuple or list of strings. UNIX and Windows.

`execve(path, args, env)`

Executes a new program like `execv()`, but additionally accepts a dictionary `env` that defines the environment in which the program runs. `env` must be a dictionary mapping strings to strings. UNIX and Windows.

`execvp(path, args)`

Like `execv(path, args)`, but duplicates the shell's actions in searching for an executable file in a list of directories. The directory list is obtained from `environ['PATH']`. UNIX and Windows.

`execvpe(path, args, env)`

Like `execvp()`, but with an additional environment variable as in the `execve()` function. UNIX and Windows.

`_exit(n)`

Exits immediately to the system with status `n`, without performing any cleanup actions. *Note:* The standard way to exit Python programs is `sys.exit(n)`. UNIX and Windows.

fork()

Creates a child process. Returns 0 in the newly created child process and the child's process ID in the original process. The child process is a clone of the original process and shares many resources such as open files. UNIX.

forkpty()

Creates a child process using a new pseudo-terminal as the child's controlling terminal. Returns a pair (*pid*, *fd*) in which *pid* is 0 in the child and *fd* is a file descriptor of the master end of the pseudo-terminal. This function is available only in certain versions of UNIX.

kill(*pid, sig*)

Sends the process *pid* the signal *sig*. A list of signal names can be found in the signal module. UNIX.

nice(*increment*)

Adds an increment to the scheduling priority (the "niceness") of the process. Returns the new niceness. Typically, users can only decrease the priority of a process, since increasing the priority requires root access. UNIX.

plock(*op*)

Locks program segments into memory, preventing them from being swapped. The value of *op* is an integer that determines which segments are locked. The value of *op* is platform-specific, but is typically one of UNLOCK, PROCLOCK, TXTLOCK, or DATLOCK. These constants are not defined by Python, but might be found in the <sys/lock.h> header file. This function is not available on all platforms and often can be performed only by a process with an effective user ID of 0 (root). UNIX.

spawnv(*mode, path, args*)

Executes the program *path* in a new process, passing the arguments specified in *args* as command-line parameters. *args* can be a list or a tuple. The first element of *args* should be the name of the program. *mode* is one of the following constants:

Constant	Description
P_WAIT	Executes the program and waits for it to terminate. Returns the program's exit code.
P_NOWAIT	Executes the program and returns the process handle.
P_NOWAITO	Same as P_NOWAIT.
P_OVERLAY	Executes the program and destroys the calling process (same as the exec functions).
P_DETACH	Executes the program and detaches from it. The calling program continues to run, but cannot wait for the spawned process.

spawnv() is available on Windows and some versions of UNIX.

spawnve(*mode, path, args, env*)

Executes the program *path* in a new process, passing the arguments specified in *args* as command-line parameters and the contents of the mapping *env* as the environment. *args* can be a list or a tuple. *mode* has the same meaning as described for spawnv(). Windows and UNIX.

startfile(*path*)

Launches the application associated with the file *path*. This performs the same action as would occur if you double-clicked the file in Windows Explorer. The function returns as soon as the application is launched. Furthermore, there is no way to wait for completion or to obtain exit codes from the application. *path* is relative to the current directory. Windows.

system(*command*)

Executes *command* (a string) in a subshell. On UNIX, the return value is the exit status of the process as returned by wait(). On Windows, the exit code is always 0. UNIX and Windows.

times()

Returns a 5-tuple of floating-point numbers indicating accumulated times in seconds. On UNIX, the tuple contains the user time, system time, children's user time, children's system time, and elapsed real time. On Windows, the tuple contains the user time, system time, and zeros for the other three values. UNIX and Windows. Not supported on Windows 95/98.

wait([*pid*])

Waits for completion of a child process and returns a tuple containing its process ID and exit status. The exit status is a 16-bit number whose low byte is the signal number that killed the process, and whose high byte is the exit status (if the signal number is zero). The high bit of the low byte is set if a core file was produced. *pid*, if given, specifies the process to wait for. If omitted, wait() returns when any child process exits. UNIX.

waitpid(*pid*, *options*)

Waits for a change in the state of a child process given by process ID *pid*, and returns a tuple containing its process ID and exit status indication, encoded as for wait(). *options* should be 0 for normal operation or WNOHANG to avoid hanging if no child process status is available immediately. This function can also be used to gather information about child processes that have only stopped executing for some reason (refer to the UNIX man pages for waitpid for details). UNIX.

The following functions take a process status code as returned by waitpid() and are used to examine the state of the process (UNIX only).

WIFSTOPPED(*status*)

Returns true if the process has been stopped.

WIFSIGNALED(*status*)

Returns true if the process exited due to a signal.

WIFEXITED(*status*)

Returns true if the process exited using the exit() system call.

WEXITSTATUS(*status*)

If WIFEXITED(*status*) is true, returns the integer parameter to the exit() system call. Otherwise, the return value is meaningless.

WSTOPSIG(*status*)

Returns the signal that caused the process to stop.

WTERMSIG(*status*)

Returns the signal that caused the process to exit.

System Configuration

The following functions are used to obtain system configuration information:

`confstr(name)`

Returns a string-valued system configuration varible. `name` is a string specifying the name of the variable. The acceptable names are platform-specific, but a dictionary of known names for the host system is found in `os.confstr_names`. If a configuration value for a specified name is not defined, the empty string is returned. If `name` is unknown, `ValueError` is raised. An `OSError` may also be raised if the host system doesn't support the configuration name. The parameters returned by this function mostly pertain to the build environment on the host machine and include paths of system utilities, compiler options for various program configurations (for example, 32-bit, 64-bit, and largefile support), and linker options. UNIX.

`sysconf(name)`

Returns an integer-valued system configuration variable. `name` is a string specifying the name of the variable. The names defined on the host system can be found in the dictionary `os.sysconf_names`. Returns -1 if the configuration name is known but the value is not defined. Otherwise a `ValueError` or `OSError` may be raised. Some systems may define well over 100 different system parameters. However, the following table lists the parameters defined by POSIX.1 that should be available on most UNIX systems:

Parameter	Description
`"SC_ARG_MAX"`	Maximum length of the arguments that can be used with `exec()`.
`"SC_CHILD_MAX"`	Maximum number of processes per user ID.
`"SC_CLK_TCK"`	Number of clock ticks per second.
`"SC_NGROUPS_MAX"`	Maximum number of simultaneous supplementary group IDs.
`"SC_STREAM_MAX"`	Maximum number of streams a process can open at one time.
`"SC_TZNAME_MAX"`	Maximum number of bytes in a timezone name.
`"SC_OPEN_MAX"`	Maximum number of files a process can open at one time.
`"SC_JOB_CONTROL"`	System supports job control.
`"SC_SAVED_IDS"`	Indicates whether each process has a saved set-user-ID and a saved set-group-ID.

Exception

`error`

Exception raised when a function returns a system-related error. This is the same as the built-in exception `OSError`. The exception carries two values: `errno` and `strerr`. The first contains the integer error value as described for the `errno` module. The latter contains a string error message. For exceptions involving the filesystem, the exception also contains a third attribute, `filename`, which is the filename passed to the function.

Appendix A   The Python Library

Example

The following example uses the os module to implement a minimalistic UNIX shell that can run programs and perform I/O redirection:

```
import os, sys, string
print 'Welcome to the Python Shell!'
while 1:
        cmd = string.split(raw_input('pysh % '))
        if not cmd: continue
        progname = cmd[0]
        outfile = None
        infile = None
        args = [progname]
        for c in cmd[1:]:
            if c[0] == '>':
                    outfile = c[1:]
            elif c[0] == '<':
                    infile = c[1:]
            else:
                    args.append(c)
        # Check for a change in working directory
        if progname == 'cd':
            if len(args) > 1:
                try:
                        os.chdir(args[1])
                    except OSError,e:
                        print e
            continue
        # Exit from the shell
        if progname == 'exit':
            sys.exit(0)
        # Spawn a process to run the command
        pid = os.fork()
        if not pid:
            # Open input file (redirection)
            if infile:
                ifd = os.open(infile,os.O_RDONLY)
                os.dup2(ifd,sys.stdin.fileno())
            # Open output file (redirection)
            if outfile:
                ofd = os.open(outfile,os.O_WRONLY | os.O_CREAT | os.O_TRUNC)
                os.dup2(ofd,sys.stdout.fileno())
            # Run the command
            os.execvp(progname, args)
        else:
            childpid,ec = os.wait(pid)
            if ec:
                print 'Exit code ',ec
```

Note

- The os.popen2(), os.popen3(), and os.popen4() functions can also be found in the popen2 module. However, the order of the returned file objects is different.

▶ **See Also** os.path (193), stat (202), statvfs (203), time (208), popen2 (195), signal (200), fcntl (161).

os.path

The os.path module is used to manipulate pathnames in a portable manner. It's imported by the os module.

abspath(*path*)

Returns an absolute version of the pathname *path*, taking the current working directory into account. For example, abspath('../Python/foo') might return '/home/beazley/Python/foo'.

basename(*path*)

Returns the basename of pathname *path*. For example, basename('/usr/local/python') returns 'python'.

commonprefix(*list*)

Returns the longest string that's a prefix of all strings in *list*. If *list* is empty, returns the empty string.

dirname(*path*)

Returns the directory name of pathname *path*. For example, dirname('/usr/local/python') returns '/usr/local'.

exists(*path*)

Returns true if *path* refers to an existing path.

expanduser(*path*)

Replaces pathnames of the form '~user' with a user's home directory. If the expansion fails or *path* does not begin with '~', the path is returned unmodified.

expandvars(*path*)

Expands environment variables of the form '$name' or '${name}' in *path*. Malformed or nonexistent variable names are left unchanged.

getatime(*path*)

Returns the time of last access as the number of seconds since the epoch (see the time module).

getmtime(*path*)

Returns the time of last modification as the number of seconds since the epoch (see the time module).

getsize(*path*)

Returns the file size in bytes.

isabs(*path*)

Returns true if *path* is an absolute pathname (begins with a slash).

isfile(*path*)

Returns true if *path* is a regular file. This function follows symbolic links, so both islink() and isfile() can be true for the same path.

isdir(*path*)

Returns true if *path* is a directory. Follows symbolic links.

islink(*path*)

Returns true if *path* refers to a symbolic link. Returns false if symbolic links are unsupported.

ismount(*path*)

Returns true if *path* is a mount point.

join(*path1* [, *path2* [, ...]])

Intelligently joins one or more path components into a pathname. For example, join('/home', 'beazley', 'Python') returns '/home/beazley/Python' on UNIX.

normcase(*path*)

Normalizes the case of a pathname. On non–case-sensitive filesystems, this converts *path* to lowercase. On Windows, forward slashes are also converted to backslashes.

normpath(*path*)

Normalizes a pathname. This collapses redundant separators and up-level references so that 'A//B', 'A/./B', and 'A/foo/../B' all become 'A/B'. On Windows, forward slashes are converted to backslashes.

samefile(*path1*, *path2*)

Returns true if *path1* and *path2* refer to the same file or directory. Macintosh and UNIX.

sameopenfile(*fp1*, *fp2*)

Returns true if the open file objects *fp1* and *fp2* refer to the same file. Macintosh and UNIX.

samestat(*stat1*, *stat2*)

Returns true if the stat tuples *stat1* and *stat2* as returned by fstat(), lstat(), or stat() refer to the same file. Macintosh and UNIX.

split(*path*)

Splits *path* into a pair (*head*, *tail*) where *tail* is the last pathname component and *head* is everything leading up to that. For example, '/home/user/foo' gets split into ('/home/user', 'foo'). This tuple is the same as would be returned by (dirname(), basename()).

splitdrive(*path*)

Splits *path* into a pair (*drive*, *filename*) where *drive* is either a drive specification or the empty string. *drive* is always the empty string on machines without drive specifications.

splitext(*path*)

Splits a pathname into a base filename and suffix. For example, splitext('foo.txt') returns ('foo', '.txt').

walk(*path*, *visitfunc*, *arg*)

This function recursively walks all the directories rooted at *path* and calls the function visitfunc(*arg*, *dirname*, *names*) for each directory. *dirname* specifies the visited directory and *names* is a list of the files in the directory as retrieved using os.listdir(*dirname*). The *visitfunc* function can modify the contents of names to alter the search process if necessary.

▶ **See Also** fnmatch (165), glob (170), os (180).

popen2

The popen2 module is used to spawn processes and connect to their input/output/error streams using pipes on UNIX and Windows. Note that these functions are also available in the os module with slightly different return values.

popen2(cmd [, bufsize [, mode]])

Executes cmd as a subprocess and returns a pair of file objects (child_stdout, child_stdin) corresponding to the input and output streams of the subprocess. bufsize specifies the buffer size for the I/O pipes. mode is one of 't' or 'b' to indicate text or binary data, which is needed on Windows.

popen3(cmd [, bufsize [, mode]])

Executes cmd as a subprocess like popen2(), but returns a triple (child_stdout, child_stdin, child_stderr) that includes the standard error stream.

popen4(cmd [, bufsize [, mode]])

Executes cmd as a subprocess like popen2(), but returns a pair of file objects (child_stdout_stderr, child_stdin) in which the standard output and standard error streams have been combined.

In addition to the functions just described, the UNIX version of this module provides the following classes that can be used to control processes:

Popen3(cmd [, capturestderr [, bufsize]])

This class represents a child process. cmd is the shell command to execute in a subprocess. The capturestderr flag, if true, specifies that the object should capture standard error output of the child process. bufsize is the size of the I/O buffers.

Popen4(cmd [, bufsize])

Like the class Popen3, but combines standard output and standard error.

An instance p of the Popen3 or Popen4 class has the following methods and attributes:

p.poll()

Returns the exit code of the child or -1 if the child process has not finished yet.

p.wait()

Waits for the child process to terminate and returns its exit code.

p.fromchild

A file object that captures the output of the child process.

p.tochild

A file object that sends input to the child process.

p.childerr

A file object that captures the standard error stream of the child process. May be None.

p.pid

Process ID of the child.

Note

- The order of file objects returned by popen2(), popen3(), and popen4() differs from the standard UNIX ordering of *stdin*, *stdout*, and *stderr*. The versions in the os module correct this.

▶ **See Also** commands (155), os.popen (185).

pwd

The pwd module provides access to the UNIX password database.

getpwuid(*uid*)

Returns the password database entry for a numeric user ID *uid*. Returns a 7-tuple (*pw_name*, *pw_passwd*, *pw_uid*, *pw_gid*, *pw_gecos*, *pw_dir*, *pw_shell*). The *pw_uid* and *pw_gid* items are integers; all others are strings. KeyError is raised if the entry cannot be found.

getpwnam(*name*)

Returns the password database entry for a username.

getpwall()

Returns a list of all available password database entries. Each entry is a tuple as returned by getpwuid().

Example

```
>>> import pwd
>>> pwd.getpwnam('beazley')
('beazley', 'x', 100, 1, 'David M. Beazley', '/home/beazley', '/usr/local/bin/tcsh')
>>>
```

▶ **See Also** grp (171), getpass (167), crypt (155).

readline

The readline module enables and provides an interface to the GNU readline library on UNIX. This library extends Python's interactive mode with command history, command completion, and advanced editing capabilities. These features are also extended to functions such as raw_input() and input().

The readline module enables the following key bindings when running interactively:

Key(s)	Description
Ctrl+a	Moves to the start of the line.
Ctrl+b	Moves back one character.
Esc b	Moves back one word.
Esc c	Capitalizes the current word.
Ctrl+d	Deletes the character under the cursor.

Key(s)	Description
Esc d	Kills to the end of the current word.
Del	Deletes the character to the left of the cursor.
Esc Del	Kills to the start of the previous word.
Ctrl+e	Moves to the end of the line.
Ctrl+f	Moves forward one character.
Esc f	Moves forward one word.
Ctrl+k	Kills the text to the end of the line.
Ctrl+l	Clears the screen.
Esc l	Converts the current word to lowercase.
Ctrl+n	Moves down through the history list.
Ctrl+p	Moves up through the history list.
Ctrl+r	Reverses incremental search through the history.
Ctrl+t	Transposes characters.
Esc t	Transposes words.
Esc u	Converts the current word to uppercase.
Ctrl+w	Kills from the cursor to the previous whitespace.
Ctrl+y	Yanks back the most recently killed text.
Esc y	Rotates the kill-ring and yanks the new top.
Esc <	Goes to the first line in history.
Esc >	Goes to the last line in history.

Notes

- Key sequences involving Esc are sometimes available using the Meta key.
- Many commands accept a numeric argument that's entered by first typing Esc *nnn*. For example, typing Esc 5 0 Ctrl+f moves forward 50 characters.
- The readline module is an optional Python feature. If you're installing from source and want to use the readline module, you'll need to enable it by following the directions given in the distribution (these vary by Python version).

   ▶ **See Also** rlcompleter (http://www.python.org/doc/lib/module-rlcompleter.html).

resource

The resource module is used to measure and control the system resources used by a program on UNIX systems. Resource usage is limited using the setrlimit() function. Each resource is controlled by a soft limit and a hard limit. The soft limit is the current limit, and may be lowered or raised by a process over time. The hard limit can be lowered to any value greater than the soft limit, but never raised (except by the superuser).

getrlimit(*resource*)

Returns a tuple (*soft*, *hard*) with the current soft and hard limits of a resource. *resource* is one of the following symbolic constants:

Constant	Description
RLIMIT_CORE	The maximum core file size (in bytes).
RLIMIT_CPU	The maximum CPU time (in seconds). If exceeded, a SIGXCPU signal is sent to the process.
RLIMIT_FSIZE	The maximum file size that can be created.
RLIMIT_DATA	The maximum size (in bytes) of the process heap.
RLIMIT_STACK	The maximum size (in bytes) of the process stack.
RLIMIT_RSS	The maximum resident set size.
RLIMIT_NPROC	The maximum number of processes that can be created.
RLIMIT_NOFILE	The maximum number of open file descriptors.
RLIMIT_OFILE	The BSD name for RLIMIT_NOFILE.
RLIMIT_MEMLOC	The maximum memory size that can be locked in memory.
RLIMIT_VMEM	The largest area of mapped memory that can be used.
RLIMIT_AS	The maximum area (in bytes) of address space that can be used.

setrlimit(*resource*, *limits*)

Sets new limits for a resource. *limits* is a tuple (*soft*, *hard*) of two integers describing the new limits. A value of -1 can be used to specify the maximum possible upper limit.

getrusage(*who*)

This function returns a large tuple that describes the resources consumed by either the current process or its children. *who* is one of the following values:

Value	Description
RUSAGE_SELF	Information about the current process
RUSAGE_CHILDREN	Information about child processes
RUSAGE_BOTH	Information about both current and child processes

The returned tuple contains system resource-usage data in the following order:

Offset	Resource
0	Time in user mode (float)
1	Time in system mode (float)
2	Maximum resident set size (pages)
3	Shared memory size (pages)
4	Unshared memory size (pages)
5	Unshared stack size (pages)
6	Page faults not requiring I/O

Offset	Resource
7	Page faults requiring I/O
8	Number of swapouts
9	Block input operations
10	Block output operations
11	Messages sent
12	Messages received
13	Signals received
14	Voluntary context switches
15	Involuntary context switches

getpagesize()

Returns the number of bytes in a system page.

Exception

error

Exception raised for unexpected failures of the getrlimit() and setrlimit() system calls.

Note

■ Not all resource names are available on all systems.

▶ **See Also** UNIX man pages for getrlimit(2).

shutil

The shutil module is used to perform high-level file operations such as copying, removing, and renaming.

copyfile(src, dst)

Copies the contents of src to dst.

copymode(src, dst)

Copies the permission bits from src to dst.

copystat(src, dst)

Copies the permission bits, last access time, and last modification time from src to dst. The contents, owner, and group of dst are unchanged.

copy(src,dst)

Copies the file src to the file or directory dst, retaining file permissions.

copy2(src, dst)

Like copy(), but also copies the last access and modification times.

copytree(src, dst [, symlinks])

Recursively copies an entire directory tree rooted at src. The destination directory dst will be created (and should not already exist). Individual files are copied using copy2(). If symlinks is true, symbolic links in the source tree are represented as symbolic links in the new tree. If symlinks is false or omitted, the contents of linked files are copied to the new directory tree. Errors are reported to standard output.

Appendix A   The Python Library

```
rmtree(path [, ignore_errors [, onerror]])
```

Deletes an entire directory tree. If `ignore_errors` is true, errors will be ignored. Otherwise, errors are handled by the `onerror` function (if supplied). This function must accept three parameters (`func`, `path`, `excinfo`), where `func` is the function that caused the error (`os.remove()` or `os.rmdir()`), `path` is the pathname passed to the function, and `excinfo` is the exception information returned by `sys.exc_info()`. If an error occurs and `onerror` is omitted, an exception is raised.

Note

- On MacOS, the resource fork is ignored on file copies.

    ▶ **See Also** os.path (193), macostools (176).

signal

The `signal` module is used to write signal handlers in Python. Signals usually correspond to asychronous events that are sent to a program due to the expiration of a timer, arrival of incoming data, or some action performed by a user. The signal interface emulates that of UNIX, although the module is supported on other platforms.

```
alarm(time)
```

If `time` is nonzero, schedules a SIGALRM signal to be sent to the program in `time` seconds. Any previously scheduled alarm is canceled. If `time` is zero, no alarm is scheduled and any previously set alarm is canceled. Returns the number of seconds remaining before any previously scheduled alarm, or zero if no alarm was scheduled. UNIX.

```
getsignal(signalnum)
```

Returns the signal handler for signal `signalnum`. The returned object is a callable Python object. The function may also return SIG_IGN for an ignored signal, SIG_DFL for the default signal handler, or None if the signal handler was not installed from the Python interpreter.

```
pause()
```

Goes to sleep until the next signal is received. UNIX.

```
signal(signalnum, handler)
```

Sets a signal handler for signal `signalnum` to the function `handler`. `handler` must be a callable Python object taking two arguments: the signal number and frame object. SIG_IGN or SIG_DFL can also be given to ignore a signal or use the default signal handler, respectively. The return value is the previous signal handler, SIG_IGN, or SIG_DFL. When threads are enabled, this function can only be called from the main thread. Otherwise, a ValueError exception is raised.

Individual signals are identified using symbolic constants of the form SIG*. These names correspond to integer values that are machine-specific. Typical values are as follows:

Signal Name	Description
SIGABRT	Abnormal termination
SIGALRM	Alarm
SIGBUS	Bus error
SIGCHLD	Change in child status
SIGCLD	Change in child status
SIGCONT	Continue
SIGFPE	Floating-point error
SIGHUP	Hangup
SIGILL	Illegal instruction
SIGINT	Terminal interrupt character
SIGIO	Asynchronous I/O
SIGIOT	Hardware fault
SIGKILL	Terminate
SIGPIPE	Write to pipe, no readers
SIGPOLL	Pollable event
SIGPROF	Profiling alarm
SIGPWR	Power failure
SIGQUIT	Terminal quit character
SIGSEGV	Segmentation fault
SIGSTOP	Stop
SIGTERM	Termination
SIGTRAP	Hardware fault
SIGTSTP	Terminal stop character
SIGTTIN	Control TTY
SIGTTOU	Control TTY
SIGURG	Urgent condition
SIGUSR1	User defined
SIGUSR2	User defined
SIGVTALRM	Virtual time alarm
SIGWINCH	Window size change
SIGXCPU	CPU limit exceeded
SIGXFSZ	File size limit exceeded

In addition, the module defines the following variables:

Variable	Description
SIG_DFL	Signal handler that invokes the default signal handler
SIG_IGN	Signal handler that ignores a signal
NSIG	One more than the highest signal number

Appendix A   The Python Library

Example

The following example illustrates a timeout on establishing a network connection:

```
import signal, socket
def handler(signum, frame):
    print 'Timeout!'
    raise IOError, 'Host not responding.'
sock = socket.socket(socket.AF_INET, socket.SOCK_STREAM)
signal.signal(signal.SIGALRM, handler)
signal.alarm(5)                      # 5-second alarm
sock.connect('www.python.org', 80)   # Connect
signal.alarm(0)                      # Clear alarm
```

Notes

- Signal handlers remain installed until explicitly reset, with the exception of SIGCHLD (whose behavior is implementation-specific).

- It's not possible to temporarily disable signals.

- Signals are only handled between the atomic instructions of the Python interpreter. The delivery of a signal can be delayed by long-running calculations written in C (as might be performed in an extension module).

- If a signal occurs during an I/O operation, the I/O operation may fail with an exception. In this case, the *errno* value is set to *errno*.EINTR to indicate an interrupted system call.

- Certain signals such as SIGSEGV cannot be handled from Python.

- Python installs a small number of signal handlers by default. SIGPIPE is ignored, SIGINT is translated into a KeyboardInterrupt exception, and SIGTERM is caught in order to perform cleanup and invoke sys.exitfunc.

- Extreme care is needed if signals and threads are used in the same program. Currently, only the main thread of execution can set new signal handlers or receive signals.

- Signal handling on Windows and Macintosh is of only limited functionality. The number of supported signals is extremely limited on these platforms.

▶ **See Also** thread (219), errno (156).

stat

The stat module defines constants and functions for interpreting the results of os.stat(), os.fstat() and os.lstat(). These functions return a 10-tuple containing file information. The following variables define the indices within the tuple for certain items:

Variable	Description
ST_MODE	Inode protection mode
ST_INO	Inode number
ST_DEV	Device the inode resides on
ST_NLINK	Number of links to the inode

Variable	Description
ST_UID	User ID of the owner
ST_GID	Group ID of the owner
ST_SIZE	File size in bytes
ST_ATIME	Time of last access
ST_MTIME	Time of last modification
ST_CTIME	Time of last status change

The following functions can be used to test file properties given the mode value returned using os.stat(*path*)[stat.ST_MODE]:

Function	Description
S_ISDIR(*mode*)	Returns nonzero if *mode* is from a directory.
S_ISCHR(*mode*)	Returns nonzero if *mode* is from a character-special device file.
S_ISBLK(*mode*)	Returns nonzero if *mode* is from a block-special device file.
S_ISREG(*mode*)	Returns nonzero if *mode* is from a regular file.
S_ISFIFO(*mode*)	Returns nonzero if *mode* is from a FIFO (named pipe).
S_ISLNK(*mode*)	Returns nonzero if *mode* is from a symbolic link.
S_ISSOCK(*mode*)	Returns nonzero if *mode* is from a socket.
S_IMODE(*mode*)	Returns the portion of the file's mode that can be set by os.chmod(). This is the file's permission bits, sticky bit, set-group-ID, and set-user-ID bits.
S_IFMT(*mode*)	Returns the portion of the file's mode that describes the file type (used by the S_IS*() functions above).

Note

- Much of the functionality in this module is also provided in a more portable form by the os.path module.

▶ **See Also** os (180), os.path (193), statvfs (203).

statvfs

The statvfs module defines constants used to interpret the result of the os.statvfs() function on UNIX. The constants defined in this module define the indices into the tuple returned by os.statvfs() for specific information.

Constant	Description
F_BSIZE	Preferred filesystem block size
F_FRSIZE	Fundamental filesystem block size
F_BLOCKS	Total number of blocks in the filesystem
F_BFREE	Total number of free blocks

continues >>

>> *continued*

Constant	Description
F_BAVAIL	Free blocks available to a non-superuser
F_FILES	Total number of file nodes
F_FFREE	Total number of free file nodes
F_FAVAIL	Free nodes available to a non-superuser
F_FLAG	Flags (system-dependent)
F_NAMEMAX	Maximum filename length

▶ **See Also** os (180), stat (202).

tempfile

The tempfile module is used to generate temporary filenames and files:

```
mktemp([suffix])
```

Returns a unique temporary filename. *suffix* is an optional file suffix to append to the filename. This function only generates a unique filename and doesn't actually create or open a temporary file.

```
gettempprefix()
```

Returns the prefix used to generate temporary files. Does not include the directory in which the file would reside.

```
TemporaryFile([mode [, bufsize [, suffix]]])
```

Creates a temporary file and returns a file-like object that supports the same methods as an ordinary file object. *mode* is the file mode and defaults to 'w+b'. *bufsize* specifies the buffering behavior and has the same meaning as for the open() function. *suffix* is the suffix to append to the filename (if any). The object returned by this function is only a wrapper around a built-in file object that's accessible in the file attribute. The file created by this function is automatically destroyed when the temporary file object is destroyed.

Two global variables are used to construct temporary names. They can be assigned to new values if desired. Their default values are system-dependent.

Variable	Description
tempdir	The directory in which filenames returned by mktemp() reside.
template	The prefix of filenames generated by mktemp(). A string of decimal digits is added to *template* to generate unique filenames.

termios

The termios module provides a POSIX-style interface for controlling the behavior of TTYs and other serial communication devices on UNIX systems. All the functions operate on integer file descriptors such as those returned by the os.open() function or the fileno() method of a file object. In addition, the module relies on a large collection of constants that are defined in the TERMIOS module, which should also be loaded.

tcgetattr(fd)

Returns a list [iflag, oflag, cflag, lflag, ispeed, ospeed, cc] of TTY attributes for a file descriptor fd. The meaning of these fields is as follows:

Field	Description
iflag	Input modes (integer)
oflag	Output modes (integer)
cflag	Control modes (integer)
lflag	Local modes (integer)
ispeed	Input speed (integer)
ospeed	Output speed (integer)
cc	A list of control characters (as strings)

The mode fields iflag, oflag, cflag, and lflag are bit fields that are interpreted using constants in TERMIOS.

Input Modes

Mode	Description
TERMIOS.IGNBRK	Ignore break condition on input.
TERMIOS.BRKINT	Generate SIGINT signal on break if IGNBRK is not set.
TERMIOS.IGNPAR	Ignore framing and parity errors.
TERMIOS.PARMRK	Mark characters with a parity error.
TERMIOS.INPCK	Enable input parity checking.
TERMIOS.ISTRIP	Strip off the eighth bit.
TERMIOS.INLCR	Translate newlines to carriage returns.
TERMIOS.IGNCR	Ignore carriage returns.
TERMIOS.ICRNL	Translate carriage returns to newlines.
TERMIOS.IUCLC	Map uppercase characters to lowercase.
TERMIOS.IXON	Enable XON/XOFF flow control on output.
TERMIOS.IXANY	Enable any character to restart output.
TERMIOS.IXOFF	Enable XON/XOFF flow control on input.
TERMIOS.IXMAXBEL	Ring bell when the input queue is full.

Output Modes

Mode	Description
TERMIOS.OPOST	Implementation-defined output processing.
TERMIOS.OLCUC	Map lowercase to uppercase on output.
TERMIOS.ONLCR	Map newlines to carriage returns.
TERMIOS.OCRNL	Map carriage returns to newlines.
TERMIOS.ONLRET	Don't output carriage returns.
TERMIOS.OFILL	Send fill characters for delay.

continues >>

Appendix A   The Python Library

>> *continued*

Mode	Description
TERMIOS.OFDEL	Set the fill character to ASCII DEL.
TERMIOS.NLDLY	Newline delay mask. Values are NL0 and NL1.
TERMIOS.CRDLY	Carriage return delay mask. Values are CR0, CR1, CR2, or CR3.
TERMIOS.TABDLY	Horizontal tab delay mask: TAB0, TAB1, TAB2, TAB3, or XTABS.
TERMIOS.BSDLY	Backspace delay mask: BS0 or BS1.
TERMIOS.VTDLY	Vertical tab delay mask: VT0 or VT1.
TERMIOS.FFDLY	Formfeed delay mask: FF0 or FF1.

Control Modes

Mode	Description
TERMIOS.CSIZE	Character size mask: CS5, CS6, CS7, or CS8.
TERMIOS.CSTOPB	Set two stop bits.
TERMIOS.CREAD	Enable receiver.
TERMIOS.PARENB	Enable parity generation and checking.
TERMIOS.PARODD	Use odd parity.
TERMIOS.HUPCL	Lower modem control lines when device is closed.
TERMIOS.CLOCAL	Ignore modem control lines.
TERMIOS.CRTSCTS	Flow control.

Local Modes

Mode	Description
TERMIOS.ISIG	Generate corresponding signals when INTR, QUIT, SUSP, or DSUSP characters are received.
TERMIOS.ICANON	Enable canonical mode.
TERMIOS.XCASE	Perform case conversion if ICANON is set.
TERMIOS.ECHO	Echo input characters.
TERMIOS.ECHOE	If ICANON is set, the ERASE character erases the preceding input character. WERASE erases the preceding word.
TERMIOS.ECHOK	If ICANON is set, the KILL character erases the current line.
TERMIOS.ECHONL	If ICANON is set, echo newline (NL) characters.
TERMIOS.ECHOCTL	If ECHO is set, echo control characters as ^X.
TERMIOS.ECHOPRT	Print characters as they're erased.
TERMIOS.ECHOKE	Echo KILL by erasing each character one at a time.
TERMIOS.FLUSHO	Output is being flushed.
TERMIOS.NOFLSH	Disable flushing the input/output queues when generating the SIGINT and SIGQUIT signals.
TERMIOS.TOSTOP	Send the SIGTTOU signal to the process group of a background process that writes to its controlling terminal.
TERMIOS.PENDIN	Reprint all characters in the input queue when the next character is typed.
TERMIOS.IEXTEN	Enable implementation-defined input processing.

Speeds

Speeds are defined by constants such as TERMIOS.B0, TERMIOS.B50, TERMIOS.B75, and TERMIOS.B230400 indicating a baud rate. The available values are implementation-specific and defined in TERMIOS.

Control Characters

The following symbols in TERMIOS are indices into the cc list. This can be used to changed various key bindings.

Character	Description
TERMIOS.VINTR	Interrupt character (typically Ctrl+C)
TERMIOS.VQUIT	Quit
TERMIOS.VERASE	Erase the preceding character (typically Del)
TERMIOS.VWERASE	Erase the preceding word (Ctrl+w)
TERMIOS.VKILL	Delete the entire line
TERMIOS.VREPRINT	Reprint all characters that have not been read yet
TERMIOS.VEOF	End of file (Ctrl+D)
TERMIOS.VNL	Line delimiter (line feed)
TERMIOS.VSUSP	Suspend (Ctrl+Z)
TERMIOS.VSTOP	Stop output (Ctrl+S)
TERMIOS.VSTART	Start output (Ctrl+Q)

tcsetattr(fd, when, attributes)

Sets the TTY attributes for a file descriptor fd. attributes is a list in the same form as returned by tcgetattr(). The when argument determines when the changes take effect:

Argument	Description
TERMIOS.TCSANOW	Changes take place immediately
TERMIOS.TCSADRAIN	After transmitting queued output
TERMIOS.TCSAFLUSH	After transmitting queued output and discarding queued input

tcsendbreak(fd, duration)

Sends a break on file descriptor fd. A duration of zero sends a break for approximately 0.25–0.5 seconds. A nonzero duration is implementation-defined.

tcdrain(fd)

Waits until all output written to file descriptor fd has been transmitted.

tcflush(fd, queue)

Discards queued data on file descriptor fd. queue determines which data to discard:

Queue	Description
TERMIOS.TCIFLUSH	Input queue
TERMIOS.TCOFLUSH	Output queue
TERMIOS.TCIOFLUSH	Both queues

Appendix A   The Python Library

tcflow(*fd*, *action*)

Suspends or resumes input or output on file descriptor *fd*. *action* is one of the following:

Action	Description
TERMIOS.TCOOFF	Suspends output
TERMIOS.TCOON	Restarts output
TERMIOS.TCIOFF	Suspends input
TERMIOS.TCION	Restarts input

Example

The following function prompts for a password with local echoing turned off:

```
def getpass():
    import termios, TERMIOS, sys
    fd = sys.stdin.fileno()
    tc = termios.tcgetattr(fd)
    old = tc[3] & TERMIOS.ECHO
    tc[3] = tc[3] & ~TERMIOS.ECHO          # Disable echo
    try:
        termios.tcsetattr(fd, TERMIOS.TCSADRAIN, tc)
        passwd = raw_input('Password: ')
    finally:
        tc[3] = tc[3] | old                # Restore old echo setting
        termios.tcsetattr(fd, TERMIOS.TCSADRAIN, tc)
    return passwd
```

▶ **See Also** tty (211), getpass (167), signal (200).

time

The time module provides various time-related functions. In Python, time is measured as the number of seconds since the "epoch." The epoch is the beginning of time (the point at which time = 0 seconds). The epoch is January 1, 1970 on UNIX and Windows, and January 1, 1900 on the Macintosh.

The following variables are defined:

accept2dyear

A Boolean value that indicates whether two-digit years are accepted. Normally this is true, but it's set to false if the environment variable $PYTHONY2K is set to a non-empty string. The value can be changed manually as well.

altzone

The timezone used during daylight saving time (DST), if applicable.

daylight

Sets to a nonzero value if a DST timezone has been defined.

timezone

The local (non–DST) timezone.

tzname

A tuple containing the name of the local timezone and the name of the local daylight saving timezone (if defined).

The following functions can be used:

asctime([*tuple*])

Converts a tuple representing a time as returned by gmtime() or localtime() to a string of the form 'Mon Jul 16 14:45:23 2001'. If no arguments are supplied, the current time is used.

clock()

Returns the current CPU time in seconds as a floating-point number.

ctime([*secs*])

Converts a time expressed in seconds since the epoch to a string representing local time. ctime(*secs*) is the same as asctime(localtime(*secs*)). If *secs* is omitted, the current time is used.

gmtime([*secs*])

Converts a time expressed in seconds since the epoch to a time tuple in UTC (Coordinated Universal Time, a.k.a. Greenwich Mean Time). The returned tuple consists of nine integers of the form (*year*, *month*, *day*, *hour*, *minute*, *second*, *weekday*, *day*, *dst*). The following numerical ranges are used for tuple elements:

Element	Value
year	A four-digit value such as 2002
month	1-12
day	1-31
hour	0-23
minute	0-59
second	0-61
weekday	0-6 (0=Monday)
day	1-366
dst	-1, 0, 1

The *dst* field is 1 if daylight saving time is in effect, 0 if not, and -1 if no information is available. If *secs* is omitted, the current time is used.

localtime([*secs*])

Returns a time tuple such as gmtime(), but corresponding to the local timezone. If *secs* is omitted, the current time is used.

mktime(*tuple*)

This function takes a time tuple representing a time in the local timezone (in the same format as returned by localtime()) and returns a floating-point number representing the number of seconds since the epoch. An OverflowError exception is raised if the input value is not a valid time.

Appendix A　The Python Library

sleep(secs)

Puts the current process to sleep for *secs* seconds. *secs* is a floating-point number.

strftime(*format* [, *tuple*])

Converts a tuple representing a time as returned by gmtime() or localtime() to a string. *format* is a format string in which the following format codes can be embedded:

Directive	Meaning
%a	Locale's abbreviated weekday name
%A	Locale's full weekday name
%b	Locale's abbreviated month name
%B	Locale's full month name
%c	Locale's appropriate date and time representation
%d	Day of the month as a decimal number [01-31]
%H	Hour (24–hour clock) as a decimal number [00-23]
%I	Hour (12–hour clock) as a decimal number [01-12]
%j	Day of the year as a decimal number [001-366]
%m	Month as a decimal number [01-12]
%M	Minute as a decimal number [00-59]
%p	Locale's equivalent of either AM or PM
%S	Seconds as a decimal number [00-61]
%U	Week number of the year [00-53] (Sunday as first day)
%w	Weekday as a decimal number [0(Sunday)-6]
%W	Week number of the year (Monday as first day)
%x	Locale's appropriate date representation
%X	Locale's appropriate time representation
%y	Year without century as a decimal number [00-99]
%Y	Year with century as a decimal number
%Z	Timezone name (or empty string if no timezone exists)
%%	The % character

The format codes can include a width and precision in the same manner as used with the % operator on strings. If *tuple* is omitted, the time tuple corresponding to the current time is used.

strptime(*string* [, *format*])

Parses a string representing a time and returns a time tuple of the same form as returned by localtime() or gmtime(). The *format* parameter uses the same specifiers as used by strftime() and defaults to '%a %b %d %H:%M:%S %Y'. This is the same format as produced by the ctime() function. If the string cannot be parsed, a ValueError exception is raised.

time()

Returns the current time as the number of seconds since the epoch in UTC (Coordinated Universal Time).

Notes

- When two-digit years are accepted, they're converted to four-digit years according to the POSIX X/Open standard, where the values 69-99 are mapped to 1969-1999 and the values 0-68 are mapped to 2000-2068.

- The functions in this module are not intended to handle dates and times far in the past or future. In particular, dates before the epoch are illegal, as are dates beyond the maximum time (2^{31} seconds since the epoch on many machines).

- In versions of Python prior to 2.1, the optional arguments to asctime(), ctime(), gmtime(), localtime(), and strftime() were required. If you're concerned with backward compatibility, remember to supply these arguments.

- The range of values for *secs* is 0 to 61 in order to account for leap seconds.

▶ **See Also** locale (172).

tty

The tty module provides functions for putting a TTY into cbreak and raw modes on UNIX systems. Raw mode forces a process to receive every character on a TTY with no interpretation by the system. Cbreak mode enables system processing for special keys such as the interrupt and quit keys (which generate signals).

setraw(fd [, when])

Changes the mode of the file descriptor *fd* to raw mode. *when* specifies when the change occurs and is TERMIOS.TCSANOW, TERMIOS.TCSADRAIN, or TERMIOS.TCSAFLUSH (the default).

setcbreak(fd [, when])

Changes the mode of file descriptor *fd* to cbreak mode. *when* has the same meaning as in setraw().

Note

- Requires the termios module.

▶ **See Also** termios (204).

_winreg

The _winreg module provides a low-level interface to the Windows Registry. The Registry is a large hierarchical tree in which each node is called a *key*. The children of a particular key are known as *subkeys* and may contain additional subkeys or values. For example, the setting of the Python sys.path variable is typically contained in the Registry as follows:

\HKEY_LOCAL_MACHINE\Software\Python\PythonCore\2.0\PythonPath

In this case, Software is a subkey of HKEY_LOCAL_MACHINE, Python is a subkey of Software, and so forth. The value of the PythonPath key contains the actual path setting.

Keys are accessed through open and close operations. Open keys are represented by special handles (which are wrappers around the integer handle identifiers normally used by Windows).

Appendix A   The Python Library

`CloseKey(key)`

Closes a previously opened registry key with handle *key*.

`ConnectRegistry(computer_name, key)`

Returns a handle to a predefined registry key on another computer. *computer_name* is the name of the remote machine as a string of the form `\\computername`. If *computer_name* is None, the local registry is used. *key* is a predefined handle such as HKEY_CURRENT_USER or HKEY_USERS. Raises EnvironmentError on failure.

`CreateKey(key, sub_key)`

Creates or opens a key and returns a handle. *key* is a previously opened key or a predefined key defined by the HKEY_* constants. *sub_key* is the name of the key that will be opened or created. If *key* is a predefined key, *sub_key* may be None, in which case *key* is returned.

`DeleteKey(key, sub_key)`

Deletes *sub_key*. *key* is an open key or one of the predefined HKEY_* constants. *sub_key* is a string that identifies the key to delete. *sub_key* must not have any sub-keys or EnvironmentError is raised.

`DeleteValue(key, value)`

Deletes a named value from a registry key. *key* is an open key or one of the predefined HKEY_* constants. *value* is a string containing the name of the value to remove.

`EnumKey(key, index)`

Returns the name of a subkey by index. *key* is an open key or one of the predefined HKEY_* constants. *index* is an integer that specifies the key to retrieve. If *index* is out of range, an EnvironmentError is raised.

`EnumValue(key, index)`

Returns a value of an open key. *key* is an open key or a predefined HKEY_* constant. *index* is an integer specifying the value to retrieve. The function returns a tuple (*name*, *data*, *type*) in which *name* is the value name, *data* is an object holding the value data, and *type* is an integer that specifies the type of the value data. The following type codes are currently defined:

Code	Description
REG_BINARY	Binary data
REG_DWORD	32-bit number
REG_DWORD_LITTLE_ENDIAN	32-bit little-endian number
REG_DWORD_BIG_ENDIAN	32-bit number in big-endian format
REG_EXPAND_SZ	Null-terminated string with unexpanded references to environment variables
REG_LINK	Unicode symbolic link
REG_MULTI_SZ	Sequence of null-terminated strings
REG_NONE	No defined value type
REG_RESOURCE_LIST	Device driver resource list
REG_SZ	Null-terminated string

FlushKey(*key*)

Writes the attributes of *key* to the Registry, forcing changes to disk. This function should only be called if an application requires absolute certainty that Registry data is stored on disk. Does not return until data is written. It is not necessary to use this function under normal circumstances.

RegLoadKey(*key*, *sub_key*, *filename*)

Creates a subkey and stores registration information from a file into it. *key* is an open key or a predefined HKEY_* constant. *sub_key* is a string identifying the subkey to load. *filename* is the name of the file from which to load data. The contents of this file must be created with the SaveKey() function and the calling process must have the SE_RESTORE_PRIVILEGE for this to work. If *key* was returned by ConnectRegistry(), filename should be a path that's relative to the remote computer.

OpenKey(*key*, *sub_key*[, *res* [, *sam*]])

Opens a key. *key* is an open key or an HKEY_* constant. *sub_key* is a string identifying the subkey to open. *res* is a reserved integer that must be zero (the default). *sam* is an integer defining the security access mask for the key. The default is KEY_READ. Other possible values for *sam*:

- KEY_ALL_ACCESS
- KEY_CREATE_LINK
- KEY_CREATE_SUB_KEY
- KEY_ENUMERATE_SUB_KEYS
- KEY_EXECUTE
- KEY_NOTIFY
- KEY_QUERY_VALUE
- KEY_READ
- KEY_SET_VALUE
- KEY_WRITE

OpenKeyEx()

Same as OpenKey().

QueryInfoKey(*key*)

Returns information about a key as a tuple (*num_subkeys*, *num_values*, *last_modified*) in which *num_subkeys* is the number of subkeys, *num_values* is the number of values, and *last_modified* is a long integer containing the time of last modification. Time is measured from January 1, 1601, in units of 100 nanoseconds.

QueryValue(*key*,*sub_key*)

Returns the unnamed value for a key as a string. *key* is an open key or an HKEY_* constant. *sub_key* is the name of the subkey to use, if any. If omitted, the function returns the value associated with *key* instead. This function returns the data for the first value with a null name. However, the type is returned (use QueryValueEx instead).

QueryValueEx(*key*, *value_name*)

Returns a tuple (*value*, *type*) containing the data and type for a key. *key* is an open key or HKEY_* constant. *value_name* is the name of the value to return. The returned type is one of the integer codes as described for the EnumValue() function.

SaveKey(*key*, *filename*)

Saves *key* and all of its subkeys to a file. *key* is an open key or a predefined HKEY_* constant. *filename* must not already exist and should not include a filename extension. Furthermore, the caller must have backup privileges for the operation to succeed.

SetValue(*key*, *sub_key*, *type*, *value*)

Sets the value of a key. *key* is an open key or HKEY_* constant. *sub_key* is the name of the subkey with which to associate the value. *type* is an integer type code, currently limited to REG_SZ. *value* is a string containing the value data. If *sub_key* does not exist, it is created. *key* must have been opened with KEY_SET_VALUE access for this function to succeed.

SetValueEx(*key*, *value_name*, *reserved*, *type*, *value*)

Sets the value field of a key. *key* is an open key or an HKEY_* constant. *value_name* is the name of the value. *type* is an integer type code as described for the EnumValue() function. *value* is a string containing the new value. When setting the values of numeric types (for example, REG_DWORD), *value* is still a string containing the raw data. This string can be created using the struct module. *reserved* is currently ignored and can be set to anything (the value is not used).

zipfile

The zipfile module is used to manipulate files encoded in the popular ZIP format. The following functions are available:

is_zipfile(*filename*)

Tests *filename* to see whether it's a valid ZIP file. Returns 1 if *filename* is a ZIP file, None otherwise.

ZipFile(*filename* [, *mode* [, *compression*]])

Opens a ZIP file *filename* and returns a ZipFile instance. *mode* is 'r' to read from an existing file, 'w' to truncate the file and write a new file, or 'a' to append to an existing file. For 'a' mode, if *filename* is an existing ZIP file, new files are added to it. If *filename* is not a ZIP file, the archive is simply appended to the end of the file. *compression* is the ZIP compression method used when writing to the archive and is one of ZIP_STORED or ZIP_DEFLATED. The default is ZIP_STORED.

PyZipFile(*filename* [, *mode*[, *compression*]])

Opens a ZIP file like ZipFile(), but returns a special PyZipFile instance with one extra method writepy() that's used to add Python source files to the archive.

ZipInfo([*filename* [, *date_time*]])

Manually creates a new ZipInfo instance, used to contain information about an archive member. Normally, it's not necessary to call this function except when using the z.writestr() method of a ZipFile instance (described below).

An instance z of ZipFile or PyZipFile supports the following methods and attributes:

z.close()

Closes the archive file. This must be called in order to flush records to the ZIP file before program termination.

`z.getinfo(`*name*`)`

Returns information about the archive member name as a `ZipInfo` instance (described below).

`z.infolist()`

Returns a list of `ZipInfo` objects for all the members of the archive.

`z.namelist()`

Returns a list of the archive member names.

`z.printdir()`

Prints the archive directory to `sys.stdout`.

`z.read(`*name*`)`

Reads archive contents for member *name* and returns the data as a string.

`z.testzip()`

Reads all the files in the archive and verifies their CRC checksums. Returns the name of the first corrupted file or `None` if all files are intact.

`z.write(`*filename*`[, `*arcname*`[, `*compress_type*`]])`

Writes *filename* to the archive with archive name *arcname*. *compress_type* is the compression parameter and is one of `ZIP_STORED` or `ZIP_DEFLATED`. By default, the compression parameter given to the `ZipFile()` or `PyZipFile()` function is used. The archive must be open in `'w'` or `'a'` mode for writes to work.

`z.writepy(`*pathname*`[, `*basename*`])`

This method, available only with `PyZipFile` instances, is used to write Python source files (`*.py` files) to a ZIP archive and can be used to easily package Python applications for distribution. If *pathname* is a file, it must end with `.py`. In this case, one of the corresponding `.pyo`, `.pyc`, or `.py` files will be added (in that order). If *pathname* is a directory and the directory is not a Python package directory, all of the corresponding `.pyo`, `.pyc`, or `.py` files are added at the top level. If the directory is a package, the files are added under the package name as a file path. If any subdirectories are also package directories, they are added recursively. *basename* is used internally and is not normally specified.

`z.writestr(`*zinfo*`, `*bytes*`)`

Writes a string of bytes to the archive. Information about the bytes is contained in the `ZipInfo` instance *zinfo*, which must minimally contain a filename, date, and time. The `ZipInfo()` function can be used to create a `ZipInfo` instance.

`z.debug`

Debugging level in the range of `0` (no output) to `3` (most output).

`ZipInfo` instances returned by the `ZipInfo()`, `z.getinfo()`, and `z.infolist()` functions have the following attributes:

zinfo`.filename`

Archive member name.

zinfo`.date_time`

Tuple `(`*year*`,`*month*`,`*day*`,`*hours*`,`*minutes*`,`*seconds*`)` containing the last modification time. *month* and *day* are numbers in the range 1-12 and 1-31, respectively. All other values start at `0`.

`zinfo.compress_type`

Compression type for the archive member. Only `ZIP_STORED` and `ZIP_DEFLATED` are currently supported by this module.

`zinfo.comment`

Archive member comment.

`zinfo.extra`

Expansion field data, used to contain additional file attributes. The data stored here depends on the system that created the file.

`zinfo.create_system`

Integer code describing the system that created the archive. Common values include those in the following table:

Value	Description
0	MS-DOS (FAT/VFAT/FAT32 filesystems)
3	UNIX
7	Macintosh
10	Windows NTFS

`zinfo.create_version`

Integer PKZIP version code that created the ZIP archive.

`zinfo.extract_version`

Minimum PKZIP version needed to extract the archive.

`zinfo.reserved`

Reserved field. Currently set to 0.

`zinfo.flag_bits`

ZIP flag bits that describe the encoding of the data, including encryption and compression.

`zinfo.volume`

Volume number of the file header.

`zinfo.internal_attr`

Describes the internal structure of the archive contents. If the low-order bit is 1, the data is ASCII text. Otherwise, binary data is assumed.

`zinfo.external_attr`

External file attributes. Operating system dependent.

`zinfo.header_offset`

Byte offset to the file header.

`zinfo.file_offset`

Byte offset to the start of the file data.

`zinfo.CRC`

CRC-32 checksum of the uncompressed file.

`zinfo.compress_size`

Size of the compressed file data.

zinfo.file_size

Size of the uncompressed file.

Notes

- This module requires the use of the zlib module.

- Detailed documentation about the internal structure of ZIP files can be found as a PKZIP Application Note at http://www.pkware.com/appnote.html.

zlib

The zlib module supports data compression by providing access to the zlib library.

adler32(*string* [, *value*])

Computes the Adler-32 checksum of *string*. *value* is used as the starting value (which can be used to compute a checksum over the concatenation of several strings). Otherwise, a fixed default value is used.

compress(*string* [, *level*])

Compresses the data in *string*, where *level* is an integer from 1 to 9 controlling the level of compression. 1 is the least (fastest) compression and 9 is the best (slowest) compression. The default value is 6. Returns a string containing the compressed data or raises error if an error occurs.

compressobj([*level*])

Returns a compression object. *level* has the same meaning as in the compress() function.

crc32(*string* [, *value*])

Computes a CRC checksum of *string*. If *value* is present, it's used as the starting value of the checksum. Otherwise, a fixed value is used.

decompress(*string* [, *wbits* [, *buffsize*]])

Decompresses the data in *string*. *wbits* controls the size of the window buffer and *buffsize* is the initial size of the output buffer. Raises error if an error occurs.

decompressobj([*wbits*])

Returns a compression object. The *wbits* parameter controls the size of the window buffer.

A compression object *c* has the following methods:

c.compress(*string*)

Compresses *string*. Returns a string containing compressed data for at least part of the data in *string*. This data should be concatenated to the output produced by earlier calls to *c*.compress() to create the output stream. Some input data may be stored in internal buffers for later processing.

c.flush([*mode*])

Compresses all pending input and returns a string containing the remaining compressed output. *mode* is Z_SYNC_FLUSH, Z_FULL_FLUSH, or Z_FINISH (the default). Z_SYNC_FLUSH and Z_FULL_FLUSH allow further compression and are used to allow partial error recovery on decompression. Z_FINISH terminates the compression stream.

A decompression object *d* has the following methods:

`d.decompress(string)`

Decompresses *string* and returns a string containing uncompressed data for at least part of the data in *string*. This data should be concatenated with data produced by earlier calls to `decompress()` to form the output stream. Some input data may be stored in internal buffers for later processing.

`d.flush()`

All pending input is processed, and a string containing the remaining uncompressed output is returned. The decompression object cannot be used again after this call.

Exception

`error`

Exception raised on compression and decompression errors.

Note

- The zlib library is available at `http://www.cdrom.com/pub/infozip/zlib`.

▶ **See Also** `gzip` (171).

Threads

This section describes modules that can be used to develop multithreaded applications. First, a little terminology and background.

Thread Basics

A running program is called a *process*. Associated with each process is a system state including memory, lists of open files, a program counter that keeps track of the instruction being executed, and a call stack used to hold the local variables of functions. Normally, a process executes statements in a single sequence of control flow. This sequence is sometimes called a *thread* (or *main thread*).

When a program creates new processes by using the `os.system()`, `os.fork()`, `os.spawnv()`, and similar system calls, these processes run as independent programs, each with its own set of system resources and main thread of execution. However, it's also possible for a program to create additional threads of execution that exist inside the calling process and share data and system resources with the original thread of execution. Threads are particularly useful when an application wants to perform tasks concurrently without spawning child processes, or when subtasks need to read and write shared data.

A multithreaded program executes by dividing its processing time between all active threads. For example, a program with 10 active threads of execution would allocate approximately 1/10 of its CPU time to each thread and cycle between threads in rapid succession.

Since threads share the same data, an extreme degree of caution is required whenever shared data structures are updated by one of the threads. In particular, attempts to update a data structure by multiple threads at approximately the same time can lead to a corrupted and inconsistent program state (a problem formally known as a *race condition*). To fix these problems, threaded programs need to lock critical sections of code by using mutual-exclusion locks and other similar synchronization primitives.

More information regarding the theory and implementation of threads and locks can be found in most operating system textbooks.

Python Threads

Python supports threads on Windows, Solaris, and systems that support the POSIX threads library (pthreads). However, threads are often disabled by default, so it may be necessary to rebuild the interpreter with thread support before using any of the modules in this section. (Beginning with Python 2.1, thread support is enabled by default.)

The scheduling of threads and thread switching is tightly controlled by a global interpreter lock that allows only a single thread of execution to be running in the interpreter at once. Furthermore, thread switching can only occur between the execution of individual bytecodes in the interpreter. The frequency with which the interpreter checks for thread switching is set by the sys.setcheckinterval() function. By default, the interpreter checks for thread switching after every 10 bytecode instructions.

When working with extension modules, the interpreter may invoke functions written in C. Unless specifically written to interact with a threaded Python interpreter, these functions block the execution of all other threads until they complete execution. Thus, a long-running calculation in an extension module may limit the effectiveness of using threads. However, most of the I/O functions in the standard library have been written to work in a threaded environment.

Finally, programmers need to be aware that threads can interact strangely with signals and interrupts. For instance, the KeyboardInterrupt exception can be received by an arbitrary thread, while signals used in conjunction with the signal module are only received by the main thread.

thread

The thread module provides low-level functions for working with threads. This module is available only on UNIX and Windows.

allocate_lock()

Creates a new lock object of type LockType. Locks are initially unlocked.

exit()

Raises the SystemExit exception. Forces a thread to exit.

get_ident()

Returns the integer "thread identifier" of the current thread.

```
start_new_thread(func, args [, kwargs])
```

Executes the function *func* in a new thread. *func* is called using apply(*func*, *args*, *kwargs*). On success, control is immediately returned to the caller. When the function *func* returns, the thread exits silently. If the function terminates with an unhandled exception, a stack trace is printed and the thread exits (other threads continue to run, however).

A lock object *lck* returned by allocate_lock() has the following methods:

```
lck.acquire([waitflag])
```

Acquires the lock, waiting until the lock is released by another thread if necessary. If *waitflag* is omitted, the function returns None when the lock is acquired. If *waitflag* is set to 0, the lock is acquired only if it can be acquired immediately without waiting. If *waitflag* is nonzero, the method blocks until the lock is released. When *waitflag* is supplied, the function returns 1 if the lock was acquired successfully, 0 if not.

```
lck.release()
```

Releases the lock.

```
lck.locked()
```

Returns the lock status: 1 if locked, 0 if not.

Example

The following example shows a simple thread that prints the current time every five seconds:

```
import thread
import time
def print_time(delay):
    while 1:
        time.sleep(delay)
        print time.ctime(time.time())

# Start the new thread
thread.start_new_thread(print_time,(5,))
# Now go do something else while the thread runs
while 1:
        pass
```

Exception

```
error
```

Exception raised on thread-specific errors.

Notes

- Calling sys.exit() or raising the SystemExit exception is equivalent to calling thread.exit().
- The acquire() method on a lock cannot be interrupted.
- When the main thread exits, whether the other threads survive depends on the system. On most systems, they're killed immediately without executing

any cleanup. Furthermore, the cleanup actions of the main thread are somewhat limited. In particular, standard I/O files are not flushed, nor are object
destructors invoked.

▶ **See Also** threading (221).

threading

The threading module provides high-level thread support with a Thread class and
classes for various synchronization primitives. It's built using the lower-level thread
module.

The following utility functions are available:

activeCount()

Returns the number of currently active Thread objects.

currentThread()

Returns the Thread object corresponding to the caller's thread of control.

enumerate()

Returns a list of all currently active Thread objects.

Thread Objects

The Thread class is used to represent a separate thread of control. A new thread can
be created as follows:

Thread(*group*=None, *target*=None, *name*=None, *args*=(), *kwargs*={})

Creates a new Thread instance. *group* is None and is reserved for future extensions.
target is a callable object invoked by the run() method when the thread starts. By
default, it's None, meaning that nothing is called. *name* is the thread name. By
default, a unique name of the form "Thread-*N*" is created. *args* is a tuple of arguments that are passed to the *target* function. *kwargs* is a dictionary of keyword
arguments that are passed to *target*.

A Thread object *t* supports the following methods:

t.start()

Starts the thread by invoking the run() method in a separate thread of control.
This method can be invoked only once.

t.run()

This method is called when the thread starts. By default, it calls the target function passed in the constructor. This method can also be redefined in subclasses of
Thread.

t.join([*timeout*])

Waits until the thread terminates or a timeout occurs. *timeout* is a floating-point
number specifying a timeout in seconds. A thread cannot join itself, and it's an
error to join a thread before it has been started.

t.getName()

Returns the thread name.

t.setName(*name*)

Sets the thread name.

t.isAlive()

Returns 1 if the thread is alive, 0 otherwise. A thread is alive from the moment the start() method returns until its run() method terminates.

t.isDaemon()

Returns the thread's daemon flag.

t.setDaemon(*daemonic*)

Sets the thread's daemon flag to the Boolean value *daemonic*. This must be called before start() is called. The initial value is inherited from the creating thread. The entire Python program exits when no active non-daemon threads are left.

A thread can be flagged as a "daemon thread" using the setDaemon() method. If only daemon threads remain, a program will exit. All programs have a main thread that represents the initial thread of control. It's not a daemon thread.

In some cases, dummy thread objects are created. These are threads of control started outside the threading module such as from a C extension module. Dummy threads are always considered alive, active, and daemonic, and cannot be joined. Furthermore, they're never deleted, so it's impossible to detect the termination of such threads.

As an alternative to explicitly creating a Thread object, the Thread class can also be subclassed. If this approach is used, the run() method can be overridden to perform the activity of the thread. The constructor can also be overridden, but it's very important to invoke the base class constructor Thread.__init__() in this case. It's an error to override any other methods of the Thread class.

Lock Objects

A *primitive lock* (or *mutual exclusion lock*) is a synchronization primitive that's in either a "locked" or "unlocked" state. Two methods, acquire() and release(), are used to change the state of the lock. If the state is locked, attempts to acquire the lock are blocked until the lock is released. If more than one thread is waiting to acquire the lock, only one is allowed to proceed when the lock is released. The order in which waiting threads proceed is undefined.

A new Lock instance is created using the following constructor:

Lock()

Creates a new lock object, initially unlocked.

A Lock object *lck* supports the following methods:

lck.acquire([*blocking* = 1])

Acquires the lock, blocking until the lock is released if necessary. If *blocking* is supplied and set to zero, the function returns immediately with a value of 0 if the lock could not be acquired, or 1 if locking was successful.

lck.release()

Releases a lock. It's an error to call this method when the lock is in an unlocked state.

RLock

A *reentrant lock* is a synchronization primitive that's similar to a Lock, but that can be acquired multiple times by the same thread. This allows the thread owning the lock to perform nested acquire() and release() operations. In this case, only the outermost release() operation resets the lock to its unlocked state.

A new RLock object is created using the following constructor:

> RLock()

Creates a new reentrant lock object.

An RLock object *rlck* supports the following methods:

> *rlck*.acquire([*blocking* = 1])

Acquires the lock, blocking until the lock is released if necessary. If no thread owns the lock, it's locked and the recursion level is set to 1. If this thread already owns the lock, the recursion level of the lock is increased by one and the function returns immediately.

> *rlck*.release()

Releases a lock by decrementing its recursion level. If the recursion level is zero after the decrement, the lock is reset to the unlocked state. Otherwise, the lock remains locked. This function should only be called by the thread that currently owns the lock.

Condition Variables

A *condition variable* is a synchronization primitive, built on top of another lock, that's used when a thread is interested in a particular change of state or event to occur. A typical use is a producer–consumer problem where one thread is producing data to be consumed by another thread. A new Condition instance is created using the following constructor:

> Condition([*lock*])

Creates a new condition variable. *lock* is an optional Lock or RLock instance. If not supplied, a new RLock instance is created for use with the condition variable.

A condition variable *cv* supports the following methods:

> *cv*.acquire(**args*)

Acquires the underlying lock. This method calls the corresponding acquire(**args*) method on the underlying lock and returns its return value.

> *cv*.release()

Releases the underlying lock. This method calls the corresponding release() method on the underlying lock.

> *cv*.wait([*timeout*])

Waits until notified or until a timeout occurs. This method is called after the calling thread has already acquired the lock. When called, the underlying lock is released, and the thread goes to sleep until it's awakened by a notify() or notifyAll() call performed on the condition variable by another thread. Once awakened, the thread reacquires the lock and the method returns. *timeout* is a floating-point number in seconds. If this time expires, the thread is awakened, the lock reacquired, and control returned.

```
cv.notify([n])
```

Wakes up one or more threads waiting on this condition variable. This method is called only after the calling thread has acquired the lock, and does nothing if no threads are waiting. n specifies the number of threads to awaken and defaults to 1. Awakened threads don't return from the wait() call until they can reacquire the lock.

```
cv.notifyAll()
```

Wakes up all threads waiting on this condition.

Examples

The following examples show a producer-consumer problem using condition variables:

```
# Consume one item
def consumer():
    cv.acquire()
    while not item_is_available():
        cv.wait()       # Wait for item
    cv.release()
    consume_item()      # Consume the item

# Produce one item
def produce():
    produce_item()      # Produce the item
    cv.acquire()
    make_item_available()
    cv.notify()         # Notify the consumer
    cv.release()
```

Semaphore

A *semaphore* is a synchronization primitive based on a counter that's decremented by each acquire() call and incremented by each release() call. If the counter ever reaches zero, the acquire() method blocks until some other thread calls release().

```
Semaphore([value])
```

Creates a new semaphore. value is the initial value for the counter. If omitted, the counter is set to a value of 1.

A Semaphore instance s supports the following methods:

```
s.acquire([blocking])
```

Acquires the semaphore. If the internal counter is larger than zero on entry, decrements it by one and returns immediately. If it's zero, blocks until another thread calls release(). The blocking argument has the same behavior as described for Lock and RLock objects.

```
s.release()
```

Releases a semaphore by incrementing the internal counter by one. If the counter is zero and another thread is waiting, that thread is awakened. If multiple threads are waiting, only one will be returned from its acquire() call. The order in which threads are released is not deterministic.

Events

Events are used to communicate between threads. One thread signals an "event" and one or more other threads wait for it. An Event instance manages an internal flag that can be set to true with the set() method and reset to false with the clear() method. The wait() method blocks until the flag is true.

Event()

Creates a new Event instance with the internal flag set to false.

An Event instance *e* supports the following methods:

e.isSet()

Returns true only if the internal flag is true.

e.set()

Sets the internal flag to true. All threads waiting for it to become true are awakened.

e.clear()

Resets the internal flag to false.

e.wait([*timeout*])

Blocks until the internal flag is true. If the internal flag is true on entry, returns immediately. Otherwise, blocks until another thread calls set() to set the flag to true, or until the optional timeout occurs. *timeout* is a floating-point number specifying a timeout period in seconds.

Example

The following example illustrates the use of the threading module by fetching a collection of URLs in separate threads. In this example, threads are defined by subclassing the Thread class.

```
import threading
import urllib
class FetchUrlThread(threading.Thread):
    def __init__(self, url,filename):
        threading.Thread.__init__(self)
        self.url = url
        self.filename = filename
    def run(self):
        print self.getName(), 'Fetching ', self.url
        urllib.urlretrieve(self.url,self.filename)
        print self.getName(), 'Saved in ', self.filename
urls = [ ('http://www.python.org','/tmp/index.html'),
         ('ftp://ftp.python.org/pub/python/2.1/Python-2.1.tgz', '/tmp/py21.tgz'),
         ('http://www.petaflop.org/p.png','/tmp/p.png'),
         ('http://www.pud.com','/tmp/pud.html')
       ]

# Go fetch a bunch of URLs in separate threads
for url,file in urls:
    t = FetchUrlThread(url,file)
    t.start()
```

▶ **See Also** thread (219), Queue (226).

Queue

The Queue module implements a multi-producer, multi-consumer FIFO queue that can be used to safely exchange information between multiple threads of execution. It's available only if thread support has been enabled.

The Queue module defines the following class:

Queue(*maxsize*)

Creates a new queue in which *maxsize* is the maximum number of items that can be placed in the queue. If *maxsize* is less than or equal to zero, the queue size is infinite.

A Queue object *q* has the following methods:

q.qsize()

Returns the approximate size of the queue. Because other threads may be updating the queue, this number is not entirely reliable.

q.empty()

Returns 1 if the queue is empty, 0 otherwise.

q.full()

Returns 1 if the queue is full, 0 otherwise.

q.put(*item* [, *block*])

Puts *item* into the queue. If optional argument *block* is 1 (the default), the caller blocks until a free slot is available. Otherwise (*block* is 0), the Full exception is raised if the queue is full.

q.put_nowait(*item*)

Equivalent to q.put(*item*, 0).

q.get([*block*])

Removes and returns an item from the queue. If optional argument *block* is 1 (the default), the caller blocks until an item is available. Otherwise (*block* is 0), the Empty exception is raised if the queue is empty.

q.get_nowait()

Equivalent to q.get(0).

Exceptions

Empty

Exception raised when nonblocking get() or get_nowait() is called on a Queue object that's empty or locked.

Full

Exception raised when nonblocking put() or put_nowait() is called on a Queue object that's full or locked.

▶ **See Also** thread (219), threading (221).

Network Programming

This section describes the modules used to implement network servers and clients. Python provides extensive network support ranging from access to low-level network interfaces to high-level clients and frameworks for writing network applications. Before beginning, a very brief (and admittedly terse) introduction to network programming is presented. Readers are advised to consult a book such as *UNIX Network Programming, Volume 1: Networking APIs - Sockets and XTI* by W. Richard Stevens (Prentice Hall, 1997, ISBN 0-13-490012-X) for many of the advanced details.

Python's network programming modules primarily support two Internet protocols: TCP and UDP. The TCP protocol is a reliable connection-oriented protocol used to establish a two-way communications stream between machines. UDP is a lower-level packet-based protocol (connectionless) in which machines send and receive discrete packets of information without formally establishing a connection. Unlike TCP, UDP communication is unreliable and thus inherently more complicated to manage in applications that require reliable communications. Consequently, most Internet protocols utilize TCP connections.

Both network protocols are handled through a programming abstraction known as a *socket*. A socket is an object similar to a file that allows a program to accept incoming connections, make outgoing connections, and send and receive data. Before two machines can establish a connection, both must create a socket object.

Furthermore, the machine receiving the connection (the server) must bind its socket object to a *port*. A port is a 16-bit number in the range 0–65535 that's managed by the operating system and used by clients to uniquely identify servers. Ports 0–1023 are reserved by the system and used by common network protocols. The following table shows the port assignments for a number of common protocols:

Service	Port Number
FTP-Data	20
FTP-Control	21
Telnet	23
SMTP (Mail)	25
Finger	79
HTTP (WWW)	80
NNTP (News)	119
HTTPS (Secure WWW)	443

The process of establishing a TCP connection involves a precise sequence of steps on both the server and client, as shown in Figure A.1.

For TCP servers, the socket object used to receive connections is not the same socket used to perform subsequent communication with the client. In particular, the accept() system call returns a new socket object that's actually used for the connection. This allows a server to manage connections from a large number of clients simultaneously.

UDP communication is performed in a similar manner except that clients and servers don't establish a "connection" with each other, as shown in Figure A.2.

Appendix A   The Python Library

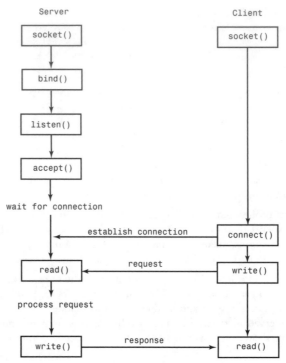

Figure A.1   *TCP connection protocol.*

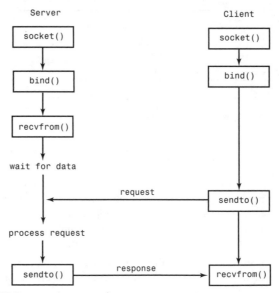

Figure A.2   *UDP connection protocol.*

The following example illustrates the TCP protocol with a client and server written using the socket module. In this case, the server simply returns the current time to the client as a string.

```
# Time server program
from socket import *
import time

s = socket(AF_INET, SOCK_STREAM)        # Create a TCP socket
s.bind(('',8888))                       # Bind to port 8888
s.listen(5)                             # Listen, but allow no more than
                                        # 5 pending connections.
while 1:
    client,addr = s.accept()    # Get a connection
    print 'Got a connection from ',addr
    client.send(time.ctime(time.time()))   # Send back to client
    client.close()
```

Here's the client program:

```
# Time client program
from socket import *
s = socket(AF_INET,SOCK_STREAM)         # Create a TCP socket
s.connect(('foo.bar.com', 8888))        # Connect to the server
tm = s.recv(1024)                       # Receive no more than 1024 bytes
s.close()
print 'The time is ', tm
```

The remainder of this section describes modules of two different flavors. First are modules and frameworks related to socket programming. Second are a variety of modules that implement the client-side interface to common Internet protocols. With the exception of HTTP, the details of these protocols are not presented. However, details can be found in the online documentation and in relevant Internet Request for Comments (RFCs) available at http://www.ietf.org. Where applicable, RFC numbers and sources for additional information are stated.

asyncore

The asyncore module is used to build network applications in which network activity is handled asynchronously as a series of events dispatched by an event loop, built using the select() system call. Such an approach is useful in network programs that want to provide concurrency, but without the use of threads or processes. This method can also provide the best performance for short transactions. All the functionality of this module is provided by the dispatcher class, which is a thin wrapper around an ordinary socket object.

　　dispatcher([sock])

Base class defining an event-driven nonblocking socket object. sock is an existing socket object. If omitted, a socket must be created using the create_socket() method (described shortly). Once created, network events are handled by special handler methods (described later). In addition, all open dispatcher objects are saved in an internal list that's used by a number of polling functions.

Appendix A　The Python Library

The following methods of the dispatcher class are called to handle network events. They should be defined in classes derived from dispatcher.

d.handle_read()

Called when new data is available to be read from a socket.

d.handle_write()

Called when an attempt to write data is made.

d.handle_expt()

Called when out-of-band (OOB) data for a socket is received.

d.handle_connect()

Called when a connection is made.

d.handle_close()

Called when the socket is closed.

d.handle_accept()

Called on listening sockets when a new connection arrives.

d.readable()

This function is used by the select() loop to see whether the object is willing to read data. Returns 1 if so, 0 if not. This method is called to see if the handle_read() method should be called with new data.

d.writable()

Called by the select() loop to see whether the object wants to write data. Returns 1 if so, 0 otherwise. This method is always called to see whether the handle_write() method should be called to produce output.

In addition to the preceding methods, the following methods are used to perform low-level socket operations. They're similar to those available on a socket object.

d.create_socket(*family*, *type*)

Creates a new socket. Arguments are the same as for socket.socket().

d.connect(*address*)

Makes a connection. *address* is a tuple (*host*, *port*).

d.send(*data*)

Sends *data*.

d.recv(*size*)

Receives at most *size* bytes.

d.listen([*backlog*])

Listens for incoming connections.

d.bind(*address*)

Binds the socket to *address*. *address* is typically a tuple (*host*, *port*).

d.accept()

Accepts a connection. Returns a pair (*client*, *addr*) where *client* is a socket object used to send and receive data on the connection and *addr* is the address of the client.

d.close()

Closes the socket.

The following functions are used to handle events:

poll([*timeout* [, *ignore_exception*]])

Polls all the open dispatcher objects for network events using select() and calls the appropriate handler functions if necessary. *timeout* is an optional timeout, 0.0 by default. *ignore_exception*, if set, causes all exceptions generated in event handlers to be ignored (the default).

loop([*timeout*])

Polls for events indefinitely. Does nothing but repeatedly call poll(). *timeout* is the timeout period and is set to 30 seconds by default.

Example

The following example implements a minimalistic Web server using asyncore. It implements two classes—asynhttp for accepting connections and asynclient for processing client requests.

```
# A minimal HTTP server with no error checking.
import asyncore, socket
import string, os, stat, mimetypes
# Class that does nothing but accept connections
class asynhttp(asyncore.dispatcher):
    def __init__(self, port):
        asyncore.dispatcher.__init__(self)
        self.create_socket(socket.AF_INET,socket.SOCK_STREAM)
        self.bind(('',port))
        self.listen(5)
    # Accept an incoming connection and create a client
    def handle_accept(self):
        client,addr = self.accept()
        print 'Connection from ', addr
        return asynclient(client)
# Handle clients
class asynclient(asyncore.dispatcher):
    def __init__(self, sock = None):
        asyncore.dispatcher.__init__(self,sock)
        self.got_request = 0         # Read HTTP request?
        self.request_data = []
        self.responsef = None        # Response file
        self.sent_headers = 0        # Send HTTP headers?
        self.clientf = sock.makefile('r+',0)  # Request file
    # Only readable if request header not read
    def readable(self):
        if not self.got_request: return 1
    # Read request header (until blank line)
    def handle_read(self):
        data = string.strip(self.clientf.readline())
        if data:
            self.request_data.append(data)
            return
        self.got_request = 1
        request = string.split(self.request_data[0])
        if request[0] == 'GET':
            filename = request[1][1:]
            self.responsef = open(filename)
```

continues >>

>> *continued*

```
                            self.content_type,enc = mimetypes.guess_type(filename)
                            self.content_length = os.stat(filename)[stat.ST_SIZE]
                    else:
                            self.close()
            # Only writable if a response is ready
            def writable(self):
                    if self.responsef: return 1
                    return 0
            # Write response data
            def handle_write(self):
                    # Send HTTP headers if not sent yet
                    if not self.sent_headers:
                            self.send('HTTP/1.0 200 OK\n')
                            if not self.content_type:
                                    self.content_type = 'text/plain'
                            self.send('Content-type: %s\n' % (self.content_type,))
                            self.send('Content-length: %d\n\n' % (self.content_length,))
                            self.sent_headers = 1
                    # Read some data and send it
                    data = self.responsef.read(8192)
                    if data:
                            sent = self.send(data)
                            # Adjust for unsent data
                            self.responsef.seek(sent-len(data),1)
                    else:
                            self.responsef.close()
                            self.close()
    # Create the server
    a = asynhttp(80)
    # Poll forever
    asyncore.loop()
```

Notes

- This module requires the select module.

  ▶ **See Also** socket (252), select (250), httplib (243), SocketServer (258).

BaseHTTPServer

The BaseHTTPServer module defines two base classes used to implement HTTP servers.

HTTPServer(*server_address*, *request_handler*)

Creates a new HTTPServer object. *server_address* is a tuple of the form (*host*, *port*) on which the server will listen. *request_handler* is a class object used to handle requests (described shortly).

The HTTPServer class is derived from SocketServer.TCPServer and supports the same methods. In particular, the following functions are most relevant:

Function	Description
h.handle_request()	Processes a single request
h.serve_forever()	Handles an infinite number of requests

Requests are handled by defining a handler derived from the following class:

BaseHTTPRequestHandler(*request, client_address, server***)**

This class is used to handle HTTP requests. When a connection is received, the request and HTTP headers are parsed. An attempt is then made to execute a method of the form do_REQUEST based on the request type. For example, a 'GET' method invokes do_GET() and a 'POST' method invokes do_POST. By default, this class does nothing, so these methods must be defined in subclasses.

The following class variables are defined for BaseHTTPRequestHandler:

BaseHTTPRequestHandler.server_version

Specifies the server software version string—for example, 'ServerName/1.2'.

BaseHTTPRequestHandler.sys_version

Python system version, such as 'Python/2.0'.

BaseHTTPRequestHandler.error_message_format

Format string used to build error messages sent to the client. The format string is applied to a dictionary containing the attributes code, message, and explain. For example:

```
'''<head>
<title>Error response</title>
</head>
<body>
<h1>Error response</h1>
<p>Error code %(code)d.
<p>Message: %(message)s.
<p>Error code explanation: %(code)s = %(explain)s.
</body>'''
```

BaseHTTPRequestHandler.protocol_version

HTTP protocol version used in responses. The default is 'HTTP/1.0'.

BaseHTTPRequestHandler.MessageClass

Class used to parse HTTP headers. The default is mimetools.Message.

BaseHTTPRequestHandler.responses

Mapping of integer error codes to two-element tuples (*message, explain*) that describe the problem.

An instance *b* of the BaseHTTPRequestHandler has the following attributes:

Attribute	Description
b.client_address	Client address as a tuple (*host, port*)
b.command	Request type such as 'GET', 'POST', 'HEAD', and so on
b.path	Contains the request path
b.request_version	HTTP version string from the request, such as 'HTTP/1.0'
b.headers	HTTP headers, typically represented as mimetools.Message object
b.rfile	Input stream for optional input data
b.wfile	Output stream for writing a response back to the client

Appendix A   The Python Library

The following methods are used:

`b.handle()`

Request dispatcher. Parses the request and calls a method of the form do_*().

`b.send_error(code [, message])`

Sends an error reply to the client. code is the numeric HTTP error code. message is an optional error message.

`b.send_response(code [, message])`

Sends a response header. The HTTP response line is sent, followed by Server and Date headers.

`b.send_header(keyword, value)`

Writes a MIME header entry to the output stream. keyword is the header keyword, value is its value.

`b.end_headers()`

Sends a blank line to signal the end of the MIME headers.

`b.log_request([code [, size]])`

Logs a successful request. code is the HTTP code and size is the size of the response in bytes (if available).

`b.log_error(format, ...)`

Logs an error message. By default, b.log_message() is called.

`b.log_message(format, ...)`

Logs an arbitrary message to sys.stderr. format is a format string applied to any additional arguments passed. The client address and current time are prefixed to every message.

`b.version_string()`

Returns the server software's version string—a combination of the server_version and sys_version variables.

`b.date_time_string()`

Returns the current date and time, formatted for a header.

`b.log_date_time_string()`

Returns the current date and time, formatted for logging.

`b.address_string()`

Performs a name lookup on the client's IP address and returns a hostname formatted for logging.

Example

The following example handles GET methods and simply echoes the request back to the client on a Web page.

```
import BaseHTTPServer
class EchoHandler(BaseHTTPServer.BaseHTTPRequestHandler):
        # Echo the request information back on a Web page
        def do_GET(self):
                self.send_response(200)
                self.send_header('Content-type','text/html')
                self.end_headers()
                self.wfile.write('''
```

```
<html><head><title>Your Request</title></head>
<body>
<pre>
You requested the following : %s
The request headers were :
%s
</pre></body></html>
''' % (self.path, self.headers))

server = BaseHTTPServer.HTTPServer(('',80),EchoHandler)
server.serve_forever()
```

Note

- The contents of this module are rarely used directly. See the SimpleHTTPServer and CGIHTTPServer modules.

▶ **See Also** SimpleHTTPServer (251), CGIHTTPServer (239), SocketServer (258), httplib (243), mimetools (266).

cgi

The cgi module is used to implement CGI scripts in Web applications. CGI scripts are programs executed by a Web server when it wants to process user input submitted through an HTML form such as the following:

```
<FORM ACTION='/cgi-bin/foo.cgi' METHOD='GET'>
Your name : <INPUT type='Text' name='name' size='30'>
Your email address: <INPUT type='Text' name='email' size='30'>
<INPUT type='Submit' name='submit-button' value='Subscribe'>
</FORM>
```

When the form is submitted, the Web server executes the CGI program foo.cgi. CGI programs receive input from two sources: sys.stdin and environment variables set by the server. The following table lists common environment variables set by Web servers:

Variable	Description
AUTH_TYPE	Authentication method
CONTENT_LENGTH	Length of data passed in sys.stdin
CONTENT_TYPE	Type of query data
DOCUMENT_ROOT	Document root directory
GATEWAY_INTERFACE	CGI revision string
HTTP_ACCEPT	MIME types accepted by the client
HTTP_COOKIE	Netscape persistent cookie value
HTTP_FROM	Email address of client (often disabled)
HTTP_REFERER	Referring URL
HTTP_USER_AGENT	Client browser
PATH_INFO	Extra path information passed

continues >>

Appendix A   The Python Library

>> *continued*

Variable	Description
PATH_TRANSLATED	Translated version of PATH_INFO
QUERY_STRING	Query string
REMOTE_ADDR	Remote IP address of the client
REMOTE_HOST	Remote hostname of the client
REMOTE_IDENT	User making the request
REMOTE_USER	Authenticated username
REQUEST_METHOD	Method ('GET' or 'POST')
SCRIPT_NAME	Name of the program
SERVER_NAME	Server hostname
SERVER_PORT	Server port number
SERVER_PROTOCOL	Server protocol
SERVER_SOFTWARE	Name and version of the server software

As output, a CGI program writes to standard output `sys.stdout`. The gory details of CGI programming can be found in a book such as *CGI Programming with Perl, 2nd Edition* by Shishir Gundavaram (O'Reilly & Associates, 1999). For our purposes, there are really only two things to know. First, the contents of an HTML form are passed to a CGI program in a sequence of text known as a *query string*. In Python, the contents of the query string are accessed using the `FieldStorage` class. For example:

```python
import cgi
form = cgi.FieldStorage()
name = form['name'].value    # Get 'name' field from a form
email = form['email'].value  # Get 'email' field from a form
```

Second, the output of a CGI program consists of two parts: an HTTP header and the raw data (which is typically HTML). A simple HTTP header looks like this:

```python
print 'Content-type: text/html'  # HTML Output
print                            # Blank line (required!)
```

The rest of the output is the raw output. For example:

```python
print '<TITLE>My CGI Script</TITLE>'
print '<H1>Hello World!</H1>'
print 'You are %s (%s)' % (name, email)
```

Most of the work in the `cgi` module is performed by creating an instance of the `FieldStorage` class. This class reads the contents of a form by reading and parsing the query string passed in an environment variable or standard input. Because input can be read from standard input, only one instance should be created. An instance `f` of `FieldStorage` has the following attributes:

Attribute	Description
f.name	The field name, if specified
f.filename	Client-side filename used in uploads
f.value	Value as a string

Attribute	Description
f.file	File-like object from which data can be read
f.type	Content type
f.type_options	Dictionary of options specified on the content-type line of the HTTP request
f.disposition	The 'content-disposition' field; None if not specified
f.disposition_options	Dictionary of disposition options
f.headers	A dictionary-like object containing all the HTTP header contents

In addition, the cgi module defines a class MiniFieldStorage that contains only the attribute's name and value. This class is used to represent individual fields of a form passed in the query string, whereas FieldStorage is used to contain multiple fields and multipart data.

Instances of FieldStorage are accessed like a Python dictionary where the keys are the field names on the form. When accessed in this manner, the objects returned are themselves an instance of FieldStorage for multipart data or file uploads, an instance of MiniFieldStorage for simple fields, or a list of such instances in cases where a form contains multiple fields with the same name.

If a field represents an uploaded file, accessing the value attribute reads the entire file into memory as a string. Because this may consume a large amount of memory on the server, it may be preferable to read uploaded data in smaller pieces by reading from the file attribute directly. For instance, the following example reads uploaded data line by line:

```
fileitem = form['userfile']
if fileitem.file:
    # It's an uploaded file; count lines
    linecount = 0
    while 1:
        line = fileitem.file.readline()
        if not line: break
        linecount = linecount + 1
```

The following functions provide a more low-level CGI interface:

escape(s [, quote])

Converts the characters '&', '<', and '>' in string s to HTML-safe sequences such as '&', '<', and '>'. If the optional flag quote is true, the double-quote character (") is also translated.

parse([fp [, environ [, keep_blank_values [, strict_parsing]]]])

Parses a form into a dictionary. fp is a file object from which data is read (defaults to stdin). environ is a dictionary containing environment variables (defaults to os.environ). keep_blank_values, if set to 1, instructs the parser to map blank entries into empty strings. Otherwise, blank entries are ignored (the default). The strict_parsing option specifies what to do with parsing errors. By default, errors are ignored. If set, parsing errors result in a ValueError exception. Returns a dictionary mapping field names to lists of values.

Appendix A   The Python Library

`parse_header(string)`

Parses the data supplied after an HTTP header field such as `'content-type'`. The data is split into a primary value and a dictionary of secondary parameters that are returned in a tuple. For example, this command:

```
parse_header("text/html; a=hello; b='world'")
```

returns this result:

```
('text/html', {'a':'hello', 'b':'world'}).
```

`parse_multipart(fp,pdict)`

Parses input of type `'multipart/form-data'` as is commonly used with file uploads. `fp` is the input file and `pdict` is a dictionary containing parameters of the content-type header. Returns a dictionary mapping field names to lists of values. This function doesn't work with nested multipart data. The `FieldStorage` class should be used instead.

`parse_qs(qs [, keep_blank_values [, strict_parsing]]):`

Parses a query string `qs`. `keep_blank_values` and `strict_parsing` have the same meaning as in `parse()`. Returns a dictionary mapping field names to lists of values.

`parse_qsl(qs [, keep_blank_values [, strict_parsing]])`

Like `parse_qs()` except that a list of (`name`, `value`) pairs is returned.

`print_directory()`

Formats the contents of the current working directory in HTML. Used for debugging.

`print_environ()`

Formats the shell environment in HTML. Used for debugging.

`print_environ_usage()`

Prints a list of useful environment variables in HTML. Used for debugging.

`print_form(form)`

Formats the data supplied on a form in HTML. `form` must be an instance of `FieldStorage`. Used for debugging.

`test()`

Writes a minimal HTTP header and prints all the information provided to the script in HTML format. Primarily used for debugging.

Notes

- The process of installing a CGI program varies widely according to the type of Web server being used. Typically programs are placed in a special `cgi-bin` directory. A server may also require additional configuration.

- On UNIX, Python CGI programs may require a line such as the following as the first line of the program:

```
#!/usr/local/bin/python
import cgi
...
```

- To simplify debugging, it's sometimes useful to set sys.stderr to sys.stdout. This will force Python error messages to be sent to the output stream (which will then appear in the text sent to the browser).

- If you invoke an external program—for example, via the os.system() or os.popen() function—be careful not to pass arbitrary strings received from the client to the shell. This is a well-known security hole that hackers can use to execute arbitrary shell commands on the server (because the command passed to these functions is first interpreted by the UNIX shell as opposed to being executed directly). In particular, never pass any part of a URL or form data to a shell command unless it has first been thoroughly checked by making sure that the string contains only alphanumeric characters, dashes, underscores, and periods.

- On UNIX, don't give a CGI program setuid mode. This is a security liability and not supported on all machines.

- Don't use 'from cgi import *' with this module. The cgi module defines a wide variety of names and symbols that you probably don't want in your namespace.

- The original CGI specification can be found at
  http://hoohoo.ncsa.uiuc.edu/cgi/interface.html.

▶ **See Also** CGIHTTPServer (239).

CGIHTTPServer

The CGIHTTPServer module provides a simple HTTP server handler that can run CGI scripts. The server is defined by the following request handler class, intended for use with the BaseHTTPServer module:

CGIHTTPRequestHandler(*request*, *client_address*, *server*)

Serves files from the current directory and all its subdirectories. In addition, the handler will run a file as a CGI script if it's located in a special CGI directory. The handler supports both GET and POST methods.

The list of valid CGI directories is contained in the following attribute:

CGIHTTPRequestHandler.cgi_directories

List of CGI directories. Defaults to ['/cgi-bin', '/htbin'].

Example

```
from BaseHTTPServer import HTTPServer
from CGIHTTPServer import CGIHTTPRequestHandler
import os
# Change to the document root
os.chdir('/home/httpd/html')
# Start the CGI server
serv = HTTPServer(('',80),CGIHTTPRequestHandler)
serv.serve_forever()
```

Appendix A   The Python Library

Notes

- For security, CGI scripts are executed with a UID of user nobody.

- Problems with the CGI script will be translated to HTTP error 403.

- Requests are handled using the do_GET and do_POST methods, both of which can be redefined in subclasses.

- To prevent problems in the execution of CGI scripts, it's usually a good idea to use CGI directory names that don't contain any embedded whitespace.

> **See Also** BaseHTTPServer (p. x), SimpleHTTPServer (p. x), cgi (p. x), httplib (p. x).

Cookie

The Cookie module provides support for managing HTTP cookies. Cookies are used to provide state management in CGI scripts that implement sessions, user logins, shopping carts, and related features. To drop a cookie on a user's browser, an HTTP server typically adds an HTTP header similar to the following to an HTTP response (see the httplib module):

```
Set-Cookie: session=8273612; expires=Sun, 18-Feb-2001 15:00:00 GMT; \
            path=/; domain=cs.uchicago.edu
```

Alternatively, a cookie can be set by embedding JavaScript in an HTML document:

```
<SCRIPT LANGUAGE="JavaScript">
document.cookie = "session=8273612; expires=Sun, 18-Feb-2001 15:00:00 GMT; \
    Path=/; Domain=cs.uchicago.edu;"
</SCRIPT>
```

The Cookie module simplifies the task of generating cookie values by providing a special dictionary-like object that stores and manages collections of cookie values known as *morsels*. Each morsel has a name, a value, and a set of optional attributes containing meta-data to be supplied to the browser {expires, path, comment, domain, max-age, secure, version}. The name is usually a simple identifier such as "*name*" and must not be the same as one of the meta-data names such as "expires" or "path". The value is usually a short string. To create a cookie, simply create a cookie object like this:

```
c = Cookie.SimpleCookie()
```

Once created, cookie values (morsels) can be set using ordinary dictionary assignment:

```
c["session"] = 8273612
c["user"] = "beazley"
```

Additional attributes of a specific morsel are set as follows:

```
c["session"]["path"] = "/"
c["session"]["domain"] = "cs.uchicago.edu"
c["session"]["expires"] = "18-Feb-2001 15:00:00 GMT"
```

To output the cookie data as a set of HTTP headers, the c.output() method is used. For example:

```
print c.output()
# Produces two lines of output
# Set-Cookie: session=8273612; expires=...; path=/; domain=...
# Set-Cookie: user=beazley
```

When a browser sends a cookie back to an HTTP server, it is encoded as a string of *key=value* pairs such as `"session=8273612; user=beazley"`. Optional attributes such as expires, path, and domain are not returned. The cookie string can usually be found in the HTTP_COOKIE environment variable, which can be read by CGI applications. To recover cookie values, use code similar to the following:

```
c = Cookie.SimpleCookie(os.environ["HTTP_COOKIE"])
session = c["session"].value
user    = c["user"].value
```

In the above example, the cookie instance c is derived from a class BaseCookie that provides the following common methods:

c.value_decode(*val*)

Takes a string *val* and returns a decoded cookie value. This function is used to interpret a cookie value returned to a server by a browser.

c.value_encode(*val*)

Takes an object *val* and returns it as an encoded string suitable for use in an HTTP header. A server would use this to encode cookie values being sent to the browser.

c.output([*attrs* [,*header* [,*sep*]]])

Generates a string suitable for use in setting cookie values in HTTP headers. *attrs* is an optional list of the optional attributes to include (`"expires"`, `"path"`, `"domain"`, and so on). *header* is the HTTP header to use, `'Set-Cookie:'` by default. *sep* is the character used to join the headers together and is a newline by default.

c.js_output([*attrs*])

Generates a string containing JavaScript code that will set the cookie if executed on a browser supporting JavaScript. *attrs* is an optional list of the attributes to include.

c.load(*rawdata*)

Loads the cookie c with data found in *rawdata*. If *rawdata* is a string, it's assumed to be in the same format as the HTTP_COOKIE environment variable in a CGI program. If *rawdata* is a dictionary, each *key-value* pair is interpreted by setting c[*key*]-*value*.

The following classes provide specialized implementations of cookie objects. Each of these classes is derived from a class BaseCookie.

SimpleCookie([*input*])

Defines a cookie object in which cookie values are interpreted as simple strings. The c.value_decode() method is the identity function and the c.value_encode() method uses the str() function to generate encoded values.

SerialCookie([*input*])

Defines a cookie object in which the cookie values are interpreted using the pickle module. The c.value_decode() method uses pickle.loads() and the c.value_encode() method uses pickle.dumps(). See the later security note.

SmartCookie([*input*])

Like SerialCookie() except that strings are left unmodified. If the cookie value cannot be successfully unpickled, c.value_decode() returns its value as a string. In addition, the c.value_encode() method only calls pickle.dumps() if the value is not a string. See the later security note.

Appendix A   The Python Library

Internally, the *key*/*value* pairs used to store a cookie value are instances of a Morsel class. An instance *m* of Morsel behaves like a dictionary and allows the optional "expires", "path", "comment", "domain", "max-age", "secure", and "version" keys to be set. In addition, a morsel *m* has the following methods and attributes:

m.value

The raw value of the cookie.

m.coded_value

The encoded value of the cookie that would be sent to or received from the browser.

m.key

The cookie name.

m.set(*key*,*value*,*coded_value*)

Sets the values of *m*.key, *m*.value, and *m*.coded_value.

m.isReservedKey(*k*)

Tests whether *k* is a reserved keyword such as "expires","path", "domain", etc.

m.output([*attrs* [,*header*]])

Produces the HTTP header string for this morsel. *attrs* is an optional list of the additional attributes to include ("expires", "path", and so on). *header* is the header string to use, 'Set-Cookie:' by default.

m.js_output([*attrs*])

Outputs JavaScript code that sets the cookie when executed.

m.OutputString([*attrs*])

Returns the cookie string without any HTTP headers or JavaScript code.

If an error occurs during the parsing or generation of cookie values, a CookieError exception is raised.

Notes

- More information about persistent cookies can be found in almost any book on CGI programming. For an official specification, see RFC-2109.

- The SerialCookie() and SmartCookie() classes have known security problems, since the pickle module allows arbitrary client-code to be executed on the server during unpickling. These should not be used unless your application has a way to validate cookie values before unpickling.

- Most browsers place limits on the size and number of cookie values. You should limit the size of cookie data to a few hundred bytes at most.

▶ **See Also** cgi (235), httplib (243).

ftplib

The ftplib module is used to implement the client side of the FTP protocol. It's rarely necessary to use this module directly, as the urllib module provides a higher-level interface. The following example illustrates the use of this module:

```
>>> import ftplib
>>> ftp = ftplib.FTP('ftp.python.org')
>>> ftp.login()
>>> ftp.retrlines('LIST')
total 40
drwxrwxr-x  12 root      4127        512 Apr  6 19:57 .
drwxrwxr-x  12 root      4127        512 Apr  6 19:57 ..
drwxrwxr-x   2 root      4127        512 Aug 25  1998 RCS
lrwxrwxrwx   1 root      bin          11 Jun 29 18:34 README -> welcome.msg
drwxr-xr-x   3 root      wheel       512 May 19  1998 bin
...
>>> ftp.retrbinary('RETR README', open('README', 'wb').write)
'226 Transfer complete.'
>>> ftp.quit()
```

Consult the online documentation for a complete description of the functionality contained in this module.

▶ **See Also** urllib (260), Internet RFC 959,
http://www.python.org/doc/lib/module-ftplib.html.

httplib

This module implements the client side of the Hypertext Transfer Protocol (HTTP) used in Web applications. Both HTTP/1.0 and HTTP/1.1 protocols are supported. In addition, if Python is configured with OpenSSL support, connections can be made using secure sockets. The HTTP/1.0 protocol is a simple text-based protocol that works as follows:

1. A client makes a connection to a Web server and sends a request header of the following form:

```
GET /document.html HTTP/1.0
Connection: Keep-Alive
User-Agent: Mozilla/4.61 [en] (X11; U; SunOS 5.6 sun4u)
Host: rustler.cs.uchicago.edu:8000
Accept: image/gif, image/x-xbitmap, image/jpeg, image/pjpeg, image/png, */*
Accept-Encoding: gzip
Accept-Language: en
Accept-Charset: iso-8859-1,*,utf-8

Data (optional)
...
```

The first line defines the request type, document (the selector), and protocol version. Following the request line are a series of header lines containing various information about the client, such as passwords, cookies, cache preferences, and client software. Following the header lines, a single blank line indicates the end of the header lines. After the header, data may appear in the event that the request is sending from a form or uploading a file. Each of the lines in the header should be terminated by a carriage return and a newline ('\r\n').

2. The server sends a response of the following form:

```
HTTP/1.0  200  OK
Content-type: text/html
Content-length:  72883 bytes
...
Header: data

Data
...
```

Appendix A The Python Library

The first line of the server response indicates the HTTP protocol version, a success code, and return message. Following the response line are a series of header fields that contain information about the type of the returned document, the document size, Web server software, cookies, and so forth. The header is terminated by a single blank line followed by the raw data of the requested document.

The following request methods are the most common:

Method	Description
GET	Get a document
POST	Post data to a form
HEAD	Return header information only
PUT	Upload data to the server

The following response codes are returned by servers:

Code	Description
Success Codes (2xx)	
200	OK
201	Created
202	Accepted
204	No content
Redirection (3xx)	
300	Multiple choices
301	Moved permanently
302	Moved temporarily
303	Not modified
Client Error (4xx)	
400	Bad request
401	Unauthorized
403	Forbidden
404	Not found
Server Error (5xx)	
500	Internal server error
501	Not implemented
502	Bad gateway
503	Service unavailable

A wide range of optional header fields can appear in both the request and response headers. These headers are specified in a format known as RFC 822, in which headers are specified in the form `Header: data`. For example:

```
Date: Fri, 16 Jul 1999 17:09:33 GMT
Server: Apache/1.3.6 (Unix)
Last-Modified: Mon, 12 Jul 1999 19:08:14 GMT
ETag: "741d3-44ec-378a3d1e"
Accept-Ranges: bytes
Content-Length: 17644
Connection: close
Content-Type: text/html
```

The following classes can be used to create HTTP/1.0 connections with a
Web server:

HTTP([*host* **[,** *port***]])**

Establishes an HTTP/1.0 connection with an HTTP server. *host* is the hostname and *port* is an optional port number. If no port number is given, the port is
extracted from the hostname if it's of the form '*host:port*'. Otherwise, port 80 is
used. If no host is passed, no connection is made and the connect() method should
be used to make the connection manually.

HTTPS([*host* **[,** *port* **[,** key_file=*kfile* **[,** cert_file=*cfile***]]])**

Establishes a secure HTTP/1.0 connection. Works like HTTP() except that the
default port is 443. In addition, optional keyword parameters key_file and
cert_file specify the names of a client private-key file and a client certificate file
to be supplied to the server.

An instance *h* of the HTTP or HTTPS class has the following methods:

h.**connect(***host* **[,** *port***])**

Connects to the server given by *host* and *port*. This should be called only if the
instance was created without a host.

h.**send(***data***)**

Sends data to the server. This should only be used after the endheaders() method.

h.**putrequest(***request, selector***)**

Sends a line to the server containing the request string, selector string, and the
HTTP version (HTTP/1.0).

h.**putheader(***header, argument* **[,** ...**])**

Sends an RFC 822–style header to the server. It sends a line to the server
consisting of the header, a colon and a space, and the first argument. If more
arguments are given, continuation lines are sent, each consisting of a tab
and an argument.

h.**endheaders()**

Sends a blank line to the server, indicating the end of the headers.

h.**getreply()**

Closes the sending end of the connection, reads the reply from the server, and
returns a triple (*replycode, message, headers*). *replycode* is the integer reply code
from the request, such as 200 on success. *message* is the message string corresponding to the reply code. *headers* is an instance of the class mimetools.Message, containing the HTTP headers received from the server.

h.**getfile()**

Returns a file object from which the data returned by the server can be read,
using the read(), readline(), or readlines() method.

Appendix A   The Python Library

Example

```
import httplib
h = httplib.HTTP('www.python.org')
h.putrequest('GET', '/index.html')
h.putheader('Accept', 'text/html')
h.putheader('Accept', 'text/plain')
h.endheaders()
errcode, errmsg, headers = h.getreply()
print errcode # Should be 200
f = h.getfile()
data = f.read() # Get the raw HTML
f.close()
```

HTTP/1.1 extends the HTTP/1.0 protocol by allowing multiple request/response data streams to be multiplexed over a single network connection. To handle multiple connections, HTTP/1.1 manages the network connection by putting it into one of three states:

State	Description
_CS_IDLE	Connection idle
_CS_REQ_STARTED	Request started
_CS_REQ_SENT	Request sent

New requests can be sent only when the connection is in the _CS_IDLE state. Once an HTTP request has been sent, the connection doesn't return to the idle state until the server response has been received and read on the client.

To support HTTP/1.1, the following classes are provided:

HTTPConnection(*host* [,*port*])

Creates an HTTP/1.1 connection. *host* is the hostname and *port* is the remote port number. The default port is 80. Returns an HTTPConnection instance.

HTTPSConnection(*host* [, *port* [, key_file=*kfile* [, cert_file=*cfile*]]])

Like HTTP/1.1, but uses a secure socket connection. The default port is 443. key_file and cert_file are optional keyword arguments that specify client private-key and certificate files. Returns an HTTPSConnection instance.

An instance *h* of HTTPConnection or HTTPSConnection supports the following methods:

h.connect()

Initializes the connection to the host and port given to HTTPConnection() or HTPPSConnection().

h.close()

Closes the connection.

h.send(*str*)

Sends a string *str* to the server. Direct use of this function with HTTP/1.1 is discouraged, because it may break the underlying response/request protocol. It's most commonly used to send data to the server after *h*.endheaders() has been called.

h.putrequest(*method*, *url*)

Sends a request to the server. *method* is the HTTP method, such as 'GET' or 'POST'. *url* specifies the object to be returned, such as '/index.html'. If *h* is not in the _CS_IDLE state, a CannotSendRequest exception is generated. Otherwise, *h* is moved to _CS_REQ_STARTED state, in which additional headers can be added to the request.

h.putheader(*header, value*)

Sends an RFC 822–style header to the server. It sends a line to the server, consisting of the header, a colon and a space, and the value. Raises a CannotSendHeader exception if *h* is not in the _CS_REQ_STARTED state.

h.endheaders()

Sends a blank line to the server, indicating the end of the header lines. Changes the connection state to _CS_REQ_SENT.

h.request(*method, url* [, *body* [, *headers*]])

Sends a complete HTTP request to the server. *method* and *url* have the same meaning as for *h*.putrequest(). *body* is an optional string containing data to upload to the server after the request has been sent. *headers* is a dictionary containing *header:value* pairs to be given to the *h*.putheader() method.

h.getresponse()

Gets a response from the server and returns an HTTPResponse instance that can be used to read data. Raises a ResponseNotReady exception if *h* is not in the _CS_REQ_STATE.

An HTTPResponse instance *r* as returned by the getresponse() method supports the following methods:

r.close()

Closes the connection. This doesn't close the underlying HTTP connection. Only the file object used to read data in this specific response is closed.

r.isclosed()

Returns true if the underlying connection has been closed.

r.read([*size*])

Reads up to *size* bytes from the server. If *size* is omitted, all the data for this request is returned.

r.getheader(*name* [, *default*])

Gets a response header. *name* is the name of the header. *default* is the default value to return if not found.

r.version

HTTP version used by server.

r.status

HTTP status code returned by the server.

r.reason

HTTP error message returned by the server.

r.length

Number of bytes left in the response.

r.will_close

Set if the server will close the connection after the response has been sent.

Appendix A   The Python Library

Example

The following example shows how the `HTTPConnection` class can be used to open an HTTP/1.1 connection and fetch several files.

```
import httplib

files = [ '/index.html', '/doc/index.html', '/News.html' ]
h = httplib.HTTPConnection("www.python.org",80)
h.connect()

for f in files:
    h.putrequest('GET','f')
    h.putheader('Accept','text/html')
    h.putheader('Accept','text/plain')
    h.endheaders()

    r = h.getresponse()
    if r.status == 200:
        data = r.read()
        print ":::: %s ::::" % f
        print data
    r.close()

h.close()
```

Notes

- This module is used by the `urllib` module, which provides a higher-level interface for accessing URLs.

- Secure HTTP is not available unless Python has also been compiled with OpenSSL support.

> **See Also** `urllib` (260), `mimetools` (266), `asyncore` (229), `BaseHTTPServer` (232), `SimpleHTTPServer` (251), `CGIHTTPServer` (239).

`imaplib`

The `imaplib` module provides a low-level client-side interface for connecting to an IMAP4 mail server using the IMAP4rev1 protocol. Documents describing the protocol, as well as sources and binaries for servers implementing it, can be found at the University of Washington's IMAP Information Center (`http://www.cac.washington.edu/imap`).

The following example shows how the module is used by opening a mailbox and printing all messages:

```
import getpass, imaplib, string
m = imaplib.IMAP4()
m.login(getpass.getuser(), getpass.getpass())
m.select()
typ, data = m.search(None, 'ALL')
for num in string.split(data[0]):
    typ, data = m.fetch(num, '(RFC822)')
    print 'Message %s\n%s\n' % (num, data[0][1])
m.logout()
```

> **See Also** `poplib` (249), `http://www.python.org/doc/lib/module-imaplib.html`, `http://www.cac.washington.edu/imap`, Internet RFC 1730, RFC 2060.

nntplib

The nntplib module provides a low-level interface to the client side of NNTP (Network News Transfer Protocol). For details about using this module, see the online documentation (http://www.python.org/doc/lib/module-nntplib.html). The following example shows how the module can be used to post a news message from a file containing valid news headers:

```
s = NNTP('news.foo.com')
f = open('article')
s.post(f)
s.quit()
```

▶ **See Also** http://www.python.org/doc/lib/module-nntplib.html, Internet RFC 977.

poplib

The poplib module provides a low-level client-side connection to a POP3 mail server. Consult the online reference at http://www.python.org/doc/lib/module-poplib.html for specific details. The following example opens a mailbox and retrieves all messages:

```
import getpass, poplib
M = poplib.POP3('localhost')
M.user(getpass.getuser())
M.pass_(getpass.getpass())
numMessages = len(M.list()[1])
for i in range(numMessages):
    for j in M.retr(i+1)[1]:
        print j
```

▶ **See Also** http://www.python.org/doc/lib/module-poplib.html, Internet RFC 1725.

robotparser

The robotparser module provides a class that can be used to fetch and query information contained in the robots.txt files that Web sites use to instruct Web crawlers and spiders. The contents of this file typically look like this:

```
# robots.txt
User-agent: *
Disallow: /warheads/designs    # Don't allow robots here
```

RobotFileParser()

Creates an object that can be used to read and query a single robots.txt file.

An instance r of RobotFileParser has the following attributes and methods:

r.set_url(*url*)

Sets the URL of the robots.txt file.

r.read()

Reads the robots.txt file and parses it.

r.parse(*lines*)

Parses a list of lines obtained from a robots.txt file.

r.can_fetch(*useragent, url*)

Returns true if *useragent* is allowed to fetch *url*.

r.mtime()

Returns the time at which the robots.txt file was last fetched.

r.modified()

Sets the time at which robots.txt was last fetched to the current time.

Note

■ Details about the robots.txt format can be found at
  http://info.webcrawler.com/mak/projects/robots/norobots.html.

select

The select module provides access to the select() system call. select() is typically used to implement polling or to multiplex processing across multiple input/output streams without using threads or subprocesses. On UNIX and Macintosh, it works for files, sockets, pipes, and most other file types. On Windows, it only works for sockets.

select(*iwtd, owtd, ewtd* [, *timeout*])

Queries the input, output, and exceptional status of a group of file descriptors. The first three arguments are lists containing either integer file descriptors or objects with a method fileno() that can be used to return a file descriptor. The *iwtd* parameter specifies objects waiting for input, *owtd* specifies objects waiting for output, and *ewtd* specifies objects waiting for an exceptional condition. Each list may be empty. *timeout* is a floating-point number specifying a timeout period in seconds. If omitted, the function waits until at least one file descriptor is ready. If *0*, the function merely performs a poll and returns immediately. The return value is a triple of lists containing the objects that are ready. These are subsets of the first three arguments. If none of the objects is ready before the timeout occurs, three empty lists are returned. If an error occurs, a select.error exception raised. Its value is the same as that returned by IOError and OSError.

Example

The following code shows how select() could be used in an event loop that wants to periodically query a collection of sockets for an incoming connection:

```
import socket, select
# Create a few sockets
s1 = socket.socket(socket.AF_INET, socket.SOCK_STREAM)
s1.bind(("",8888))
s1.listen(5)
s2 = socket.socket(socket.AF_INET, socket.SOCK_STREAM)
s2.bind(("",8889))
s2.listen(5)
# Event loop
while 1:
        ... processing ...
        # Poll the sockets for activity
        input,output,exc = select.select([s1,s2],[],[],0)
        # Loop over all of the sockets that have pending input
        for sock in input:
            # Accept an incoming connection
```

```
        client = sock.accept()
        ... handle client ...
        client.close()
# Done. Carry on.
... more processing ...
```

Note

- There's usually an upper limit on the number of file selectors that can be given to select(). It's often 64 for Windows and 256 for UNIX.

▶ **See Also** asyncore (229), socket (252), os (180).

SimpleHTTPServer

The SimpleHTTPServer module provides a simple HTTP server handler that can serve files from the current directory. The module defines the following handler class, intended for use with the BaseHTTPServer module:

SimpleHTTPRequestHandler(*request, client_address, server*)

Serves files from the current directory and all its subdirectories. The class implements the do_HEAD() and do_GET() methods to support HEAD and GET requests, respectively. All IOError exceptions result in a 404 File not found error. Attempts to access a directory result in a 403 Directory listing not supported error.

The following class attributes are available:

SimpleHTTPRequestHandler.server_version

Server version string.

SimpleHTTPRequestHandler.extensions_map

A dictionary mapping suffixes into MIME types. Unrecognized file types are considered to be of type 'text/plain'.

Example
```
from BaseHTTPServer import HTTPServer
from SimpleHTTPServer import SimpleHTTPRequestHandler
import os
# Change to the document root
os.chdir("/home/httpd/html")
# Start the SimpleHTTP server
serv = HTTPServer(("",80),SimpleHTTPRequestHandler)
serv.serve_forever()
```

▶ **See Also** BaseHTTPServer (232), CGIHTTPServer (239), httplib (243).

smtplib

The smtplib module provides a low-level SMTP client interface that can be used to send mail. For specific details about the module, see the online reference at http://www.python.org/doc/lib/module-smtplib.html. The following example shows how the module might be used by prompting the user for an address and sending a message:

Appendix A   The Python Library

```
import string, sys
import smtplib
def prompt(prompt):
    sys.stdout.write(prompt + ": ")
    return string.strip(sys.stdin.readline())
fromaddr = prompt("From")
toaddrs  = string.splitfields(prompt("To"), ',')
print "Enter message, end with ^D:"
msg = ""
while 1:
    line = sys.stdin.readline()
    if not line:
        break
    msg = msg + line
print "Message length is " + `len(msg)`
server = smtplib.SMTP('localhost')
server.sendmail(fromaddr, toaddrs, msg)
server.quit()
```

▶ **See Also** poplib (249), http://www.python.org/doc/lib/module-smtplib.html, imaplib (248), Internet RFC 821 (Simple Mail Transfer Protocol), Internet RFC 1869 (SMTP Service Extensions).

socket

The socket module provides access to the BSD socket interface. Although it's based on UNIX, this module is available on all platforms.

fromfd(*fd*, *family*, *type* [, *proto*])

Creates a socket object from an integer file descriptor *fd*. The address family, socket type, and protocol number are the same as for socket(). The file descriptor must refer to a previously created socket. Returns an instance of SocketType.

getfqdn([*name*])

Returns the fully qualified domain name of *name*. If *name* is omitted, the local machine is assumed. For example, getfqdn("stonecrusher") might return "stonecrusher.cs.uchicago.edu".

gethostbyname(*hostname*)

Translates a hostname such as 'www.python.org' to an IP address. The IP address is returned as a string, such as '132.151.1.90'.

gethostbyname_ex(*hostname*)

Translates a hostname to an IP address, but returns a triple (*hostname*, *aliaslist*, *ipaddrlist*) in which *hostname* is the primary hostname, *aliaslist* is a list of alternative hostnames for the same address, and *ipaddrlist* is a list of IP addresses for the same interface on the same host. For example, gethostbyname_ex('www.python.org') returns ('parrot.python.org', ['www.python.org'], ['132.151.1.90']).

gethostname()

Returns the hostname of the local machine.

gethostbyaddr(*ip_address*)

Returns the same information as gethostbyname_ex(), given an IP address such as '132.151.1.90'.

`getprotobyname(protocolname)`

Translates an Internet protocol name such as `'icmp'` to a protocol number (such as the value of `IPPROTO_ICMP`) that can be passed to the third argument of the `socket()` function.

`getservbyname(servicename, protocolname)`

Translates an Internet service name and protocol name to a port number for that service. For example, `getservbyname('ftp', 'tcp')` returns 21. The protocol name should be `'tcp'` or `'udp'`.

`ntohl(x)`

Converts 32-bit integers from network (big-endian) to host byte order.

`ntohs(x)`

Converts 16-bit integers from network to host byte order.

`htonl(x)`

Converts 32-bit integers from host to network byte order.

`htons(x)`

Converts 16-bit integers from host to network byte order.

`ssl(sock, key_file, cert_file)`

Creates a client-side secure socket. `sock` is an existing socket instance that has already established a connection using its `connect()` method. `key_file` is the name of a client private-key file. `cert_file` is the name of a client certificate file. `key_file` and `cert_file` must both be set to `None` or set to the names of PEM format files containing the client key and certificate. This function is available only if Python has been configured with OpenSSL support. In addition, this function cannot be used to create server-side secure sockets. See the notes.

`socket(family, type [, proto])`

Creates a new socket using the given address family, socket type, and protocol number. `family` is one of the following constants:

Constant	Description
`AF_INET`	IPv4 protocols (TCP, UDP)
`AF_UNIX`	UNIX domain protocols

The socket type is one of the following constants:

Constant	Description
`SOCK_STREAM`	Stream socket (TCP)
`SOCK_DGRAM`	Datagram socket (UDP)
`SOCK_RAW`	Raw socket (available with `AF_INET` only)
`SOCK_SEQPACKET`	Sequenced connection-mode transfer of records

The protocol number is usually omitted (and defaults to 0). It's usually used only in conjunction with raw sockets (`SOCK_RAW`) and is set to one of the following constants when used: `IPPROTO_ICMP`, `IPPROTO_IP`, `IPPROTO_RAW`, `IPPROTO_TCP`, `IPPROTO_UDP`.

To open a TCP connection, use socket(AF_INET, SOCK_STREAM). To open a UDP connection, use socket(AF_INET, SOCK_DGRAM). To open a raw IP socket, use socket(AF_INET, SOCK_RAW). Access to raw sockets is privileged and will only succeed if the effective user ID is 0 (root) on UNIX systems. The function returns an instance of SocketType (described shortly).

Sockets are represented by an instance of type SocketType. The following methods are available on a socket s:

s.accept()

Accepts a connection and returns a pair (conn, address) where conn is a new socket object that can be used to send and receive data on the connection, and address is the address of the socket on the other end of the connection.

s.bind(address)

Binds the socket to an address. The format of address depends on the address family. In most cases, it's a tuple of the form (hostname, port). For IP addresses, the empty string represents INADDR_ANY, and the string '<broadcast>' represents INADDR_BROADCAST. The INADDR_ANY hostname (the empty string) is used to indicate that the server allows connections on any Internet interface on the system. This is often used when a server is multihomed. The INADDR_BROADCAST hostname ('<broadcast>') is used when a socket is being used to send a broadcast message.

s.close()

Closes the socket. Sockets are also closed when they're garbage-collected.

s.connect(address)

Connects to a remote socket at address. The format of address depends on the address family, but it's normally a pair (hostname, port). Raises socket.error if an error occurs.

If you're connecting to a server on the same computer, you can use the name 'localhost' as the first argument to s.connect().

s.connect_ex(address)

Like connect(address), but returns 0 on success or the value of errno on failure.

s.fileno()

Returns the socket's file descriptor.

s.getpeername()

Returns the remote address to which the socket is connected as a pair (ipaddr, port). Not supported on all systems.

s.getsockname()

Return the socket's own address as a pair (ipaddr, port).

s.getsockopt(level, optname [, buflen])

Returns the value of a socket option. level defines the level of the option and is SOL_SOCKET for socket-level options or a protocol number such as IPPROTO_IP for protocol-related options. optname selects a specific option. If buflen is omitted, an integer option is assumed and its integer value is returned. If buflen is given, it specifies the maximum length of the buffer used to receive the option. This buffer is returned as a string, where it's up to the caller to decode its contents using the struct module or other means. The following list shows commonly used option names for level SOL_SOCKET:

Option Name	Value	Description
SO_KEEPALIVE	0, 1	Periodically probes the other end of the connection and terminates if it's half-open
SO_RCVBUF	int	Size of receive buffer (in bytes)
SO_SNDBUF	int	Size of send buffer (in bytes)
SO_REUSEADDR	0, 1	Allows local address reuse
SO_RCVLOWAT	int	Number of bytes read before select() returns the socket as readable
SO_SNDLOWAT	int	Number of bytes available in send buffer before select() returns the socket as writable
SO_RCVTIMEO	tvalue	Timeout on receive calls in seconds
SO_SNDTIMEO	tvalue	Timeout on send calls in seconds
SO_OOBINLINE	0, 1	Places out-of-band data into the input queue
SO_LINGER	linger	Lingers on close() if the send buffer contains data
SO_DONTROUTE	0, 1	Bypasses routing table lookups
SO_ERROR	int	Gets error status
SO_BROADCAST	0, 1	Allows sending of broadcast datagrams
SO_TYPE	int	Gets socket type
SO_USELOOPBACK	0, 1	Routing socket gets copy of what it sends

tvalue is a binary structure that's decoded as

(*second*, *microsec*) = struct.unpack("ll", *tvalue*).

linger is a binary structure that's decoded as

(*linger_onoff*, *linger_sec*) = struct.unpack("ii", *linger*).

The following options are available for level IPPROTO_IP:

Option Name	Value	Description
IP_ADD_MEMBERSHIP	ipmreg	Join multicast group (set only)
IP_DROP_MEMBERSHIP	ipmreg	Leave a multicast group (set only)
IP_HDRINCL	int	IP header included with data
IP_MULTICAST_IF	inaddr	Outgoing interface
IP_MULTICAST_LOOP	uchar	Loopback
IP_MULTICAST_TTL	uchar	Time to live
IP_OPTIONS	char[44]	IP header options
IP_TOS	int	Type of service
IP_TTL	int	Time to live

inaddr is a 32-bit binary structure containing an IP address (struct.unpack('bbbb', *inaddr*)). *ipmreg* is a 64-bit binary structure containing two IP addresses in the same format as *inaddr*. *uchar* is a one-byte unsigned integer as created by struct.pack('b',*uvalue*). *char[44]* is a string containing at most 44 bytes.

Not all options are available on all machines. Refer to an advanced networking book for specific details about each option.

s.listen(*backlog*)

Starts listening for incoming connections. *backlog* specifies the maximum number of pending connections the operating system should queue before connections are refused. The value should be at least 1, with 5 being sufficient for most applications.

s.makefile([*mode* [, *bufsize*]])

Creates a file object associated with the socket. *mode* and *bufsize* have the same meaning as with the built-in open() function. The file object uses a duplicated version of the socket file descriptor, created using os.dup(), so the file object and socket object can be closed or garbage-collected independently.

s.recv(*bufsize* [, *flags*])

Receives data from the socket. The data is returned as a string. The maximum amount of data to be received is specified by *bufsize*. *flags* provides additional information about the message and is usually omitted (in which case it defaults to zero). If used, it's usually set to one of the following constants (system-dependent):

Constant	Description
MSG_PEEK	Look at data, but don't discard (receive only)
MSG_WAITALL	Don't return until the requested number of bytes have been read (receive only)
MSG_OOB	Receive/send out-of-band data
MSG_DONTROUTE	Bypass routing table lookup (send only)

s.recvfrom(*bufsize* [, *flags*])

Like the recv() method except that the return value is a pair (*data*, *address*) in which *data* is a string containing the data received and *address* is the address of the socket sending the data. The optional *flags* argument has the same meaning as for recv(). This function is primarily used in conjunction with the UDP protocol.

s.send(*string* [, *flags*])

Sends data in *string* to a connected socket. The optional *flags* argument has the same meaning as for recv(), described earlier. Returns the number of bytes sent.

s.sendto(*string* [, *flags*], *address*)

Sends data to the socket. *flags* has the same meaning as for recv(). *address* is a tuple of the form (*host*, *port*) that specifies the remote address. The socket should not already be connected. Returns the number of bytes sent. This function is primarily used in conjunction with the UDP protocol.

s.setblocking(*flag*)

If *flag* is zero, the socket is set to nonblocking mode. Otherwise, the socket is set to blocking mode (the default). In nonblocking mode, if a recv() call doesn't find any data or if a send() call cannot immediately send the data, the socket.error exception is raised. In blocking mode, these calls block until they can proceed.

s.setsockopt(*level, optname, value*)

Sets the value of the given socket option. *level* and *optname* have the same meaning as for getsockopt(). The value can be an integer or a string representing the contents of a buffer. In the latter case, it's up to the caller to ensure that the string contains the proper data. See getsockopt() for socket option names, values, and descriptions.

s.shutdown(*how*)

Shuts down one or both halves of the connection. If *how* is 0, further receives are disallowed. If *how* is 1, further sends are disallowed. If *how* is 2, further sends and receives are disallowed.

Exception

error

This exception is raised for socket or address-related errors. It returns a pair (*errno, mesg*) with the error returned by the underlying system call.

Example

A simple example of a TCP connection is shown on page 226 (in the introduction to network programming). The following example illustrates a simple UDP client and server:

```
# UDP message server
# Receive small packets from anywhere and print them out
import socket
s = socket.socket(socket.AF_INET, socket.SOCK_DGRAM)
s.bind(("",10000))
while 1:
      data, address = s.recvfrom(256)
      print address[0], "said : ", data

# UDP message client
# Send a message packet to the server
import socket
s = socket.socket(socket.AF_INET, socket.SOCK_DGRAM)
while 1:
      msg = raw_input("Say something : ")
      if msg:
            s.sendto(msg, ("servername",10000))
      else:
            break
s.close()
```

Notes

- Not all constants and socket options are available on all platforms.
- The socket module currently doesn't support a number of other network protocols such as IPX and IPv6. However, a number of additions to the socket module are likely to appear in future Python releases.

▶ **See Also** SocketServer (258), asyncore (229), select (250).

Appendix A   The Python Library

SocketServer

The SocketServer module is used to write TCP, UDP, and UNIX domain socket servers. Rather than having to implement servers using the low-level socket module, this module provides four classes that implement the above protocols:

TCPServer(address, handler)

A server supporting the TCP protocol. address is a 2-tuple of the form (host, port), where host is the hostname and port is the port number. Typically, host is set to the empty string. handler is an instance of a subclass of the BaseRequestHandler class described later.

UDPServer(address, handler)

A server supporting the Internet UDP protocol. address and handler are the same as for TCPServer().

UnixStreamServer(address, handler)

A server implementing a stream-oriented protocol using UNIX domain sockets.

UnixDatagramServer(address, handler)

A server implementing a datagram protocol using UNIX domain sockets.

Instances of all four server classes have the following methods and attributes:

s.fileno()

Returns the integer file descriptor for the server socket.

s.handle_request()

Waits for a request and handles it by creating an instance of the handler class (described shortly) and invoking its handle() method.

s.serve_forever()

Handles an infinite number of requests.

s.address_family

The protocol family of the server, either socket.AF_INET or socket.AF_UNIX.

s.RequestHandlerClass

The user-provided request handler class that was passed to the server constructor.

s.server_address

The address on which the server is listening, such as ('127.0.0.1', 80).

s.socket

The socket object being used for incoming requests.

In addition, the server classes define the following class attributes (<ServerClass> should be filled in with the name of one of the four available classes):

<ServerClass>.request_queue_size

The size of the request queue that's passed to the socket's listen() method. The default value is 5.

<ServerClass>.socket_type

The socket type used by the server, such as socket.SOCK_STREAM or socket.SOCK_DGRAM.

Requests are handled by defining a subclass of the class BaseRequestHandler. When the server receives a connection, it creates an instance *h* of the handler class and invokes the following methods:

h.finish()

Called to perform cleanup actions after the handle() method has completed. By default, it does nothing. It's not called if either the setup() or handle() method generates an exception.

h.handle()

This method is called to perform the actual work of a request. It's called with no arguments, but several instance variables are set to useful values. *h*.request contains the request, *h*.client_address contains the client address, and *h*.server contains an instance of the server that called the handler. For stream services such as TCP, the *h*.request attribute is a socket object. For datagram services, it's a string containing the received data.

h.setup()

This method is called before the handle() method to perform initialization actions. By default, it does nothing.

The process of creating a server involves the following steps:

1. Define a request handler class by subclassing BaseRequestHandler.

2. Create an instance of one of the server classes by passing the server's address and the request handler class.

3. Call the handle_request() or serve_forever() method of the server to process connections.

The following code illustrates the process for a very simple HTTP server that simply echoes the HTTP request back in a Web page:

```
import SocketServer
import socket
import string
# Read an HTTP request from a client and bounce it back in a Web page
class EchoHandler(SocketServer.BaseRequestHandler):
    def handle(self):
            f = self.request.makefile()
            self.request.send("HTTP/1.0 200 OK\r\n")
            self.request.send("Content-type: text/plain\r\n\r\n\r\n")
            self.request.send("Received connection from %s\r\n\r\n\r\n" %
                              (self.client_address,))
            while 1:
                line = f.readline()
                self.request.send(line)
                if not string.strip(line):
                        break
            f.close()
# Create the server and start serving
serv = SocketServer.TCPServer(("",80),EchoHandler)
serv.serve_forever()
```

By default, the server classes process requests one at a time in a synchronous manner. The servers can alternatively handle requests in a subprocess, using os.fork(), or as a separate thread by instantiating one of the following server classes instead of the four classes listed earlier:

- ForkingUDPServer(*address, handler*)

- ForkingTCPServer(*address, handler*)

- ThreadingUDPServer(*address, handler*)

- ThreadingTCPServer(*address, handler*)

Finally, two additional classes can be used as base classes for handlers: StreamRequestHandler and DatagramRequestHandler. When used, these classes override the setup() and finish() methods of the handle to provide two file attributes, self.rfile and self.wfile, that can be used to read and write data to and from the client, respectively. For example:

```
# Read an HTTP request from a client and bounce it back
class EchoHandler(SocketServer.StreamRequestHandler):
    def handle(self):
        self.wfile.write("HTTP/1.0 200 OK\r\n")
        self.wfile.write("Content-type: text/plain\r\n\r\n")
        self.wfile.write("Received connection from %s\r\n\r\n" %
                         (self.client_address,))
        while 1:
            line = self.rfile.readline()
            self.wfile.write(line)
            if not string.strip(line):
                break
```

Note

- All the server classes can be specialized by subclassing. The online documentation contains more information about this topic.

▶ **See Also** socket (252), BaseHTTPServer (232), SimpleHTTPServer (251), CGIHTTPServer (239), thread (219), os (180).

urllib

The urllib module is used to fetch data from the Web.

urlopen(*url* [, *data*])

Given a uniform resource locator (URL) such as http://www.python.org or ftp://foo.com/pub/foo.tar, this function opens a network connection and returns a file-like object. If the URL doesn't have a scheme identifier such as ftp: or http:, or if it's file:, a local file is opened. If a connection cannot be made or an error occurs, an IOError exception is raised. If the URL is an HTTP request, the optional *data* argument specifies that the request should be made using a POST method, in which case the data is uploaded to the server. In this case, the data must be encoded in an 'application/x-www-form-urlencoded' format as produced by the urlencode() function.

urlretrieve(*url* [, *filename* [, *hook*]])

Opens a URL and copies its data to a local file, if necessary. If *url* is a local file or a cached copy of the data exists, no copying is performed. *filename* specifies the name of the local file in which data will be saved. If omitted, a temporary filename will be generated. *hook* is a function called after a connection has been made and after each block of data has been read. It's called with three arguments: the number of blocks transferred so far, the block size in bytes, and the total size of the file in bytes. The function returns a tuple (*filename, headers*) in which *filename* is the name of the local file where the data was saved and *headers* is the information returned by the info() method as described for urlopen(). If the URL corresponds to a local file or if a cached copy was used, *headers* will be None. Raises an IOError if an error occurs.

urlcleanup()

Clears the local cache created by urlretrieve().

quote(*string* [, *safe*])

Replaces special characters in *string* with escape sequences suitable for including in a URL. Letters, digits, and the underscore (_), comma (,) period (.), and hyphen (·) characters are unchanged. All other characters are converted into escape sequences of the form '%xx'. *safe* provides additional characters that should not be quoted and is '/' by default.

quote_plus(*string* [, *safe*])

Calls quote() and additionally replaces all spaces with plus signs.

unquote(*string*)

Replaces escape sequences of the form '%xx' with their single-character equivalent.

unquote_plus(*string*)

Like unquote(), but also replaces plus signs with spaces.

urlencode(*dict*)

Converts a dictionary to a URL-encoded string suitable for use as the *data* argument of the urlopen() function. The resulting string is a series of '*key=value*' pairs separated by '&' characters, where both *key* and *value* are quoted using quote_plus().

The file-like object returned by urlopen() supports the following methods:

Method	Description
u.read([*nbytes*])	Reads *nbytes* of data.
u.readline()	Reads a single line of text.
u.readlines()	Reads all input lines and returns a list.
u.fileno()	Returns the integer file descriptor.
u.close()	Closes the connection.
u.info()	Returns the mimetools.Message object containing meta-information associated with the URL. For HTTP, the HTTP headers included with the server response are returned. For FTP, the headers include 'content-length'. For local files, the headers include a date, 'content-length', and 'content-type' field.
u.geturl()	Returns the real URL of the returned data, taking into account any redirection that may have occurred.

Notes

- The only supported protocols are HTTP, FTP, Gopher, and local files. Although the httplib module supports HTTP/1.1, this module uses HTTP/1.0 retrieve documents.

Appendix A   **The Python Library**

- If Python is configured with OpenSSL support, secure HTTP (`https://name`) is also supported.
- The `urlopen()` function works transparently with proxies that don't require authentication. On UNIX and Windows, proxy servers should be set with the `$http_proxy`, `$ftp_proxy`, and `$gopher_proxy` environment variables.
- Caching is currently not implemented.
- If a URL points to a local file but the file cannot be opened, the URL is opened using the FTP protocol.
- The `urllib2` module (available with Python 2.1) provides more advanced support for fetching URLs, dealing with redirection, and handling user authentication. Details about this module are available at `http://www.python.org/doc/current/lib/module-urllib2.html`.

▶ **See Also** `httplib` (243), `ftplib` (242), `urlparse` (262), `mimetools` (266).

urlparse

The `urlparse` module is used to manipulate URL strings such as `"http://www.python.org"`. The general form of a URL is as follows:

`"scheme://netloc/path;parameters?query#fragment"`

urlparse(`urlstring` [, `default_scheme` [, `allow_fragments`]])

Parses the URL in `urlstring` and returns a tuple (`scheme`, `netloc`, `path`, `parameters`, `query`, `fragment`). `default_scheme` specifies the scheme (`"http"`, `"ftp"`, and so on) to be used if none is present in the URL. If `allow_fragments` is zero, fragment identifiers are not allowed.

urlunparse(`tuple`)

Constructs a URL string from a tuple as returned by `urlparse()`.

urljoin(`base`, `url` [, `allow_fragments`])

Constructs an absolute URL by combining a base URL `base` with a relative URL `url`. `allow_fragments` has the same meaning as for `urlparse()`. If the last component of the base URL is not a directory, it's stripped.

Examples

```
>>> urlparse("http://www.python.org/index.html")
('http', 'www.python.org', '/index.html', '', '', '')

>>> urlunparse(('http', 'www.python.org', '/index.html', '', '', ''))
'http://www.python.org/index.html'

>>> urljoin("http://www.python.org/index.html","Help.html")
'http://www.python.org/Help.html'
```

▶ **See Also** `urllib` (260), Internet RFC 1738, Internet RFC 1808.

webbrowser

The `webbrowser` module provides functions for opening documents in a Web browser in a platform-independent manner. The module tries to determine the current browser using the environment of the local machine.

open(*url* [, *new*])

Displays *url* with the default browser. If *new* is set, a new browser window is opened.

open_new(*url*)

Displays *url* in a new window of the default browser.

get([*name*])

Returns a controller object for manipulating a browser. *name* is the name of the browser type and is typically one of 'netscape', 'kfm', 'grail', 'windows-default', 'internet-config', or 'command-line'.

register(*name*, *constructor*[, *controller*])

Registers a new browser type for use with the get() function. *name* is the name of the browser. *constructor* is called without arguments to create a controller object for manipulating the browser. *controller* is a controller instance to use instead. If supplied, *constructor* is ignored and may be None.

A controller instance *c* returned by the get() function has the following methods:

c.open(*url*[, *new*])

Same as the open() function.

c.open_new(*url*)

Same as the open_new() function.

Note

- If set, the $BROWSER environment variable determines the name of the default browser.

Internet Data Handling and Encoding

The modules in this section are used to encode and decode data formats that are widely used in Internet applications.

base64

The base64 module is used to encode and decode data using base64 encoding. base64 is commonly used to encode binary data in mail attachments.

decode(*input*, *output*)

Decodes base64–encoded data. *input* is a filename or a file object open for reading. *output* is a filename or a file object open for writing.

decodestring(*s*)

Decodes a base64–encoded string *s*. Returns a string containing the decoded binary data.

encode(*input*, *output*)

Encodes data using base64. *input* is a filename or a file object open for reading. *output* is a filename or a file object open for writing.

encodestring(*s*)

Encodes a string *s* using base64.

▶ **See Also** binascii (264), Internet RFC 1421.

binascii

The `binascii` module is used to convert data between binary and a variety of ASCII encodings such as base64, binhex, and uuencode.

a2b_uu(*string*)

Converts a line of uuencoded data to binary. Lines normally contain 45 (binary) bytes, except for the last line. Line data may be followed by whitespace.

b2a_uu(*data*)

Converts a string of binary data to a line of uuencoded ASCII characters. The length of *data* should not be more than 45 bytes.

a2b_base64(*string*)

Converts a string of base64-encoded data to binary.

b2a_base64(*data*)

Converts a string of binary data to a line of base64-encoded ASCII characters. The length of *data* should not be more than 57 bytes.

a2b_hex(*string*)

Converts a string of hex digits to a string of binary data. *string* must contain an even number of digits.

b2a_hex(*data*)

Converts a string of binary data to a string of hex digits.

a2b_hqx(*string*)

Converts a string of binhex4-encoded data to binary without performing RLE decompression.

rledecode_hqx(*data*)

Performs an RLE (Run-Length Encoding) decompression of the binary data in *data*. Returns the decompressed data unless the data input is incomplete, in which case the `Incomplete` exception is raised.

rlecode_hqx(*data*)

Performs a binhex4 RLE compression of *data*.

b2a_hqx(*data*)

Converts the binary data to a string of binhex4-encoded ASCII characters. *data* should already be RLE coded and have a length divisible by three.

crc_hqx(*data*, *crc*)

Computes the binhex4 CRC checksum of the data. *crc* is a starting value of the checksum.

crc32(*data* [, *oldcrc*])

Computes the CRC-32 checksum of *data*. If supplied, the *oldcrc* parameter allows for incremental calculation of the checksum.

Exceptions

Error

Exception raised on errors.

`Incomplete`

Exception raised on incomplete data. This exception occurs when multiple bytes of data are expected, but the input data has been truncated.

▶ **See Also** `base64` (263), `binhex` (265), `uu` (277).

binhex

The `binhex` module is used to encode and decode files in binhex4, a format commonly used to represent files on the Macintosh.

`binhex(input, output)`

Converts a binary file with name *input* to a binhex file. *output* is a filename or an open file-like object supporting `write()` and `close()` methods.

`hexbin(input [, output])`

Decodes a binhex file. *input* is either a filename or a file-like object with `read()` and `close()` methods. *output* is the name of the output file. If omitted, the output name is taken from the binhex file.

Notes

■ Both the data and resource forks are handled on the Macintosh.

■ Only the data fork is handled on other platforms.

▶ **See Also** `binascii` (264), `macostools` (176).

mailcap

The `mailcap` module is used to read UNIX mailcap files. Mailcap files are used to tell mail readers and Web browsers how to process files with different MIME types. The contents of a mailcap file typically look something like this:

```
video/mpeg; xmpeg %s
application/pdf; acroread %s
```

When data of a given MIME type is encountered, the mailcap file is consulted to find an application for handling that data.

`getcaps()`

Reads all available mailcap files and returns a dictionary mapping MIME types to a mailcap entry. Mailcap files are read from `$HOME/.mailcap`, `/etc/mailcap`, `/usr/etc/mailcap`, and `/usr/local/etc/mailcap`.

`findmatch(caps, mimetype [, key [, filename [, plist]]])`

Searches the dictionary *caps* for a mailcap entry matching *mimetype*. *key* is a string indicating an action and is typically `'view'`, `'compose'`, or `'edit'`. *filename* is the name of the file that's substituted for the `%s` keyword in the mailcap entry. *plist* is a list of named parameters and is described further in the online documentation at `http://www.python.org/doc/lib/module-mailcap.html`. Returns a tuple (*cmd*, *mailcap*) containing the command from the mailcap file and the raw mailcap entry.

Example

```
import mailcap
import urllib
import os
# Go fetch a document
urllib.urlretrieve("http://www.swig.org/Doc1.1/PDF/Python.pdf", "/tmp/tmp1234")

caps = mailcap.getcaps()
cmd, mc = mailcap.findmatch(caps,'application/pdf',filename='/tmp/tmp1234')
if cmd:
    os.system(cmd + " &")
else:
    print "No application for type application/pdf"
```

▶ **See Also** http://www.python.org/doc/lib/module-mailcap.html,
mimetypes (268), Internet RFC 1524.

mimetools

The `mimetools` module provides a number of functions for manipulating MIME-encoded messages. MIME (Multipurpose Internet Mail Extensions) is a standard for sending multipart multimedia data through Internet mail. Parts of the standard are also used in other settings, such as the HTTP protocol. A MIME-encoded message looks similar to this:

```
Content-Type: multipart/mixed; boundary="====_931526447=="
Date: Fri, 06 Jul 2001 03:20:47 -0500
From: John Doe <johndoe@foo.com>
To: Jane Doe (janedoe@foo.com>
Subject: Important Message From John Doe

--====_931526447==
Content-Type: text/plain; charset="us-ascii"

Here is that document you asked for ... don't show anyone else ;-)

--====_931526447==
Content-Type: application/msword; name="list.doc"
Content-Transfer-Encoding: base64
Content-Disposition: attachment; filename="list.doc"

SXQgd2FzIGEgbG9uZyBob3QgZGF5IGluIHRoZSBtb250aCBvbiBiKdWx5LCB3aGVuIExhcnJ5IHN0
YXJ0ZWQgdGFsa2luZwphYm91dCBzb2Npby1wb2xpdGljYWwgc2NhbGibGUgaW1tZXJzaXZlIHZp
cnR1YWwgdGcG9yYWwKY29sbGFib3JhdGl2ZSBwYXJhbGxlbCBoaWdoIHBlcmZvcm1hbmNlIHdl
Yi1iYXNlZCBtb2JpbGUKb2JqZWN0LW9yaWVudGVkIHNlaWVudGlmaWMgY29tcHV0aW5nIGVudmly
b25tZW50cy4gIEZvcnR1bmF0ZWx5LCBQZXRlICmhhZCByZWFsbWJlcmVkIHRvIGJyaW5nIGhpcyAu
NDUuI4KCg==

--====_931526447==--
```

MIME messages are broken into parts delimited by a line separator such as `--====_931526447==` above. This separator always starts with a double hyphen as shown. The final separator has a trailing double hyphen (--) appended to indicate the end of the message. Immediately following each separator is a set of RFC 822 headers describing the content-type and encoding. Data is separated from the headers by a single blank line.

The mimetools module defines the following functions to parse headers and decode data:

Message(*file* [, *seekable*])

Parses MIME headers and returns a Message object derived from the rfc822.Message class. *file* and *seekable* have the same meaning as for rfc822.Message.

choose_boundary()

Creates a unique string of the form `'hostipaddr.uid.pid.timestamp.random'` that can be used as a part boundary when generating a message.

decode(*input*, *output*, *encoding*)

Reads encoded data from the open file object *input* and writes the decoded data to the open file object *output*. *encoding* specifies the encoding method: `'base64'`, `'quoted-printable'`, or `'uuencode'`.

encode(*input*, *output*, *encoding*)

Reads data from the open file object *input*, encodes it, and writes it to the open file object *output*. Encoding types are the same as for decode().

copyliteral(*input*, *output*)

Read lines of text from the open file *input* until EOF and writes them to the open file *output*.

copybinary(*input*, *output*)

Read blocks of binary data from the open file *input* until EOF and writes them to the open file *output*.

Instances of the Message class support all the methods described in the rfc822 module. In addition, the following methods are available:

m.getplist()

Returns the parameters for the content-type header as a list of strings. If the message contains the header `'Content-type: text/html; charset=US-ASCII'`, for example, this function returns `['charset=US-ASCII']`. For parameters of the form `'key=value'`, key is converted to lowercase, while *value* is unchanged.

m.getparam(*name*)

Returns the value of the first parameter of the form `'name=value'` from the `'content-type'` header. If *value* is surrounded by quotes of the form `'<...>'` or `"..."`, they're removed.

m.getencoding()

Returns the encoding specified in the `'content-transfer-encoding'` message header. If no such header exists, returns `'7bit'`.

m.gettype()

Returns the message type from the `'content-type'` header. Types are returned as a string of the form `'type/subtype'`. If no content-type header is available, `'text/plain'` is returned.

m.getmaintype()

Returns the primary type from the `'content-type'` header. If no such header exists, returns `'text'`.

`m.getsubtype()`

Returns the subtype from the `'content-type'` header. If no such header exists, returns `'plain'`.

▶ **See Also** `rfc822` (274), `mimetypes` (268), `MimeWriter` (271), `multifile` (272), `mailcap` (265), Internet RFC 1521.

mimetypes

The `mimetypes` module is used to guess the MIME type associated with a file, based on its filename extension. It also converts MIME types to their standard filename extensions. MIME types consist of a type/subtype pair. The following table shows the MIME types currently recognized by this module:

File Suffix	MIME Type
`.a`	application/octet-stream
`.ai`	application/postscript
`.aif`	audio/x-aiff
`.aifc`	audio/x-aiff
`.aiff`	audio/x-aiff
`.au`	audio/basic
`.avi`	video/x-msvideo
`.bcpio`	application/x-bcpio
`.bin`	application/octet-stream
`.cdf`	application/x-netcdf
`.cpio`	application/x-cpio
`.csh`	application/x-csh
`.dll`	application/octet-stream
`.dvi`	application/x-dvi
`.exe`	application/octet-stream
`.eps`	application/postscript
`.etx`	text/x-setext
`.gif`	image/gif
`.gtar`	application/x-gtar
`.hdf`	application/x-hdf
`.htm`	text/html
`.html`	text/html
`.ief`	image/ief
`.jpe`	image/jpeg
`.jpeg`	image/jpeg
`.jpg`	image/jpeg
`.latex`	application/x-latex
`.man`	application/x-troff-man

File Suffix	MIME Type
.me	application/x-troff-me
.mif	application/x-mif
.mov	video/quicktime
.movie	video/x-sgi-movie
.mpe	video/mpeg
.mpeg	video/mpeg
.mpg	video/mpeg
.ms	application/x-troff-ms
.nc	application/x-netcdf
.o	application/octet-stream
.obj	application/octet-stream
.oda	application/oda
.pbm	image/x-portable-bitmap
.pdf	application/pdf
.pgm	image/x-portable-graymap
.pnm	image/x-portable-anymap
.png	image/png
.ppm	image/x-portable-pixmap
.py	text/x-python
.pyc	application/x-python-code
.ps	application/postscript
.qt	video/quicktime
.ras	image/x-cmu-raster
.rgb	image/x-rgb
.rdf	application/xml
.roff	application/x-troff
.rtf	application/rtf
.rtx	text/richtext
.sgm	text/x-sgml
.sgml	text/x-sgml
.sh	application/x-sh
.shar	application/x-shar
.snd	audio/basic
.so	application/octet-stream
.src	application/x-wais-source
.sv4cpio	application/x-sv4cpio
.sv4crc	application/x-sv4crc
.t	application/x-troff
.tar	application/x-tar

continues >>

>> continued

File Suffix	MIME Type
.tcl	application/x-tcl
.tex	application/x-tex
.texi	application/x-texinfo
.texinfo	application/x-texinfo
.tif	image/tiff
.tiff	image/tiff
.tr	application/x-troff
.tsv	text/tab-separated-values
.txt	text/plain
.ustar	application/x-ustar
.wav	audio/x-wav
.xbm	image/x-xbitmap
.xml	text/xml
.xsl	application/xml
.xpm	image/x-xpixmap
.xwd	image/x-xwindowdump
.zip	application/zip

guess_type(*filename*)

Guesses the MIME type of a file based on its filename or URL. Returns a tuple (*type*, *encoding*) in which *type* is a string of the form type/subtype and *encoding* is the program used to encode the data (for example, compress or gzip). Returns (None, None) if the type cannot be guessed.

guess_extension(*type*)

Guesses the standard file extension for a file based on its MIME type. Returns a string with the filename extension including the leading dot (.). Returns None for unknown types.

init([*files*])

Initializes the module. *files* is a sequence of filenames that are read to extract type information. These files contain lines that map a MIME type to a list of acceptable file suffixes such as the following:

```
image/jpeg:   jpe jpeg jpg
text/html:    htm html
...
```

read_mime_types(*filename*)

Loads type mapping from a given filename. Returns a dictionary mapping filename extensions to MIME type strings. Returns None if *filename* doesn't exist or cannot be read.

knownfiles

List of common names for mime.types files.

suffix_map

Dictionary mapping suffixes to suffixes. This is used to allow recognition of encoded files for which the encoding and the type are indicated by the same extension. For example, the .tgz extension is mapped to .tar.gz to allow the encoding and type to be recognized separately.

encodings_map

Dictionary mapping filename extensions to encoding types.

types_map

Dictionary mapping filename extensions to MIME types.

▶ **See Also** mimetools (266).

MimeWriter

The MimeWriter module defines the class MimeWriter that's used to generate MIME-encoded multipart files.

MimeWriter(fp)

Creates a new instance of the MimeWriter class. fp is an open file object to be used for writing. A StringIO object can also be used.

An instance m of the MimeWriter class has the following methods:

m.addheader(key, value [, prefix])

Adds a header line of the form "key: value" to the MIME message. prefix determines where the header is inserted; 0 appends to the end (the default) and 1 inserts at the start.

m.flushheaders()

Writes all the headers accumulated so far.

m.startbody(ctype [, plist [, prefix]])

Returns a file-like object that's used to write to the body of the message. ctype specifies the content type and plist is a list of tuples of the form (name, value) containing additional parameters for the content-type declaration. prefix has the same meaning as for the addheader() method except that its default value is set to insert at the start.

m.startmultipartbody(subtype [, boundary [, plist [, prefix]]])

Returns a file-like object that's used to write the body of a multipart message. subtype specifies the multipart subtype such as 'mixed' and boundary can be used to provide a user-defined boundary specifier. plist is a list containing optional parameters for the subtype, and prefix is the same as in the startbody() method. Subparts are created using nextpart().

m.nextpart()

Returns a new instance of MimeWriter that represents an individual part in a multipart message. startmultipartbody() must be called prior to calling this method.

m.lastpart()

Used to indicate the last part of a multipart message. Should always be called to terminate a multipart message.

Example

The following example takes a list of files passed on the command line and produces a multipart MIME document in which each file is encoded using base64 encoding:

```
import sys
import mimetools, mimetypes, MimeWriter
# Open the output file and create a MimeWriter
out = open("output.txt","w")
writer = MimeWriter.MimeWriter(out)
# Start a multipart message
writer.startmultipartbody("mixed")
writer.flushheaders()
# Iterate over files passed on the command line
for file in sys.argv[1:]:
    subpart = writer.nextpart()  # Create a new subpart
    # Attempt to guess the file's MIME type and encoding
    type,encoding = mimetypes.guess_type(file)
    if encoding:
            subpart.addheader("Content-encoding",encoding)
            subpart.addheader("Content-transfer-encoding", "base64")
    if type:
            pout = subpart.startbody(type, [("name",file)])
    else:
            pout = subpart.startbody("text/plain",[("name",file)])
    infile = open(file,"rb")
    # Encode the raw data using base64
    mimetools.encode(infile,pout,'base64')
    infile.close()

# Clean up
writer.lastpart()
out.close()
```

▶ **See Also** mimetypes (268), mimetools (266), rfc822 (274), multifile (272).

multifile

The multifile module defines an object that can be used to read multipart text files as found in MIME-encoded messages. The multifile object works by splitting a file into a series of logical file-like objects that are delimited by a unique boundary string such as the following:

```
--216.150.6.70.100.4397.932677969.082.3036
Part 1
...
--216.150.6.70.100.4397.932677969.082.3036
Part 2
...
--216.150.6.70.100.4397.932677969.082.3036--
```

In this case, the boundary string is of the form returned by the mimetools.choose_boundary() function. The last boundary string (with a trailing --) marks the end of the multipart data.

> **MultiFile(*fp* [, *seekable*])**

Creates a multifile object. *fp* is a file-like object containing input data. The input object's readline() method is used to read data. If the *seekable* option is set, the multifile object allows random access using the seek() and tell() methods.

A MultiFile object *m* supports the following methods:

***m*.push(*str*)**

Pushes a boundary string into the reader. When this string is encountered in the input, it signals an end of section or end of message. More than one boundary marker can be pushed to handle nested multipart data. However, encountering any other boundary than the most recently pushed value raises an error.

***m*.readline()**

Reads a line of text. If the line matches the most recently pushed boundary, '' is returned to indicate the end of the part. Furthermore, if the boundary corresponds to an end marker, the m.last attribute is set to 1. Raises Error if an EOF is encountered before all boundary strings have been popped.

***m*.readlines()**

Returns all lines remaining in the current part as a list of strings.

***m*.read()**

Reads all lines remaining in the current part and returns as a single string.

***m*.next()**

Skips to the next section. Returns true if a next section exists, false if an end marker is encountered.

***m*.pop()**

Pops a section boundary. This boundary will no longer be interpreted as EOF.

***m*.seek(*pos* [, *whence*])**

Seeks to a new position within the current section. The *pos* and *whence* arguments are interpreted as for a file seek.

***m*.tell()**

Returns the file position relative to the start of the current section.

Finally, MultiFile instances have two public-instance variables:

***m*.level**

Nesting depth of the current part.

***m*.last**

True if the last end-of-file was an end-of-message marker.

Example

```
# Unpack a MIME encoded mail message into parts
import mimetools, multifile, sys
def unpack_part(file,partno=0):
    headers = mimetools.Message(file)      # Get headers
    type = headers.getmaintype()           # Get main content type
    if type == 'multipart':                # Multipart?
        boundary = headers.getparam("boundary")
        file.push(boundary)
        file.readlines()
        while not file.last:
            file.next()
            partno = partno + 1
            unpack_part(file,partno)
        file.pop()
        return
    name = headers.getparam("name")         # Get filename
    if not name: name = "part%d" % (partno,)
```

continues >>

>> *continued*

```
        encoding = headers.getencoding()
        print "Unpacking '%s'. Encoding = %s" % (name, encoding)
        if encoding == '7bit':
            outfile = open(name,"w")
            mimetools.copyliteral(file,outfile)
        else:
            outfile = open(name,"wb")
            mimetools.decode(file,outfile,encoding)
        outfile.close()
# Read a filename from options and unpack it
f = open(sys.argv[1])
mf = multifile.MultiFile(f,0)
unpack_part(mf)
```

Note

- The MultiFile class defines a number of methods that can be specialized in a
  subclass. Please refer to the online library reference at
  http://www.python.org/doc/lib/module-multifile.html.

▶ **See Also** mimetools (266), MimeWriter (271),
http://www.python.org/doc/lib/module-multifile.html.

quopri

The quopri module performs quoted-printable transport encoding and decoding.
This format is used primarily to encode text files.

  decode(*input*, *output*)

Decodes. *input* and *output* are file objects.

  encode(*input*, *output*, *quotetabs*)

Encodes. *input* and *output* are file objects. *quotetabs*, if set to true, forces tab characters to be quoted in addition to the normal quoting rules.

▶ **See Also** binascii (264), Internet RFC 1521.

rfc822

The rfc822 module is used to parse email headers presented in a format defined
by the Internet standard RFC 822. Headers of this form are used in a number of
contexts, including mail handling and in the HTTP protocol. A collection of
RFC 822 headers looks like this:

```
Return-Path: <beazley@cs.uchicago.edu>
Date: Sun, 15 Apr 03:18:21 -0500 (CDT)
Message-Id: <199907171518.KAA24322@gargoyle.cs.uchicago.edu>
Reply-To: beazley@cs.uchicago.edu
References: <15065.6056.897223.775915@empire-builder.cs.uchicago.edu>
        <20010415041130.008D1D1D8@smack.cs.uchicago.edu>
Mime-Version: 1.0 (generated by tm-edit 7.78)
Content-Type: text/plain; charset=US-ASCII
From: David Beazley <beazley@cs.uchicago.edu>
To: techstaff@cs
Subject: Modem problem

I'm having some trouble running MPI over the ultra-scalable modem array on our
Beowulf cluster. Can someone take a look at it?
```

Each header line is of the form 'headername: values' and may span multiple lines provided that additional lines are indented with whitespace. Header names are not case sensitive, so a field name of 'Content-Type' is the same as 'content-type'. A list of headers is terminated by a single blank line.

RFC 822 headers are parsed by creating an instance of the Message class.

Message(file [, seekable])

Reads RFC 822 headers from the file-like object *file* and returns a Message object. Headers are read using file.readline() until a blank line is encountered. *seekable* is a flag that's set to zero if *file* is unseekable (such as a file created from a socket).

A Message object *m* behaves like a dictionary except that its key values are not case sensitive and it doesn't support certain dictionary operations, including update() and clear().

Method	Description
m[name]	Returns the value for header name.
m[name]=value	Adds a header.
m.keys()	Returns a list of header names.
m.values()	Returns a list of header values.
m.items()	Returns a list of header (name, value) pairs.
m.has_key(name)	Tests for the existence of a header name.
m.get(name [, default])	Gets a header value. Returns *default* if not found.
len(m)	Returns the number of headers.
str(m)	Converts headers to an RFC 822–formatted string.

In addition, the following methods are available:

m.getallmatchingheaders(name)

Returns a list of all lines with headers that match *name*, including continuation lines (if any).

m.getfirstmatchingheader(name)

Returns the list of lines for the first header matching *name*, including any continuation lines. Returns None if *name* doesn't match any headers.

m.getrawheader(name)

Returns a string containing the raw text after the colon for the first header matching *name*. Returns None if no match is found.

m.getheader(name [, default])

Like getrawheader(name), but strips all leading and trailing whitespace. *default* specifies a default value to return if no matching header is found.

m.getaddr(name)

Returns a pair (full_name, email_address) for a header containing an email address. If no header matches *name*, (None, None) is returned.

m.getaddrlist(name)

Parses a header containing a list of email addresses and returns a list of tuples as returned by the getaddr() method. If multiple headers match the named header, all are parsed for addresses (for example, multiple 'cc' headers).

`m.getdate(name)`

Parses a header containing a date and returns a 9-tuple compatible with `time.mktime()`. Returns `None` if no match is found or the date cannot be parsed.

`m.getdate_tz(name)`

Parses a header containing a date and returns a 10-tuple in which the first nine elements are the same as returned by `getdate()` and the tenth is a number with the offset of the date's timezone from UTC (Greenwich Mean Time). Returns `None` if no match is found or the date is unparsable.

Finally, messages have two instance attributes:

`m.headers`

A list containing the entire set of header lines.

`m.fp`

The file-like object passed when the `Message` was created.

In addition to `Message`, the `rfc822` module defines the following utility functions:

`parsedate(date)`

Parses an RFC 822–formatted date such as `'Mon, 16 Apr 2001 17:30:08 -0600'` and returns a 9-tuple that's compatible with the `time.mktime()` function. Returns `None` if `date` cannot be parsed.

`parsedate_tz(date)`

Parses a date, but returns a 10-tuple where the first nine elements are the same as returned by `parsedate()` and the tenth item is the offset of the date's timezone from UTC. Returns `None` if `date` cannot be parsed.

`mktime_tz(tuple)`

Turns a 10-tuple as returned by `parsedate_tz()` into a UTC timestamp. If the timezone item is `None`, assumes local time.

`AddressList(addrlist)`

Converts a string containing a list of email addresses into an `AddressList` object. The following operations can be performed on `AddressList` objects:

Operation	Description
`len(a)`	Number of addresses in a list
`str(a)`	Converts a back into a string of email addresses
`a + b`	Combines two lists of addresses, removing duplicates
`a - b`	Removes all addresses in list b from list a

Example

```
import rfc822
# Open a mail message
f = open("mailmessage")
# Read the headers
m = rfc822.Message(f)
# Extract a few fields
m_from = m["From"]
m_to = m.getaddr("To")
m_subject = m["Subject"]
```

Note

■ The Message class defines a few additional methods that can be specialized in a subclass. For details, please refer to the online documentation at http://www.python.org/doc/lib/module-rfc822.html.

▶ **See Also** mimetools (266), MimeWriter (271), mimetypes (268), mailcap (265), Internet RFC 822, http://www.python.org/doc/lib/module-rfc822.html.

uu

The uu module is used to encode and decode files in uuencode format, commonly used for transferring binary data over an ASCII-only connection.

encode(input, output [, name [, mode]])

Uuencodes a file. *input* is a file object opened for reading or a filename. *output* is a file object opened for writing or a filename. *name* specifies the name of the file that's encoded in the uuencoded file. *mode* specifies the mode of the file. By default, *name* and *mode* are taken from the input file.

decode(input [, output [, mode]])

Decodes a uuencoded file. *input* is a file object opened for reading or a filename. *output* is a file object opened for writing or a filename. *mode* is used to set permission bits and overrides the setting encoded in the input file.

▶ **See Also** binascii (264).

xdrlib

xdrlib is used to encode and decode data in the Sun XDR (External Data Representation) format. XDR is often used as a portable way to encode binary data for use in networked applications. It's used extensively in applications involving remote procedure calls (RPC).

Encoding and decoding is controlled through the use of two classes:

Packer()

Creates an object for packing data into an XDR representation.

Unpacker(data)

Creates an object for unpacking XDR-encoded data. *data* is a string containing XDR-encoded data values.

An instance *p* of the Packer class supports the following methods:

p.get_buffer()

Returns the current pack buffer as a string.

p.reset()

Resets the pack buffer to the empty string.

p.pack_uint(x)

Packs a 32-bit unsigned integer *x*.

p.pack_int(x)

Packs a 32-bit signed integer *x*.

`p.pack_enum(x)`

Packs an enumeration *x* (an integer).

`p.pack_bool(x)`

Packs a Boolean value *x*.

`p.pack_uhyper(x)`

Packs a 64-bit unsigned integer *x*.

`p.pack_hyper(x)`

Packs a 64-bit signed integer *x*.

`p.pack_float(x)`

Packs a single-precision floating-point number.

`p.pack_double(x)`

Packs a double-precision floating-point number.

`p.pack_fstring(n, s)`

Packs a fixed-length string of length *n*.

`p.pack_fopaque(n, data)`

Packs a fixed-length opaque data stream. Similar to `pack_fstring()`.

`p.pack_string(s)`

Packs a variable-length string *s*.

`p.pack_opaque(data)`

Packs a variable-length opaque data string *data*. Similar to `pack_string()`.

`p.pack_bytes(bytes)`

Packs a variable-length byte stream *bytes*. Similar to `pack_string()`.

`p.pack_list(list, pack_func)`

Packs a list of homogeneous items. *pack_func* is the function called to pack each data item (for example, `p.pack_int`). For each item in the list, an unsigned integer 1 is packed first, followed by the data item. An unsigned integer 0 is packed at the end of the list.

`p.pack_farray(n, array, pack_func)`

Packs a fixed-length list of homogeneous items. *n* is the list length, *array* is a list containing the data, and *pack_func* is the function called to pack each data item.

`p.pack_array(list, pack_func)`

Packs a variable-length list of homogeneous items by first packing its length and then calling the `pack_farray()` method.

An instance *u* of the Unpacker class supports the following methods:

`u.reset(data)`

Resets the string buffer with the given data.

`u.get_position()`

Returns the current unpack position in the data buffer.

`u.set_position(position)`

Sets the data buffer unpack position to *position*.

`u.get_buffer()`

Returns the current unpack data buffer as a string.

u.done()

Indicates unpack completion. Raises an Error exception if all the data has not been unpacked.

In addition, every data type that can be packed with a Packer can be unpacked with an Unpacker. Unpacking methods are of the form unpack_type(), and take no arguments. They return the unpacked object.

u.unpack_int()

Unpacks and returns a 32-bit signed integer.

u.unpack_uint()

Unpacks and returns a 32-bit unsigned integer. If the unsigned value is larger than sys.maxint, it's returned as an unsigned long integer.

u.unpack_enum()

Unpacks and returns an enumeration (an integer).

u.unpack_bool()

Unpacks a Boolean value and returns it as an integer.

u.unpack_hyper()

Unpacks and returns a 64-bit signed integer as a Python long integer.

u.unpack_uhyper()

Unpacks and returns a 64-bit unsigned integer as a Python long integer.

u.unpack_float()

Unpacks and returns a single-precision floating-point number. The value will be converted to double precision when it is returned as a Python floating-point number.

u.unpack_double()

Unpacks and returns a double-precision floating-point number.

u.unpack_fstring(*n*)

Unpacks and returns a fixed-length string. *n* is the number of characters expected.

u.unpack_fopaque(*n*)

Unpacks and returns a fixed-length opaque data stream, similarly to unpack_fstring().

u.unpack_string()

Unpacks and returns a variable-length string.

u.unpack_opaque()

Unpacks and returns a variable-length opaque data string.

u.unpack_bytes()

Unpacks and returns a variable-length byte stream.

u.unpack_list(*unpack_func*)

Unpacks and returns a list of homogeneous items as packed by pack_list(). *unpack_func* is the function called to perform the unpacking for each item (for example, *u*.unpack_int).

Appendix A   The Python Library

> *u*.`unpack_farray(`*n*, `unpack_func`)

Unpacks and returns (as a list) a fixed-length array of homogeneous items. *n* is the number of list elements to expect and `unpack_func` is the function used to unpack each item.

> *u*.`unpack_array(`*unpack_func*)

Unpacks and returns a variable-length list of homogeneous items. `unpack_func` is the function used to unpack each item.

Exceptions

> `Error`

The base exception class. `Error` has a single public data member *msg* containing the description of the error.

> `ConversionError`

Class derived from `Error`. Contains no additional instance variables.

Note

- Objects created with `xdrlib` can be pickled using the `pickle` module.

> ▶ **See Also** `struct` (144), `array` (127), Internet RFC 1014.

Restricted Execution

Normally, a Python program has complete access to the machine on which it runs. In particular, it can open files and network connections, and perform other potentially sensitive operations. In certain applications, however, this is undesirable—especially in Internet applications, in which a program may be subject to attackers or when code from an untrusted source is executed.

To provide some measure of safety, Python provides support for restricted execution. Restricted execution is based on the notion of separating trusted and untrusted code. In particular, a program running in trusted mode (a *supervisor*) can create an execution environment (or *sandbox*) in which untrusted code can be executed with limited privileges. The capabilities of the untrusted code are tightly controlled by the supervisor, which can restrict the set of objects that can be accessed as well as the behavior of individual functions.

Python's restricted execution mode is implemented by playing a number of tricks with dictionaries, namespaces, and the environment in which untrusted code executes. As a result, untrusted code uses the same set of function names and modules that would be used in a normal program (as opposed to separate, secure APIs). The only difference is that certain modules and built-in functions may be unavailable (or redefined to secure versions).

Internally, the interpreter determines whether a piece of code is restricted by looking at the identity of the `__builtins__` object in its global namespace. If it's the same as the standard `__builtin__` module, the code is unrestricted. Otherwise, it's restricted. When running in restricted mode, the interpreter imposes a number of further restrictions that are designed to prevent untrusted code from becoming privileged:

- The __dict__ attribute of classes and instances is not accessible.
- The func_globals attribute of functions is not accessible.

These restrictions are imposed to prevent untrusted code from altering its global namespace (which is used by the supervisor to restrict the set of objects that are accessible).

Finally, it should be noted that although the Python restricted execution environment prevents access to critical operations, it doesn't prevent denial-of-service attacks, in which an untrusted program might try to exhaust memory or use an unlimited amount of CPU time.

Restricted execution is supported through the use of two modules: rexec and Bastion. rexec restricts the environment in which code runs. Bastion restricts the access that untrusted code has to objects created by the supervisor.

rexec

The rexec module is used to run code in a restricted environment. The environment is encapsulated in a class RExec that contains attributes specifying the capabilities for the code to execute.

RExec([*hooks* [, *verbose*]])

Creates an instance of the REexec class that represents a restricted environment. *hooks* is an instance of a class used to implement nonstandard methods for importing modules and is not described here. *verbose* is a flag that causes some debugging output to be printed to standard output.

The following class variables are used by the __init__() method when an instance of the REexec class is created. Changing them on an instance has no effect, so it's better to create a subclass of RExec that modifies their values.

REExec.nok_builtin_names

A tuple of strings containing the names of built-in functions not available to restricted programs. The default value is ('open', 'reload', '__import__').

REExec.ok_builtin_modules

A tuple of strings containing the names of built-in modules that can be safely imported. The default value is as follows:

```
('audioop', 'array', 'binascii', 'cmath', 'errno', 'imageop', 'marshal',
'math', 'md5', 'operator', 'parser', 'pcre', 'regex', 'rotor',
'select', 'strop', 'struct', 'time')
```

REExec.ok_path

The list of directories that are searched when an import is performed in the restricted environment. The default value is the same as sys.path.

REExec.ok_posix_names

A tuple of names for functions in the os module that are available to restricted programs. The default value is as follows:

```
('error', 'fstat', 'listdir', 'lstat', 'readlink',
'stat', 'times', 'uname', 'getpid', 'getppid',
'getcwd', 'getuid', 'getgid', 'geteuid', 'getegid')
```

`RExec.ok_sys_names`

A tuple of names for functions and variables in the sys module that are available to restricted programs. The default value is as follows:

`('ps1', 'ps2', 'copyright', 'version', 'platform', 'exit', 'maxint')`

An instance *r* of RExec uses the following methods to execute restricted code:

`r.r_eval(code)`

Like eval() except that code is executed in the restricted environment. *code* is a string or a compiled code object. Returns the value of the resulting expression.

`r.r_exec(code)`

Like the exec statement except that execution is performed in the restricted environment. *code* is a string or a compiled code object.

`r.r_execfile(filename)`

Like execfile() except that code is executed in the restricted environment.

`r.s_eval(code)`

Like r_eval() except that access to sys.stdin, sys.stdout, and sys.stderr is allowed.

`r.s_exec(code)`

Like r_exec() except that access to sys.stdin, sys.stdout, and sys.stderr is allowed.

`r.s_execfile(code)`

Like r_execfile() except that access to sys.stdin, sys.stdout, and sys.stderr is allowed.

The following methods are called implicitly by code executing in the restricted environment and can be redefined in subclasses of RExec:

`r.r_import(modulename [, globals [, locals [, fromlist]]])`

Imports a module *modulename*. An ImportError exception should be raised if the module is unsafe.

`r.r_open(filename [, mode [, bufsize]])`

Opens a file in the restricted environment. The arguments are the same as the built-in open() function. By default, files can be opened for reading, but not for writing.

`r.r_reload(module)`

Reloads the module object *module*.

`r.r_unload(module)`

Unloads the module object *module*.

`r.s_import(modulename [, globals [, locals [, fromlist]]])`

Like r_import(), but with access to standard I/O streams.

`r.s_reload(module)`

Like r_reload(), but with access to standard I/O streams.

`r.s_unload(module)`

Like r_unload(), but with access to standard I/O streams.

Example

The following program executes Python code submitted through a CGI script in a restricted environment along with limits on CPU and memory usage:

```
#!/usr/local/bin/python
import rexec
import cgi, StringIO, sys, string, resource
form = cgi.FieldStorage()
code = form["code"].value          # Get some arbitrary code to execute
code = string.replace(code,"\015","")
sys.stderr = sys.stdout      # Make error messages appear

print "Content-type: text/plain\n\n"
print "The output of your program is : \n\n"
class CGIExec(rexec.RExec):
      def r_open(*args):
          raise SystemError, "open not supported"
r = CGIExec()               # Create sandbox
# Restrict memory usage to 4 Mbytes
resource.setrlimit(resource.RLIMIT_DATA,(4000000,4000000))
# Set CPU time limit to 10 seconds
resource.setrlimit(resource.RLIMIT_CPU,(10,10))
# Go run the code
r.s_exec(code)              # Execute the untrusted code
```

▶ **See Also** Bastion (283).

Bastion

The Bastion module restricts access to attributes of objects. It's primarily used in conjunction with the rexec module when a privileged program wants to allow restricted programs to access attributes of unrestricted objects. The idea behind a Bastion is simple—a wrapper is placed around an object, causing every method access to be redirected through a filter function that's responsible for accepting or rejecting the access. Furthermore, all access to data attributes (non-methods) is prohibited.

   Bastion(*object* [, *filter* [, *name* [, *class*]]])

Returns a bastion for the object *object*. *filter* is a function that accepts a string containing a method name and returns true or false if access to the method is permitted or denied, respectively. *name* is the name of the object that's printed by the bastion's str() method. *class* is the class object that implements Bastion objects and is not described here (it's rarely necessary to supply this).

Example

In this example, you want to restrict access to a StringIO object so that only read operations are permitted (see the StringIO module):

```
import StringIO, Bastion

str = StringIO("")
...
strbast = Bastion.Bastion(str, lambda x: x in ['read','readline','readlines'])
strbast.readline()          # Okay
strbast.write("Ha ha")      # Fails. AttributeError : write
```

Notes

- If the *filter* function is omitted, a bastion limits access to all methods beginning with an underscore.
- Bastions cannot be placed around built-in types such as files and sockets.

Miscellaneous Modules

The modules in this category are used for miscellaneous tasks that don't fit into any of the other categories.

bisect

The bisect module provides support for keeping lists in sorted order. It uses a bisection algorithm to do most of its work.

bisect(*list*, *item* [, *low* [, *high*]])

Returns the index of the proper insertion point for *item* to be placed in *list* in order to maintain *list* in sorted order. *low* and *high* are indices specifying a subset of the list to be considered.

insert(*list*, *item* [, *low* [, *high*]])

Inserts *item* into *list* in sorted order.

cmd

The cmd module provides a class Cmd that's used as a framework for building a line-oriented command interpreter. The Cmd class is never instantiated directly, but is used as a base class for a class that actually implements the interpreter. An instance c of the Cmd class provides the following methods:

c.cmdloop([*intro*])

Prints a banner message contained in *intro* and repeatedly issues a prompt, reads a line of input, and dispatches an appropriate action. For each line of text, the first word is stripped off and used as a command name. For a command name of 'foo', an attempt is made to invoke a method do_foo() with the remainder of the input line as a string argument. If a line contains only the character '?', a predefined method do_help() is dispatched. If the command name is '!', a method do_shell() is invoked (if defined). An end-of-file is converted into a string 'EOF' and dispatched to a command do_EOF.

Subclasses of Cmd inherit a predefined method do_help(). When this method is invoked with an argument 'bar', it tries to invoke the method help_bar(). With no arguments, do_help() lists all the available help topics by listing all commands with corresponding help_* methods, undocumented commands (commands without corresponding help_* methods), and miscellaneous topics (help methods without a corresponding command). Each of the command methods should return an integer code indicating success or failure. A negative value indicates an error and causes the interpreter to return. Otherwise, the interpreter continues to read input after each command. If the readline module has been loaded, the command interpreter will have line editing and history capabilities.

c.onecmd(*str*)

Interprets *str* as a single line of input.

c.emptyline()

This method is called when an empty line of input is typed. It should be defined by the user. If not overridden, it repeats the last nonempty command entered.

```
c.default(line)
```

Called when an unrecognized command is typed. By default, it prints an error message and exits.

```
c.precmd()
```

Method executed just before the input prompt is issued. It should be overridden by derived classes.

```
c.postcmd()
```

Method executed immediately after a command dispatch has finished.

```
c.preloop()
```

Method executed once when cmdloop() is executed.

```
c.postloop()
```

Method executed when cmdloop() is about to return.

The following instance variables should also be defined by a subclass of cmd.

Variable	Description
c.prompt	Prompt printed to solicit input.
c.identchars	String of characters accepted for the command prefix.
c.lastcmd	Last nonempty command seen.
c.intro	Intro text banner; overridden using the argument to cmdloop().
c.doc_header	Header to issue if the help section has a section for documented commands.
c.misc_header	Header to issue for miscellaneous help topics.
c.undoc_header	Header for undocumented commands.
c.ruler	Character used to draw separator lines under help message headers. If empty, no ruler line is drawn. The default is '='.

Example

The following example shows how this module can be used to implement an interpreter wrapper around the callable objects of a module. It also shows the interesting feature of code being executed in a class definition.

```
# cmdhelp.py
# Builds a command interpreter that allows arbitrary Python
# commands to be typed, but reads their doc strings to create
# a collection of help commands.  Just do an execfile(cmdhelp.py)
# in a module to utilize this.

import cmd, sys, traceback

# Define the interpreter class
class Interpreter(cmd.Cmd):
    symbols = globals()
    prompt = "?>> "
    intro  = "Interpreter for " + __name__

    # Find all of the callable objects and look for
    # their doc strings
```

continues >>

>> *continued*

```
                    for n in symbols.keys():
                        c = symbols[n]
                        if callable(c):
                            if c.__doc__:
                                exec """
        def help_%s(self):print %s.__doc__
        """ % (n,n)

                    # Execute an arbitrary statement
                    def default(self,l):
                        try:
                            exec self.lastcmd in globals()
                        except:
                            traceback.print_exc()

                    # Do nothing on empty line
                    def emptyline(self):
                        pass

                    def do_EOF(self,arg):
                        return -1


        # Create an instance
        interp = Interpreter()
```

The following code shows how this code might be used:

```
Python 2.0 (#1, Feb 25 2001, 07:54:16)
[GCC 2.95.2 19991024 (release)] on sunos5
Type "copyright", "credits" or "license" for more information.
>>> from socket import *
>>> execfile("cmdhelp.py")
>>> interp.cmdloop()
Interpreter for __main__
?>> help
Miscellaneous help topics:
==========================
getservbyname      gethostbyaddr    htons       socket
ntohs              gethostbyname    fromfd      getprotobyname
gethostname        htonl
Undocumented commands:
======================
EOF                help
?>> help socket
socket(family, type[, proto]) -> socket object
Open a socket of the given type.  The family argument
specifies the address family; it is normally AF_INET,
sometimes AF_Unix.  The type argument specifies whether this
is a stream (SOCK_STREAM) or datagram (SOCK_DGRAM) socket.
The protocol argument defaults to 0, specifying the default
protocol.
?>> s = socket(AF_INET, SOCK_STREAM)
?>> s.connect("www.python.org",80)
...
```

▶ **See Also** shlex (288).

md5

The md5 module implements RSA's MD5 message-digest algorithm. MD5 takes a sequence of input text and produces a 128-bit hash value. To compute the hash value, create an md5 object using the new() function, feed data to it using the update() method, and then call the digest() method to get the hash value.

new([arg])

Returns a new md5 object. If arg is present, the method call update(arg) is also made.

An md5 object m has the following methods:

m.update(arg)

Updates the md5 object m with the string arg. Repeated calls are equivalent to a single call with the concatenation of all the arguments.

m.digest()

Returns the digest of all data passed to the object using the update() method so far. Returns a 16-byte string that may contain nonprintable characters, including null bytes.

m.copy()

Returns a copy of the md5 object.

Example

```
import md5
m = md5.new()              # Create a new MD5 object
m.update("Hello")
m.update("World")
d = m.digest()             # Get the digest
```

The following shortcut can also be used:

```
d = md5.new("Hello World").digest()
```

▶ **See Also** sha (287), Internet RFC 1321.

sha

The sha module implements the secure hash algorithm (SHA). SHA takes a sequence of input text and produces a 160-bit hash value. To compute the hash value, create an sha object using the new() function and feed data to it.

new([string])

Returns a new sha object. If string is present, the method call update(string) is made.

blocksize

Size of the blocks fed into the hash function. This is always 1.

digestsize

The size of the resulting digest in bytes. This is always 20.

An instance s of an sha object has the following methods:

s.update(arg)

Updates the sha object with the string arg. Repeated calls are equivalent to a single call with the concatenation of all the arguments.

s.digest()

Returns the digest of all data passed to the object using the update() method so far. Returns a 20-byte string that may contain nonprintable characters, including null bytes.

`s.copy()`

Returns a copy of the sha object.

`s.hexdigest()`

Returns the digest value as a string of hexadecimal digits.

Note

- The SHA algorithm is defined by NIST document FIPS PUB 180-1: Secure Hash Standard. It's available online at `http://csrc.nist.gov/fips/fip180-1.ps`.

▶ **See Also** md5 (286).

shlex

The shlex module provides a class shlex that can be used to build lexical analyzers for simple syntaxes such as shells.

`shlex([stream])`

Creates an instance of the shlex class. *stream* specifies a file or stream-like object where characters will be read. This object must provide read() and readline() methods. If omitted, input is taken from sys.stdin.

An instance s of the shlex class supports the following methods:

`s.get_token()`

Returns a token (as a string). If tokens have been saved with push_token(), a token is popped off the stack. Otherwise, the token is read from the input stream. An end-of-file returns an empty string.

`s.push_token(str)`

Pushes a token onto the token stack.

In addition, the following instance variables can be set:

Variable	Description
s.commenters	String of characters recognized as starting a comment. Comments continue to the end of the line. Includes '#' by default.
s.wordchars	String of characters that form multi-character tokens. Includes all ASCII alphanumeric characters and the underscore by default.
s.whitespace	String of whitespace characters that will be skipped.
s.quotes	Characters that will be considered to be string quotes. Includes single and double quotes by default.
s.lineno	Source line number.
s.token	The token buffer.

Note

- Any character not declared to be a word character, whitespace, or a quote is returned as a single-character token. Also, words must be delimited by whitespace. Special symbols such as quotes and comments are not recognized within words. Thus, a word such as isn't is returned as a single token.

▶ **See Also** cmd (284).

The Python Debugger

The Python debugger is loaded by importing the `pdb` module. The `pdb` module provides an interactive source code debugger that allows post-mortem debugging, inspection of stack frames, breakpoints, single stepping of source lines, and code evaluation.

The debugger is started by loading the `pdb` module and issuing one of the following functions:

run(*statement* [, *globals* [, *locals*]])

Executes the string *statement* under debugger control. The debugger prompt will appear immediately before any code executes. Typing 'continue' will force it to run. *globals* and *locals* define the global and local namespaces in which the code runs.

runeval(*expression* [, *globals* [, *locals*]])

Evaluates the *expression* string under debugger control. The debugger prompt will appear before any code executes, as with `run()`. On success, the value of the expression is returned.

runcall(*function* [, *argument*, ...])

Calls a function within the debugger. *function* is a callable object. The debugger prompt will appear before any code executes. The return value of the function is returned upon completion.

set_trace()

Starts the debugger at the point at which this function is called. This can be used to hard-code a debugger breakpoint into a specific code location.

post_mortem(*traceback*)

Starts post-mortem debugging of a traceback object.

pm()

Enters post-mortem debugging using the traceback in `sys.last_traceback`.

When the debugger starts, it will present a prompt such as the following:

```
>>> import pdb
>>> import buggymodule
>>> pdb.run('buggymodule.start()')
> <string>(0)?()
(Pdb)
```

`(Pdb)` is the debugger prompt at which the following commands are recognized. *Note:* Some commands have a short and a long form. In this case, parentheses are used to indicate both forms. For example, `h(elp)` means that either `h` or `help` is acceptable.

h(elp) [*command*]

Shows the list of available commands. Specifying a command returns help for that command.

w(here)

Prints a stack trace.

d(own)

Moves the current frame one level down in the stack trace.

`u(p)`

Moves the current frame one level up in the stack trace.

`b(reak) [loc [, condition]]`

Sets a breakpoint at location `loc`. `loc` is one of the following:

Setting	Description
`n`	A line number in the current file
`filename:n`	A line number in another file
`function`	A function name in the current file
`filename:function`	A function name in another file

If `loc` is omitted, all the current breakpoints are printed. `condition` is an expression that must evaluate to true before the breakpoint is honored.

`tbreak [loc [, condition]]`

Sets a temporary breakpoint that's removed after its first hit.

`cl(ear) [bpnumber [bpnumber ...]]`

Clears a list of breakpoint numbers. If breakpoints are not specified, all breaks are cleared.

`disable [bpnumber [bpnumber ...]]`

Disables the set of specified breakpoints. Unlike with clear, they can be reenabled later.

`enable [bpnumber [bpnumber ...]]`

Enables a specified set of breakpoints.

`ignore bpnumber [count]`

Ignores a breakpoint for `count` executions.

`condition bpnumber [condition]`

Places a condition on a breakpoint. `condition` is an expression that must evaluate to true before the breakpoint is recognized. Omitting the condition clears any previous condition.

`s(tep)`

Executes a single source line and stops inside called functions.

`n(ext)`

Executes until the next line of the current function. Skips the code contained in function calls.

`r(eturn)`

Runs until the current function returns.

`c(ont(inue))`

Continues execution until the next breakpoint is encountered.

`l(ist) [first [, last]]`

Lists source code. Without arguments, lists 11 lines around the current line. With one argument, lists 11 lines around that line. With two arguments, lists lines in a given range. If `last` is less than `first`, it's interpreted as a count.

a(rgs)

Prints the argument list of the current function.

p expression

Evaluates the expression in the current context and prints its value.

alias [*name* [*command*]]

Creates an alias called *name* that executes *command*. The substrings '%1','%2', and so forth are replaced by parameters when the alias is typed. '%*' is replaced by all parameters. If no command is given, the current alias list is shown. Aliases can be nested and can contain anything that can be legally typed at the Pdb prompt. For example:

```
#Print instance variables (usage "pi classInst")
alias pi for k in %1.__dict__.keys(): print "%1.",k,"=",%1.__dict__[k]
#Print instance variables in self
alias ps pi self
```

unalias *name*

Deletes the specified alias.

[!]*statement*

Executes the (one-line) *statement* in the context of the current stack frame. The exclamation point can be omitted unless the first word of the statement resembles a debugger command. To set a global variable, you can prefix the assignment command with a "global" command on the same line:

```
(Pdb) global list_options; list_options = ['-l']
(Pdb)
```

q(uit)

Quits from the debugger.

Notes

- Entering a blank line repeats the last command entered.
- Commands that the debugger doesn't recognize are assumed to be Python statements and are executed in the context of the program being debugged.
- If a file .pdbrc exists in the user's home directory or in the current directory, it's read in and executed as if it had been typed at the debugger prompt.

The Python Profiler

This section describes the Python profiler—a tool that can be used to analyze the runtime performance of a program.

profile

The profile module is used to collect profiling information.

run(*command* [, *filename*])

Executes the contents of *command* using the exec statement under the profiler. *filename* is the name of a file in which raw profiling data is saved. If omitted, a report such as the following is printed to standard output:

```
126 function calls (6 primitive calls) in 5.130 CPU seconds
Ordered by: standard name
ncalls   tottime   percall   cumtime   percall   filename:lineno(function)
     1     0.030     0.030     5.070     5.070   <string>:1(?)
 121/1     5.020     0.041     5.020     5.020   book.py:11(process)
     1     0.020     0.020     5.040     5.040   book.py:5(?)
     2     0.000     0.000     0.000     0.000   exceptions.py:101(__init__)
     1     0.060     0.060     5.130     5.130   profile:0(execfile('book.py'))
     0     0.000               0.000             profile:0(profiler)
```

Different parts of the report generated by run() are interpreted as follows:

Section	Description
primitive calls	Number of nonrecursive function calls
ncalls	Total number of calls (including self-recursion)
tottime	Time spent in this function (not counting subfunctions)
percall	tottime/ncalls
cumtime	Total time spent in the function
percall	cumtime/(primitive calls)
filename:lineno(function)	Location and name of each function

When there are two numbers in the first column (for example, "121/1"), the latter is the number of primitive calls, and the former is the actual number of calls.

Notes

- Analysis of saved profile data is performed by the pstats module.
- To obtain accurate information, it may be necessary to calibrate the profiler. Please refer to http://www.python.org/doc/lib/profile.html for details.

pstats

The pstats module defines a class Stats that's used to analyze the data saved by the profile module.

Stats(*filename*)

Reads profiling data from *filename*—a file previously created by the profile.run() function. Returns a statistics object that can be used to print reports.

A statistics object s has the following methods:

s.strip_dirs()

Removes leading path information from filenames.

s.add(*filename* [, ...])

Accumulates additional profiling information into the current profile. *filename* is the name of a file containing data previously saved by profile.run().

s.sort_stats(*key* [, ...])

Sorts statistics according to a series of keys. Each key can be one of the following values:

Key Name	Description
'calls'	Call count
'cumulative'	Cumulative time
'file'	Filename
'module'	Filename
'pcalls'	Primitive call count
'line'	Line number
'name'	Function name
'nfl'	Name/file/line
'stdname'	Standard name
'time'	Internal time

Time values and call counts are sorted in descending order. Line numbers and filenames are sorted in ascending order.

> s.print_stats(*restriction* [, ...])

Prints a profile report to standard output. The order is the same as produced by the last sort_stats() method. The arguments are used to eliminate entries in the report. Each restriction can be an integer to select a maximum line count, a decimal to select a percentage of the lines, or a regular expression to pattern-match against the names that are printed.

> s.print_callers(*restrictions* [, ...])

Prints a list of all functions that called each function in the profile database. The ordering is identical to print_stats(). *restrictions* has the same meaning as for print_stats().

> s.print_callees(*restrictions* [, ...])

Prints a list of a functions that were called by each function. *restrictions* has the same meaning as for print_stats().

Note

- If the pstats module is run as a script, it launches an interactive profile statistics browser. Type 'help' for a list of the available commands. This is a new Python 2.1 feature.

Undocumented Modules

The modules listed in this section are not covered in detail in this book, but have descriptions in the online library reference and elsewhere.

Python Services

Module	Description
code	Code object support
codeop	Compiles Python code

continues >>

Appendix A   The Python Library

>> continued

Module	Description
compileall	Byte-compiles Python files in a directory
dis	Disassembler
fpectl	Floating-point exception control
imp	Provides access to the implementation of the import statement
inspect	Inspects live objects
keyword	Tests whether a string is a Python keyword
linecache	Retrieves lines from files
parser	Accesses parse-trees of Python source code
pprint	Prettyprinter for objects
pyclbr	Extracts information for class browsers
py_compile	Compiles Python source to bytecode files
repr	Alternate implementation of the repr() function
symbol	Constants used to represent internal nodes of parse trees
tabnanny	Detection of ambiguous indentation
token	Terminal nodes of the parse tree
tokenize	Scanner for Python source code
user	User configuration file parsing

String Processing

Module	Description
difflib	Functions for computing deltas
fpformat	Floating-point number formatting
regex	Regular expression matching (obsolete)
regsub	Regular expression substitution (obsolete)

Operating System Modules

Module	Description
curses	Curses library interface
dl	Access to UNIX shared libraries
dircache	Directory cache
mutex	Mutual exclusion locks
pty	Pseudo-terminal handling
pipes	Interface to shell pipelines
posixfile	File locking
nis	Interface to Sun's NIS
rlcompleter	Completion function for GNU readline

Module	Description
sched	Event scheduler
statcache	Caching version of stat() function
syslog	Interface to UNIX syslog daemon

Network

Module	Description
gopherlib	Gopher protocol
telnetlib	Telnet protocol
urllib2	Extensible library for opening URLs

Internet Data Handling

Module	Description
formatter	Generic output formatting
htmllib	HTML parsing
mailbox	Reading various mailbox formats
mhlib	Access to MH mailboxes
mimify	MIME processing of mail messages
netrc	Netrc file processing
sgmllib	Simple SGML parsing
xml	XML parsing package
xmllib	Simple XML parsing

Multimedia Services

Module	Description
audioop	Manipulates raw audio data
imageop	Manipulates raw image data
aifc	Reads and writes AIFF and AIFC files
sunau	Reads and writes Sun AU files
wave	Reads and writes WAV files
chunk	Reads IFF chunked data
colorsys	Conversions between color systems
rgbimg	Reads and writes SGI RGB files
imghdr	Determines the type of an image
sndhdr	Determines the type of a sound file

Appendix A   The Python Library

SGI Irix

Module	Description
al	Audio functions on SGI
cd	CD-ROM access on SGI
fl	FORMS library
flp	FORMS design loader
fm	Font manager interface
gl	Graphics library interface
imgfile	Support for SGI imglib files
jpeg	Reads and writes JPEG files

Sun-Specific Services

Module	Description
sunaudiodev	Access to Sun audio hardware

Miscellaneous

Module	Description
ConfigParser	Configuration file parser
calendar	Calendar-generation functions
doctest	Testing support based on docstrings
unittest	Unit testing framework
whrandom	Random number generation
winsound	Playing sounds on Windows
xreadlines	Efficient iteration over a file

B

Extending and Embedding Python

This appendix covers the C API used to build extension modules and embed the Python interpreter into other applications. It's not intended to be a tutorial, so readers may want to consult the "Embedding and Extending the Python Interpreter" document available at http://www.python.org/doc/ext, as well as the "Python/C API Reference Manual" available at http://www.python.ord/doc/api. The functions described in this section are current as of Python 2.1 and are likely to be compatible with future releases of Python 2.x.

Enabling Optional Modules

A number of modules in the standard library are disabled due to system differences and dependencies on third-party packages. To enable these modules, you must edit a configuration file and rebuild the interpreter (note that this is primarily an issue for UNIX systems).

For versions of Python prior to 2.1, the file Modules/Setup in the Python source distribution contains configuration data for modules built into the Python interpreter. It contains entries of this form:

```
signal signalmodule.c          # signal(2)
...
#readline readline.c -lreadline -ltermcap
```

Each line indicates the name of a module, followed by source files, compiler options, and link libraries needed to compile that module. A line starting with # is a comment and denotes modules that have been disabled. Long lines can be broken into multiple lines by placing a backslash (\) at the end of lines to be continued. To enable an optional module, the Setup file should be edited to reflect the installation locations of required third-party libraries. For example, to enable the readline module, the Setup file might be modified as follows:

```
...
readline readline.c -I/usr/local/include -L/usr/local/lib \
         -lreadline -ltermcap
```

The interpreter must be rebuilt and reinstalled by typing make and make install in the top-level directory of the source tree for the changes to Setup to take effect.

Beginning with Python 2.1, much of the need to edit the setup file has been removed because the Python installation process has been modified to compile only a core of necessary modules into the Python executable. Most modules are now configured as dynamic modules and some effort is made to detect them automatically if it's possible to build them. For instance, a build of Python 2.1 will automatically enable the readline module if it can detect that the necessary libraries are installed during its configuration process. If it's necessary to manually modify the build process, changes should be made to the setup.py file in the main Python 2.1 source directory.

Extension Module Example

Extension modules are used to extend the interpreter with functions in C. For example, suppose you wanted to access the following C functions in a Python module named spam:

```
/* Compute the greatest common divisor of positive
   integers x and y */
int gcd(int x, int y) {
    int g;
    g = y;
    while (x > 0) {
        g = x;
        x = y % x;
        y = g;
    }
    return g;
}
/* Print some data */
void print_data(char *name, char *email, char *phone) {
    printf("Name    : %s\n", name);
    printf("Email   : %s\n", email);
    printf("Phone   : %s\n", phone);
}
```

To access these functions from an extension module, you must write code such as that in Listing B.1:

Listing B.1   Accessing Functions from an Extension Module

```
/* "spam" module */

/* Include the Python C API */
#include "Python.h"

/* External declarations */
extern int gcd(int,int);
extern void print_data(char *, char *, char *);

/* Wrapper for the gcd() function */
PyObject *spam_gcd(PyObject *self, PyObject *args) {
    int x, y, g;
    /* Get Python arguments */
    if (!PyArg_ParseTuple(args,"ii",&x,&y)) {
        return NULL;
    }
    /* Call the C function */
    g = gcd(x,y);
    return Py_BuildValue("i",g);
}
```

```
/* Wrapper for the print_data() function */
PyObject *
spam_print_data(PyObject *self, PyObject *args, PyObject *kwargs)
{
    char *name = "None";
    char *email = "None";
    char *phone = "None";
    static char *argnames[] = {"name","email","phone",NULL};

    /* Get Python arguments */
    if (!PyArg_ParseTupleAndKeywords(args,kwargs,"|sss",argnames,
        &name,&email,&phone)) {
        return NULL;
    }
    /* Call the C function */
    print_data(name,email,phone);
    return Py_BuildValue("");         /* Return None */
}
/* Method table mapping names to wrappers */
static PyMethodDef spammethods[] = {
    {"gcd", spam_gcd, METH_VARARGS},
    {"print_data", spam_print_data, METH_VARARGS | METH_KEYWORDS },
    {NULL, NULL}
};
/* Module initialization function */
initspam(void) {
    Py_InitModule("spam", spammethods);
}
```

Extension modules always need to include "Python.h". For each C function to be
accessed, a wrapper function is written. These wrapper functions either accept two
arguments (self and args, both of type PyObject *) or three arguments (self, args,
and kwargs, all of type PyObject *). The self parameter is used when the wrapper
function is implementing a built-in method to be applied to an instance of some
object. In this case, the instance is placed in the self parameter. Otherwise, self is
set to NULL. args is a tuple containing the function arguments passed by the interpreter. kwargs is a dictionary containing keyword arguments.

Arguments are converted from Python to C using the PyArg_ParseTuple() or
PyArg_ParseTupleAndKeywords() function. Similarly, the Py_BuildValue() function is used to
construct an acceptable return value. These functions are described in later sections.

Functions signal an error by returning NULL. If a function has no return value
(that is, void), the None object must be returned. For example:

```
PyObject *wrap_foo(PyObject *self, PyObject *args) {
    ...
    /* Return None */
    return Py_BuildValue("");
}
```

None can also be returned as follows:

```
PyObject *wrap_foo(PyObject *self, PyObject *args) {
    ...
    /* Return None */
    Py_INCREF(Py_None);
    return Py_None;
}
```

The method table spammethods in Listing B.1 is used to associate Python names
with the C wrapper functions. These are the names used to call the function from
the interpreter. The METH_VARARGS flag indicates the calling conventions for a wrapper.

In this case, only positional arguments in the form of a tuple are accepted. It can also be set to METH_VARARGS ¦ METH_KEYWORDS to indicate a wrapper function accepting keyword arguments.

The module initialization function initspam is used to initialize the contents of the module. In this case, the Py_InitModule("spam",spammethods) function creates a module spam and populates it with built-in function objects corresponding to the functions listed in the method table.

Compilation of Extensions

Extension modules are usually compiled into shared libraries or DLLs that can be dynamically loaded by the interpreter. The low-level details of this process vary by machine, but the distutils module in the Python library can be used to simplify the process. To create an extension module using distutils, follow these steps:

1. Create a file called setup.py that starts with the following code:

```
# setup.py
from distutils.core import setup, Extension
```

2. Add some source information about your extension as follows:

```
setup(name="spam", version="1.0",
      ext_modules=[Extension("spam", ["spam.c", "spamwrapper.c"])])
```

3. To build your extension, type the following:

```
python setup.py build
```

At this point, a shared library such as spammodule.so (or some variant of this name such as spammodule.sl or spammodule.dll) will be created in a special "build" directory. If you want to install the extension, you can type python setup.py install. This command will copy the shared library to the site-packages directory (for example, /usr/local/lib/python2.1/site-packages).

If you need to supply additional build information such as include directories, libraries, and preprocessor macros, they can also be included in the setup.py file as follows:

```
setup(name="spam", version="1.0",
   ext_modules=[
     Extension(
       "spam",
       ["spam.c", "spamwrapper.c"],
       include_dirs = ["/usr/include/X11","/opt/include"],
       define_macros = [('DEBUG',1),
                        ('NEED_CPLUSPLUS',0)],
       undef_macros = ['HAVE_FOO','HAVE_NOT'],
       library_dirs= ["/usr/lib/X11", "/opt/lib"],
       libraries = ["X11", "Xt", "blah"]
     )
   ]
 )
```

At this point, it's worth noting that the distutils module can more generally be used to create Python packages suitable for distribution and installation by other users. For instance, it allows packages to be distributed as a mix of scripts and compiled extensions. It also knows how to create RPM spec files and self-extracting

ZIP files on Windows. Further details about the distutils module are available at http://www.python.org/doc/current/dist/dist.html.

In some situations, you may want to build an extension module manually. This almost always requires advanced knowledge of various compiler and linker options. The following is an example on Linux:

```
linux % gcc -c -fpic -I/usr/local/include/python2.1 spam.c spamwrapper.c
linux % gcc -shared spam.o spamwrapper.o -o spammodule.so
```

When building a module, it's important to note that the name of the shared library must match the name of the module used in the wrapper code. For example, if the module is named spam, the initialization function must be named initspam and the shared library must be called spammodule.so (possibly with a different file extension, depending on your machine).

Once compiled, an extension module is used like any other module, by simply using the import statement:

```
% python
Python 2.0 (#1, Oct 27 2000, 14:34:45)
[GCC 2.95.2 19991024 (release)] on sunos5
Type "copyright", "credits" or "license" for more information.
>>> import spam
>>> spam.gcd(63,56)
7
>>> spam.gcd(71,89)
1
>>> spam.print_data(name="Dave",phone="555-1212")
Name   : Dave
Email  : None
Phone  : 555-1212
>>>
```

When searching for an extension module, Python uses the same search path as it uses for .py files. Thus, to properly find an extension module, it should be located in the current working directory or in one of the directories in sys.path.

Converting Data from Python to C

The following functions are used to convert arguments passed from Python to C.

```
int PyArg_ParseTuple(PyObject *args, char *format, ...);
```

Parses a tuple of objects in *args* into a series of C variables. *format* is a format string containing zero or more of the specifier strings from Table B.1, which describes the expected contents of *args*. All the remaining arguments contain the addresses of C variables into which the results will be placed. The order and types of these arguments must match the specifiers used in *format* and use the C datatypes listed in Table B.1. Zero is returned if the arguments could not be parsed.

```
int PyArg_ParseTupleAndKeywords(PyObject *args, PyObject *kwdict,
                                char *format, char **kwlist, ...);
```

Parses both a tuple of arguments and a dictionary containing keyword arguments contained in *kwdict*. *format* has the same meaning as for PyArg_ParseTuple(). The only difference is that *kwlist* is a null-terminated list of strings containing the names of all the arguments. Returns 1 on success, 0 on error.

Note: In Table B.1, results of a conversion (for example, in `char *r` or `char **r`) are always placed in the parameter labeled *r*. When applicable, a length is stored in `len`.

Table B.1   Base Format Specifiers and Associated C Datatypes for `PyArg_Parse*`

Format	Python Type	C Type
`"s"`	String or Unicode	`char **r`
`"s#"`	String or Unicode	`char **r, int *len`
`"z"`	String, Unicode, or None	`char **r`
`"z#"`	String, Unicode, or None	`char **r, int *len`
`"u"`	Unicode	`Py_UNICODE **r`
`"u#"`	Unicode	`Py_UNICODE **r, int *len`
`"es"`	String, Unicode, or buffer	`const char *enc, char **r`
`"es#"`	String, Unicode, or buffer	`const char *enc, char **r, int *len`
`"b"`	Integer	`char *r`
`"h"`	Integer	`short *r`
`"i"`	Integer	`int *r`
`"l"`	Integer	`long int *r`
`"c"`	String of length 1	`char *r`
`"f"`	Float	`float *r`
`"d"`	Float	`double *r`
`"D"`	Complex	`Py_complex *r`
`"O"`	Any	`PyObject **r`
`"O!"`	Any	`PyTypeObject *type, PyObject **r`
`"O&"`	Any	`int (*converter)(PyObject *, void *), void *r`
`"S"`	String	`PyObject **r`
`"U"`	Unicode	`PyObject **r`
`"t#"`	Read-only buffer	`char **r, int *len`
`"w"`	Read-write buffer	`char **r`
`"w#"`	Read-write buffer	`char **r, int *len`

When converting integer values, an `OverflowError` exception is raised if the Python integer is too large to fit into the requested C datatype. Long integers may also be used anyplace an integer is expected, provided that they're small enough to fit.

When converting strings with the `"s"`, `"s#"`, `"z"`, or `"z#"` specifiers, both standard and Unicode strings may be used. The `"z"` specifiers also allow `None` to be passed, in which case a `NULL` pointer is returned. In both cases, it's unnecessary to allocate space for the returned string—a pointer to the raw string data stored in the Python interpreter is returned. When Unicode strings are passed, they're first converted to an 8-bit string using the default Unicode encoding. The `"u"` and `"u#"` specifiers require a Unicode string and return a pointer to raw Unicode string data, where each character is of type `Py_UNICODE` (which is currently the same as the

C wchar_t type). The "s#", "z#", and "u#" specifiers return the string length in addition to the string data.

The "es" and "es#" specifiers are used to read a string or Unicode string that has
been encoded according to a specific encoding rule. For example:

```
char *buffer;
PyArg_ParseTuple(args,"es","utf-8",&buffer);
```

In this case, PyArg_ParseTuple() first reads an encoding name and then returns a
pointer to a buffer in which an encoded version of the string has been placed. This
buffer contains dynamically allocated memory and must be explicitly deallocated
using PyMem_Free() after the caller has finished using the encoded contents. The "es#"
specifier optionally accepts a buffer length. In this case, a user can pass the address
and length of a preallocated buffer in which encoded string data will be placed. The
len parameter is always set to the actual length of the encoded data upon return.

The "t#", "w", and "w#" specifiers are similar to the string-conversion specifiers,
but return a pointer to byte-oriented data stored in a Python object implementing the buffer interface. String and Unicode objects provide this interface, as do
selected types in the standard library, such as arrays created with the array module
and mmap objects created by the mmap module.

The "O", "S", and "U" specifiers return raw Python objects of type PyObject *. "S"
and "U" restrict this object to be a string or Unicode string, respectively.

The "O!" conversion requires two C arguments: a pointer to a Python type object
and a pointer to a PyObject * into which a pointer to the object is placed. A TypeError
is raised if the type of the object doesn't match the type object. For example:

```
/* Parse a List Argument */
PyObject *listobj1;
PyArg_ParseTuple(args,"O!", &PyList_Type, &listobj1);
```

The "O&" conversion takes two arguments (converter, addr) and uses a function to
convert a PyObject * to a C datatype. converter is a pointer to a function with the
prototype int converter(PyObject *obj, void *addr), where obj is the passed Python
object, and addr is the address supplied as the second argument. converter() should
return 1 on success, 0 on failure. On error, the converter should also raise an
exception. For example:

```
struct Point {
    int x;
    int y;
};

int convert_point(PyObject *obj, void *addr) {
    Point *p = (Point *) addr;
    return PyArg_ParseTuple(obj,"ii", &p->x, &p->y);
}
...
PyObject *wrapper(PyObject *self, PyObject *args) {
    Point p;
    ...
    /* Get a point */
    if (!PyArg_ParseTuple(args,"O&",convert_point, &p))
        return NULL;
    ...
}
```

Table B.2 lists format modifiers that can also be used in format strings.

Table B.2   Format String Modifiers

Format String	Description
`"(items)"`	A tuple of objects
`"¦"`	Start of optional arguments
`":"`	End of arguments (the remaining text is the function name)
`";"`	End of arguments (the remaining text is the error message)

`"¦"` specifies that all remaining arguments are optional. This can appear only once in a format specifier and cannot be nested. `":"` indicates the end of the arguments. Any text that follows is used as the function name in any error messages. `";"` signals the end of the arguments. Any following text is used as the error message. *Note:* Only one of : and ; should be used. Listing B.2 shows some examples:

Listing B.2   Format Specifiers

```
int      ival, ival2, len;
double   dval;
char     *sval;
PyObject *o1, *o2;

/* Parse an integer, double, and a string */
PyArg_ParseTuple(args,"ids", &ival, &dval, &sval);

/* Parse a string and length */
PyArg_ParseTuple(args,"s#", &sval, &len);

/* Parse optional arguments */
PyArg_ParseTuple(args,"id¦s", &ival, &dval, &sval);

/* Parse with an error message */
PyArg_ParseTuple(args,"ii; gcd requires 2 integers", &ival, &ival2);

/* Parse two tuples */
PyArg_ParseTuple(args,"(ii)(ds)", &ival, &ival2, &dval, &sval);
```

Converting Data from C to Python

The following function is used to convert the values contained in C variables to a Python object:

```
PyObject *Py_BuildValue(char *format, ...)
```

This constructs a Python object from a series of C variables. *format* is a string describing the desired conversion. The remaining arguments are the values of C variables to be converted.

The *format* specifier (see Table B.3) is similar to that used with the `PyArg_Parse*` functions.

Table B.3   Format Specifiers for `Py_BuildValue()`

Format	PyType	C Type	Description
`"s"`	String	`char *`	Null-terminated string. If the C string pointer is NULL, None is returned.
`"s#"`	String	`char *, int`	String and length. May contain null bytes. If the C string pointer is NULL, None is returned.
`"z"`	String or None	`char *`	Same as `"s"`.
`"z#"`	String or None	`char *, int`	Same as `"s#"`.
`"u"`	Unicode	`Py_UNICODE *`	Null-terminated Unicode string. If the C string pointer is NULL, None is returned.
`"u#"`	Unicode	`Py_UNICODE *, int`	Unicode string and length.
`"b"`	Integer	`char`	8-bit integer.
`"h"`	Integer	`short`	Short 16-bit integer.
`"i"`	Integer	`int`	Integer.
`"l"`	Integer	`long`	Long integer.
`"c"`	String	`char`	Single character. Creates a Python string of length 1.
`"f"`	Float	`float`	Single-precision floating point.
`"d"`	Float	`double`	Double-precision floating point.
`"O"`	Any	`PyObject *`	Any Python object. The object is unchanged except for its reference count, which is incremented by 1. If a NULL pointer is given, a NULL pointer is returned.
`"O&"`	Any	`converter, any`	C data processed through a converter function.
`"S"`	String	`PyObject *`	Same as `"O"`.
`"U"`	Unicode	`PyObject *`	Same as `"O"`.
`"N"`	Any	`PyObject *`	Same as `"O"` except that the reference count is not incremented.
`"(items)"`	Tuple	`vars`	Creates a tuple of items. `items` is a string of format specifiers from this table. `vars` is a list of C variables corresponding to the items in `items`.
`"[items]"`	List	`vars`	Creates a list of items. `items` is a string of format specifiers. `vars` is a list of C variables corresponding to the items in `items`.
`"{items}"`	Dictionary	`vars`	Creates a dictionary of items.

Examples:

```
Py_BuildValue("")                      None
Py_BuildValue("i",37)                  37
Py_BuildValue("ids",37,3.4,"hello")    (37, 3.5, "hello")
Py_BuildValue("s#","hello",4)          "hell"
Py_BuildValue("()")                    ()
Py_BuildValue("(i)",37)                (37,)
Py_BuildValue("[ii]",1,2)              [1,2]
Py_BuildValue("[i,i]",1,2)             [1,2]
Py_BuildValue("{s:i,s:i}","x",1,"y",2) {'x':1, 'y':2}
```

Error Handling

Errors are indicated by returning NULL to the interpreter. Prior to returning NULL, an exception should be set or cleared using one of the following functions:

```
void PyErr_Clear()
```

Clears any previously raised exceptions.

```
PyObject *PyErr_Occurred()
```

Checks to see whether an error has been generated. If so, returns the current exception object. Otherwise, returns NULL.

```
void PyErr_NoMemory()
```

Raises a MemoryError exception.

```
void PyErr_SetFromErrno(PyObject *exc)
```

Raises an exception. *exc* is an exception object. The value of the exception is taken from the errno variable in the C library.

```
void PyErr_SetFromErrnoWithFilename(PyObject *exc, char *filename)
```

Like PyErr_SetFromErrno() but includes the filename in the exception value as well.

```
void PyErr_SetObject(PyObject *exc, PyObject *val)
```

Raises an exception. *exc* is an exception object and *val* is an object containing the value of the exception.

```
void PyErr_SetString(PyObject *exc, char *msg)
```

Raises an exception. *exc* is an exception object and *msg* is a message describing what went wrong.

The *exc* argument in these functions can be set to one of the following:

C Name	Python Exception
PyExc_ArithmeticError	ArithmeticError
PyExc_AssertionError	AssertionError
PyExc_AttributeError	AttributeError
PyExc_EnvironmentError	EnvironmentError
PyExc_EOFError	EOFError
PyExc_Exception	Exception
PyExc_FloatingPointError	FloatingPointError
PyExc_ImportError	ImportError
PyExc_IndexError	IndexError

C Name	Python Exception
PyExc_IOError	IOError
PyExc_KeyError	KeyError
PyExc_KeyboardInterrupt	KeyboardInterrupt
PyExc_LookupError	LookupError
PyExc_MemoryError	MemoryError
PyExc_NameError	NameError
PyExc_NotImplementedError	NotImplementedError
PyExc_OSError	OSError
PyExc_OverflowError	OverflowError
PyExc_RuntimeError	RuntimeError
PyExc_StandardError	StandardError
PyExc_SyntaxError	SyntaxError
PyExc_SystemError	SystemError
PyExc_SystemExit	SystemExit
PyExc_TypeError	TypeError
PyExc_UnicodeError	UnicodeError
PyExc_ValueError	ValueError
PyExc_ZeroDivisionError	ZeroDivisionError

The following example shows how an exception is typically set and an error returned in extension code:

```
PyErr_SetString(PyExc_ValueError,"Expected a positive value!");
return NULL;
```

An extension module can define a new exception type by using the following function:

PyObject *PyErr_NewException(char *excname, PyObject *base, PyObject *dict)

Creates a new exception object. *excname* is the name of the exception in the form "*modulename.excname*", *base* is an optional base class for the exception, and *dict* is an optional dictionary used as the __dict__ attribute of the resulting exception class. Both of these arguments are normally set to NULL. The returned object is a class object.

The following example shows how a new exception is created in an extension module:

```
static PyObject *SpamError;
...

/* Module initialization function */
initspam(void) {
    PyObject *m, *d;
    m = Py_InitModule("spam",SpamMethods);
    d = PyModule_GetDict(m);
    SpamError = PyErr_NewException("spam.error", NULL, NULL);
    PyDict_SetItemString(d,"error",SpamError);
    ...
}
```

Reference Counting

Unlike programs written in Python, C extensions have to manipulate the reference count of Python objects. This is done using the following macros:

Macro	Description
Py_INCREF(*obj*)	Increments the reference count of *obj*, which must be non-NULL
Py_DECREF(*obj*)	Decrements the reference count of *obj*, which must be non-NULL
Py_XINCREF(*obj*)	Increments the reference count of *obj*, which may be NULL
Py_XDECREF(*obj*)	Decrements the reference count of *obj*, which may be NULL

Manipulating the reference count of Python objects in C is a delicate topic, and readers are strongly advised to consult the "Extending and Embedding the Python Interpreter" document available at http://www.python.org/doc/ext before proceeding any further. With this in mind, all Python objects are manipulated in C through the use of pointers of type PyObject *. Furthermore, these pointers are classified into two categories: owned references and borrowed references. An *owned reference* is a pointer to a Python object in which the reference count of that object has been updated to reflect the fact that some piece of C code or a C data structure is holding a pointer to it. A *borrowed reference*, on the other hand, is simply a bare pointer to a Python object in which the reference count of the object has not been updated.

Owned references are most commonly created by functions that create new Python objects, such as Py_BuildValue(), PyInt_FromLong(), and PyList_New(). When called, a new Python object is created and the object is said to be *owned* by the calling function. Borrowed references often appear when a function obtains a pointer to a Python object from elsewhere or when the contents of Python objects such as lists and dictionaries are extracted. For example, the self and args parameters of a wrapper function are borrowed references, as is the pointer returned by functions such as PyList_GetItem().

The owner of a reference must either give up ownership using the Py_DECREF() macro or transfer ownership elsewhere. For example, temporary objects created inside a wrapper function should be destroyed using Py_DECREF(), whereas the return value of a wrapper is an owned reference that's given back to the interpreter. Likewise, the holder of a borrowed reference can obtain ownership using the Py_INCREF() macro. However, special care is in order. For example, decrementing the reference count of a borrowed reference may cause the interpreter to crash with a segmentation fault at a later time during execution. Likewise, failure to release an owned reference or inadvertently increasing the reference count of an object will lead to memory leaks.

Figuring out Python's reference-counting scheme is tricky because there are several inconsistencies in its treatment of references. However, here are a few general rules:

- Functions that create new Python objects always return owned references.
- If you want to save a reference to a Python object, use Py_INCREF() to increase the reference count.
- To dispose of an owned reference, use Py_DECREF().
- Many (but not all) functions that return pointers to objects contained in sequences and mapping objects return owned references.
- Many (but not all) functions that store objects in containers such as sequences and mappings increase the reference count of objects they contain.
- All C wrapper functions must return an owned reference.

Exceptions to these rules are noted in later sections of this appendix.

Calling Python from C

Sometimes it's useful to call Python functions from C programs. To do this, the following functions can be used:

```
PyObject *PyEval_CallObject(PyObject *func, PyObject *args)
```

Call *func* with arguments *args*. *func* is a Python callable object (function, method, class, and so on). *args* is a tuple of arguments.

```
PyObject *PyEval_CallObjectWithKeywords(PyObject *func, PyObject *args, PyObject *kwargs)
```

Call *func* with positional arguments *args* and keyword arguments *kwargs*. *func* is a callable object, *args* is a tuple, and *kwargs* is a dictionary.

The following example illustrates the use of these functions:

```
/* Call a python function */

PyObject *func;    /* Callable object. */
PyObject *args;
PyObject *result;
int      arg1, arg2;

func = get_python_function() /* See below */
args = Py_BuildValue("(ii)", arg1, arg2);  /* Build argument list */
result = PyEval_CallObject(func,args);     /* Call function       */
```

The only remaining problem is that C code, at compile time, cannot know the address of a Python object that has not yet been created, since Python is dynamic. One approach is to let Python create the function object and then register the address with a callback function. To deal with this, extension code such as the following can be used to set the callback function:

```
static PyObject *func = 0;    /* Callback function */

static PyObject *
set_callback(PyObject *self, PyObject *args) {
    PyObject *f;
    if (PyArg_ParseTuple(args,"O",&f)) {
        if (!PyCallable_Check(f)) {
            PyErr_SetString(PyExc_TypeError, "expected a callable");
            return NULL;
        }
```

continues >>

>> *continued*

```
                    Py_XINCREF(f);        /* Save reference to callback */
                    Py_XDECREF(func);     /* Release any previous callback */
                    func = f;
                    Py_INCREF(Py_None);
                    return Py_None;
                }
            return NULL;
        }
```

This function would then be invoked from the interpreter as follows:

```
# Some function
def foo(x,y):
    return x+y
...
set_callback(foo)
```

Alternatively, it might be possible to obtain Python callable objects using functions in the embedding API, described later in this appendix.

Abstract Object Layer

The functions in Tables B.4 through B.8 are used to manipulate objects from C, in much the same manner as from the interpreter. All the functions in this section that return an int return -1 if an error occurs. Likewise, functions that return a PyObject * return NULL on failure. Note that an "error" in this context is not the same as the false result of a test. For instance, the PyNumber_Check(PyObject *obj) function returns 0 if obj is not a number, but this isn't the same as an error. Finally, unless otherwise noted, all functions in this section that return a PyObject * return ownership with the object. It's up to the caller to decrement the reference count of the returned object if necessary.

Table B.4   Objects

Type	Function
int	PyCallable_Check(PyObject *o)
PyObject *	PyObject_CallFunction(PyObject *callable_object, char *format,...)
PyObject *	PyObject_CallMethod(PyObject *o, char *methodname, char *format, ...)
PyObject *	PyObject_CallObject(PyObject *callable_object, PyObject *args)
void	PyObject_ClearWeakRefs(PyObject *obj)
int	PyObject_Cmp(PyObject *o1, PyObject *o2, int *result)
int	PyObject_Compare(PyObject *o1, PyObject *o2)
int	PyObject_DelAttr(PyObject *o, PyObject *attr_name)
int	PyObject_DelAttrString(PyObject *o, char *attr_name)
int	PyObject_DelItem(PyObject *o, PyObject *key)
PyObject *	PyObject_GetAttr(PyObject *o, PyObject *attr_name)
PyObject *	PyObject_GetAttrString(PyObject *o, char *attr_name)
PyObject *	PyObject_GetItem(PyObject *o, PyObject *key)

Type	Function
int	PyObject_HasAttr(PyObject *o, PyObject *attr_name)
int	PyObject_HasAttrString(PyObject *o, char *attr_name)
int	PyObject_Hash(PyObject *o)
int	PyObject_IsTrue(PyObject *o)
int	PyObject_Length(PyObject *o)
int	PyObject_Print(PyObject *o, FILE *fp, int flags)
PyObject *	PyObject_Repr(PyObject *o)
PyObject *	PyObject_RichCompare(PyObject *o1, PyObject *o2, int op)
int	PyObject_RichCompareBool(PyObject *o1, PyObject *o2, int op)
int	PyObject_SetAttr(PyObject *o, PyObject *attr_name, PyObject *v)
int	PyObject_SetAttrString(PyObject *o, char *attr_name, PyObject *v)
int	PyObject_SetItem(PyObject *o, PyObject *key, PyObject *v)
PyObject *	PyObject_Str(PyObject *o)
PyObject *	PyObject_Type(PyObject *o)

The *flags* argument of PyObject_Print() is used to select printing options. Currently, the only option is Py_PRINT_RAW, which forces PyObject_Print() to produce output using PyObject_Str() as opposed to PyObject_Repr() (the default).

PyObject_Hash() and PyObject_Length() return a positive integer result on success and -1 on error.

The *op* argument to PyObject_RichCompare() and PyObject_RichCompareBool() is one of Py_EQ, Py_NE, Py_LT, Py_GT, Py_GE, or Py_LE.

Table B.5   Numbers

Type	Function
PyObject *	PyNumber_Absolute(PyObject *o)
PyObject *	PyNumber_Add(PyObject *o1, PyObject *o2)
PyObject *	PyNumber_And(PyObject *o1, PyObject *o2)
int	PyNumber_Check(PyObject *o)
PyObject *	PyNumber_Coerce(PyObject **p1, PyObject **p2)
PyObject *	PyNumber_Divide(PyObject *o1, PyObject *o2)
PyObject *	PyNumber_Divmod(PyObject *o1, PyObject *o2)
PyObject *	PyNumber_Float(PyObject *o)
PyObject *	PyNumber_Int(PyObject *o)
PyObject *	PyNumber_Invert(PyObject *o)
PyObject *	PyNumber_Long(PyObject *o)
PyObject *	PyNumber_Lshift(PyObject *o1, PyObject *o2)

continues >>

Table B.5   Continued

Type	Function
PyObject *	PyNumber_Multiply(PyObject *o1, PyObject *o2)
PyObject *	PyNumber_Negative(PyObject *o)
PyObject *	PyNumber_Or(PyObject *o1, PyObject *o2)
PyObject *	PyNumber_Positive(PyObject *o)
PyObject *	PyNumber_Power(PyObject *o1, PyObject *o2, PyObject *o3)
PyObject *	PyNumber_Remainder(PyObject *o1, PyObject *o2)
PyObject *	PyNumber_Rshift(PyObject *o1, PyObject *o2)
PyObject *	PyNumber_Subtract(PyObject *o1, PyObject *o2)
PyObject *	PyNumber_Xor(PyObject *o1, PyObject *o2)
PyObject *	PyNumber_InPlaceAdd(PyObject *o1, PyObject *o2)
PyObject *	PyNumber_InPlaceSubtract(PyObject *o1, PyObject *o2)
PyObject *	PyNumber_InPlaceMultiply(PyObject *o1, PyObject *o2)
PyObject *	PyNumber_InPlaceDivide(PyObject *o1, PyObject *o2)
PyObject *	PyNumber_InPlaceRemainder(PyObject *o1, PyObject *o2)
PyObject *	PyNumber_InPlacePower(PyObject *o1, PyObject *o2)
PyObject *	PyNumber_InPlaceLshift(PyObject *o1, PyObject *o2)
PyObject *	PyNumber_InPlaceRshift(PyObject *o1, PyObject *o2)
PyObject *	PyNumber_InPlaceAnd(PyObject *o1, PyObject *o2)
PyObject *	PyNumber_InPlaceXor(PyObject *o1, PyObject *o2)
PyObject *	PyNumber_InPlaceOr(PyObject *o1, PyObject *o2)

Table B.6   Sequences

Type	Function
int	PySequence_Check(PyObject *o)
PyObject *	PySequence_Concat(PyObject *o1, PyObject *o2)
int	PySequence_Contains(PyObject *o, PyObject *value)
int	PySequence_Count(PyObject *o, PyObject *value)
int	PySequence_DelItem(PyObject *o, int i)
int	PySequence_DelSlice(PyObject *o, int i1, int i2)
PyObject *	PySequence_GetItem(PyObject *o, int i)
PyObject *	PySequence_GetSlice(PyObject *o, int i1, int i2)
int	PySequence_In(PyObject *o, PyObject *value)
int	PySequence_Index(PyObject *o, PyObject *value)
PyObject *	PySequence_List(PyObject *o)
PyObject *	PySequence_Repeat(PyObject *o, int count)
int	PySequence_SetItem(PyObject *o, int i, PyObject *v)
int	PySequence_SetSlice(PyObject *o, int i1, int i2, PyObject *v)

Type	Function
PyObject *	PySequence_Tuple(PyObject *o)
PyObject *	PySequence_InPlaceConcat(PyObject *o1, PyObject *o2)
PyObject *	PySequence_InPlaceRepeat(PyObject *o1, int count)
PyObject *	PySequence_Fast(PyObject *o, const char *errmsg)
PyObject *	PySequence_Fast_GET_ITEM(PyObject *o, int i)

The PySequence_Fast() function returns o unmodified if it's already a tuple or a list
and increases its reference count. Otherwise, o must be a sequence type. If it's not
a sequence, a TypeError is raised and errmsg is used as the error message. The
PySequence_Fast_GET_ITEM() function should only be used with objects returned by
PySequence_Fast().

Table B.7   Mappings

Type	Function
int	PyMapping_Check(PyObject *o)
int	PyMapping_Clear(PyObject *o)
int	PyMapping_DelItem(PyObject *o, PyObject *key)
int	PyMapping_DelItemString(PyObject *o, char *key)
PyObject *	PyMapping_GetItemString(PyObject *o, char *key)
int	PyMapping_HasKey(PyObject *o, PyObject *key)
int	PyMapping_HasKeyString(PyObject *o, char *key)
PyObject *	PyMapping_Items(PyObject *o)
PyObject *	PyMapping_Keys(PyObject *o)
int	PyMapping_Length(PyObject *o)
int	PyMapping_SetItemString(PyObject *o, char *key, PyObject *v)
PyObject *	PyMapping_Values(PyObject *o)

Table B.8   Buffer Interface

Type	Function
int	PyObject_AsCharBuffer(PyObject *, const char **buffer, int *len)
int	PyObject_AsReadBuffer(PyObject *, const void **buffer, int *len)
int	PyObject_AsWriteBuffer(PyObject *, void **buffer, int *len)

The buffer interface is used by objects that want to expose the raw bytes used to
store data to the caller without having to make a copy. Typically this is only used
by strings, Unicode strings, and arrays as created in the array module. The size and
interpretation of the data depends on the underlying object.

Appendix B   Extending and Embedding Python

Low-Level Functions on Built-in Types

The functions in Tables B.9 through B.21 can be used to manipulate various built-in types. Functions of the form Py<*type*>_Check() are used to check the type of an object and return 1 if an object is the correct type, 0 otherwise. Functions of the form Py<*type*>_From<*type*> are used to create a Python object from a C datatype. Functions of the form Py<*type*>_As<*type*> are used to convert from Python to C. These functions are presented without further description.

Table B.9   Integers

Type	Function
long	PyInt_AsLong(PyObject *iobj)
int	PyInt_Check(PyObject *obj)
PyObject *	PyInt_FromLong(long)
long	PyInt_GetMax(void)

Table B.10   Long Integers

Type	Function
double	PyLong_AsDouble(PyObject *lobj)
long	PyLong_AsLong(PyObject *lobj)
long long	PyLong_AsLongLong(PyObject *lobj)
unsigned long	PyLong_AsUnsignedLong(PyObject *lobj)
unsigned long long	PyLong_AsUnsignedLongLong(PyObject *lobj)
void *	PyLong_AsVoidPtr(PyObject *lobj)
int	PyLong_Check(PyObject *obj)
PyObject *	PyLong_FromDouble(double)
PyObject *	PyLong_FromLong(long)
PyObject *	PyLong_FromLongLong(long long)
PyObject *	PyLong_FromUnsignedLong(unsigned long)
PyObject *	PyLong_FromUnsignedLongLong(unsigned long long)
PyObject *	PyLong_FromVoidPtr(void *)

Table B.11   Floats

Type	Function
int	PyFloat_Check(PyObject *obj)
double	PyFloat_AsDouble(PyObject *fobj)
PyObject *	PyFloat_FromDouble(double)

Table B.12   Complex

Type	Function
Py_complex	PyComplex_AsCComplex(PyObject *cobj)
int	PyComplex_Check(PyObject *obj)
PyObject *	PyComplex_FromCComplex(Py_complex *cobj)
PyObject *	PyComplex_FromDoubles(double real, double imag)
double	PyComplex_ImagAsDouble(PyObject *cobj)
double	PyComplex_RealAsDouble(PyObject *cobj)

Table B.13   Strings

Type	Function
char *	PyString_AsString(PyObject *str)
PyObject *	PyString_AsEncodedString(PyObject *unicode, const char *encoding, const char *errors)
int	PyString_Check(PyObject *obj)
void	PyString_Concat(PyObject **str, PyObject *newpart)
void	PyString_ConcatAndDel(PyObject **str, PyObject *newpart)
PyObject *	PyString_Decode(const char *s, int size, const char *encoding, const char *errors)
PyObject *	PyString_Encode(const Py_UNICODE *s, int size, const char *encoding, const char *errors)
PyObject *	PyString_Format(PyObject *format, PyObject *args)
PyObject *	PyString_FromString(char *str)
PyObject *	PyString_FromStringAndSize(char *str, int len)
int	PyString_Resize(PyObject **str, int newsize)
int	PyString_Size(PyObject *str)

Note: Encode and Decode functions expect encoding and error parameters that are the same as the built-in unicode() function.

Table B.14   Unicode

Type	Function
int	PyUnicode_Check(PyObject *o)
PyObject *	PyUnicode_FromUnicode(Py_UNICODE *, int size)
Py_UNICODE *	PyUnicode_AsUnicode(PyObject *o)
int	PyUnicode_GetSize(PyObject *o)
PyObject *	PyUnicode_FromEncodedObject(PyObject *obj, const char *encoding, const char *errors)
PyObject *	PyUnicode_FromObject(PyObject *o)
PyObject *	PyUnicode_FromWideChar(const wchar_t *, int size)
int	PyUnicode_AsWideChar(PyObject *o, wchar_t *buf, int maxlen)

Appendix B   Extending and Embedding Python

Table B.15   Lists

Type	Function
int	PyList_Append(PyObject *list, PyObject *obj)
PyObject *	PyList_AsTuple(PyObject *list)
int	PyList_Check(PyObject *obj)
PyObject *	PyList_GetItem(PyObject *list, int index)
PyObject *	PyList_GetSlice(PyObject *list, int i, int j)
int	PyList_Insert(PyObject *list, int index, PyObject *obj)
PyObject *	PyList_New(int size)
int	PyList_Reverse(PyObject *list)
int	PyList_SetItem(PyObject *list, int index, PyObject *obj)
int	PyList_SetSlice(PyObject *list, int i, int j, PyObject *slc)
int	PyList_Size(PyObject *list)
int	PyList_Sort(PyObject *list)

Note: PyList_GetItem() returns a borrowed reference.

Table B.16   Tuples

Type	Function
int	PyTuple_Check(PyObject *obj)
PyObject *	PyTuple_GetItem(PyObject *tup, int index)
PyObject *	PyTuple_GetSlice(PyObject *tup, int i, int j)
PyObject *	PyTuple_New(int size)
int	PyTuple_SetItem(PyObject *tup, int index, PyObject *obj)
int	PyTuple_Size(PyObject *tup)

Note: PyTuple_SetItem() increments the reference count of *obj* even if it fails, and PyTuple_GetItem() returns a borrowed reference.

Table B.17   Dictionaries

Type	Function
int	PyDict_Check(PyObject *obj)
void	PyDict_Clear(PyObject *dict)
int	PyDict_DelItem(PyObject *dict, PyObject *key)
int	PyDict_DelItemString(PyObject *dict, char *key)
PyObject *	PyDict_GetItem(PyObject *dict, PyObject *key)
PyObject *	PyDict_GetItemString(PyObject *dict, char *key)
PyObject *	PyDict_Items(PyObject *dict)
PyObject *	PyDict_Keys(PyObject *dict)
PyObject *	PyDict_New(void)

Type	Function
int	PyDict_SetItem(PyObject *dict, PyObject *key, PyObject *value)
int	PyDict_SetItemString(PyObject *dict, char *key, PyObject *value)
int	PyDict_Size(PyObject *dict)
PyObject *	PyDict_Values(PyObject *dict)

Note: PyDict_GetItem() and PyDict_GetItemString() return borrowed references.

Table B.18   Buffer Objects

Type	Function
int	PyBuffer_check(PyObject *o)
PyObject *	PyBuffer_FromObject(PyObject *base, int offset, int size)
PyObject *	PyBuffer_FromReadWriteObject(PyObject *base, int offset, int size)
PyObject *	PyBuffer_FromMemory(void *ptr, int size)
PyObject *	PyBuffer_FromReadWriteMemory(void *ptr, int size)
PyObject *	PyBuffer_New(int size)

Table B.19   Files

Type	Function
FILE *	PyFile_AsFile(PyObject *file)
int	PyFile_Check(PyObject *obj)
PyObject *	PyFile_FromFile(FILE *, char *, char *, int (*)(FILE *))
PyObject *	PyFile_FromString(char *name, char *mode)
PyObject *	PyFile_GetLine(PyObject *file, int)
PyObject *	PyFile_Name(PyObject *file)
void	PyFile_SetBufSize(PyObject *file, int size)
int	PyFile_SoftSpace(PyObject *file, int)
int	PyFile_WriteObject(PyObject *file, PyObject *obj, int)
int	PyFile_WriteString(char *str, PyObject *file)

Table B.20   Modules

Type	Function
int	PyModule_Check(PyObject *obj)
PyObject *	PyModule_GetDict(PyObject *mod)
char *	PyModule_GetFilename(PyObject *mod)
char *	PyModule_GetName(PyObject *mod)
PyObject *	PyModule_New(char *name)

Table B.21   CObjects

Type	Function
int	`PyCObject_Check(PyObject *o)`
PyObject *	`PyCObject_FromVoidPtr(void *cobj, void (*destr)(void *))`
PyObject *	`PyCObject_FromVoidPtrAndDesc(void *cobj, void *desc,` `void (*destr)(void *, void *))`
void *	`PyCObject_AsVoidPtr(PyObject *self)`
void *	`PyCObject_GetDesc(PyObject *self)`

Note: The CObject interface is typically used to provide a wrapper around an arbitrary C pointer. These objects are mostly used by extension-building tools such as SWIG.

Defining New Types

New types of objects can also be defined in extension modules. However, this process is considerably more advanced than simply accessing a few C functions. Because of this complexity, you should consider implementing a new type only in the following situations:

- The type is not easily constructed from existing Python types.
- The type requires interaction with the operating system or another special feature not provided by the interpreter or the standard library.
- The type hasn't already been implemented elsewhere. For example, efficient matrix types have already been implemented, so it would make little sense to reinvent them. It's always a good idea to check the Python libraries and newsgroups before implementing a new type. The Vaults of Parnassas Python Resources (http://www.vex.net/parnassus) is also an excellent resource for finding previously implemented extension modules.

The process of creating a new Python type involves the following steps:

1. Define a data structure that contains the actual data stored in the type—for example, the List type has an array of elements containing the list items.
2. Define the functions that are going to serve as methods of the type—for example, the append() method of a List object.
3. Define a pair of functions for creating and destroying the type.
4. Define a set of functions that implement the special methods such as __add__() and __getitem__() that are supported by the type, as described in Chapter 3, "Types and Objects."
5. Fill in a data structure containing pointers to the numeric operations of a type.
6. Fill in a data structure containing pointers to the sequence operations of the type.
7. Fill in a data structure containing pointers to the mapping operators of the type.
8. Define a type object that contains all the properties of the object and its associated methods.
9. Register methods and any additional functions with the interpreter in the module initialization function.

Listing B.3 illustrates the process of creating a new Python type by implementing a `SharedBuffer` object. A shared buffer is a special data structure that contains data shared by multiple Python interpreters running as different processes. Whenever a change is made by one interpreter, it's automatically reflected in shared buffers of the other interpreters. This implementation of a shared buffer utilizes an operating system feature known as *memory-mapped files*, in which the contents of a "file" are mapped into the address space of a process and can be accessed as ordinary memory. Memory-mapped files are supported on both UNIX and Windows, although Listing B.3 shows only the UNIX implementation. Also, this example is only intended to illustrate the process of creating a new type—if you really want to use memory-mapped files, it might be easier to use the `mmap` module in the standard library.

Listing B.3   Shared Buffer Type

```
/***************************************************************
 * sbuffer.c
 *
 * A shared buffer object implemented using mmap().
 ***************************************************************/
#include "Python.h"
#include <unistd.h>
#include <fcntl.h>
#include <sys/mman.h>
#include <sys/stat.h>

/***************************************************************
 * sbufferobject information
 ***************************************************************/
typedef struct {
    PyObject_HEAD
    char        *buffer;    /* Memory buffer */
    int         size;       /* Size of the structure */
    int         fd;         /* File descriptor */
    int         prot;       /* Protection bits */
    int         offset;     /* File offset */
} sbufferobject;

/* Exception object used by this module */
static PyObject *AccessError;

/* Forward declaration of type descriptor.
   staticforward is a macro defined in Python.h that
   provides a portable way of creating forward references
   to static functions */
staticforward PyTypeObject SharedBufferType;

/***************************************************************
 * Instance methods
 *      sbuffer.lock()      - Lock the shared buffer
 *      sbuffer.unlock()    - Unlock the shared buffer
 *      sbuffer.get()       - Get data as a NULL-terminated string
 *      sbuffer.store()     - Store data as a NULL-terminated string
 ***************************************************************/
static PyObject *
sbuffer_lock(sbufferobject *self, PyObject *args) {
  if (!PyArg_ParseTuple(args,"")) return NULL;
  lockf(self->fd,F_LOCK,0);
  return Py_BuildValue("");
}
```

continues >>

>> *continued*

```c
static PyObject *
sbuffer_unlock(sbufferobject *self, PyObject *args) {
  if (!PyArg_ParseTuple(args,"")) return NULL;
  lockf(self->fd,F_ULOCK,0);
  return Py_BuildValue("");
}

static PyObject *
sbuffer_get(sbufferobject *self, PyObject *args) {
  int i;
  if (!PyArg_ParseTuple(args,"")) return NULL;
  if (self->prot & PROT_READ) {
    for (i = 0; i < self->size; i++) {
      if (!self->buffer[i]) break;
    }
    return PyString_FromStringAndSize(self->buffer,i);
  } else {
    return PyString_FromString("");
  }
}

static PyObject *
sbuffer_store(sbufferobject *self, PyObject *args) {
  char *str;
  int len;
  if (!PyArg_ParseTuple(args,"s",&str)) return NULL;
  if (self->prot & PROT_WRITE) {
    len = strlen(str)+1;
    if (len > self->size) len = self->size;
    memcpy(self->buffer,str,len);
  } else {
    PyErr_SetString(AccessError,"SharedBuffer is read-only");
    return NULL;
  }
  return Py_BuildValue("");
}

/* Instance methods table.  Used by sbuffer_getattr() */
static struct PyMethodDef sbuffer_methods[] = {
  {"lock",    sbuffer_lock,   METH_VARARGS},
  {"unlock",  sbuffer_unlock, METH_VARARGS},
  {"get",     sbuffer_get,    METH_VARARGS},
  {"store",   sbuffer_store,  METH_VARARGS},
  { NULL,     NULL }
};

/*************************************************************
 * Basic Operations
 *************************************************************/

/* Create a new shared buffer object */
static sbufferobject *
new_sbuffer(int fd, int size, int offset, int prot)
{
  sbufferobject *self;
  void *buffer;
  buffer = mmap(0,size,prot,MAP_SHARED,fd,offset);
  if (buffer <= 0) {
    PyErr_SetFromErrno(PyExc_OSError);
    return NULL;
  }
  self = PyObject_NEW(sbufferobject, &SharedBufferType);
  if (self == NULL) return NULL;
  self->buffer = (char *) buffer;
  self->size = size;
  self->offset = offset;
  self->prot = prot;
```

```
  self->fd = fd;
  return self;
}

/* Release a shared buffer */
static void
sbuffer_dealloc(sbufferobject *self) {
  munmap(self->buffer, self->size);
  close(self->fd);
  PyMem_DEL(self);
}

/* Get an attribute */
static PyObject *
sbuffer_getattr(sbufferobject *self, char *name) {
  if (strcmp(name,"prot") == 0) {
    return Py_BuildValue("i", self->prot);    /* self.prot */
  } else if (strcmp(name,"fd") == 0) {
    return Py_BuildValue("i", self->fd);      /* self.fd  */
  }
  /* Look for a method instead */
  return Py_FindMethod(sbuffer_methods, (PyObject *)self, name);
}

/* repr() function */
static PyObject *
sbuffer_repr(sbufferobject *self) {
  char rbuffer[256];
  sprintf(rbuffer,"<SharedBuffer, fd = %d, length = %d, prot = %d at %x>",
          self->fd, self->size, self->prot, self);
  return PyString_FromString(rbuffer);
}

/***************************************************************
 * Sequence operations
 ***************************************************************/

/* len() */
static int
sbuffer_length(sbufferobject *self) {
  return self->size;
}

/* getitem - Get a single character */
static PyObject *
sbuffer_getitem(sbufferobject *self, int index) {
  if (index < 0 || index >= self->size) {
    PyErr_SetString(PyExc_IndexError, "index out-of-bounds");
    return NULL;
  }
  if (!(self->prot & PROT_READ)) {
    PyErr_SetString(AccessError,"SharedBuffer is not readable");
    return NULL;
  }
  return Py_BuildValue("c",self->buffer[index]);
}

/* setitem - Store a single character */
static int
sbuffer_setitem(sbufferobject *self, int index, PyObject *obj)
{
  char *str;
  int   strsize;
  if (!PyString_Check(obj)) {
    PyErr_SetString(PyExc_TypeError, "Expected a string.");
```

continues >>

>> *continued*

```
                return 1;
              }
              if (PyString_Size(obj) != 1) {
                PyErr_SetString(PyExc_ValueError,"Expected a one character string.");
                return 1;
              }
              if (index < 0 || index >= self->size) {
                PyErr_SetString(PyExc_IndexError, "index out-of-bounds");
                return 1;
              }
              if (!(self->prot & PROT_WRITE)) {
                PyErr_SetString(AccessError,"SharedBuffer is read-only");
                return 1;
              }
              self->buffer[index] = *(PyString_AsString(obj));
              return 0;
            }

            /* getslice - Get a slice out of the buffer */
            static PyObject *
            sbuffer_getslice(sbufferobject *self, int start, int end) {
              if (start < 0) start = 0;
              if (end > self->size) end = self->size;
              if (end < start) end = start;
              if (!(self->prot & PROT_READ)) {
                PyErr_SetString(AccessError,"SharedBuffer is not readable");
                return NULL;
              }
              return PyString_FromStringAndSize(self->buffer+start, (end-start));
            }

            /* setslice - Set a slice in the buffer */
            static int
            sbuffer_setslice(sbufferobject *self, int start, int end, PyObject *obj)
            {
              int size;
              if (start < 0) start = 0;
              if (end > self->size) end = self->size;
              if (end < start) end = start;
              if (!PyString_Check(obj)) {
                PyErr_SetString(PyExc_TypeError, "Expected a string.");
                return 1;
              }
              if (!(self->prot & PROT_WRITE)) {
                PyErr_SetString(AccessError,"SharedBuffer is read-only");
                return 1;
              }
              size = PyString_Size(obj);
              if (size < (end-start)) end = start+size;
              memcpy(self->buffer+start,PyString_AsString(obj),(end-start));
              return 0;
            }

            /* Sequence methods table */
            static PySequenceMethods sbuffer_as_sequence = {
              (inquiry)          sbuffer_length,    /* sq_length   : len(x)      */
              (binaryfunc)       0,                 /* sq_concat   : x + y       */
              (intargfunc)       0,                 /* sq_repeat   : x * n       */
              (intargfunc)       sbuffer_getitem,   /* sq_item     : x[i]        */
              (intintargfunc)    sbuffer_getslice,  /* sq_slice    : x[i:j]      */
              (intobjargproc)    sbuffer_setitem,   /* sq_ass_item : x[i] = v    */
              (intintobjargproc) sbuffer_setslice,  /* sq_ass_slice : x[i:j] = v */
            };

            /* Type object for shared buffer objects */
            static PyTypeObject SharedBufferType = {
              PyObject_HEAD_INIT(&PyType_Type) /* Required initialization */
```

```
  0,                             /* ob_size      : Usually 0    */
  "SharedBuffer",                /* tp_name      : Type name    */
  sizeof(sbufferobject),         /* tp_basicsize : Object size  */
  0,                             /* tp_itemsize  : Usually 0    */

  /* Standard methods */
  (destructor) sbuffer_dealloc,  /* tp_dealloc,  : refcount = 0 */
  (printfunc)  0,                /* tp_print     : print x      */
  (getattrfunc) sbuffer_getattr, /* tp_getattr   : x.attr       */
  (setattrfunc) 0,               /* tp_setattr   : x.attr = v   */
  (cmpfunc)    0,                /* tp_compare   : x > y        */
  (reprfunc)   sbuffer_repr,     /* tp_repr      : repr(x)      */

  /* Type categories */
  0,                             /* tp_as_number  : Number methods   */
  &sbuffer_as_sequence,          /* tp_as_sequence: Sequence methods */
  0,                             /* tp_as_mapping : Mapping methods  */
  (hashfunc)   0,                /* tp_hash      : dict[x]       */
  (ternaryfunc) 0,               /* tp_call      : x()          */
  (reprfunc)   0,                /* tp_str       : str(x)       */
};

/***************************************************************
 * Module level functions
 ***************************************************************/

/* Create a new shared buffer object as
   SharedBuffer(filename,size,offset,prot) */
static PyObject *
sbufferobject_new(PyObject *self, PyObject *args) {
  char *filename;
  int size;
  int fd, flags;
  int prot = PROT_READ | PROT_WRITE;
  int offset = 0;
  struct stat finfo;

  if (!PyArg_ParseTuple(args,"si|ii",&filename,&size,&offset,&prot)) {
    return NULL;
  }
  if (stat(filename,&finfo) < 0) {
    PyErr_SetFromErrno(PyExc_OSError);
    return NULL;
  }
  if (size + offset > finfo.st_size) {
    PyErr_SetString(PyExc_IndexError,
                    "Requested size and offset is too large.");
    return NULL;
  }
  if ((fd = open(filename,O_RDWR, 0666)) < 0) {
    PyErr_SetFromErrno(PyExc_OSError);
    return NULL;
  }
  return (PyObject *) new_sbuffer(fd,size,offset,prot);
}

/* Module Methods Table */
static struct PyMethodDef sbuffertype_methods[] = {
  { "SharedBuffer", sbufferobject_new, METH_VARARGS },
  { NULL, NULL }
};

/* Module initialization function */
void initsbuffer() {
  PyObject *m, *d;
```

continues >>

>> continued

```
                m = Py_InitModule("sbuffer",sbuffertype_methods);
                d = PyModule_GetDict(m);

                /* Add a few useful constants for the prot parameter */
                PyDict_SetItemString(d,"PROT_READ",PyInt_FromLong(PROT_READ));
                PyDict_SetItemString(d,"PROT_WRITE",PyInt_FromLong(PROT_WRITE));

                /* Define the exception */
                AccessError = PyErr_NewException("sbuffer.AccessError",NULL,NULL);
                PyDict_SetItemString(d,"AccessError",AccessError);
            }
```

Finally, Listing B.4 uses the new SharedBuffer type. In this case, a shared buffer is used to exchange data between a parent and a child process created with os.fork(). The example (motivated by a problem posted to the Python mailing list) performs a hostname-to-IP address translation with a timeout.

Listing B.4   Python Program Using a SharedBuffer

```
            # Hostname lookup with a timeout.
            # (with apologies to Andy D.)

            import sbuffer, socket, os, sys, signal

            # Create the memory mapped region
            buffer = open("address","w")
            buffer.write(" "*2048)
            buffer.close()

            # Open the file as a shared buffer object
            buffer = sbuffer.SharedBuffer("address",2048)

            # Return hostname or "" if it can't be resolved
            # in less than 1 second.
            def gethostbyname(hostname):
                buffer.store("")          # Clear the address buffer
                pid = os.fork()           # Create a subprocess
                if pid == 0:
                    # Child process
                    signal.alarm(1)       # Start the clock
                    try:
                        name = socket.gethostbyname(hostname)
                    except:
                        sys.exit()
                    buffer.store(name)    # Save the name in the buffer
                    sys.exit()            # Done
                else:
                    os.wait()             # Wait for completion
                    return buffer.get()   # Get the address
            # Try it out
            ip = gethostbyname("www.python.org")
```

Special Methods for Types

This section describes the C data structures used to implement types. This is an advanced topic and the presentation here is only intended to be a quick reference.

Types are defined by a structure with the following fields. Many of the fields in this structures use typedef names such as hashfunc, binaryfunc, intargfunc, and so forth. These types are defined later in this appendix in Table B.26.

```
typedef struct _typeobject {
    PyObject_VAR_HEAD
    char             *tp_name;
    int              tp_basicsize;
    int              tp_itemsize;
    destructor       tp_dealloc;
    printfunc        tp_print;
    getattrfunc      tp_getattr;
    setattrfunc      tp_setattr;
    cmpfunc          tp_compare;
    reprfunc         tp_repr;

    PyNumberMethods   *tp_as_number;
    PySequenceMethods *tp_as_sequence;
    PyMappingMethods  *tp_as_mapping;

    hashfunc         tp_hash;
    ternaryfunc      tp_call;
    reprfunc         tp_str;
    getattrofunc     tp_getattro;
    setattrofunc     tp_setattro;

    PyBufferProcs    *tp_as_buffer;
    long             tp_flags;
    traverseproc     tp_traverse;
    inquiry          tp_clear;
    richcmpfunc      tp_richcompare;
    long             tp_weaklistoffset;
} PyTypeObject;
```

Most of the special methods for a type are encapsulated in four data structures: PySequenceMethods, PyMappingMethods, PyNumberMethods, and PyBufferProcs. Tables B.22 through B.26 show the contents of these structures.

Table B.22 PySequenceMethods Structure

C Datatype	Name	Python Method
(inquiry)	sq_length	__len__(x)
(binaryfunc)	sq_concat	__add__(x,y)
(intargfunc)	sq_repeat	__mul__(x,n)
(intargfunc)	sq_item	__getitem__(x,n)
(intintargfunc)	sq_slice	__getslice__(x,i,j)
(intobjargproc)	sq_ass_item	__setitem__(x,n,v)
(intintobjargproc)	sq_ass_slice	__setslice__(x,i,j,v)
(objobjproc)	sq_contains	__contains__(x,o)
(binaryfunc)	sq_inplace_concat	__iadd__(x,y)
(intargfunc)	sq_inplace_repeat	__imul__(x,n)

Table B.23 PyMappingMethods Structure

C Datatype	Name	Python Method
(inquiry)	mp_length	__len__(x)
(binaryfunc)	mp_subscript	__getitem__(x,key)
(objobjargproc)	mp_ass_subscript	__setitem__(x,key,value)

Table B.24   `PyNumberMethods` Structure

C Datatype	Name	Python Method
(binaryfunc)	nb_add	__add__(x,y)
(binaryfunc)	nb_subtract	__sub__(x,y)
(binaryfunc)	nb_multiply	__mul__(x,y)
(binaryfunc)	nb_divide	__div__(x,y)
(binaryfunc)	nb_remainder	__mod__(x,y)
(binaryfunc)	nb_divmod	__divmod__(x,y)
(ternaryfunc)	nb_power	__pow__(x,y,n)
(unaryfunc)	nb_negative	__neg__(x)
(unaryfunc)	nb_positive	__pos__(x)
(unaryfunc)	nb_absolute	__abs__(x)
(inquiry)	nb_nonzero	__zero__(x)
(unaryfunc)	nb_invert	__invert__(x)
(binaryfunc)	nb_lshift	__lshift__(x,y)
(binaryfunc)	nb_rshift	__rshift__(x,y)
(binaryfunc)	nb_and	__and__(x,y)
(binaryfunc)	nb_xor	__xor__(x,y)
(binaryfunc)	nb_or	__or__(x,y)
(coercion)	nb_coerce	__coerce__(x,y)
(unaryfunc)	nb_int	__int__(x)
(unaryfunc)	nb_long	__long__(x)
(unaryfunc)	nb_float	__float__(x)
(unaryfunc)	nb_oct	__oct__(x)
(unaryfunc)	nb_hex	__hex__(x)
(binaryfunc)	nb_inplace_add	__iadd__(x,y)
(binaryfunc)	nb_inplace_subtract	__isub__(x,y)
(binaryfunc)	nb_inplace_multiply	__imul__(x,y)
(binaryfunc)	nb_inplace_divide	__idiv__(x,y)
(binaryfunc)	nb_inplace_remainder	__imod__(x,y)
(ternaryfunc)	nb_inplace_power	__ipow__(x,y,n)
(binaryfunc)	nb_inplace_lshift	__ilshift__(x,y)
(binaryfunc)	nb_inplace_rshift	__irshift__(x,y)
(binaryfunc)	nb_inplace_and	__iand__(x,y)
(binaryfunc)	nb_inplace_xor	__ixor__(x,y)
(binaryfunc)	nb_inplace_or	__ior__(x,y)

Table B.25   `PyBufferProcs` Methods

C Datatype	Python Method
(getreadbufferproc)	bf_getreadbuffer
(getwritebufferproc)	bf_getwritebuffer

C Datatype	Python Method
(getsegcountproc)	bf_getsegcount
(getcharbufferproc)	bf_getcharbuffer

Table B.26   C Prototypes for Methods Defined in This Section

C Datatype	Prototype
(inquiry)	int (*)(PyObject *)
(unaryfunc)	PyObject (*)(PyObject *)
(binaryfunc)	PyObject (*)(PyObject *, PyObject *)
(ternaryfunc)	PyObject (*)(PyObject *, PyObject *, PyObject *)
(coercion)	int (*)(PyObject **, PyObject **)
(intargfunc)	PyObject (*)(PyObject *, int)
(intintargfunc)	PyObject (*)(PyObject *, int, int)
(intobjargproc)	int (*)(PyObject *, int, PyObject *)
(intintobjargproc)	int (*)(PyObject *, int, int, PyObject *)
(destructor)	void (*)(PyObject *)
(printfunc)	int (*)(PyObject *, FILE *, int)
(getattrfunc)	PyObject (*)(PyObject *, char *)
(getattrofunc)	PyObject (*)(PyObject *, PyObject *)
(setattrfunc)	int (*)(PyObject *, char *, PyObject *)
(setattrofunc)	int (*)(PyObject *, PyObject *, PyObject *)
(cmpfunc)	int (*)(PyObject *, PyObject *)
(reprfunc)	PyObject (*)(PyObject *)
(hashfunc)	long (*)(PyObject *)
(objobjfunc)	int (*)(PyObject *, PyObject *)
(getreadbufferproc)	int (*)(PyObject *, int, void **)
(getwritebufferproc)	int (*)(PyObject *, int, void **)
(getsegcountproc)	int (*)(PyObject *, int *)
(getcharbufferproc)	int (*)(PyObject *, int, const char **)
(richcmpfunc)	PyObject *(*)(PyObject *, PyObject *, int);
(visitproc)	int (*)(PyObject *, void *)
(traverseproc)	int (*)(PyObject *, visitproc, void *)

Threads

When using threads, a global interpreter lock is used to prevent more than one thread from executing in the interpreter at once. If a function written in an extension module executes for a long time, it will block the execution of other threads until it completes. This is because the lock is held whenever an extension function is invoked. If the extension module is thread-safe, the following macros can be used to release and reacquire the global interpreter lock:

`Py_BEGIN_ALLOW_THREADS`

Releases the global interpreter lock and allows other threads to run in the interpreter. The C extension must not invoke any functions in the Python C API while the lock is released.

`Py_END_ALLOW_THREADS`

Reacquires the global interpreter lock. The extension will block until the lock can be acquired successfully in this case.

The following example illustrates the use of these macros:

```
PyObject *spamfunction(PyObject *self, PyObject *args) {
        ...
        PyArg_ParseTuple(args, ...)
        Py_BEGIN_ALLOW_THREADS
        result = run_long_calculation(args);
        Py_END_ALLOW_THREADS
        ...
        return Py_BuildValue(fmt,result);
}
```

Many more subtle aspects of threads are not covered here. Readers are strongly advised to consult the C API Reference Manual. In addition, you may need to take steps to make sure that your C extension is thread-safe, as it could be invoked by other Python threads shortly after the interpreter lock is released.

Embedding

The Python interpreter can also be embedded into other applications. When embedding the interpreter on UNIX, you must include the file config.c (usually found in a place such as *<python>*/lib/python2.1/config/config.c, where *<python>* is the directory where Python was installed) and link against the library libpython2.1.a. (A comparable but more complex process is required on Windows and the Macintosh. Consult the online documentation for details.) The following functions are used to call the interpreter to execute code and control its operation:

int PyRun_AnyFile(FILE *fp, char *filename)

If *fp* is an interactive device such as TTY in UNIX, this function calls PyRun_InteractiveLoop(). Otherwise, PyRun_SimpleFile() is called. If *filename* is NULL, a default string of "???" is used as the filename.

int PyRun_SimpleString(char *command)

Executes *command* in the __main__ module of the interpreter. Returns 0 on success, -1 if an exception occurred.

int PyRun_SimpleFile(FILE *fp, char *filename)

Similar to PyRun_SimpleString(), except that the program is read from a file *fp*.

int PyRun_InteractiveOne(FILE *fp, char *filename)

Executes a single interactive command.

int PyRun_InterativeLoop(FILE *fp, char *filename)

Runs the interpreter in interactive mode.

```
int PyRun_String(char *str, int start, PyObject *globals, PyObject *locals)
```

Executes the code in *str* in the global and local namespaces defined by globals and locals. *start* is a start token to use when parsing the source code. Returns the result of execution or NULL if an error occurred.

```
int PyRun_File(FILE *fp, char *filename, int start, PyObject *globals,
               PyObject *locals)
```

Like PyRun_String() except that code is read from the file *fp*.

```
PyObject *Py_CompileString(char *str, char *filename, int start)
```

Compiles code in *str* into a code object. *start* is the starting token and *filename* is the filename that will be set in the code object and used in tracebacks. Returns a code object on success, NULL on error.

```
Py_Initialize(void)
```

Initializes the Python interpreter. This function should be called before using any other functions in the C API, with the exception of Py_SetProgramName(), PyEval_InitThreads(), PyEval_ReleaseLock(), and PyEval_AcquireLock().

```
int Py_IsInitialized(void)
```

Returns 1 if the interpreter has been initialized, 0 if not.

```
Py_Finalize(void)
```

Cleans up the interpreter by destroying all of the sub-interpreters and objects that were created since calling Py_Initialize(). Normally, this function frees all the memory allocated by the interpreter. However, circular references and extension modules may introduce memory leaks that cannot be recovered by this function.

```
void Py_SetProgramName(char *name)
```

Sets the program name that's normally found in the argv[0] argument of the sys module. This function should only be called before Py_Initialize().

```
char *Py_GetProgramName(void)
```

Returns the program name as set by Py_SetProgramName(void).

```
char *Py_GetPrefix(void)
```

Returns the prefix for installed platform-independent files.

```
char *Py_GetExecPrefix(void)
```

Returns the exec-prefix for installed platform-dependent files.

```
char *Py_GetProgramFullPath(void)
```

Returns the full pathname of the Python executable.

```
char *Py_GetPath(void)
```

Returns the default module search path. The path is returned as a string consisting of directory names separated by a platform-dependent delimiters (: on UNIX, ; on DOS/Windows, and '\n' on Macintosh).

```
const char *Py_GetVersion(void)
```

Returns the version of the interpreter as a string.

```
const char *Py_GetPlatform(void)
```

Returns the platform identifier string for the current platform.

```
const char *Py_GetCopyright(void)
```

Returns the official copyright string.

Appendix B   Extending and Embedding Python

```
const char *Py_GetCompiler(void)
```

Returns the compiler string.

```
const char *Py_GetBuildInfo(void)
```

Returns build information about the interpreter.

```
int PySys_SetArgv(int argc, char **argv)
```

Sets command-line options used to populate the value of sys.argv. This should only be called by Py_Initialize().

Extension Building Tools

A number of tools are available to simplify the construction of Python extensions.

Extension Classes

Extension classes, written by Jim Fulton and available at http://www.digicool.com/releases/ExtensionClass/, provide a mechanism for defining extension types that are more class-like. In particular, they can be subclassed in C or Python, and provide better interaction with documentation strings and other aspects of the interpreter.

CXX

The cxx extension, developed by Paul Dubois, simplifies the process of creating extension modules in C++ (http://cxx.sourceforge.net).

pyfort

pyfort, also developed by Paul Dubois, can be used to build Python extension modules from Fortran code. Details are available at http://pyfortran.sourceforge.net.

f2py

f2py is a Fortran-to-Python interface generator developed by Pearu Peterson. Details are available at http://cens.ioc.ee/projects/f2py2e/.

Boost Python Library

The Boost Python Library provides a tool for wrapping C++ libraries into Python extensions. The library provides a number of advanced features, including support for overloaded functions and operators. Details are available at http://www.boost.org/libs/python/doc/index.html.

SWIG

swig (Simplified Wrapper and Interface Generator), developed by the author and available at http://www.swig.org, can be used to create Python extensions automatically from annotated C header files.

Summary of Changes

C

This appendix briefly describes some of the more important changes to Python since the first edition of *Python Essential Reference*, which described Python 1.5.2. The primary focus here is on core language changes that may cause incompatibilities between Python versions.

Detailed changes to individual library modules are not covered. For a more comprehensive list of changes, readers are encouraged to consult the documentation at http://www.python.org. The Misc/NEWS file in the Python source distribution also contains a very detailed list of language changes.

Python 1.6

Python 1.6 was released only about a week before the release of Python 2.0. The story behind this release is complicated and somewhat political. However, the bottom line is that there is very little reason to use this release, given its similarity to Python 2.0.

Python 2.0

- Unicode support.
- List comprehensions.
- Augmented assignment operators (+=, -=, *=, /=, %=, **=, &=, |=, ^=, >>=, and <<=) and associated special methods __iadd__, __isub__, etc.
- The syntax f(*args,**kwargs) can now be used to call a function with positional arguments *args* and keyword arguments *kwargs*. Previously, the built-in apply() function was used for this purpose.
- Garbage collection of cyclical data structures and the gc module.
- Enhanced print statement. print >>f, obj now redirects its output to the file object f.
- The import statement has been enhanced with the as modifier; for example, import foo as bar. However, as is not a new Python reserved word.

- String methods added to both standard and Unicode strings. These methods replace most of the functionality in the `string` module.

- `d.setdefault()` method added to dictionaries.

- New built-in functions: `zip()`, `unichr()`, `unicode()`.

- New modules described in Appendix A, "The Python Library": `gc`, `UserString`, `_winreg`, `zipfile`, `unicodedata`, `encodings`, `codecs`, `atexit`, `filecmp`, `gettext`, `mmap`, `robotparser`, `webbrowser`.

- New exceptions: `UnboundLocalError`, `UnicodeError`.

Python 2.1

- Functions now define nested scopes. Currently, this feature must be enabled by including `from __future__ import nested_scopes` in your program. In future releases, this feature will be enabled by default.

- Rich comparisons and the associated `__le__()`, `__lt__()`, `__eq__()`, `__ne__()`, `__gt__()`, and `__ge__()` methods.

- `d.popitem()` method added to dictionaries.

- `f.xreadline()` method added to files to support fast iteration over lines.

- Functions and methods can now have attributes attached to them.

- Support for weak references added. A new module, `weakref`, provides an interface.

  ▶ **See Also** `weakref` (124).

- Warning framework added. The `warnings` module provides an interface.

  ▶ **See Also** `warnings` (121).

- Case-sensitive import now supported on non–case-sensitive platforms.

- Interactive display hook (`sys.displayfunc`) added.

- Uncaught exception hook (`sys.exceptfunc`) added.

- `from __future__` directive added to allow optional use of new features.

- Complex numbers can now only be compared for equality. Comparisons of `<`, `>`, `<=`, or `>=` raise a `TypeError` exception.

- The `continue` statement can now be used inside `try` blocks. This was previously illegal.

- New modules described in Appendix A: `warnings`, `weakref`.

- Modules can now specify a list of symbols to export in the `from module import *` statement by specifying a list `__all__`.

- Many minor changes to output formatting. The `%x`, `%X`, and `%o` format codes now always produce a sign character for negative long integers. The `repr()` function uses standard character escape codes such as `"\n"` instead of `"\012"`.

Index

C

F

H

M

O

U

X

Y

Z

HOW TO CONTACT US

VISIT OUR WEB SITE

WWW.NEWRIDERS.COM

On our Web site, you'll find information about our other books, authors, tables of contents, and book errata. You will also find information about book registration and how to purchase our books, both domestically and internationally.

EMAIL US

Contact us at: **nrfeedback@newriders.com**

- If you have comments or questions about this book
- To report errors that you have found in this book
- If you have a book proposal to submit or are interested in writing for New Riders
- If you are an expert in a computer topic or technology and are interested in being a technical editor who reviews manuscripts for technical accuracy

Contact us at: **nreducation@newriders.com**

- If you are an instructor from an educational institution who wants to preview New Riders books for classroom use. Email should include your name, title, school, department, address, phone number, office days/hours, text in use, and enrollment, along with your request for desk/examination copies and/or additional information.

Contact us at: **nrmedia@newriders.com**

- If you are a member of the media who is interested in reviewing copies of New Riders books. Send your name, mailing address, and email address, along with the name of the publication or Web site you work for.

BULK PURCHASES/CORPORATE SALES

If you are interested in buying 10 or more copies of a title or want to set up an account for your company to purchase directly from the publisher at a substantial discount, contact us at 800-382-3419 or email your contact information to corpsales@pearsontechgroup.com. A sales representative will contact you with more information.

WRITE TO US

New Riders Publishing
201 W. 103rd St.
Indianapolis, IN 46290-1097

CALL/FAX US

Toll-free (800) 571-5840
If outside U.S. (317) 581-3500
Ask for New Riders
FAX: (317) 581-4663

VOICES THAT MATTER

New Riders

ISBN: 0735710201
1152 pages
US $49.99

Inside XML

Steven Holzner

Inside XML is a foundation book that covers both the Microsoft and non-Microsoft approach to XML programming. It covers in detail the hot aspects of XML, such as DTD's vs. XML Schemas, CSS, XSL, XSLT, Xlinks, Xpointers, XHTML, RDF, CDF, parsing XML in Perl and Java, and much more.

ISBN: 0735710074
400 pages
US $34.99

Solaris 8 Essential Reference

John Mulligan

A great companion to the solarisguide.com Web site, *Solaris 8 Essential Reference* assumes readers are well-versed in general UNIX skills and simply need some pointers on how to get the most out of Solaris. This book provides clear and concise instruction on how to perform important administration and management tasks.

ISBN: 0735710643
700 pages
US $49.99

Berkeley DB

Sleepycat Software

Berkeley DB is a tutorial on using the Berkeley DB embedded database, covering methods, architecture, data applications, memory, and configuring the APIs in Perl, Java, and Tcl, etc. The second part of the book is a reference section of the various Berkeley DB APIs.

ISBN: 0735710430
400 pages
US $49.99

Advanced Linux Programming

Code Sourcery, LLC

An in-depth guide to programming Linux from the most recognized leaders in the Open Source community, this book is the ideal reference for Linux programmers who are reasonably skilled in the C programming language and who are in need of a book that covers the Linux C library (glibc).

Exerpt from Bestselling title—
Berkeley DB

Sleepycat Software
ISBN: 0735710643
700 pages

3

Access Method Configuration

BERKELEY DB CURRENTLY OFFERS FOUR ACCESS METHODS: Btree, Hash, Queue, and Recno. Each is discussed in the following sections.

Btree

The Btree access method is an implementation of a sorted, balanced tree structure. Searches, insertions, and deletions in the tree all take O(log base_b N) time, where base_b is the average number of keys per page, and N is the total number of keys stored. Often, inserting ordered data into Btree implementations results in pages that are only half-full. Berkeley DB makes ordered (or inverse-ordered) insertion the best case, resulting in nearly full-page space utilization.

Hash

The Hash access method data structure is an implementation of Extended Linear Hashing, as described in "Linear Hashing: A New Tool for File and Table Addressing," by Witold Litwin in the *Proceedings of the 6th International Conference on Very Large Databases (VLDB)*, 1980.

Queue

The Queue access method stores fixed-length records with logical record numbers as keys. It is designed for fast inserts at the tail, and has a special cursor consume operation that deletes and returns a record from the head of the queue. The Queue access method uses record-level locking.

Recno

The Recno access method stores both fixed- and variable-length records with logical record numbers as keys, optionally backed by a flat text (byte stream) file.

Selecting an Access Method

The Berkeley DB access method implementation unavoidably interacts with each application's data set, locking requirements, and data access patterns. For this reason, one access method may result in a dramatically better performance for an application than another one. Applications whose data can be stored using more than one access method may want to benchmark their performance using the different candidates.

One of the strengths of Berkeley DB is that it provides multiple access methods with nearly identical interfaces to the different access methods. This means that it is simple to modify an application to use a different access method. Applications can easily benchmark the different Berkeley DB access methods against each other for their particular data set and access pattern.

Most applications choose between using the Btree or Hash access methods, or between using the Queue and Recno access methods because each of the two pairs offer similar functionality.

Hash or Btree?

The Hash and Btree access methods should be used when logical record numbers are not the primary key used for data access. (If logical record numbers are a secondary key used for data access, the Btree access method is a possible choice because it supports simultaneous access by a key and a record number.)

Keys in Btrees are stored in sorted order, and the relationship between them is defined by that sort order. For this reason, the Btree access method should be used when there is locality of reference among keys. *Locality of reference* means that accessing one particular key in the Btree implies that the application is more likely to access keys near the key being accessed, where *near* is defined by the sort order. For example, if keys are timestamps, and it is likely that a request for an 8 a.m. timestamp will be followed by a request for a 9 a.m. timestamp, the Btree access method is generally the right choice. Or, if the keys are names, for example, and the application wants to review all entries with the same last name, the Btree access method is again a good choice.

There is little difference in performance between the Hash and Btree access methods on small data sets in which all or most of the data set fits into the cache. However, when a data set is large enough that significant numbers of data pages no longer fit into the cache, the Btree locality of reference described previously becomes important for performance reasons. For example, there is no locality of reference for the Hash access method, so key "AAAAA" is as likely to be stored on the same database page with key "ZZZZZ" as with key "AAAAB." In the Btree access method, key "AAAAA" is far more likely to be near key "AAAAB" than key "ZZZZZ" because items are sorted. So, if the application exhibits locality of reference in its data requests, the Btree page read into the cache to satisfy a request for key "AAAAA" is much more likely to be useful to satisfy subsequent requests from the application than the Hash page read into the cache to satisfy the same request. This means that for applications with locality of reference, the cache is generally much more effective for the Btree access method than the Hash access method, and the Btree access method will make many fewer I/O calls.

However, when a data set becomes even larger, the Hash access method can outperform the Btree access method because Btrees contain more metadata pages than Hash databases. The data set can grow so large that metadata pages begin to dominate the cache for the Btree access method. If this happens, the Btree can be forced to do an I/O for each data request because the probability that any particular data page is already in the cache becomes quite small. Because the Hash access method has fewer metadata pages, its cache stays "hotter" longer in the presence of large data sets. In addition, once the data set is so large that both the Btree and Hash access methods are almost certainly doing an I/O for each random data request, the fact that Hash does not have to walk several internal pages as part of a key search becomes a performance advantage for the Hash access method.

Application data access patterns strongly affect all of these behaviors. For example, accessing the data by walking a cursor through the database will greatly mitigate the large data set behavior described previously because each I/O into the cache will satisfy a fairly large number of subsequent data requests.

In the absence of information on application data and data access patterns, either the Btree or Hash access methods will suffice for small data sets. For data sets larger than the cache, we normally recommend using the Btree access method. If you have truly large data, the Hash access method may be a better choice. The **db_stat** utility is a useful tool for monitoring how well your cache is performing.

Queue or Recno?

The Queue or Recno access methods should be used when logical record numbers are the primary key used for data access. The advantage of the Queue access method is that it performs record-level locking; for this reason, it supports significantly higher levels of concurrency than the Recno access method. The advantage of the Recno access method is that it supports a number of additional features beyond those supported by the Queue access method, such as variable-length records and support for backing flat-text files.

Logical record numbers can be mutable or fixed: Mutable where logical record numbers can change as records are deleted or inserted, and fixed where record num bers never change, regardless of the database operation. It is possible to store and retrieve records based on logical record numbers in the Btree access method. However, those record numbers are always mutable, and the logical record number other records in the database will change as records are deleted or inserted. The Q access method always runs in fixed mode, and logical record numbers never chang regardless of the database operation. The Recno access method can be configured run in either mutable or fixed mode.

In addition, the Recno access method provides support for databases whose per nent storage is a flat text file, and the database is used as a fast temporary storage a while the data is being read or modified.

Logical Record Numbers

The Berkeley DB Btree, Queue, and Recno access methods can operate on logica record numbers. Logical record numbers are 1-based, not 0-based; that is, the first record in the database is record number 1. In all cases for the Queue and Recno a methods (and when calling the Btree access method using the **DB→get** and **DBcursor→c_get** functions with the DB_SET_RECNO flag specified), the **data** field of the key must be a pointer to a memory location of type **db_recno_t**, as ty def'd in the standard Berkeley DB include file. This type is a 32-bit unsigned type. which limits the number of logical records in a Queue or Recno database; and the maximum logical record, which may be directly retrieved from a Btree database, to 4,294,967,296. The **size** field of the key should be the size of that type (for exam **sizeof(db_recno_t** in the C programming language). In the case of Btree suppor duplicate data items, the logical record number refers to a key and all of its data ite

Record numbers in Recno databases can be configured to run in either mutab fixed mode: *mutable*, in which logical record numbers change as records are delete inserted; and *fixed*, in which record numbers never change, regardless of the databa operation. Record numbers in Queue databases are always fixed and never change regardless of the database operation. Record numbers in Btree databases are always mutable, and as records are deleted or inserted, the logical record number for othe records in the database can change. See "Logically Renumbering Records" for mc information.

Configuring Btree databases to support record numbers can severely limit the throughput of applications with multiple concurrent threads writing the database because locations used to store record counts often become hot spots that many different threads all need to update.

Selecting a Page Size

The size of the pages used in the underlying database can be specified by calling the **DB→set_pagesize** function. The minimum page size is 512 bytes, and the maximum page size is 64K bytes and must be a power of two. If no page size is specified by the application, a page size is selected based on the underlying filesystem I/O block size. (A page size selected in this way has a lower limit of 512 bytes and an upper limit of 16K bytes.) There are four issues to consider when selecting a page size: overflow record sizes, locking, I/O efficiency, and recoverability.

First, the page size implicitly sets the size of an overflow record. *Overflow records* are key or data items that are too large to fit on a normal database page because of their size, and are therefore stored in overflow pages. *Overflow pages* are pages that exist outside of the normal database structure. For this reason, there is often a significant performance penalty associated with retrieving or modifying overflow records. Selecting a page size that is too small and forces the creation of large numbers of overflow pages can seriously impact the performance of an application.

Second, in the Btree, Hash, and Recno access methods, the finest-grained lock that Berkeley DB acquires is for a page. (The Queue access method generally acquires record level locks rather than page-level locks.) Selecting a page size that is too large and causes threads or processes to wait because other threads of control are accessing or modifying records on the same page can impact the performance of your application.

Third, the page size specifies the granularity of I/O from the database to the operating system. Berkeley DB gives a page-sized unit of bytes to the operating system to be scheduled for writing to the disk. For many operating systems, there is an internal **block size** that is used as the granularity of I/O from the operating system to the disk. If the page size is smaller than the block size, the operating system may be forced to read a block from the disk, copy the page into the buffer it read, and then write out the block to disk. Obviously, it will be much more efficient for Berkeley DB to write filesystem-sized blocks to the operating system and for the operating system to write those same blocks to the disk. Selecting a page size that is too small and causes the operating system to coalesce or otherwise manipulate Berkeley DB pages can impact the performance of your application. Alternatively, selecting a page size that is too large may cause Berkeley DB and the operating system to write more data than is strictly necessary.

Fourth, when using the Berkeley DB Transactional Data Store product, the page size may affect the errors from which your database can recover. See "Berkeley DB Recoverability" for more information.

Selecting a Cache Size

The size of the cache used for the underlying database can be specified by calling t**DB→set_cachesize** function. Choosing a cache size is, unfortunately, an art. Your cache must be at least large enough for your working set plus some overlap for une pected situations.

When using the Btree access method, you must have a cache big enough for the minimum working set for a single access. This includes a root page, one or more in nal pages (depending on the depth of your tree), and a leaf page. If your cache is an smaller than that, each new page will force out the least-recently-used page, and Berkeley DB will reread the root page of the tree anew on each database request.

If your keys are of moderate size (a few tens of bytes), and your pages are on the order of 4K to 8K, most Btree applications will be only three levels. For example, using 20 byte keys with 20 bytes of data associated with each key, an 8KB page can hold roughly 400 keys and 200 key/data pairs. Thus, a fully populated three-level B holds 32 million key/data pairs, and a tree with only a 50% page-fill factor still hole 16 million key/data pairs. We rarely expect trees to exceed five levels, although Berkeley DB supports trees up to 255 levels.

The rule-of-thumb is that cache is good and more cache is better. Generally, app cations benefit from increasing the cache size up to a point when the performance will stop improving as the cache size increases. When this point is reached, one of t things have happened: either the cache is large enough that the application is almos never having to retrieve information from disk; or your application is doing truly ra dom accesses, so increasing the size of the cache doesn't significantly increase the o of finding the next requested information in the cache. The latter is fairly rare—alm all applications show some form of locality of reference.

That said, it is important not to increase your cache size beyond the capabilities your system because it will result in reduced performance. Under many operating s tems, tying down enough virtual memory will cause your memory and potentially your program to be swapped. This is especially likely on systems without unified O buffer caches and virtual memory spaces because the buffer cache was allocated at boot time and so cannot be adjusted based on application requests for large amoun of virtual memory.

For example, even if accesses are truly random within a Btree, your access patter will favor internal pages to leaf pages, so your cache should be large enough to hol all internal pages. In the steady state, this requires at most one I/O per operation to retrieve the appropriate leaf page.

You can use the **db_stat** utility to monitor the effectiveness of your cache. The lowing output is excerpted from the output of that utility's **-m** option:

```
prompt: db_stat -m
131072   Cache size (128K).
4273     Requested pages found in the cache (97%).
134      Requested pages not found in the cache.
18       Pages created in the cache.
```

```
116     Pages read into the cache.
93      Pages written from the cache to the backing file.
5       Clean pages forced from the cache.
13      Dirty pages forced from the cache.
0       Dirty buffers written by trickle-sync thread.
130     Current clean buffer count.
4       Current dirty buffer count.
```

The statistics for this cache say that there have been 4,273 requests of the cache, and only 116 of those requests required an I/O from disk. This means that the cache is working well, yielding a 97% cache hit rate. The **db_stat** utility will present these statistics both for the cache as a whole and for each file within the cache separately.

Selecting a Byte Order

Database files created by Berkeley DB can be created in either little- or big-endian formats. The byte order used for the underlying database is specified by calling the **DB→set_lorder** function. If no order is selected, the native format of the machine on which the database is created will be used.

Berkeley DB databases are architecture-independent, and any format database can be used on a machine with a different native format. In this case, each page that is read into or written from the cache must be converted to or from the host format, and databases with non-native formats will incur a performance penalty for the run-time conversion.

It is important to note that the Berkeley DB access methods do no data conversion for application-specified data. Key/data pairs written on a little-endian format architecture will be returned to the application exactly as they were written when retrieved on a big-endian format architecture.

Non-Local Memory Allocation

Berkeley DB can allocate memory for returned key/data pairs, which then become the responsibility of the application. See DB_DBT_MALLOC or DB_DBT_REAL-LOC for further information.

On systems where there may be multiple library versions of malloc (notably Windows NT), the Berkeley DB library could allocate memory from a different heap than the application will use to free it. To avoid this problem, the allocation routine to be used for allocating such key/data items can be specified by calling the **DB→set_malloc** or **DB→set_realloc** functions. If no allocation function is specified, the underlying C library functions are used.

Btree Comparison

The Btree data structure is a sorted, balanced tree structure storing associated key/data pairs. By default, the sort order is lexicographical, with shorter keys collating before longer keys. The user can specify the sort order for the Btree by using the **DB→set_bt_compare** function.

Sort routines are passed pointers to keys as arguments. The keys are represented as **DBT** structures. The routine must return an integer less than, equal to, or greater than zero if the first argument is considered to be respectively less than, equal to, or greater than the second argument. The only fields that the routines may examine in the **DBT** structures are the **data** and **size** fields.

An example routine that might be used to sort integer keys in the database is as follows:

```
int
compare_int(dbp, a, b)
        DB *dbp;
        const DBT *a, *b;
{
        int ai, bi;

        /*
         * Returns:
         *      < 0 if a < b
         *      = 0 if a = b
         *      > 0 if a > b
         */
        memcpy(&ai, a→data, sizeof(int));
        memcpy(&bi, b→data, sizeof(int));
        return (ai - bi);
}
```

Note that the data must first be copied into memory that is appropriately aligned because Berkeley DB does not guarantee any kind of alignment of the underlying data, including for comparison routines. When writing comparison routines, remember that databases created on machines of different architectures may have different integer byte orders, for which your code may need to compensate.

An example routine that might be used to sort keys based on the first five bytes of the key (ignoring any subsequent bytes) is as follows:

```
int
compare_dbt(dbp, a, b)
        DB *dbp;
        const DBT *a, *b;
{
        u_char *p1, *p2;

        /*
         * Returns:
         * < 0 if a < b
         * = 0 if a = b
         * > 0 if a > b
         */
        for (p1 = a→data, p2 = b→data, len = 5; len—; ++p1, ++p2)
                if (*p1 != *p2)
                        return ((long)*p1 - (long)*p2);
        return (0);
}
```

All comparison functions must cause the keys in the database to be well-ordered. The most important implication of being well-ordered is that the key relations must be transitive; that is, if key A is less than key B and key B is less than key C, the comparison routine must also return that key A is less than key C. In addition, comparisons will be able to return 0 only when comparing full-length keys; partial key comparisons must always return a result less than or greater than 0.

Btree Prefix Comparison

The Berkeley DB Btree implementation maximizes the number of keys that can be stored on an internal page by storing only as many bytes of each key as are necessary to distinguish it from adjacent keys. The prefix comparison routine is what determines this minimum number of bytes (that is, the length of the unique prefix) that must be stored. A prefix comparison function for the Btree can be specified by calling **DB→set_bt_prefix**.

The prefix comparison routine must be compatible with the overall comparison function of the Btree because what distinguishes any two keys depends entirely on the function used to compare them. This means that if a prefix comparison routine is specified by the application, a compatible overall comparison routine must also have been specified.

Prefix comparison routines are passed pointers to keys as arguments. The keys are represented as **DBT** structures. The prefix comparison function must return the number of bytes of the second key argument that are necessary to determine if it is greater than the first key argument. If the keys are equal, the length of the second key should be returned. The only fields that the routines may examine in the **DBT** structures are **data** and **size** fields.

An example prefix comparison routine follows:

```
u_int32_t
compare_prefix(dbp, a, b)
        DB *dbp;
        const DBT *a, *b;
{
        size_t cnt, len;
        u_int8_t *p1, *p2;

        cnt = 1;
        len = a→size > b→size ? b→size : a→size;
        for (p1 =
                a->data, p2 = b→data; len--; ++p1, ++p2, ++cnt)
                        if (*p1 != *p2)
                                return (cnt);
        /*
         * They match up to the smaller of the two sizes.
         * Collate the longer after the shorter.
         */
        if (a→size < b→size)
                return (a→size + 1);
```

```
        if (b→size < a→size)
                return (b→size + 1);
        return (b→size);
}
```

The usefulness of this functionality is data-dependent, but in some datasets, it can produce significantly reduced tree sizes and faster search times.

Minimum Keys Per Page

The number of keys stored on each page affects the size of a Btree and how it is maintained. Therefore, it also affects the retrieval and search performance of the tree. For each Btree, Berkeley DB computes a maximum key and data size. This size is a function of the page size and the fact that at least two key/data pairs must fit on any Btree page. Whenever key or data items exceed the calculated size, they are stored on overflow pages instead of in the standard Btree leaf pages.

Applications may use the **DB→set_bt_minkey** function to change the minimum number of keys that must fit on a Btree page from two to another value. Altering this value in turn alters the on-page maximum size, and can be used to force key and data items that would normally be stored in the Btree leaf pages onto overflow pages.

Some data sets can benefit from this tuning. For example, consider an application using large page sizes, with a data set almost entirely consisting of small key and data items, but with a few large items. By setting the minimum number of keys that must fit on a page, the application can force the outsized items to be stored on overflow pages. That in turn can potentially keep the tree more compact; that is, with fewer internal levels to traverse during searches.

The following calculation is similar to the one performed by the Btree implementation. (The **minimum_keys** value is multiplied by 2 because each key/data pair requires two slots on a Btree page.)

```
maximum_size = page_size / (minimum_keys * 2)
```

Using this calculation, if the page size is 8KB and the default **minimum_keys** value of 2 is used, any key or data items larger than 2KB will be forced to an overflow page. If an application were to specify a **minimum_key** value of 100, any key or data items larger than roughly 40 bytes would be forced to overflow pages.

It is important to remember that accesses to overflow pages do not perform as well as accesses to the standard Btree leaf pages, so setting the value incorrectly can result in overusing overflow pages and decreasing the application's overall performance.

Retrieving Btree Records by Number

The Btree access method optionally supports retrieval by logical record numbers. To configure a Btree to support record numbers, call the **DB→set_flags** function with the DB_RECNUM flag.

Configuring a Btree for record numbers should not be done lightly. Although often useful, it requires that storing items into the database be single-threaded, which can severely impact application throughput. Generally, it should be avoided in trees with a need for high write concurrency.

To determine a key's record number, use the DB_GET_RECNO flag to the **DBcursor→c_get** function. To retrieve by record number, use the DB_SET_RECNO flag to the **DB→get** and **DBcursor→c_get** functions.

Page Fill Factor

The density, or *page fill factor*, is an approximation of the number of keys allowed to accumulate in any one bucket, determining when the hash table grows or shrinks. If you know the average sizes of the keys and data in your dataset, setting the fill factor can enhance performance. A reasonable rule to use to compute fill factor is the following:

```
(pagesize - 32) / (average_key_size + average_data_size + 8)
```

The desired density within the hash table can be specified by calling the **DB→set_h_ffactor** function. If no density is specified, one will be selected dynamically as pages are filled.

Specifying a Database Hash

The database hash determines in which bucket a particular key will reside. The goal of hashing keys is to distribute keys equally across the database pages; therefore, it is important that the hash function work well with the specified keys so that the resulting bucket usage is relatively uniform. A hash function that does not work well can effectively turn into a sequential list.

No hash performs equally well on all possible datasets. It is possible that applications may find that the default hash function performs poorly with a particular set of keys. The distribution resulting from the hash function can be checked using the **db_stat** utility. By comparing the number of hash buckets and the number of keys, one can decide if the entries are hashing in a well-distributed manner.

The hash function for the hash table can be specified by calling the **DB→set_h_hash** function. If no hash function is specified, a default function will be used. Any application-specified hash function must take a reference to a DB object, a pointer to a byte string and its length as arguments, and return an unsigned 32-bit hash value.

Hash Table Size

When setting up the hash database, knowing the expected number of elements that will be stored in the hash table is useful. This value can be used by the Hash access method implementation to more accurately construct the necessary number of buckets that the database will eventually require.

The anticipated number of elements in the hash table can be specified by calling the **DB→set_h_nelem** function. If not specified or set too low, hash tables will expand gracefully as keys are entered, although a slight performance degradation may be noticed. In order for the estimated number of elements to be a useful value to Berkeley DB, the **DB→set_h_ffactor** function must also be called to set the page fill factor.

Managing Record-Based Databases

When using fixed- or variable-length record-based databases, particularly with flat-text backing files, there are several items that the user can control. The Recno access method can be used to store either variable- or fixed-length data items. By default, the Recno access method stores variable-length data items. The Queue access method can store only fixed-length data items.

Record Delimiters

When using the Recno access method to store variable-length records, records read from any backing source file are separated by a specific byte value that marks the end of one record and the beginning of the next. This delimiting value is ignored except when reading records from a backing source file; that is, records may be stored into the database that include the delimiter byte. However, if such records are written out to the backing source file and the backing source file is subsequently read into a database, the records will be split where delimiting bytes were found.

For example, UNIX text files can usually be interpreted as a sequence of variable-length records separated by ASCII newline characters. This byte value (ASCII 0x0a) is the default delimiter. Applications may specify a different delimiting byte using the **DB→set_re_delim** interface. If no backing source file is being used, there is no reason to set the delimiting byte value.

Record Length

When using the Recno or Queue access methods to store fixed-length records, the record length must be specified. Because the Queue access method always uses fixed-length records, the user must always set the record length prior to creating the database. Setting the record length is what causes the Recno access method to store fixed-length records, not variable-length records.

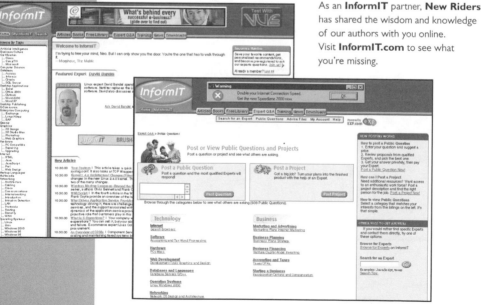
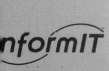

Colophon

The image on the cover of this book, captured by photographer John P. Blair, is that of the Great Kiva of Pueblo Bonito Ruins in Chaco Canyon, New Mexico. Chaco Canyon was the center of Pueblon culture between AD 850 and 1250, and is considered the greatest architectural achievement of northern American Indians. The architectural structure at Chaco Canyon included more than 600 rooms, many two- and three-story buildings, and several *kivas*— circular subterranean chambers used for ceremonial purposes. To construct such a site required careful planning and the integration of landscaping, astronomical alignments, geometry, and engineering.

Named a National Historic Monument on March 11, 1907, and a National Historic Park on December 19, 1980, the site is protected by the Antiquities Act of 1906, making it illegal to excavate or alter any part of the site, or to remove objects without a permit. The park attracts 90,000–100,000 visitors per year.

This book was written and edited in Microsoft Word, and laid out in QuarkXPress on Power Macintosh G3 computers. The index was created by the author with the assistance of a few Python scripts. The fonts used for the body text are Bembo, Rotis Sans Serif, and MCPdigital. It was printed on 50# Husky Offset Smooth paper at R.R. Donnelley & Sons in Crawfordsville, Indiana. Prepress consisted of PostScript computer-to-plate technology (filmless process). The cover was printed at Moore Langen Printing in Terre Haute, Indiana, on Carolina, coated on one side.